THE INTERNATIONAL PSYCHO - ANALYTICAL LIBRARY

No. 13

SELECTED PAPERS OF
KARL ABRAHAM M.D.

THE BASIC CLASSICS IN PSYCHIATRY

SELECTED PAPERS OF
KARL ABRAHAM M.D.

WITH AN INTRODUCTORY MEMOIR BY
ERNEST JONES

TRANSLATED BY
DOUGLAS BRYAN and
ALIX STRACHEY

First American Edition

BASIC BOOKS, INC., PUBLISHERS
59 FOURTH AVENUE, NEW YORK 3, N.Y.

PUBLISHED BY

The Hogarth Press Ltd

LONDON

*

Clarke, Irwin & Co. Ltd

TORONTO

*

Basic Books, Inc.

NEW YORK

First Published	1927
Second Impression	1942
Third Impression	1948
Fourth Impression	1949
First American Edition	1953

PRINTED IN GREAT BRITAIN BY
LOWE AND BRYDONE (PRINTERS) LTD., LONDON, N.W.10

TRANSLATORS' NOTE

THE Papers and Essays translated in this volume include the whole of Abraham's more important psycho-analytic work, except his *Traum und Mythus*, which has already appeared in English, and his study on Amenhotep, for which room could not, unfortunately, be found.

With an occasional exception, where the continuity of the subject-matter seemed to require it, the chapters are arranged in chronological order.

The references in the foot-notes usually only give the title and date of first publication of the works referred to. In that case further information will be found at the end of the volume in the 'List of Books and Papers referred to'. In addition, a complete and numbered bibliography of Abraham's publications has been appended, and these works are referred to by their number, together with the initials A. B. (Abraham Bibliography).

D. B.
A. S.

INTRODUCTORY MEMOIR [1]

THERE can be no doubt that of all the blows the science of psycho-analysis has yet suffered the death of Karl Abraham is much the most cruel and severe. We have once before lost by death a President of a Branch Society, and we miss a number of other valued workers whose names will always live in our memory. Blows of another sort have several times affected the psycho-analytical movement, one of which even brought with it the loss, by another way than death, of a President of the International Psycho-Analytical Association. But, with all due respect to the memory of our other dead colleagues, none of them meant to psycho-analysis what Karl Abraham did; for he was at once a master of its theory and practice, a pioneering contributor to our growing knowledge, a leader and organizer of the rarest order, as well as a loyal friend and colleague to all. Some of the reasons why the loss we have just sustained is so great will appear from the following record of his life and activities.

The main *events of Abraham's life*, considered externally, are as follows. He was born in Bremen on May 3, 1877, so that he was forty-eight when he died. He came of an old Jewish family that had long been resident in the Hanseatic towns of North Germany; there was an older brother, but no sister. He attended the high school at home until 1896, when he entered on the medical curriculum.

In his later school years Abraham developed an intense fondness for comparative linguistics and philology. Had he had the opportunity he would have preferred to devote himself entirely to such studies, and his interest in them persisted all his life. He certainly possessed an unusual

[1] Published in the *International Journal of Psycho-Analysis*, April 1926.

talent in this direction. Besides his mother tongue he could speak English, Spanish, Italian, and some Rhæto-Romanic; he analysed patients in the first two of these, and his paper at the International Congress of Psychology in Oxford was delivered (unwritten) in English. He also had a respectable knowledge of Danish, Dutch and French, being doubtless accustomed to hearing something of the two former languages in his childhood. He was thoroughly at home in the classics and eagerly seized the opportunity of his children's school studies to revive his familiarity with them. No one who was present at the Hague Congress in 1920 will forget the astonishment with which we heard him deliver a speech in a Latin that had to be brought up to date for the occasion.

He pursued his medical studies at Würzburg (a town for which he retained a great affection, hence perhaps the choice of it for the first German Psycho-Analytical Congress), Berlin, and Freiburg-im-Breisgau. He obtained his state doctorate in 1901 from the last-named university.

During these studies his principal interest was in biology, a fact which had a profound influence on his later work and general scientific outlook. It was while he was at Freiburg that he first became acquainted with Switzerland, the country which ever after he loved above all others. He liked the Swiss people and mode of life, but it was certainly the high mountains, which contrasted so much with his home scenery, that constituted the principal attraction. As soon as he had the chance he became an enthusiastic alpinist and made a number of first-class climbs. Like Segantini, who had died just before Abraham's first visit to Switzerland and in whose personality he was so deeply interested, he preferred the Upper Engadine to all other places on earth, and he returned there time and again. His last holiday, the convalescence from which we all hoped so much, was spent there in the summer of 1925, and he was able to carry out fairly arduous climbs even at that time. He had long cherished the desire to build a villa in that locality (near Sils Maria), and the last letter he ever wrote was a business one connected with this project.

While at Freiburg he conceived the wish to obtain a post at Burghölzli, partly so as to be in his beloved Switzerland, partly because he had been impressed by Professor Bleuler's work in psychiatry and esteemed it higher than that of any other psychiatrist. He had, however, to wait a few years before this wish could be gratified, and so in April, 1901, he accepted the post of assistant at the Berlin Municipal Asylum at Dalldorf. For his chief here, Professor Liepmann, he always preserved the greatest respect, and two scientific contributions dating from this time were in Liepmann's special field, that of aphasia and apraxia. He worked for nearly four years at Dalldorf, thus laying a sound foundation in clinical psychiatry; but in December, 1904, he was made happy by obtaining an appointment at Burghölzli, with the title of Assistant at the University Psychiatric Clinic of Zürich. Here his attention was soon turned in a more definitely psychological direction, and through Bleuler and Jung he became acquainted with Freud's works. His first contribution to psycho-analysis dates from this period, a paper (9)[1] read before an annual meeting of the German Psychiatric Society at Frankfurt. By a sad coincidence his last appearance in public was in a suburb of the same town eighteen years later, when he presided over the Ninth International Psycho-Analytical Congress.

About this time also occurred an event which was the main reason for the happiness and delight in life so characteristic of the man, and which was largely responsible for the energy and whole-hearted enjoyment with which he was able to devote himself to his work. Obtaining the appointment at Zürich coincided with his becoming engaged; and, as his position there steadily improved, he was able to marry, in January, 1906. His choice of helpmeet was supremely fortunate, for he found a partner who shared his life to the full and possessed a capacity for happiness equal to his own. A daughter was born at Zürich at the end of 1906, and a son a few years later in Berlin.

Abraham's own hope was to be able to work permanently

---

[1] Such numbers, in brackets, refer to the appended bibliography.

in Switzerland, but experience soon showed him that the
chances of a regular psychiatric career there were very
remote for a foreigner, so that he had to look elsewhere.
His decision to leave was doubtless hastened by the uncomfortable atmosphere resulting from the tension between
Bleuler and Jung. He therefore resigned his post in
November, 1907. In the same month he met Professor
Freud for the first time, on a visit he paid to him in Vienna;
the last time the two met was in the August of 1924 on
the Semmering. The conversations that then took place
bore early fruit in an important paper (11), to which we
shall have occasion to recur. The personal relations thus
established ripened into a friendship which remained un
clouded till the end. Abraham was one of a small group
who regularly visited Professor Freud during the holiday
season; on one occasion he organized a tour in which they
took part in a region, the Harz, which he knew well.

In December, 1907, Abraham settled in Berlin and began
a private psychiatric practice. He was helped somewhat
at first by Professor Oppenheim, a relative by marriage,
and he worked for a time at Oppenheim's neurological
clinic; but their divergent attitude towards Freud's theories
soon brought about a distance between the two men. Of
more lasting assistance was that rendered by Dr. Wilhelm
Fliess, whom Abraham got to know a few years later and for
whom he conceived a great regard; it was Fliess who was
mainly responsible for his treatment during his last illness.

Abraham was thus the first true psycho-analyst in
Germany; for one can hardly call such the few men,
Muthmann, Warda, etc., who had gone only a little way with
Freud's theories. He immediately began, by means of
private gatherings and lectures in his own house, to interest
other physicians in the work. Of those whom he managed
to interest at that time, however, only one, Dr. Koerber,
has persevered to the present day. He also tried for a few
years to present the subject at meetings of the various
medical societies, where he displayed great courage and
pertinacity in facing alone bitter and even fierce opposition.
In spite of these qualities, however, and his characteristic

hopefulness, even Abraham had ultimately to recognize the futility of such an undertaking. But the clouds began to lift. In the autumn of 1909 Dr. Eitingon, who had also worked at Burghölzli, joined him in Berlin, and from that time on Abraham had a colleague after his own heart.

The International Psycho-Analytical Association was formally established in March, 1910, and the Berlin Psycho-Analytical Society was founded in the same month. It was the first branch of the International Association to be constituted, the Vienna and Zürich branches following in April and June respectively; both these cities had of course informal groups for years before Berlin. Of the nine original members (which included Dr. Warda, the first physician independently to give support to Freud's theories) only two still remain in the Society, Drs. Eitingon and Koerber. Something will be said later about what Abraham meant to the Berlin Society, but a few simple facts may be related at this point. He held the Presidency of the Society from its foundation until his death. He gave freely and of his best to the Society; its interests always stood first with him. He was unremitting in his attendance, in leadership and criticism. Nearly all his chief works were communicated first of all to the Society. In all he read no fewer than forty-six communications to it in the fifteen years of his Presidency, in several of which he was unavailable owing to either war or illness; twelve communications were delivered in a single year (1923). His capacities in the training and teaching of analysts found scope also outside the activities of the Society. He conducted a number of training analyses, and among his most distinguished pupils may be mentioned Helene Deutsch, Edward Glover, James Glover, Melanie Klein, Sándor Radó, and Theodor Reik. Obvious disadvantages presented themselves, however, in local workers being analysed by the President of the Society, and it was a relief to Abraham when this difficulty was brilliantly solved by Dr. Hanns Sachs being invited to Berlin in 1920 and being given an official appointment in connection with this side of the work. On the other hand, Abraham freely devoted himself to delivering courses of lectures, and he rendered invaluable services in Berlin in this respect. The first course given under the auspices of the Society was a four weeks' one delivered in March, 1911; from then on he played a prominent part in every series arranged by the Society and later by the Lehrinstitut. Abraham was also active, though in a very minor way as compared with Eitingon, in founding and supporting the Berlin Polyclinic. From its inception in 1920 he was a prominent member of the Commission for the Education of Psycho-Analysts. In this field he was active in selecting suitable candidates, in training selected ones, particularly from abroad, and in general helpfulness in matters of organization. His time was of course too much in demand for him to engage in actual daily work at the Polyclinic itself.

Similarly Abraham's relation to the International Association was throughout a close one. He was one of the five or six who have attended every Congress so far held. The first Congress, in April, 1908, though actually organized by Dr. Jung, was mainly Austro-Hungarian in *personnel*; Abraham was one of the three ' foreigners ' to speak at it (the other two being Jung and the present writer). He read a paper at every Congress except the last one, where he was deterred by ill-health together with the duties of presiding; this is a record equalled only by Professor Freud and Dr. Ferenczi. The eight papers in question are among the most valuable of his contributions to psycho-analysis, and we shall presently mention them all when considering his scientific work. At and after the Munich Congress, in 1913, Abraham led the opposition against Jung, and after the latter resigned, the Advisory Council of the Association appointed Abraham to act as provisional President until the next Congress could be held. He made all the preparations for one to take place in Dresden in the September of 1914, and did in fact preside in this provisional capacity when it finally met in Budapest in the September of 1918. At the Seventh Congress, in 1922, he was made Secretary of the International Association, and at the Eighth, in 1924, he was finally elected, amid great applause, to the position of President. At the Ninth Congress, held the year after, he was unanimously re-elected.

Abraham was on the editorial staff of the *Zentralblatt* and *Zeitschrift* from the beginnings of these journals, and in 1919 was one of the editors of the latter. His activity here, however, was confined to matters of general policy and to contributing original papers and reviews. When Dr. Jung resigned the editorship of the *Jahrbuch* he was succeeded by Drs. Abraham and Hitschmann, who produced Band VI. in 1914. They would doubtless have continued in this capacity had it not been decided to discontinue the *Jahrbuch*.

Almost throughout the course of the war Abraham served at Allenstein, in East Prussia, where he was chief physician to the psychiatric station of the Twentieth Army Corps. The experience there gained enabled him to contribute to the psychology of war neurosis (57), and two of his most valuable other papers (52, 54) also date from this period. The war left him with a disastrous legacy of ill-health which quite possibly was the ultimate cause of his death. Toward the end of his service he contracted a severe dysentery which it cost him a great effort to throw off. Even afterwards he suffered from recurrent attacks, of which the last was in the spring of 1924. His health then appeared to be perfectly restored. In May, 1925, he accidentally inhaled a small foreign body; it was presumably infected, for within a fortnight he underwent an alarming attack of septic broncho-pneumonia that very nearly proved fatal. This left a local bronchiectasis which never entirely disappeared. A convalescence of several weeks in the Engadine was followed by the strain of presiding at the Homburg Congress, which was evidently too much for him. In the autumn, however, he appeared to be better, and even made tentative efforts to resume his work. But the condition got worse, obscure complications set in, and in November he had to enter a hospital. A fortnight later he underwent a serious operation which did not have the hoped-for effect. He gradually sank, and finally succumbed on Christmas Day, 1925. Throughout his long and painful illness he never evinced any doubts about the outcome, and he was full of optimistic plans to the very end. His tenacity of life, strength of will, and power of bodily recuperation were all of a most extraordinary order and astounded the physicians in charge. Several times it seemed impossible that a human being could survive the appalling stress that the affliction imposed on his body, but his will and courage refused to surrender until he ceased to breathe.

*   *   *   *   *   *

In order to obtain a fresh and unitary view of Abraham's *scientific works* I have just re-read the whole of them and will record my impressions of them here. In a personal appraisement of this general nature it will be understood that no attempt will be made to abstract or review the works themselves in any detail. The observations that will be offered may be divided under the headings of quantity, quality, and content.

Abraham was not a voluminous writer and the actual amount of what he wrote is less than one might expect from one's sense of their significance. His printed publications, excluding merely verbal communications, consist of four small books, containing altogether less than 300 pages, and forty-nine other papers amounting to about 400 pages; in addition there will be at least one posthumous paper. Very many of these were only a page or two long, and only five exceeded twenty pages.

The fact just mentioned is doubtless to be correlated with what was perhaps the most salient feature of all Abraham's writings, namely, a remarkable conciseness. Abraham never wasted a word in saying what he had to; every sentence was pregnant with meaning, and this meaning was expressed with completely unambiguous lucidity. He had an intense feeling for the concrete; he kept close to his clinical data and never indulged in remote hypotheses. These qualities, together with an unusual degree of objectivity, were also of great value in reviewing the work of others.   The collective reviews he wrote (15, 16, 51, 73) were models of what such things should be and are of permanent value in rapidly orienting the student of psycho-analysis;   the same qualities are to be observed in the numerous reviews he wrote for the *Zentralblatt* and *Zeitschrift*, which are not listed in the bibliography.   Abraham was a master of exposition and especially excelled in the difficult art of presenting case-histories.   It is well known how hard it is to enter into a report of someone else's cases, which is apt to be so incomplete as to be useless or else so long and confused as to be boring.   Abraham's smooth and easy style, combined with his feeling for the essential, enabled him to initiate the reader into the gist of a case in a page or two, and the clinical data with which he fortified his con-clusions were always as interesting as they were instructive. Few writers on psycho-analysis have equalled him in the gift of clear and attractive style, a gift all the more valuable in dealing with such a complicated subject-matter.

Coming now to the nature and content of Abraham's writings, we should constantly bear in mind, in estimating their significance, the date at which they were written.   It is a testimonial to the general accuracy of his work that so much of it has become incorporated into our daily knowledge as to make it not easy to appreciate the novelty it once had. His writings fall in a general way into four groups.   There are first those pioneering works to which reference has just been made;   among them may be mentioned those on the psychology of dementia præcox (11), the sexual aspects of alcoholism (12), the influence of incestuous fixations in the choice of a mate (13), and his book on dreams and myths (14).   Secondly, there is a number of neat and finished studies, classics which we can always re-read with enjoy-ment and instruction;   such are his essays on hysterical dream phantasies (17), Segantini (30), Amenhotep (34), the transformations of scoptophilia (43), ejaculatio præcox (54), war neuroses (57), and the castration complex in women (67).   Thirdly, we have his most original works, which constitute a valuable and permanent addition to our knowledge;   prominent among these one would place his

B

investigations into the pregenital stage of development
(52) with his two books on the evolution of the libido (105)
and character formation (106) respectively. The fourth
and last group would comprise a large number of shorter
papers always containing data that illustrated, confirmed
or expanded our knowledge of psycho-analytical theory
and practice.

In reviewing Abraham's writings as a whole one is
especially struck with the remarkable many-sidedness of
them. They cover the whole field of psycho-analysis and
there are few parts of that vast field which they do not
illuminate. Even on the aspects of psycho-analysis on
which he wrote least, *e.g.* homosexuality, dream interpretation, and education, enough is implied in his other works
to show that he was thoroughly conversant with the problems
involved. The variety of his writings makes it expedient
to divide them into different groups, and for the present
purpose five main headings have been chosen.

1. *Childhood* (including Infantile Sexuality). Abraham's
first two papers on psycho-analysis dealt with infantile
traumata (9, 10), and from the first he was concerned to
point out the dynamic aspects of the individual's reaction
to the trauma. He showed how the repeated experiencing
of sexual assaults constitutes with some children a regular
form of their sexual activity, an aspect of the subject quite
ignored by criminologists, and indeed by psychologists.
In the same connection, with special reference to the
traumatic neuroses, he dealt with unconscious impulses
directed against the self (injury or death), a theme which
recurs many times in his works. These impulses, which
we should now describe in terms of hostility against the
ego or against some renounced object which has been
incorporated into the ego, he attributed at that time to
unconscious masochism.

We pass now from his first writings to some of his last,
which may well be called his most important ones. I refer
to his work on the pregenital stage of libidinal development.
Already in 1913 the title of a communication to the Berlin
Society (41) tells us that he was preoccupied with the inter-

relation of the nutritional and sexual instincts, and in 1916 he published one of the two most brilliant contributions he ever made to psycho-analysis (52). With the aid of an astonishing case material, containing examples of infantile oral habits persisting to an age when their erotic nature could be put beyond doubt by direct introspection, he confirmed to the full Freud's conclusions about oral erotism. Adopting Freud's terms ' pregenital ' and ' cannibalistic ', he greatly enriched our knowledge of this phase in development, particularly as regards the phenomena in later life derived from it. Notable in the latter connection are the important relationships he established between oral erotism on the one hand and sleep and speech on the other. Many disturbances in eating were traced to a similar source. He distinguished between the cases where a disjunction has been effected between the two forms of mouth activity (nutritional and erotic), which are at first so closely united, and those where the union has persisted; and he pointed out that adult thumb-suckers, etc., belong to the former class, *i.e.* are in a more advanced stage of development than the person afflicted with neurotic disturbances of the eating function. The clinical parts of this paper, on manic-depressive insanity, will be mentioned in a later connection.

The continuation of this work, which took the form of a book published only last year (105), contains such a wealth of thought and investigation that no summary could do it justice. It is Abraham's weightiest contribution to psychoanalysis. In it he subdivides the three main stages in libidinal development into six: oral (1, sucking; 2, biting); anal-sadistic (1, destructive and expulsive; 2, mastering and retaining); genital (1, partial love or phallic; 2, adult). None of these subdivisions was entirely original on his part, but the detailed and explicit way in which he analysed them and showed the precise relation of one to the other constitutes a masterly piece of work which must always rank highly in psycho-analytical literature. In conjunction with van Ophuijsen he clarified the problems of the infant's relation to its object on the alimentary level (incorporation, expulsion, etc.), and threw a flood of light on the obscure problems of pregenital sexual life altogether.

Among other contributions to the study of childhood may be mentioned his papers on the part played by grandparents in infantile phantasy (40), the effects of overheard coitus (42; see also 43, Sect. ii.), the narcissistic attitude of infants towards excretory processes (63), and a series of pretty observations on infantile sexual theories (83, 94, 110); Nos. 38, 85, and 93 also belong to this group.

2. *Sexuality*. Abraham's interest in pregenital development was paralleled by that in the component instincts out of which adult sexuality is evolved. In an early paper on a case of foot and corset fetishism (18), he showed how the osphresiolagniac, scoptolagniac and sadistic impulses could undergo a complicated process of intertwining and displacement so as to produce a manifest perversion.

His lengthiest single paper was concerned with the restrictions and transformations that the scoptophilic impulse may undergo (43). Using a rich case material on which to found his conclusions, he dealt with the various forms of anxiety in regard to the visual function, other disturbances of this function, and neurotic affections of the visual organ itself. He traced the neurotic dread of light to displacements from an ambivalent attitude towards the parental genitalia, particularly the paternal ones; one case of hysteria and two of dementia præcox were described in this connection and the therapeutic results recorded. Further themes in the same paper are ophthalmic pain and other neurotic eye symptoms, the symbolic significance of darkness (which will be described presently), phobias relating to ghosts and the sun, and a number of problems belonging to applied psycho-analysis which will be mentioned in their appropriate connection.

A clever paper written in the middle of the war solved many problems relating to ejaculatio præcox (54). Again illustrating his points throughout from his ample clinical experience, he demonstrated how this symptom results from a failure in the evolution of urethral erotism. It is not, however, simply a fixation on this form of erotism, for it does not occur in masturbation, but depends on some feature in the object relationship. The cowardice characteristic of the condition, and the dread of hurting women, indicate repressed sadism. Such patients have a narcissistic over-estimation of the penis as being the urinary organ; they wish to exhibit urination in front of the woman, and because of her supposed contempt for the performance they react in a hostile manner by the impulse to pollute her. Disappointed love in respect of the mother, and consequently hostility towards her, furnish the key to the situation, as so often with the problems Abraham studied.

Another extremely valuable paper is concerned with the obverse of this attitude, *i.e.* with the hostility of women towards men as displayed in what Abraham termed the female castration complex (67). This contribution, which is extremely rich and suggestive, constitutes the basis of our knowledge of an obscure topic and has already opened the way to important later investigations. After discussing the various ways in which the girl may react to the belief that she has been castrated, the replacement of the wish for a penis by that for a child (confirmed by Freud's latest contribution on the subject at the Homburg Congress), and so on, Abraham distinguished two neurotic types, which are, however, evidently not to be too sharply separated. They result respectively from repression of the wish to take over the man's part in a positive direction and of the wish to avenge themselves by castrating the man; he called them the wish-fulfilling and the revenge types respectively. He contrasted these neuroses with the more positive ex-pressions in character formation, the former corresponding with female homosexuality and the latter with the archaic sadistic reaction. The motivating impulse in the second type is to bite off the man's penis, or at least to diminish his potency by disappointing him with frigidity and in other complicated hostile ways that will bring him into a posi-tion of contempt. This attitude logically culminates in a strong depreciation of the penis, and of men in general. Abraham showed the connection of the complex with various neurotic symptoms, such as vaginismus, enuresis, conjunctivitis neurotica, etc., and also pointed out the numerous ways in which it may influence women in their object choice. Last, but not least, he showed how such women can transmit their complex-conditioned reactions to their children.

Abraham's contributions in the sphere of love relationships in the usual sense are less extensive. In one of his first papers (13) he showed how marriages among relatives are often the expression of an incestuous fixation, a fact of importance in connection with the transmission of neurotic tendencies. In this connection he also pointed out (at the same time as Ferenczi) the part played by such fixations in the ætiology of psychical impotence and frigidity. Another manifestation of this fixation he saw in the undue tendency to monogamy. Some years later he published a pendant to this study in which he discussed the obverse manifestation of neurotic exogamy (45). Incestuous fixation was the theme of several other papers (e.g. 20, 22, 23, 53, 97, 98, 107, 112), and was of course extensively taken into account in all his analytic work.

Other papers on purely sexual topics are two on sadism (21 and 33), one on the ear passage as an erotogenic zone (46), two on anal erotism (48 and 70) which will be mentioned later, and a number of shorter ones (66, 86, 88, 89, 103).

3. *Clinical Subjects*. As was to be expected from a clinician of Abraham's rank, his contributions in this sphere are of special importance. The first one of note marked a turning-point in our knowledge of the psychology of dementia præcox (11) and the differentiation between neuroses and psychoses in general. It is a matter for wonderment that a professional psychiatrist such as he was never returned to this subject later; presumably it was because his interest in this field was concentrated in the attempt to unravel another psychosis. Jealous colleagues in Zürich unjustly accused him of not sufficiently acknowledging his indebtedness to Jung in connection with this paper, but events showed clearly that Jung never accepted the main idea of the paper, which, as Abraham himself

avowed, emanated from a conversation with Freud (his first one). The main idea in question was the suggestion that disturbances of the ego functions could be purely secondary to disturbances in the sphere of the libido, in which event it might be possible to apply Freud's libido theory to the elucidation of dementia præcox. After discussing the relation between sublimation and transference, Abraham pointed out that the capacity for both these processes is diminished in dementia præcox, and that the so-called dementia is simply the result of this state of affairs. In it the libido is withdrawn from objects—the opposite of hysteria, where there is an exaggerated object cathexis—and applied to the self. To this he traced the delusions of persecution and megalomania, the latter being an expression of auto-erotic sexual overestimation (of what later became termed narcissism). In contradistinction from hysteria, the psycho-sexual peculiarity of dementia præcox lies in an inhibited development at the auto-erotic level, with consequently a tendency to regress to this level.

Abraham's most systematic, and probably his most important, contribution to psychopathology consists in his three works on manic-depressive insanity. The brilliance of Freud's essay in the same field, and the striking manner in which he found the central key to the problems, have doubtless obscured some of the credit which Abraham deserved, as genius always does when brought side by side with talent; and this was probably heightened by a purely accidental circumstance: *Trauer und Melancholie*, that is to say, was written at a time when no reference could be made in it to some valuable contributions which Abraham had recently made (52), although, owing to war conditions, it was not actually published until a year later than the latter. No works of Abraham's reveal his scientific characteristics, as regards both his capacities and his limitations, better than these on manic-depressive insanity. It was also the study which evidently fascinated him more than any other, although it is probable, as indeed is hinted by the titles of two out of the three works, that he was more interested in the light the disease throws on certain early stages of libidinal development than in the clinical problems as such.

In his first paper on the subject (*Ansätze, etc.*, 26), which was read at the Weimar Congress in 1911, Abraham started from the assumption that depression must bear a relation to grief similar to that of anxiety to fear, and he came to the conclusion that the despair about life is the result of a renunciation of the sexual goal. He narrated six cases, in all of which he found both clinical and psychological features very much akin to those of the obsessional neurosis. Thus, the patients showed many characteristics of the latter condition in the so-called free interval, and in both conditions there is a mutual paralysis of the love and hate instincts. In manic-depressive insanity the libido shows predominantly an attitude of hatred. It is as though the patient said: " I cannot love because of my hate; the result is that I am hated and so I am depressed and hate back " (return of the repressed sadism). The sense of guilt and sin corresponds with repressed hate. The delusion of poverty is an expression of the same fact (money = love). In mania the complexes overcome the inhibitions and the patient reverts to the carefree state of childhood. He related the beneficial effects of his therapeutic endeavours and regarded them as justifying the hope that it would fall to psycho-analysis to free psychiatry from the nightmare of therapeutic nihilism.

His treatment of these clinical problems is more incidental in the second contribution (*Untersuchungen über die früheste prägenitale Entwicklungsstufe der Libido*, 52), but none the less important. He here clearly recognized the oral fixation in melancholia and was able to explain a number of clinical features on that basis. Thus the refusal of food is due to regression to the old connection between eating and oral erotism, as is also the dread of starvation. He was further able to formulate the distinction between manic-depressive insanity and the closely allied obsessional neurosis in terms of pregenital libidinal organization. In the latter condition, with its anal-sadistic fixation, the attitude towards the object is one of mastering, whereas in the former condition it is one of annihilating through swallowing (late oral stage). The most striking feature of melancholia, the intense self-reproaches and self-depreciation, Abraham regarded as self-punishment induced by horror at the repressed cannibalistic impulses. In this he was partly right, for a certain number of these do emanate in this way from a guilty conscience, but he failed to make the much more important observation, which Freud said was 'not at all hard to perceive', to the effect that these reproaches are chiefly directed against the image of the lost love-object which has been erected within the ego. In a later paper he described his difficulty in understanding the point when he first read it in Freud's essay, and gave some personal explanation for his inhibition; it is not likely, however, that the explanation was a complete one. For a man of his rigid ethical standards it was evidently easier to grasp the fact that a person could inflict on himself severe suffering as a punishment for having had hostile wishes directed against a love-object than to believe that such a person was still torturing the image of that object.

His third and most complete study of the problem (105) took full cognizance of Freud's epoch-making essay, and Abraham was able to confirm all Freud's conclusions in detail and even to amplify some of them. He identified the incorporating of the object to which Freud had called attention with the swallowing impulse dating from the oral stage, and in this connection he developed some interesting considerations about the process of introjection in general. The facts that in the free interval the melancholiac can advance to an obsessional (*i.e.* anal-sadistic) level, and further, that an essential difference between the two conditions is that the melancholiac gives up his object relationship whereas the obsessional neurotic retains his (Freud), brought him to the conclusion that the anal-sadistic phase must have two sub-stages (see above). He suggested that the line of demarcation between these two sub-stages may be of great practical importance in psychiatry as indicating the point where true object-relationship sets in, thus pointing to one of the main distinctions between neurosis and psychosis. The ætiology of manic-depressive insanity he sought in a constitutionally strong oral erotism, with a special fixation at this level induced by severe disappointments in relation to the mother ; he distinguished between disappointments of this kind that occur before, during, and after the Oedipus stage.   The melancholiac's hatred is predominantly directed against the mother, but in a later passage Abraham pointed out that some of this originally referred to the father, there being in this disorder an unusual tendency to invert the Oedipus complex.   This feature, and the ambivalence concerning both parents lead to complicated forms of introjection, and he could distinguish between reproaches emanating from either introjected love-object against the self and those directed by the self against the image of the object; the latter are, of course, the principal and more characteristic ones.

Abraham drew an interesting parallel between melancholia and the processes of archaic grief as elucidated by Róheim.   He further threw much light on the obscure matter of the curious course run by manic-depressive insanity.   He regarded the incorporating of the object in the oral phase as being partly determined by an endeavour to preserve it from annihilation and considered that then, after the sadistic attack had worn itself out, the image of the love-object is once more expelled—by the anal route.   He drew a picture of what he called the ' primal depression ' of infancy, the precursor of later melancholia, and suggested that patients affected with mania not preceded by melancholia were still engaged in shaking off this primal depression and the heightened sexual desire that follows the working through of grief, particularly as seen in primitive ceremonies.

In an early work on hysterical dream states (17) Abraham brought this syndrome, described by Löwenfeld, into relation with Freud's work on hysterical attacks and traced the genesis of them to masturbation phantasies which have undergone repression.   Such patients linger in the stage of preliminary pleasure because end pleasure is associated with anxiety.   He narrated six cases of the kind.   In one of them he was able to trace the symptom of macropsia to a regression to childhood.   His study of the condition furnished a link between allo- and hetero-suggestion, inasmuch as the attacks could be shown to occur either quite spontaneously or in the presence of people by whom the patients felt themselves to be hypnotically influenced. Several of Abraham's short papers were on the subject of phantasy life, and his pretty analysis of the father-saving type of phantasy (76) is specially worthy of remembrance in this connection.

Abraham published two papers on locomotor anxiety (39 and 44), a condition of which he had suffered slight symptoms himself in early life. He showed that the sexual origin of the anxiety could be demonstrated by re-converting it therapeutically, when the same patients took an unusual pleasure in locomotor acts (both active and passive). In the same paper (44) he threw light on the common symptom of ' dread of dread ' by connecting it with repression of ' fore-pleasure '.

His war experience enabled him to confirm independently the view that had been put forward by the present writer concerning the narcissistic origin of the so-called ' war-shock ' cases (57), as did also Ferenczi shortly afterwards. Criticism is often made of the supposedly subjective nature of psycho-analytic work, but this may be quoted as an experimental demonstration of the contrary. When faced with entirely novel problems observers in different countries, quite cut off from one another by war conditions, investigated them and came to substantially the same conclusions.

In a discussion on Ferenczi's work on tic, Abraham threw out the interesting suggestion that the condition represents a conversion symptom on the anal-sadistic level to be contrasted with the symptoms of conversion-hysteria developed on the phallic level (72).

Abraham's contributions on the subject of therapeutics were few, but important. The chief one was certainly his study of a special and difficult type of reaction characteristic of some patients (58). They are mostly obsessional neurotics who show a high degree of narcissistic defiance and who tend to avoid transference by identifying themselves with the analyst. They insist on conducting their analysis themselves, a tendency which Abraham connected with anal-sadistic reactions. Forbidden masturbation plays an important part in the ætiology of such cases. Abraham discussed helpfully the special therapeutic technique needed to deal with this difficult type. His paper on psycho-analytic treatment in advanced years (62) may be summed up in the dictum that the prognosis depends more on the age of the neurosis (*i.e.* the age of the patient at which the neurosis became severe) than on the actual age of the patient. Special measures are necessary, however, in these older cases, such as more active pressure and help on the part of the analyst. In this connection may also be mentioned the clear way in which he illustrated the value of Freud's advice not to encourage patients to write down their dreams before analysis (37). Finally, Abraham's work on the treatment of psychotic patients is the best we yet possess, and he must certainly be regarded as a pioneer in this difficult field. He showed a rare degree of scepticism and critical honesty in recording his results (26, 105), and he suggested useful criteria (*e.g.* transitory symptoms) for determining what proportion of a given change in mental state could be ascribed to the actual therapeutic endeavours of the physician. He demonstrated that manic-depressive insanity can, in favourable cases, be radically affected by psycho-analysis, and he was very hopeful of further progress along these lines.

Abraham took a special interest in the problems of alcoholism and drug habits. Almost the only papers he wrote in pre-analytical days, apart from those evidently inspired by his teacher's interests, were on the effects of drug-taking (3 and 4). His early paper on the relations between alcoholism and sexuality (12) showed the essential nature of the connection between the two and was the foundation of all our later knowledge on the subject. Indeed the only important later contribution that has been made on this matter has dealt with the inherent relation between alcoholism and homosexuality, a connection which, curiously enough, Abraham pointed out only in regard to women. He missed also the homosexual basis of alcoholic delusions of jealousy, ascribing these only to the displacement of guilt on to the mate. He showed, however, that the motive of drinking was temporarily to heighten sexual potency by undoing repressions and sublimations and releasing especially the component impulses, and further that alcohol betrays its user later by diminishing his potency. He also revealed the unconscious identification of alcohol with semen, and of syringe with phallus. The connection between morphinism and repressed sexuality was insisted on in the same contribution, as also in later passages (17, S. 14 ; 52, S. 84), where the oral basis of both smoking and morphinism was pointed out.

The numerous short communications on clinical subjects (24, 31, 32, 36, 49, 55, 68, 71, 90, 91, 104, 111) mostly contain notable observations and suggestions. One may remark that Abraham's interest in the obsessional neurosis seems to have been greater than that in hysteria. A clinical paper on Coué's teachings (115), not available at the moment of writing, is being prepared from notes left by Abraham, and will be published at the same time as this obituary.

4. *General Topics*. By far the most important work of a general nature that Abraham contributed to psycho-analysis was his investigation of characterology. Two of the three studies were published separately, and then all three united in a single volume (106). In his essay on the anal character Abraham expanded the extensive work that had been done on this subject and added a number of fresh observations of considerable clinical and characterological value. We may especially note the two types he distinguished of excessive docility and defiance respectively, both of which may be present in the same person. He showed also how the two types react in the analytic situation: the latter one produces a resistance very similar to the characteristic one he had described in another connection (58, see above), whereas the former one, on the other hand, insists on the analyst doing the whole work himself; in both cases the result is a refusal to enter upon free associations. The details of regression from the genital to the anal level were also dealt with in an illuminating way.

The second essay, on the contributions made by oral erotism to character-formation, was one of Abraham's most original contributions to psycho-analysis. The indirect effects of oral erotism in later life are in great part produced through the connection between it and anal erotism, and here Abraham showed how primordial is the triangular relationship between the functions of acquiring, possessing and expending, the economy of which varies greatly among different persons. Direct gratification of oral erotism is of course permitted to a considerable extent in the adult, so that sublimation is less extensive than it is with some other erotogenic zones. The most typical form of sublimation seems to be the character trait of optimism, one which Abraham himself possessed in a high degree; it contrasts with the seriousness and pessimism of certain anal types, particularly those associated with early disappointments of oral gratification. If this disappointment occurs during the second—biting—phase of the oral stage, then the later love will be characterized by great ambivalency due to the cannibalistic and hostile attitude towards the mother persisting. Abraham threw a great deal of light on the genesis and interrelation of other traits concerned with oral-erotic displacements, notably greed, envy, thrift, avarice, and impatience.

The third essay in this series dealt with the ‘ genital character ’, and so was concerned with the problems of normality. Abraham disclaimed any attempt to set up absolute standards in this respect, and indeed insisted at length on the impossibility of doing so, but he nevertheless gave us a very valuable point of view by inquiring which of the pregenital features are the last to be relinquished. He found that the most severe way of testing genital normality was to ascertain the extent to which the subject has overcome his narcissism and the attitude of ambivalency that runs through most of the earlier stages. In his discussion of the importance of aim-deflected feelings of genital origin for a satisfactory relationship with the outer world, Abraham dwelt on the supreme necessity of love in childhood and the injurious effects that may result from the child receiving too little of this essential pabulum.

In the same connection may perhaps be mentioned Abraham's attempts to solve the problems of grief (105). This also he considered to have an important connection with oral attitudes. Whereas Freud lays stress on the gradual and painful tearing of oneself away from the loved object under the demands of reality, Abraham paid more attention to the incorporation of the image of this object, and he regarded this as being carried out by the oral mechanism. (It is doubtful, however, whether this is a regular process in the 'grief-work'.)

As a general contribution to psycho-analysis should also be mentioned the numerous social implications that belong to Abraham's work on the female castration complex (67, see above). These will be of very great importance sociologically in the future, and when they are more fully worked out the part that Abraham played in indicating them will not be forgotten.

Abraham's contributions to our knowledge of individual symbolisms were fairly extensive, and they have now for the most part been incorporated in the general body of science. Among them may be noted: house and garden as symbols of the mother, new house as that of the strange woman or baby (25 and 96); snake as a symbol of the *father's* penis, with the fear of death as a manifestation of dread of the father (32); spider as a symbol of the feared mother (80); his beautiful analysis of the forked road in connection with the Oedipus saga, as well as of the number three (76 and 82); and darkness (or anything mysterious and obscure) as a symbol of the mother's womb (including bowel) (43).

Abraham confirmed Stekel's observation about the significance of personal names (28), though he added little new on the point. He also made several contributions to the psychopathology of every-day life, both throughout his clinical writings and in a few special notes (*e.g.* 78, 79, etc.).

5. *Applied Psycho-Analysis.* Abraham's first work in this field was of historical importance (14), for it opened the way for much of the later research that has been carried out in the application of psycho-analysis to mythology, by Otto

Rank, Theodor Reik, and others. It was of course mainly inspired by the Oedipus analysis in the *Traumdeutung*. Justifying the attempt to correlate dreams and myths on the ground that they are both products of human phantasy, he showed the far-reaching connections between the two. With both the essence of the phantasy is a wish-fulfilment and the wishes in both cases are unconscious and infantile. The egocentricity of the individual in the one corresponds with the egocentricity of the people in the other. The phenomena of censorship, repression and the formation of neologisms are common to both, as are the mechanisms of condensation, displacement, and secondary elaboration. He illustrated these conclusions by presenting some dream analyses side by side with a most interesting study of the Prometheus myth and the legend of the divine drinks; incidentally the sexual nature of the latter, soma, nectar and ambrosia, was clearly pointed out. Making good use of his philological knowledge, Abraham pointed out the resemblances between the etymological and the psycho-analytic points of view and showed how our knowledge of symbolism could be derived from investigation of the one field as well as from the other. His final conclusion was that 'myths are relics from the infantile mental life of the people, and dreams constitute the myths of the individual'. The universal validity of determinism in mental life was also insisted on. The book is written with extraordinary skill, and illustrates Abraham's lucidity and simplicity at their best. Although the contents are now fully assimilated in analytical circles, it is still a pleasure to re-read it and enjoy the powers of exposition which Abraham possessed in so high a degree.

Abraham's next work in this field also took book form, an interesting study of the Swiss painter Segantini (30). It was almost the first time that an attempt was made to analyse the personality of a painter and to correlate in detail the painter's unconscious trends with his choice of theme, composition, and mode of presentation. He demonstrated the enormous influence the painter's mother exercised on both his life and his work, and he was able to trace in detail the ambivalent attitude of love and hate the painter bore to her; once more we have a study of the 'evil mother'. The closing pages of this book contain a remarkable foreshadowing of Freud's conception of the death instinct in its investigation of the unconscious motives leading to self-destruction. Abraham's interest in this study was evidently with the psychology of the artist rather than in the psychology of art itself, but in a later paper (100), unfortunately never printed, he took up the question of the tendencies in modern art as seen from a psycho-analytic point of view.

Abraham's analysis of Amenhotep IV. (Echnaton) (34) is not only of great interest in itself, but is noteworthy as being the first occasion when it was shown how a knowledge of psycho-analysis could contribute to the elucidation of purely historical problems. To attempt the psychoanalysis of someone who died some twenty-three centuries ago may have seemed a desperate undertaking, but Abraham's painstaking study had nothing of the hypothetical about it, and the conclusions he reached will be hard ever to impugn. Echnaton, 'the first great man in the spiritual realm to be recorded by history', was a forerunner of the Christian teachers of the doctrine of love and an ethical revolutionary who reserved his hate for his father only. Abraham was able to show how all Echnaton's innovations, iconoclasms and reforms could be directly traced to the effects of his Oedipus complex.

Abraham's wide education and general knowledge were turned to good account in many of his psycho-analytical studies. In his detailed investigation of scoptophilia (43, see above) he expounded his general conclusions with the help of a mass of mythological and folk-loristic material. His equating of beliefs and fears concerning the sun and ghosts respectively was a noteworthy achievement in this paper, and in it he also clearly indicated the ambivalence of the motives that led to man displacing the father on to the heavens (exaltation and relegation to a distance). In the same paper he made a practical contribution to our knowledge of sublimation in science, philosophy and

c

religion by showing how chafing solicitude for the solving of questions that cannot be answered, such as those to do with the aim of life, the length of life, and the outcome of life after death, is largely the result of unconscious displacement from questions that may not or dare not be answered.

The same wide range of knowledge comes to expression in a number of shorter papers in the field of applied psychoanalysis, such as those on the significance of the ' day of atonement ' rites (64), the note on the Russian sect of yoni worshippers (25), the clever analysis of the details in the Oedipus legend (76 and 82), and many others (29, 56, 59, 64, 69, 84). The last paper ever published by Abraham (95), a most interesting study of a rogue he had come across, was a thoughtful contribution to one of the chief problems in criminology.

Summary. In attempting to summarize in a few words the essential characteristics of Abraham's written work, one would select the features of many-sidedness, one which speaks for itself in the review just made, and the high general average of excellence he maintained in his writings; hardly anything he wrote was of merely ephemeral value, and his work throughout was marked by the valuable qualities of sobriety, cautious scepticism and good judgement.

This evenness in quality may perhaps be correlated with an important feature of Abraham's mode of thought, namely, his consistently biological outlook. This gave a stable background to all his work and furnished a criterion by which the inherent probability or validity of any general conclusion could be measured. One may be permitted the reflection that of all the many ways in which Abraham will be missed in psycho-analysis, the one that may well have the weightiest consequences for the future will be in connection with this very feature. Psycho-analysis has not even yet come to the most decisive turning-point in its development, although it has successfully survived important preliminary ones. That will come, and very likely within the next twenty years, when the question of incorporating psycho-analysis into the general body of science seriously arises. There the most severe test for the young science will present itself, for much will depend on the alternatives of whether it will be absorbed by a process of partial acceptance and continual attenuation, or whether it will display sufficient vitality to preserve its essential qualities and impart them to the other branches of science with which it will come into contact. Just in this task which lies before us Abraham's characteristic qualities would undoubtedly have been of peculiar value, for he possessed a breadth and sanity of outlook over science and life as a whole combined in a rare degree with a single-minded vision of the depths of psycho-analytic truths.

On studying his original contributions one is struck by the preponderance of themes dealing with the pregenital stages of development, including auto-erotism and the component instincts, and with the element of repressed hate, especially in regard to the mother. The latter theme recurs again and again in his works and far outweighs in extent his contributions in the sphere of love, transference, and akin problems. It is similarly remarkable that such a first-class clinician, a man with whom the clinical point of view was always the dominant one, contributed less to our knowledge of purely clinical problems, such as problems of the transference neuroses or even the psychoses (in spite of his work on manic-depressive insanity, which was the outstanding one in this field), than to genetic problems of libidinal development. It is likely that he will be remembered longer for his contributions in the genetic than for those in the clinical field.

If one had to select Abraham's most important single piece of work, though never forgetting the variety of his valuable contributions to all aspects of psycho-analysis, it would probably be that on oral erotism. Here he described in full its various manifestations, traced clearly its internal development and its evolution into succeeding libidinal phases, worked out its relation to both love and hate, demonstrated its clinical importance in respect of alcoholism, drug-taking, and especially manic-depressive insanity, and

—last but not least—gave us a revealing picture of the significant part it plays in the formation of character. Perhaps the most outstanding lesson in psychology we owe to Abraham is the vast importance of the suckling period and the fateful consequences that antagonism aroused to the mother during this period may have for later life.

* * * * *

It remains to say something about Karl Abraham's personality, about his personal value to psycho-analysis. We have attempted to present an objective estimate of what Abraham's scientific writings have meant and mean for the development of our knowledge, but his value to psycho-analysis greatly transcended even this. The nature of it may be hinted at by a single consideration: just as he was the central fulcrum through which the advance of psycho-analysis operated in Berlin, and in Germany altogether, so his influence insensibly made Berlin in many important respects the centre of the whole international psycho-analytical movement. To understand the secret of this achievement is to know Abraham. For the dominating position he attained in psycho-analysis was not in the smallest degree the result of any personal ambition or striving; it proceeded altogether from the automatic consequence of his intrinsic worth, and therein lay the greatness of the man.

Some men are born to be leaders. It is in their nature to command others. Abraham was not such a man. To the very end, as he remarked to me at the Homburg Congress, he found it strange that he should occupy a prominent position; it was, as he said, foreign to his nature, and it was not easy for him to apprehend and accept the evident fact. His influence over his fellows and the important part he played sprang not from any desire for eminence, but from more solid qualities, from a surpassing worth that could not but be recognized. What were those qualities?

This question can be answered only by resolving an antinomy. Prominent among Abraham's character traits were a refreshing youthfulness and a sanguine optimism. Now these are not traits that usually inspire implicit reliance, nor do they generally go with such qualities as cautious scepticism and calm, sober judgement on which we laid stress when considering Abraham's scientific work. Nevertheless both descriptions are profoundly true. To comprehend this paradox is to hold the key to Abraham's personality.

Even in the qualities that gave Abraham his great personal and social charm there were hints of stouter ones which formed the basis of his character. He was singularly youthful, and even boyish at moments when the circumstances were appropriate; though he could be decidedly witty at times, a quiet fun, often very shrewd, was his more characteristic form of humour. This gave his personality, so winning to women and attractive to men, a freshness and vigour that always made him a stimulating companion or colleague. His demeanour was invariably cheerful, courteous and friendly. But these qualities were not to be presumed on. Behind them was a firmness impervious to the blandishments of man or woman. He could afford to be easy and pliant in his intercourse with others, just because he had himself so completely in hand; knowing that he could not be unduly influenced from either within or without, he was confident in any situation. This complete confidence was ultimately rooted in self-mastery.

The same is true of one of his most characteristic traits, what his friends called his incurable optimism. He was always hopeful, however irksome or sinister the prospect, and his buoyancy, together with the confidence that went with it, often contributed materially to bringing about a more successful issue than at first seemed possible. As a rule this optimism was very nicely balanced with a keen sense of reality, so that its effect was purely invigorating, but once or twice in his life it played him false, marring what was otherwise a perfection of stability.

Abraham's capacity for reserve was to be discerned in the quiet punctiliousness of his manner. Probably, however, few even of his friends knew how deep this was.

They only felt that somewhere there was a barrier beyond which one might not penetrate. For the purposes of life Abraham had compassed a peculiarly stable mental organization, but the very depths were not to be plumbed, perhaps even by himself.

No one could know Abraham well without realizing that he was one of those men who are endowed with quite exceptional powers of sublimation, and that he had attained an unusually advanced measure of emotional and instinctual development. It is not chance that it was he who taught us what is perhaps the best criterion of full mental development: the overcoming of narcissism and of ambivalence. For we shall not know many men who would emerge as he did when tried by this severe test.

Abraham had been able to transmute his egocentric trends in a very remarkable degree, with the result that he could devote himself quite single-heartedly to the one goal of his life, namely, the advancement of psycho-analysis. With a solitary exception, the nature of which was such as to prove the rule, it was impossible to detect in him a trace of any personal ambition whatever; the exception was a rather odd desire to become a Docent at the University of Berlin, and this was itself obviously bound up with the prestige of psycho-analysis. His colleagues in Berlin will best know how completely he identified himself with the interests of the Society there—from the moment he founded it, in March 1910, to the time of his last attendance, on May 9 of last year. His rare gifts as a teacher, investigator and lecturer were indispensable to the development of the Society, but of still greater value were his qualities as a leader, of which we have still to speak.

His transmutation of purely personal interest, together with his native shrewdness of mind, gave Abraham an unusual capacity for viewing problems, personalities, and events in a detached and objective way. This to a great extent accounts for the marked sobriety of his judgement, but it had a further value. It gave him a social ease and friendliness of manner that made it possible for him to approach his fellows with unusual directness, so that no one would well take amiss whatever he might have to say. Any criticisms he might wish to make were at once transferred from any personal basis to a purely objective one, and this attitude rarely failed in its effect of allaying emotion and conducing to a reasoned consideration of the matter. Courteously firm and, when his mind was made up, inflexible, he was never in the smallest way overbearing; his quiet decisiveness was in itself authoritative. He was a delightful colleague to work with, as I had ample opportunity to observe when we were associated together in the Central Executive of the Association as well as in many other connections. He was always accessible to any ideas presented to him, and one could count on their not being refracted by any subjective elements; an answer to any proposal would be clear, concise, and concrete. All these qualities made him an admirable referee in matters of personal or scientific disputation. A great part, therefore, of both his sanity of judgement and his sagacity in human relationships proceeded from his capacity for impersonal objectivity.

Ambivalence was entirely foreign to Abraham's nature, both intellectually and emotionally. He seemed to be altogether devoid of hate. He sometimes disliked certain individuals, usually on the impersonal ground of regarding their activities as harmful to the cause of psycho-analysis; but even so I have never known of his hating anyone. He was even at times curiously oblivious to the strength of hostile emotions in other people; I have seen him cheerfully reasoning with someone who was glowering with anger and resentment, apparently blandly ignoring the emotion and full of hope that a quiet exposition would change the situation. In controversy, even when heated, he would be unbending, but his temper never frayed. Abraham could please charmingly, help gladly and generously, love devotedly; he could withstand stubbornly and fight valiantly; but he could not hate. Consequently, though he occasionally excited criticism and opposition, he never provoked hatred: he had his opponents, and of course jealous rivals, but he had no enemies.

Abraham's profound sense of confidence was thus

founded in the stability of his own mind.   With his evenly
balanced mental organization and his securely firm self-
control, one inclining slightly even towards austerity, he
could freely give rein to his innate tendencies, knowing they
would carry him only the ways he desired.   When we say
that Abraham was a *normally developed* member of society,
we are using words which, though cold to the uninitiated,
are rich with significance for all psycho-analysts.

We can now see how inevitable it was that Abraham
should be a leader in psycho-analysis, and why he was so
successful in that position.   His tireless energy and his
demeanour of intrepid confidence, always fresh and un-
perturbed, were bracing to others and inspired them with
the assurance necessary for accomplishing difficult tasks.
His shrewd perspicacity enabled him to criticize in a
peculiarly cool way any inaccuracies or exuberances and to
exercise a steadying influence on the divagations of fancy.
His constantly benevolent and at the same time impersonal
attitude made it possible to convey such criticisms
without wounding or disheartening the person affected.
His brightness and friendliness, aided by his general
optimism, inclined him always to make prominent the best
features of a colleague's work and, when commenting on
it, insensibly to modify the weak features so as to present
the work in the most favourable light.   The result was
that he always got the best out of his colleagues and pupils.
And all the while it was plain to them that in Abraham they
had a rallying point, a touchstone of objectivity, to which
they rarely applied in vain.

This last feature leads us to what were, in my opinion,
the most salient of all Abraham's valuable qualities—his
fearlessness and his integrity.   That he displayed a tenacious
courage when ringed round with hostility in his lonely
pioneering days is generally known, though it needs a similar
experience fully to appreciate what that means.   But few
know that there were even more striking evidences of his
courageous disregard for painful consequences; at more
than one important juncture in his life I have known him
risk the friendship of those very near to him by pursuing a

course which seemed to him the only right one, even when he knew it was one that could readily lend itself to serious misinterpretation.

For integrity with Abraham came before everything else. Honesty of purpose was so built into his nature that he invariably and unhesitatingly did what he felt to be the only right thing, and he never swerved from his course. This high degree of integrity produced on those around him such a sense of certainty and security that they came to rely on him as on a rock. Amid the turmoils of personal emotions and the clash of discordant tendencies Abraham stood always firm, a central steadiness in the shifting eddies around. And this was his greatest value to psychoanalysis. Karl Abraham was in truth *un preux chevalier* of Science, *sans peur et sans reproche.*

ERNEST JONES.

TABLE OF CONTENTS

CHAPTERS XXIII., XXIV., XXV.
Psycho-Analytical Studies on Character-Formation

CHAPTER I

THE EXPERIENCING OF SEXUAL TRAUMAS AS A FORM OF SEXUAL ACTIVITY (1907)[1]

FREUD's original theory of the ætiology of hysteria has undergone important alterations in the course of time. As he himself has pointed out,[2] however, two important points remain unchanged in it, namely, sexuality and infantilism, the significance of which he has investigated more and more deeply.

Among other things, the problem of sexual traumas in youth has been affected by the alterations that the general theory of sexuality and of the neuroses has undergone. For some time Freud regarded those traumas as the ultimate source of hysterical phenomena, and assumed that they were discoverable in all cases of hysteria. But he has not been able to maintain this view in its original form. In the paper referred to he assigns a secondary rôle to sexual traumas in youth and assumes the presence of an abnormal psycho-sexual constitution as the primary cause of a neurosis. This view accords with the fact that not all children who experience a sexual trauma suffer later on from hysteria. According to Freud, children who are disposed to hysteria react in an abnormal manner to sexual impressions of all kinds in consequence of their abnormal disposition. I recently showed that infantile sexual traumas occurred in the psychoses [3] as well; and I put forward the view that the trauma could not be regarded as the cause of the disease,

---

[1] [No. 10, A. B.]
[2] ' My Views on the Part played by Sexuality in the Ætiology of the Neuroses ' (1905).   [3] [Cf. No. 9, A. B.]

but that it exercised an influence on the form taken by it. I agreed with Freud's assumption of an abnormal psycho-sexual constitution in the patient.

Nevertheless this assumption only takes us one step forward, and stops before a second, more important difficulty. It certainly explains why a sexual trauma in childhood is of such great significance in the history of many individuals. On the other hand, the problem remains why so many neurotic and psychotic persons can produce a sexual trauma in the anamnesis of their childhood. If we can solve this problem we shall gain some information at least as to the nature of the abnormal constitution which we have assumed to exist.

In this paper I intend to go more closely into these questions. I shall more particularly try to establish the view that in a great number of cases the trauma was desired by the child unconsciously, and that we have to recognize it as a form of infantile sexual activity.

Anyone who is interested in the psychology of children will have observed that whereas one child will resist temptation or seduction another will easily yield to it. There are children who will hardly oppose any resistance to the invitation of an unknown person to follow him; others who react in an opposite way in the same circumstances. Presents and sweets, or the mere expectation of them, influence children very differently. Further, there are children who quite definitely provoke adults in a sexual manner. With regard to this the reports of cases brought against persons charged with immoral conduct towards children are very instructive. In two cases in which a senile dement had assaulted a child I happen to know that the child had behaved in a provocative way; and in a number of other cases I had good grounds for suspecting a similar state of affairs. Even among brothers and sisters one finds striking differences in this respect. I know of many cases of this kind. In a family of several sisters, for instance, one allowed herself to be enticed by a strange person to go with him; and on another occasion, when playing with an older boy, she followed him into a distant room and allowed him to kiss her. Her two sisters showed the opposite tendency. This girl, of whom many similar episodes could be related, exhibited neurotic traits even in childhood and later became ill with pronounced hysteria. This example is not exceptional but typical. For the present we may say quite generally that certain children respond more readily than others to sexual or other kinds of seduction, and we may make use of this fact so as to classify sexual traumas, diverse as they are, into two groups. We can distinguish sexual traumas which take the child unawares from those which it has itself provoked or which are due to temptation or seduction, or which it could at any rate have foreseen and avoided. In the first group there are no grounds for assuming a compliance on the part of the child; in the second we cannot avoid assuming that there was a compliance of this sort. But the cases do not all belong to one or other of these two groups. If a sexual assault takes place unexpectedly, the person attacked may either defend itself actively and in earnest, or it may submit to the attack. In the latter case we again find a response, *i.e.* a yielding on the part of the person attacked. We might say that the person succumbs to a '*vis haud ingrata*' —to use an expression of Roman law.

The subject of '*vis haud ingrata*' has always attracted the attention of legislators, especially where it enters into the regulations for the punishment of sexual crimes. The Mosaic law, for instance, has taken it most carefully into account. In *Deuteronomy* xxii. 23-27 we read:

' 23. If a damsel that is a virgin be betrothed unto a husband, and a man find her in the city, and lie with her;

' 24. Then shall ye bring them both out unto the gate of that city and ye shall stone them with stones that they die; the damsel, because she cried not, being in the city; and the man, because he hath humbled his neighbour's wife: so thou shalt put away evil from among you.

' 25. But if a man find a betrothed damsel in the field, and the man force her and lie with her: then the man only that lay with her shall die:

' 26. But unto the damsel thou shalt do nothing; there

D

is in the damsel no sin worthy of death: for as when a man riseth against his neighbour, and slayeth him, even so is this matter:

' 27. For he found her in the field, and the betrothed damsel cried, and there was none to save her.'

I will also refer to the excellent little story out of *Don Quixote*, which Freud[1] has quoted:

A woman brought a man before the judge and accused him of having robbed her of her honour by force. Sancho indemnified her with a purse full of money which he took from the accused; but after she had gone he gave the man permission to follow her and take back the purse from her. Both came back struggling with each other; and the woman boasted that the villain had been unable to seize the purse from her. Thereupon Sancho said: ' Had you fought to keep your virtue half as valiantly as you did to keep your purse, this man could not have robbed you of it '.

It is true that these examples refer to adults; but we shall find later on that in this respect there is no difference between children and grown-up people.

The Mosaic law makes the punishment of the girl dependent upon whether she had called for help or not, that is to say, upon whether she had done all she possibly could to prevent the occurrence. I have examined the cases which I have previously published [2] with reference to this point, and find that in all of them the trauma could have been prevented. The children could have called for help, run away, or offered resistance instead of yielding to the seduction. And I was able to establish the same thing in a number of other cases.

What confirms us in our assumption of compliance on the part of the child is not only its conduct while the assault is in preparation and while it is actually going on, but after it has happened. In pointing out that hysterics are suffering from ' reminiscences ', Breuer and Freud have already called attention to the fact that as children they did not tell their relatives about the sexual trauma at the time, but kept

---

[1] *Zur Psychopathologie des Alltagslebens*, Zweite Auflage, S. 87.
[2] [No. 9, A.B.]

it secret; and that they did so not only while the impression of it was fresh in their minds, but that they repressed it into the unconscious so that they could not voluntarily recall it. I have found[1] similar conduct in children who later suffered from dementia præcox; though at the time I did not investigate the problem further.

It is a remarkable thing that a child who has experienced a sexual trauma should keep it secret from its parents in spite of the emotion associated with it. For a child who has been, say, chased and beaten by another one will come and complain to its mother. The objection will probably be raised that conventional prudishness prevents the child from speaking about it, since it has naturally been brought up to avoid talking about anything relating to sex. This objection, however, does not hold. To begin with, a child is not troubled by considerations of conventionality under the stress of violent emotion. And then not all children by any means behave in this way when they have had a sexual experience.

I will give two examples to illustrate this difference. The first is this.—A water-pipe had to be attended to in the cellar of a house. A workman came and asked for the key of the cellar. A woman who was living in the house told him to go down the stairs and said that she would send him the key. He went down and the woman's little daughter brought him the key. The man went into the cellar and came out again shortly afterwards. The child was waiting on the dimly lighted stairs in order to take back the key. Before she knew what was happening the man attempted an indecent act. The child ran terrified up the stairs and immediately told her mother what had happened. The man was followed and arrested.

A case that I have previously published will serve as the second example. A girl of nine years old was enticed by a neighbour into a wood. She followed him quite willingly. He then attempted to rape her. It was only when he had almost or quite attained his purpose that the child succeeded in getting free. She hurried home, but said nothing about

[1] *Loc. cit.*

what had happened; nor did she ever speak about it afterwards to her family.

The conduct of these two children after the trauma is quite opposite. Why is this? Let us first compare the conduct of children on other occasions. A child, for example, who has hurt itself in a game which it has been forbidden to play will suppress the pain, and will not go to its mother for comfort as it would normally do. The reason is clear: the child had yielded to the attraction of doing something forbidden, and it now has the feeling that the accident is its own fault.

This sense of guilt in children is extraordinarily sensitive. The following story from the childhood of a lady is an interesting illustration of the problem under discussion. She was out one day picking flowers with a friend, when a strange man came up and spoke to them, asking them to go with him, and saying that he would show them where more beautiful flowers were to be found. They went a little way with him. Presently she began to have scruples about going further with the stranger and suddenly turned round and ran off. Her friend did likewise. Now although nothing had taken place between the man and the children except that they had walked a certain distance together, the lady definitely remembered having felt a great dislike of speaking about the affair at home at the time. She kept it absolutely secret from her family, and never even spoke about it to her friend afterwards. The child's silence can only be explained by a sense of guilt. She evidently had a more or less definite feeling that the guilt was not only on the side of the seducer, but also on the side of the person who lets himself be seduced.

The same explanation obviously fits the two examples given before. The one child was taken completely by surprise and found herself in a situation which she had not sought. It was her mother who had sent her into the cellar. No one could reproach her, and therefore she immediately found words in which to tell her mother what had happened. The other child, on the contrary, had allowed herself to be seduced. She had followed the neighbour into the wood and allowed him to go a long way in carrying out his purpose before she freed herself from him and ran off. It is not to be wondered at that this child kept the occurrence secret.

It is the *pleasure-gain* present in every sexual activity which is the temptation. Freud [1] distinguishes between a *fore-pleasure* and *satisfaction-pleasure* in every sexual act. The fore-pleasure can be produced in a physical way through direct tactile stimulation of erotogenic zones of the body; or it can be called forth by other sensory stimuli, for instance through visual impressions; or, lastly, in a purely mental way by means of images—as, for instance, through the tension and excitement of the situation. It is difficult to say which of the two kinds of pleasure plays the greater part in children. Undoubtedly there are marked individual differences in this respect. In some of the cases I have observed it seemed to me as though the unusualness and secrecy of the situation, that is, the adventure as such, were the chief attraction for the child. On the other hand, I must again refer to the cases in which children directly provoke adults to sexual acts. Here we obviously have to presume a desire for satisfaction-pleasure as well.

When the child yields to the trauma it is because its libido is striving to obtain sexual fore-pleasure or satisfaction-pleasure. This fact of a pleasure-gain is the secret which the child guards so anxiously; it alone explains its sense of guilt and the psychological events which follow upon a sexual trauma. I will here refer to Freud's view concerning the early phases of sexuality. Freud has effectually destroyed the myth of a sexual latency period extending up to puberty. We learn from his investigations that the first traces of sexual activity appear very early and that for some time they are of an auto-erotic character. A stage follows in which the child turns to ' object-love '; but its sexual object need not be of the opposite sex. In addition to heterosexual and homosexual impulses certain other impulses, of a sadistic and masochistic character, find

---

[1] *Drei Abhandlungen zur Sexualtheorie* (1905).

expression. Hence Freud speaks of a polymorpho-perverse stage. All these early impulses in the child originate in the unconscious and naturally do not come into consciousness in their true form; they tend towards a definite sexual aim without the child becoming clearly aware of this tendency. For a child disposed to hysteria or dementia præcox a sexual experience constitutes a sexual aim of this kind. It undergoes the trauma in consequence of a tendency in its unconscious. If there is an underlying unconscious wish for it, the experiencing of a sexual trauma in childhood is a masochistic expression of the sexual impulse. It represents therefore one form of infantile sexual activity.

In the sphere of sexuality as elsewhere, there is every degree of transition from the normal to the abnormal. Nevertheless, I consider that we may in general regard any craving for sexual excitation which leads to a submission to sexual traumas as an abnormal kind of sexual activity. It is a striking fact that we meet with it precisely in the early history of neurotic or mentally afflicted individuals, in whose later life numerous sexual abnormalities are found. At the time when I was attempting [1] to apply Freud's theory of the psycho-sexual basis of hysteria to dementia præcox, I had already roughly worked out the respects in which the sexuality of children who later succumbed to those illnesses was abnormal. I arrived at the conclusion that their sexual development was precocious and their libido itself quantitatively abnormal, and that their imagination was prematurely occupied with sexual matters to an abnormal degree. This idea can now be expressed more definitely. We can say that children belonging to this category show an abnormal desire for obtaining sexual pleasure, and in consequence of this undergo sexual traumas.

If we now observe what happens to the images associated with the trauma in the child's mind we shall find new evidence in support of our view. A feeling of guilt cannot be tolerated by its consciousness any more than by that of adults. It therefore attempts to deal with the displeasur-

[1] [No. 9, A. B.]

able recollections in some way or other in order to eliminate their disturbing effect. They are split off from the rest of the contents of consciousness and thenceforward lead a separate existence as a 'complex'.

The case is different with those children who have suffered a sexual trauma without having been in any way responsive to it. These children can speak freely; they do not need to force out of their field of consciousness the recollection of that occurrence.

The process of eliminating displeasurable ideas from consciousness is the same in hysteria and dementia præcox (or in persons who suffer later from one or other of those diseases). Moreover, we can observe this process going on daily in healthy persons. But sooner or later it turns out that repression is only a make-shift measure. The complex can, no doubt, remain in the unconscious for a long time; but one day some event analogous to the primary sexual trauma takes place and the repressed material is roused to activity. Its conversion into symptoms of hysteria or dementia præcox then follows. In dementia præcox, it is true, there exists another possibility, namely, that a new wave of the illness may come on from endogenous sources and that this material will be elaborated into symptoms.

Freud has also drawn our attention to other mechanisms which fundamentally serve the same purpose as repression. One is the transposition of an affect on to indifferent ideas. If this takes place, obsessional symptoms develop. Like repression, this process of transposition on to indifferent ideas occurs in dementia præcox just as it does in the 'neuroses'. An example of the first sort is the imaginary pregnancies which are so common in dementia præcox, and which in their psychological genesis are entirely similar to hysterical pregnancies. An example of the second sort is the fact that in many cases of dementia præcox in which the diagnosis is quite clear obsessive ideas constitute the most prominent characteristic of the illness. Hysteria and dementia præcox have therefore two methods in common of expressing a sense of sexual guilt. There is yet a third method available in dementia præcox. This is to produce a delusion of having sinned, and to displace it on to an indifferent set of ideas. I cannot in this place bring forward evidence from case-histories to show that delusions of sin are in a great measure based on self-reproaches with a sexual content. I referred in a preceding paper[1] to the fact that a number of patients sooner or later connect a delusion of sin with the fact that in their youth they had not been truthful and had said nothing to their relatives about some sexual experience they had had. They displace their sense of guilt, which is in reality associated with having submitted to a sexual trauma without resistance, on to the far more venial ' sin ' of having been dishonest. It seems to me that this psychic mechanism of displacement on to a less affective idea is closely related to the process of transposition which underlies the formation of obsessional ideas. The result, however, is different. In the one case an obsessional idea is formed ; in the other, a delusion. I can in this place only mention in passing certain other mechanisms, also discovered by Freud, which are of a similar nature and serve similar purposes. There is, for instance, the very common process of ' displacement ' which occurs in hysteria and dementia præcox and also in dreams. An example of this is the displacement of a genital sensation on to the mouth.

Thus the later history of the complex and the subsequent forms it takes bear out the view put forward above as to the nature of sexual traumas in youth. Children who later suffer from hysteria or dementia præcox show a certain peculiarity which, however, is quite explicable from our point of view and goes to support our belief that their unconscious responds to the sexual trauma. This peculiarity is the fact that they very often have experienced not merely a single trauma. One would expect that a burnt child would dread the fire, *i.e.* would avoid any repetition or even the bare possibility of a repetition of a sexual trauma, since besides pleasure the experience caused it pain or other displeasurable feelings either directly or indirectly.

[1] [Cf. No. 9, A. B.]

Observation, however, shows the opposite. Individuals who have once suffered a sexual trauma, of which they were partly guilty through their compliant behaviour and which at the same time afforded them pleasure, show a tendency to expose themselves to further occurrences of the same nature. If they suffer a second trauma, they assimilate it in their unconscious to the first trauma which has already been repressed. The additional trauma acts in an auxiliary manner in disturbing the psychic balance, and the illness breaks out, either in the form of hysteria or dementia præcox according to the person's congenital disposition.

The tendency to experience sexual traumas repeatedly is a peculiarity which we can often observe in adult hysterics. We might even speak of a traumatophilic diathesis, which, moreover, is not limited to sexual traumas. Hysterics are those interesting people to whom something is always happening. Female hysterics in particular are constantly meeting with adventures. They are molested in the public street, outrageous sexual assaults are made on them, etc. It is part of their nature that they must expose themselves to external traumatic influences. There is in them a need to appear to be constantly subjected to external violence. In this we recognize a general psychological characteristic of women in an exaggerated form.[1] The fact that in pronounced hysteria a tendency to experience traumas is also found in adults is valuable evidence in support of the assumption that people of this kind have a similar tendency in childhood.

In his *Psychopathologie des Alltagslebens* Freud has directed our attention to the fact that awkward behaviour, blunders, self-injuries, accidents, and similar occurrences in every-day life are often due to an unconscious purpose on the part of the subject. I have quoted above an anecdote related by Freud which shows that sexual 'accidents', too, can come from an unconscious wish. This theory of

---

[1] Incidentally we may allude to the dreams of healthy girls and women in which they are stabbed or murdered in some way by a man. Freud has shown that these dreams are to be recognized as symbolic representations of a sexual wish. In the dream the man is the assailant and the dreamer adopts the passive rôle; she is not even guilty of the *symbolic* sexual act.

Freud gives further very important support to my view that infantile sexual traumas of the kind I have specified are brought about by an unconscious wish on the part of the child. In order to justify my use of Freud's results I will give a few illustrations from my own experience in confirmation of the truth of his conclusions.

A girl of nineteen was knocked down in the street by a soldier trotting past on a horse. It was broad daylight when this happened, and the thoroughfare was a wide and straight one. The girl was unconscious for a short time, but suffered no severe bodily injury. Shortly afterwards symptoms of a so-called traumatic neurosis appeared.

The previous history of the girl was as follows : Since her childhood she had been through all sorts of experiences of a depressing nature. To begin with, she had been witness of quarrels between her parents. When they had separated she had been allocated to her mother. She did not like her mother, however, who was an uneducated woman without refinement. She was fond of her father, who carried on literary activities in spite of being a simple artizan. When she was twelve years old she ran away from her mother and went to her father. She was one of the best pupils in her school, and began to write poetry quite early on. She wanted to become a school-mistress, and her wish seems to have arisen from her admiration for a certain male teacher as well as from natural inclination. As her father had not the means to send her to a proper training college she had to leave school early and take work as a servant in one place after another. She was very unhappy because she could not gratify her desire to become educated or get into a higher social sphere. She remained a year and a half in one situation. Then she attempted to improve her position by learning shorthand and typewriting; but her financial resources failed before she had attained her end, and she had to go to work in a factory, where the association with uneducated women was not at all to her taste. She had been on bad terms with her mother ever since she had believed herself justified in the suspicion that her younger sister was the offspring of an illicit relationship on the part of her mother before the divorce. She stood quite alone, especially as even her father troubled himself very little about her. She had to do work that she hated and live in a social sphere that was distasteful to her. Her younger sister, whom she supported out of her earnings in order to enable her to learn an occupation, rewarded her sacrifice with ingratitude. All these circumstances, and probably an unfortunate love affair in addition, had such a depressing effect upon her that she lost all interest in life. During the time before the accident she wrote some poetry in which she gave expression to her weariness of life. Then the above-mentioned accident occurred.

When, as in this case, a person has lost all pleasure in life, and the thought is obviously present in his mind that it would be better to die than go on living under such conditions; and when that person meets with an accident under circumstances which suggest that it might have been avoided, then I consider that we are justified in assuming that there is an unconscious intention of suicide. The girl did not deliberately throw herself in front of the horse. That would have been conscious suicide. But she did not perceive the possibility of getting out of the way clearly enough. Freud has already given this explanation in similar cases of suicide or attempted suicide which appeared on a superficial view to be accidents. It is worth noting that the girl's condition improved when she was given an occupation which lay in the direction of her complex, and when efforts were made to get her a better position.

What strange and yet effective means the unconscious employs to attain its ends is shown in the following history of an accident met with by a lady suffering from dementia præcox. The patient suffered principally from a delusion of sin which was the result of long-continued masturbation. She declared that her masturbation was traceable to an accident which had happened to her a number of years before, when she had slipped and fallen so that her genital region had knocked against the corner of a table. Her description of the accident made it impossible to picture it

otherwise than as the result of an unconscious purpose.   At
that time the patient obviously felt a sexual excitation which
she could not gratify in the normal way.   She struggled
against the longing to masturbate.   But the gratification
her conscious forbade her to obtain her unconscious procured for her through her 'accident'.

Another patient had from childhood had an exceedingly
strong affection for her brother.   When she was grown up
she measured every man by the standard of her brother.
She did fall in love with a man later on, but the affair ended
badly.   Shortly after this, while she was still very much
depressed, she twice got into serious danger through her
carelessness on a climbing party.   As she was a good
climber, her falling twice in safe and easy places remained
a mystery to her friends.   It appeared later that at that
time she was playing with ideas of suicide.   After her
unfortunate love affair she turned her whole affection back
again to her brother, who some time afterwards became
engaged.   Soon after this she fell ill with dementia præcox.
(Probably the illness had been developing gradually.)   In
the initial stage of depression she attempted to throw herself
out of the window—obviously the same thing as her falls
in climbing.   Her condition very slowly improved in the
asylum, until at last she was able to go for walks in the park
with an attendant.   A ditch was being dug in the garden
and she used to cross it by a plank bridge, although she
could quite easily have jumped over it.   At that time she
was told the date on which her brother was to be married.
She continually spoke of his wedding.   On the day before it
was to happen, as she was out walking as usual, she sprang
over the ditch instead of crossing by the bridge, and did
it so clumsily that she sprained her ankle.   Later on, too,
these self-injuries occurred so frequently that even the
attendant began to suspect that there was something intentional in them.   In these minor accidents her unconscious
was obviously expressing the intention to commit suicide.

Events of this kind appear in quite a new light as soon
as we know something about the circumstances which precede and accompany them.   The more one subjects such

events to psychological analysis, the more room one is obliged to give to the significance of unconscious volition. Of course no strict line can be drawn between unconscious and conscious purpose in this connection.

Adult neurotics and mental patients offer us highly interesting examples of frequent traumatic experiences (not only of a sexual kind). At this point we must make a slight digression into an allied field of interest. The fact that a traumatic hysteria is very often a ' pension-hysteria ' is beyond dispute. It is the patient's desire to obtain compensation that prevents his symptoms from disappearing. If the patient has got better and a reduction or entire withdrawal of the pension is threatened as a consequence, then his symptoms which have disappeared or become less severe will once more reappear or grow more acute. Here we obtain an insight into the numerous ways in which the unconscious mind is able to realize wishes without their having to become conscious at all. It is not uncommon for persons who have just had an accident to meet with another, often a quite insignificant one, which comes just in the nick of time to support their claim to a pension. I have noticed this happen very frequently among a class of people especially disposed to hysteria, namely, Polish workmen employed under the German Workmen's Compensation Act. It is well known that these people defend their claim to a pension with a peculiar tenacity, and that their traumatic-hysterical symptoms take an exceptionally firm hold on them. The number of Polish workmen who claim pensions on account of more than one accident is surprisingly large.

The tendency to reinforce the first accident by means of a second one is even manifested in cases where the person is laid up with his hysterical symptoms and so has no opportunity of having another one while at work. An Italian workman upon whom I had recently to give an opinion had been injured through an iron clamp falling on his head from some scaffolding. I got him to tell me his dreams. He repeatedly told me that in his dream someone had beaten him over the head with a stick, or that some other accident had happened to him. His unconscious clearly wished to keep the traumatic symptom complex alive, and gave expression to this wish in his dreams. The fact that his dreams were accompanied by anxiety is no evidence against this view, if we accept Freud's theory of dreams. I consider that in this way the very frequent anxiety-dreams of persons injured accidentally fall into line with Freud's theory of wish-fulfilment. The unconscious is untiring in its efforts to give expression to a complex. It takes care that the affective value of the trauma suffered shall not be lost, and from time to time it brings the occurrence back to memory by means of an anxiety dream.

The observation both of adults and children, and the analysis of dreams of healthy persons, as well as neurotics and mental cases, and of the symptoms of hysteria and dementia præcox, lead us to the conclusion that at the back of sexual traumas, particularly infantile ones, and of other traumas as well, there often lies an unconscious purpose on the part of the apparently passive party. We have traced back to supposed abnormalities in their infantile sexuality the fact that persons who later fall ill with hysteria or dementia præcox show in their youth an abnormal response to sexual traumas; and we have come to regard such behaviour as a form of abnormal infantile sexual activity. Thus Freud's original view has undergone an important alteration. Infantile sexual traumas play no ætiological rôle in hysteria and dementia præcox. The experiencing of such traumas indicates rather that the child already has a disposition to neurosis or psychosis in later life. Instead of an *ætiological* significance, the infantile sexual trauma now receives a *formative* one, and we can understand how it is able to lay down a definite course for the subsequent illness and to determine the individual character of many symptoms.

Our investigations have once more brought before us the far-reaching similarity between the symptomatology of hysteria and dementia præcox. We have not yet arrived at the solution of the differences that undoubtedly exist between the two diseases. These are to be found for the most part in the psycho-sexual sphere, and will form the subject of a further inquiry.

Postscript (1920)

This paper, which was written in 1907, contains certain errors in its rendering of Freud's views. At the time of writing I had only recently begun to interest myself in the psycho-analytic method of thought. I consider it better to point out this fact in a general way than to make the necessary corrections in each place in the text, particularly since those errors do not invalidate the results of my investigations.

Chapter II

THE PSYCHO - SEXUAL DIFFERENCES BE-TWEEN HYSTERIA AND DEMENTIA PRÆCOX [1] (1908)

THE psycho-analytic method has enabled us to recognize important analogies in the structure of hysteria and dementia præcox.[2] It will be sufficient in this paper to mention the most outstanding ones. The symptoms of both diseases originate in repressed sexual complexes. In both cases normal as well as perverse impulses can determine the formation of symptoms. The means of expression employed by both diseases are to a considerable extent the same. (I need only refer to sexual symbolism.)

But that in spite of these common characteristics there exists a fundamental antithesis between the two diseases, all observers agree. Up to the present, however, they have not defined this antithesis satisfactorily. They have only described differences of degree, and these only bring out once more the similarity between the two forms of illness. Seeing that certain important characteristics common to hysteria and dementia præcox are of a psycho-sexual nature, the question arises as to where this analogy ends. And so, in seeking to discover the fundamental differences between the two illnesses, we are again brought back to the psycho-sexual sphere.

Freud's *Drei Abhandlungen zur Sexualtheorie* (1905) offers us a basis for an investigation of this kind, and in

---

[1] [No. 11, A. B.]
[2] See particularly Jung, *Über die Psychologie der Dementia Præcox* (1907).

particular his views on the sexuality of children, sexual perversions, and the sexual impulse of neurotics. The theoretical considerations that I am about to bring forward concerning the sexuality of chronic mental patients stand or fall by Freud's sexual theories.[1]

The earliest sexual impulses in the child are, according to Freud, connected with a single erotogenic zone—the mouth. During the first years of its life other parts of the body assume the function of erotogenic zones in addition to the oral zone. The earliest expressions of its libido are auto-erotic. At this stage the child knows no sexual object as yet except itself. In the subsequent period of develop- ment it turns to object-love. But its object-love does not immediately have a fixed and definite direction towards persons of the opposite sex. There are a number of com- ponent-instincts in the child, and in the normal course of events one of these, the heterosexual one, acquires and retains the place of supremacy; whereas the energy derived from the other component-instincts is withdrawn from sexual use and applied to important social aims. This latter process is termed sublimation. It may be said in general that feelings of disgust originate from the sublimation of homosexual components; shame from the sublimation of infantile scoptophilia and exhibitionism; and horror, pity and similar feelings from the sublimation of the sadistic and masochistic components.

Learning to transfer its libido to persons of the opposite sex and converting its remaining component-instincts into social feelings are not all the child's psychosexual develop- ment. Both sexual transference and sublimation of sexual energy go far beyond these limits; and both processes normally work together in harmony. Artistic,[2] scientific, and to a certain extent many other occupational activities, depend upon sublimatory processes. Persons with un-

[1] In this paper many of the ideas which go some way beyond Freud's published views I owe in the first instance to written and oral communications from Freud himself. And I have also been able to formulate many points more clearly through discussion with Prof. Bleuler and Dr. Jung in the course of my work at the Zürich Psychiatric Clinic.

[2] Cf. Rank, *Der Künstler, Ansätze zu einer Sexualpsychologie* (1907).

gratified libido frequently convert their free sexual energy into feverish activity in their work, or they direct their surplus libido to social activities and find in them their satisfaction. This is the best source from which flows the interest in sick nursing and the care of infants, in public charities, in societies for the protection of animals, etc.

Man's social conduct depends upon his capacity for adaptation. This, however, is a sublimated sexual transference. A positive or negative mental *rapport* develops between people after they have been together for a certain length of time, and it expresses itself in feelings of sympathy or antipathy. It is the basis of sentiments of friendship and mental harmony. The behaviour of a human being in social life is entirely in accord with the way in which he reacts to sexual stimuli. In both cases a given person shows himself easy or difficult of access, coarse or refined in his manner, fastidious or easy-going as to his choice. What we characterize in the behaviour of one person as stiff, awkward, or clumsy, and in another as graceful, adroit, etc., are signs of a lesser or greater capacity for adaptation, *i.e.* capacity for transference.

In psycho-analysis we make use of the transference for therapeutic purposes as we do in all forms of mental treatment.[1] Suggestion, the effects of which are seen in their highest degree in hypnosis, is a very pronounced form of sexual transference.

Man transfers his libido not only to animate but also to inanimate objects. He has a personal relation to almost all the objects of his environment, and this relation originates in his sexuality. In my monograph, *Traum und Mythus*,[2] I have discussed this question in detail, and I will only mention here a few essential considerations on this point. Our German language gives a gender to inanimate objects, because it compares them with male and female by reason of definite characteristics. 'The human being sexualizes

---

[1] Cf. Freud, 'Fragment of an Analysis of a Case of Hysteria' (1905). Also Sadger, 'Die Bedeutung der psychoanalytischen Methode nach Freud' (1907).

[2] [No. 14, A. B.]

the universe ', says Kleinpaul.[1]   The sexual symbolism of language which we meet again in dreams and mental disorders originates in the same source.   To objects we have grown to like through use or because of their æsthetic value we obviously have a personal relationship which is quite analogous to sexual attraction.   The direction taken by our taste in the choice of objects completely conforms to our sexual object-choice.   There are many different degrees of this kind of object-love.   Many persons have almost no needs in this respect, while others are completely under the dominion of their passion for certain objects. With a delicate perception of these psychological connections the German language terms a man who shrinks from no sacrifice in the attainment of a desired object a ' *Liebhaber* ' [' lover '], thus likening him to a man who is in love with a woman.   The most pronounced type of such a ' *Liebhaber* ' is the collector.   The excessive value he places on the object he collects corresponds completely to the lover's over-estimation of his sexual object.   A passion for collecting is frequently a direct surrogate for a sexual desire; and in that case a delicate symbolism is often concealed behind the choice of objects collected.   A bachelor's keenness for collecting often diminishes after he has married; and it is well known that interest in collecting varies in different periods of life.

The sexual impulse of the neurotic is distinguishable in the first place from that of the normal person by the excessive strength of his desire.   Furthermore, the neurotic lacks internal harmony.   His component-instincts are only incompletely subjected to his heterosexual one; and there exists on the other hand a tendency to repress this latter instinct.   Ideas associated with normal sexual activities occasion repugnance and disgust in him.   Throughout his life one component-instinct is opposing another, and excessive desire for a thing wars with an extreme rejection of it.   From this conflict the neurotic takes flight into illness. With the outbreak of his neurosis, repressed material comes into his consciousness and is converted into hysterical

[1] Kleinpaul, *Stromgebiet der Sprache*, S. 468.

symptoms. The conversion serves as a discharge for repressed impulses which may be normal but are more
especially of a perverse kind. The symptoms are themselves abnormal sexual activities. Apart from periods of
illness in the strict sense the neurotic libido manifests itself
in an intensified transference. It cathects its objects in an
abnormally high degree; and it shows more than the average
tendency towards sublimation.

In the light of this knowledge we may go on to compare the psychosexual conduct of persons suffering from
dementia præcox with that of healthy persons and of
neurotics. For this purpose we will select a few types
from that large group of chronic mental cases which,
in accordance with Kraepelin, we classify as dementia
præcox.

Let us suppose ourselves in a mental hospital. We
see before us a patient suffering from a severe form of the
illness and in an advanced stage of it. He is standing in
a corner of a room or running about restlessly. He stares
vacantly before him, hallucinates, whispers a couple of
words, and gesticulates in a strange manner. He speaks to
nobody and avoids everyone. He has no desire to occupy
himself, neglects his appearance, eats noisily, is dirty,
smears himself with excrement and masturbates openly
without shame. It is as though his surroundings did not
exist for him.

We come to a less severe case who yet exhibits fundamentally the same behaviour, though not in such an extreme degree. He, too, is unsocial and reserved and has
persecutory and grandiose ideas. His conduct and manner
of speech are peculiar, affected, and unnatural. He complains bitterly about his internment, but he utters these
complaints, like all others, without adequate affect. He
takes cognizance of events in the external world but has no
real interest in them. He will do a little mechanical work,
but it gives him no satisfaction.

Here is another patient whose illness does not show
any very marked symptoms and who need not necessarily
be certified. He easily feels himself injured by others,

does not get on with his relatives, makes no friends, and does not want any. He feels no need for human relationships, and is devoid of tact and finer feelings. We cannot get into friendly relations with him. He may perhaps possess more than average intelligence, but everything he does is as a rule without value. His intellectual productions are generally peculiar and unnatural, violating the laws of good taste and being quite devoid of normal feeling.

All these forms of the disease [1] have in common the same anomalies in regard to the patient's emotional life. (For the differences are only a matter of degree: a slight form can turn into a severe one, and a severe one can show considerable remissions.) Whereas the ideas of healthy persons are accompanied by adequate feeling, such an association of feeling is lacking in these patients. But since we have traced back all transference of feeling to sexuality we must come to the conclusion that dementia præcox destroys the person's capacity for sexual transference, *i.e.* for object-love.

The child's first unconscious sexual inclination is towards its parents, and particularly towards the one of the opposite sex. A lively transference also occurs between brothers and sisters in the same family. At the same time, however, feelings of rebellion and hate are present, especially between members of the same sex. These feelings succumb to the influence of education and other exogenous factors of repression. Under normal conditions there exists between parents and children an affectionate relationship and a feeling of unity. In hysterics we often find this affection morbidly increased towards one person, and changed into violent aversion towards another. Such family affection is usually lacking in dementia præcox patients; and we find in its place indifference or pronounced hostility passing into delusions of persecution.

An educated patient, whose mother had never ceased

---

[1] In using the words 'slight' and 'severe' nothing is implied about the morbid process of the disease, but only about its practical (social) effects.

her tender care for him during his long illness in spite of his coldness towards her, reacted to the news of her death with the remark, ' Is that the latest ? '   In the same way it is an every-day experience that in dementia præcox parents leave off having any feelings for their children.

I had under my observation a young man in whom this mental trouble had developed very early.   In early child-hood he had such a marked transference towards his mother that at three years old he once exclaimed: ' Mother, if you die I shall hit my head with a stone and then I shall be dead too '.   He would not allow his mother to be with his father for a single moment.   He used to insist on being taken walks by her alone, watched over her jealously, and was spiteful towards his brother.   He had shown an abnormal tendency to contradiction from infancy.   His mother said of him that even at that time he was ' the spirit that always denies '.[1]   He had not associated with other boys, but had clung to his mother alone.   When he was thirteen years old he had become so uncontrollable at home that his parents had had to entrust him to other hands.   From the moment that his mother had taken him to his new home and had gone away he had changed completely.   The excessive love and tenderness for his mother changed into feelings of absolute coldness.   He wrote stiff, formal letters in which he never mentioned her.   He gradually developed a severe hallucinatory psychosis in which the process of decay of his affective life became more and more apparent.

Psycho-analytic investigation has shown that in mental patients excessive affection often turns to violent hostility. This revulsion of the libido from an object upon which it was at one time transferred with particular intensity is an irrevocable one in dementia præcox.

In the anamnesis of cases of dementia præcox we are very frequently told that the patient had always been quiet and inclined to brood, had never associated with anyone, had avoided company and amusements, and had never

[1] ' Der Geist der stets verneint.'   [This is said of Mephistopheles in Goethe's *Faust*, Pt. I.]

been really gay like other people. These persons have in fact never had a proper capacity for transferring their libido to the external world. It is they who form the unsocial element in asylums. Their words are without affective content. They speak of the most sacred things and the merest trivialities in the same tone of voice and with the same gestures. It is only if the conversation touches on a complex that an affective reaction, sometimes a very violent one, may occur.

Dementia præcox patients are in a certain sense very suggestible, and this may seem to contradict the idea of a weak sexual transference. Their suggestibility, however, is quite different to that of hysteria. It seems to me to consist simply in this, that they do not struggle against this or that influence, because at the moment they are too indifferent to oppose it (Kraepelin's 'automatic obedience'). The disturbance in their capacity for attention is certainly of great significance here in this connection. It seems to me therefore that this suggestibility is simply an absence of resistance. But it very easily changes into resistance. The negativism of dementia præcox is the most complete antithesis to transference. In contrast to hysteria, these patients are only in a very slight degree accessible to hypnosis. In attempting to psycho-analyse them we notice the absence of transference again. Hence psycho-analysis hardly comes into consideration as a therapeutic procedure in this kind of illness.

We can notice the failure of transference in these patients in many ways. We never see them really happy. They have no sense of humour; their laughter is unreal or convulsive, or grossly erotic, but never hearty. And it often means, not that they are in good spirits but that a complex has been touched. This is the case, for example, in the stereotyped laughter of the patient who is hallucinating, for his hallucinations are always concerned with his complex. The demeanour of such patients is clumsy and stiff; it shows very clearly their lack of adaption to their environment. Kraepelin speaks very significantly of a 'loss of gracefulness' in them. They have lost the need to make their environment comfortable and cheerful. Their attachment to their activities and occupation disappears in the same manner as their attachment to people. They readily become absorbed in themselves; and, what seems to me especially characteristic, they do not know what boredom is. It is true that most of these patients in institutions can be educated to do quite useful work by making a constant suggestion in this direction; but they take no pleasure in what they do, and as soon as the suggestion ceases they give it up. An apparent exception is seen in those patients who work from early morning till late at night without needing any rest or recreation. Such indefatigable industry invariably springs from a complex. One patient I know, for instance, is exceedingly active on the asylum farm because he regards the entire grounds as his own property. Another, a very old man, works untiringly in the scullery of his section and will not allow anyone else to help him. This is because he hears elves speaking out of the water in the sink, and they once prophesied to him that he should come to them if he washed 100,000 more pieces of crockery before his death. This octogenarian takes no interest in anything else but this work, which he performs to the accompaniment of secret ceremonies.

These patients no longer take any real interest in objects, or in their property; and nothing that surrounds them has any attraction for them. It is true that they often express intense longing for some object, but if they get it it has no effect on them. It is also true that they take great care of certain things, but occasion will show that they have no real feeling for them. A certain patient collected a large quantity of common stones; he said they were precious stones, and set an enormous value upon them. The drawer in which he kept them finally broke in consequence of their weight. When the stones were taken away the patient protested against this interference with his rights; but he did not grieve after his lost treasures, but collected fresh stones. They did just as well as symbols of his supposed riches. The very frequent destructive mania of patients undoubtedly springs in part from their lack of pleasure in objects.

In very many cases the mental disturbance affects not only those finer social sublimations which are gradually evolved in the course of the person's whole life, but also those which originated in his early childhood, such as shame, disgust, moral feelings, pity, etc. Careful investigation would probably show that these feelings are, at any rate to some extent, obliterated in every case of dementia præcox; and in all severe cases it is quite evident that this is so. The most pronounced manifestations of such a process are smearing with excreta, drinking urine, dirtiness, etc., all of which point to the loss of feelings of disgust; while obtrusive erotic conduct, such as exhibiting, implies a loss of feelings of shame. We are reminded of the behaviour of infants who have as yet no disgust of excreta, and no feelings of shame at nakedness. Other manifestations are the freedom with which many patients speak of the intimacies of their former life. They reject memories only when they have lost value or interest for them. Their attitude in regard to cruel acts committed by themselves shows most clearly of all that they have lost all sentiment of pity. I once saw a patient a few hours after he had shot an innocent neighbour dead and severely injured his wife. He was talking quite calmly about the motive of the deed and about the deed itself, and at the same time contentedly eating the meal that had been put before him.

So far we can recognize two groups of phenomena in dementia præcox: one in which the libido of the patient is turned away from animate and inanimate objects, and the other in which he has lost those feelings which arise through sublimation. Thus we see that this illness involves a cessation of object-love [1] and of sublimation. Only one similar sexual condition is known to us, namely, that of early childhood; we term it, with Freud, 'auto-erotism'. In this period, too, interest in objects and sublimation is lacking. The psychosexual characteristic of dementia præcox is the

---

[1] A patient whom I was observing addressed himself as ' you ' in his numerous writings; for he himself was the only object in which he was interested.

return of the patient to auto-erotism, and the symptoms of his illness are a form of auto-erotic sexual activity.

This of course does not mean that every sexual impulse in these patients is purely auto-erotic. But it does mean that every attraction to another person is, as it were, sicklied o'er with the pale cast of auto-erotism. When a female patient seems to have very intense feelings of love and expresses them with great violence, her singular lack of shame in showing them surprises us at the same time. The loss of feelings of shame, which are an effect of sublimation, is a step in the direction of auto-erotism. Moreover, we see such patients falling in love with some one quite suddenly and indiscriminately, and then as quickly exchanging that person for another. In every asylum there are always some women who are in love with whoever is their physician at the time; and each of them soon has the delusion of being engaged or married to him, imagines herself with child by him, and sees a sign of love in every word he utters. If the physician leaves, his successor very quickly takes his place in the emotional life of those patients. They are therefore still able to direct their sexual desire on to a person, but are no longer capable of any steady attachment to him. Other patients cherish for years an imaginary love, which only exists in their minds; and they have probably never even seen their sexual object. In real life they keep away from any human contact. In short, there is always some evidence of their auto-erotic attitude. In those cases which on account of an extensive remission of symptoms give the impression of a cure, the deficient capacity for a continued interest in the external world is, as a rule, the morbid trait which is most clearly visible.

The patient whose libido has turned away from objects has set himself against the world. He is alone, and faces a world which is hostile to him. It seems as though his ideas of persecution [1] were directed especially against that person upon whom he had at one time transferred his libido

---

[1] The turning away of the libido from the external world is the basis for the formation of delusions of persecution in general. I cannot in this place go into the further factors which come into consideration in this connection.

in a marked degree.   In many cases, therefore, the persecutor would be his original sexual object.

The auto-erotism of dementia præcox is the source not only of delusions of persecution but of megalomania. Under normal conditions, when two persons have transferred their libido on to one another each over-estimates the value of the other whom he loves (Freud calls this ' sexual over-estimation '). The mental patient transfers on to himself alone as his only sexual object the whole of the libido which the healthy person turns upon all living and inanimate objects in his environment, and accordingly his sexual over-estimation is directed towards himself alone and assumes enormous dimensions.   For he is his whole world.   The origin of megalomania in dementia præcox is thus a reflected or auto-erotic sexual over-estimation—an over-estimation which is turned back on to the ego.[1]   Delusions of persecution and megalomania are therefore closely connected with each other. Every delusion of persecution in dementia præcox is accompanied by megalomania.

The patient's auto-erotic isolation from the external world not only affects his reactive behaviour but also his receptive attitude.   He shuts himself off from the sense-perceptions of reality that flow towards him.   His unconscious produces sense-perceptions of a hallucinatory nature, and these correspond to repressed wishes.   He thus carries his self-isolation so far that in a certain measure he boycotts the external world.   He no longer gives it anything, or accepts anything from it.   He grants himself a monopoly for the supply of sense-impressions.

The patient who has no interest in the external world, who vegetates in complete absorption in himself, and whose apathetic expression gives an appearance of utter insensibility, seems to ordinary observation to be devoid of mental or emotional activity.   It is customary to use the term ' dementia ' for this condition.   But the same expression is used for the condition that follows on other psychoses, on

---

[1] I regard auto-erotic sexual over-estimation as the source of megalomania *in general* in dementia præcox. The special idea in which it may take shape is determined by a definite repressed wish in this connection.

epileptic, paralytic, and senile dementia. The two conditions are in reality of quite a different nature, and it is only their *effect*—the diminution of intellectual capacity—which is the same in both, and even so only up to a certain point. In using the term ' dementia ', therefore, we should bear this fact in mind. Above all, we should be careful not to fall into the common error of calling delusions ' feebleminded ' because they are absurd; if so, we should have to call the deeply significant absurdities that occur in dreams ' feeble-minded '. Both paralytic and senile dementia utterly destroy the patient's intellectual powers, and cause gross symptoms of mental deterioration in him; while epileptic dementia leads to an extraordinarily impoverished and monotonous ideational life, and an increased difficulty in comprehension. These diseases may become stationary for a time, but in general they are progressive. In dementia præcox, on the other hand, the dementia is based on a ' blocking ' of feeling. The patient retains his intellectual capacities—at any rate, although the reverse has frequently been asserted it has never been proved. But in consequence of this auto-erotic ' blocking ', the patient does not receive any new impressions, and reacts to the external world either in an abnormal manner or not at all. But remissions may take place at any time, and even go so far that hardly any suspicion of a mental defect is left.

The ' dementia ' of dementia præcox is an auto-erotic phenomenon in which the patient is without normal affective reactions to the external world. Epileptic or organic dements, on the other hand, react with very lively feelings in so far as they are capable of comprehending what is taking place. The epileptic never behaves with indifference; he shows a superabundance of affect, both in loving and hating. He transfers his libido on to people and objects in an extraordinary degree, and shows both affection and gratitude towards his relatives. He takes pleasure in his work and clings to his property with great tenacity, carefully preserving every scrap of paper and never ceasing to contemplate his treasures with great satisfaction.

Auto-erotism is also the feature which distinguishes dementia præcox from hysteria. In the one case the libido is withdrawn from objects, in the other it cathects objects in an excessive degree. On the one hand there is loss of the capacity for sublimation, and on the other increased capacity for it.

Whereas we can often already recognize the psychosexual characteristics of hysteria in children, the severer pathological symptoms usually only develop much later. Nevertheless some of these cases do show outspoken signs of illness even in childhood. We conclude from this that the psychosexual constitution of hysteria is congenital. The same conclusion is true of dementia præcox. We very frequently find in the anamnesis that the patients were always peculiar and dreamy, and never associated with anyone. Long before the actual outbreak of the illness they were unable to transfer their libido, and therefore carried out all their love adventures in the realm of phantasy. In all probability there is hardly a case which does not exhibit these characteristics. Such persons are also especially prone to onanism. They have therefore never completely overcome their infantile auto-erotism. Object-love has not fully developed in them, and when the disease becomes manifest they turn to auto-erotism once more. The psychosexual constitution of dementia præcox is based, therefore, on an inhibition in development. The few cases which show psychotic phenomena in a gross form in childhood corroborate this view in a striking manner; for they clearly show a pathological persistence in auto-erotism. One of my patients had shown a pronounced negativism at the early age of three. When he was being washed he would close his fist and not allow his fingers to be dried. He showed the same behaviour as a fifth-form boy at school. In his third year the same patient could not be induced to empty his bowels for months at a time, and his mother had to ask him every day to give up this habit. This example shows an abnormal fixation to an erotogenic zone—a typical auto-erotic phenomenon. The young patient previously mentioned, who suddenly withdrew his libido from his mother when he was thirteen years old, had also behaved in a negativistic manner in earliest childhood.

Inhibition of a person's psychosexual development is not only expressed in his failure to overcome his auto-erotism completely, but also in an abnormal persistence of his component-instincts. This characteristic, which deserves a separate and detailed investigation, can only be illustrated in this place by a single instance taken from the patient about whose negativistic and auto-erotic behaviour I have already spoken. When he was twenty-seven years old his physician had once had to feed him through a stomach-tube because he refused to eat anything. He conceived this measure as a pederastic act, and from that time regarded the physician as his homosexual persecutor. This example brings to light the homosexual component-instinct with displacement from the anal zone to another erotogenic zone ('displacement from below upwards', Freud), and shows us at the same time the erotogenic origin of an idea of persecution.

An abnormal persistence of the component-instincts is also characteristic of the neuroses, and shows that they too have undergone inhibitions in development. But in them the auto-erotic tendency is absent. In dementia præcox the disturbance is much more deeply rooted; a person who has never completely passed out of the primary stage of his psychosexual development is thrown back more and more into the auto-erotic stage as the disease progresses.

A great part of the pathological manifestations of dementia præcox would, it seems to me, be explicable if we assumed that the patient has an abnormal psychosexual constitution in the direction of auto-erotism. Such an assumption would render the recently discussed toxin theory unnecessary.

It is naturally impossible to deal in a short paper with all the numerous phenomena of the disease that can be traced back to such an inhibition in development; and even a much longer work could not do this, for analysis of the psychoses on the basis of Freudian theories is still in its infancy.   And yet Freud's method will, I think, give us some knowledge which is not obtainable in any other way. What I have chiefly had in view in this paper has been to find a differential diagnosis between dementia præcox, hysteria, and the obsessional neuroses.   It furthermore seems to me that psycho-analytic research will be able to tackle the problem of the genesis of the various forms of delusions.   Perhaps the method will also help to elucidate the intellectual disturbances seen in the clinical picture of dementia præcox—disturbances which we are still far from understanding at present.

Chapter III

THE PSYCHOLOGICAL RELATIONS BETWEEN
SEXUALITY AND ALCOHOLISM (1908)[1]

IT is an undisputed fact that, generally speaking, men are more prone to taking alcohol than women. Even though in many countries women daily take alcohol as a matter of course just like men, and though in many places intoxicated women are often seen in the streets, still alcohol is never associated with the social life of women to anything like the extent that it is with that of men. There are wide circles in which to be a hard drinker is looked upon as a sign of manliness, even as a matter of honour. Society never demands in this way that women should take alcohol. It is the custom with us rather to condemn drinking as unwomanly; nor is drinking ever a matter of boasting among normal women as it is among men.

It seems to me worth inquiring whether this difference in the attitude of men and women towards alcohol rests on sexual differences. But such an inquiry must start from the newer conceptions of the psycho-sexual constitution of men and women as laid down in Freud's works [2] in especial.

It is a biological fact that the human body contains the genital organs of both sexes in a rudimentary form. In the course of its normal development one of the two sets of organs is suppressed or takes over other activities, whilst the other goes on developing until it is capable of performing its true functions. An analogous process takes

[1] [No. 12, A. B.]   [2] *Drei Abhandlungen zur Sexualtheorie*, 1905.

place in the psychosexual sphere. Here, too, the differentiation of the sexes proceeds from an original state of
bi-sexuality. In childhood the expressions of the sexual
instincts in boys and girls are still very much alike.

We have learned, particularly through Freud's investigations, that sexual activities are by no means lacking in
childhood. Only the function of procreation does not as
yet appear; that instinct only gradually finds its definitive
form. According to Freud the infantile libido is without
an object; it is ' auto-erotic '. It obtains gratification by
the stimulation of certain parts of the body which serve as
erotogenic zones. Nevertheless in the pre-pubertal period
not the whole of the child's sexual energy is employed in
auto-erotic pleasure-gain. A large part of it is repressed
out of consciousness. It is no longer applied to sexual
ends, but takes over important social functions. This
concept of ' repression ', introduced by Freud, is indispensable for the understanding of many psychological
processes, both normal and pathological. The deflection
of repressed sexual ideas and feelings on to social spheres
is termed by us, following Freud, ' sublimation '; and this
process serves to set up the barriers which restrain the
sexual instincts of both sexes.

On arrival at maturity the boy, like the girl, acquires
the marked bodily and physical characteristics of his sex;
and in the psychosexual sphere the important process of
object-finding commences. The libido is now directed on
to the other sex. But the male and female libido is
differentiated not only in this respect but in another, and
one which especially interests us here. The female sexuality
shows a greater tendency to repression and to the formation
of resistances. The infantile sexual repression in women
receives a strong reinforcement at puberty. This gives
rise to the greater passivity of the sexual instinct in woman.
The male libido is of a more active nature. It overcomes
by means of its aggressive components the psychical
resistances with which it meets in its sexual object. In
the German language two expressions characterize the
psychosexual differences of the sexes. The man is said

F

to 'make a conquest' in love; the woman, to 'yield her-self' up to it.

Alcohol acts on the sexual instinct by removing the resistances and increasing sexual activity. These facts are generally known, but their real nature is not inquired into as a rule.

The more we study the subject the more complicated does the sexual instinct appear. Besides 'normal' hetero-sexual love, it includes a number of 'perverse' impulses. In the child we see those impulses in a state of complete chaos; for the child is a 'polymorpho-perverse' being (Freud). The 'component-instincts' are only gradually subordinated to the single heterosexual one. They succumb to repression and sublimation, and from them originate shame and disgust, moral, æsthetic and social feelings, pity and horror, the child's filial devotion to its parents, and the parents' fond care of their child. Artistic and scientific activities, too, are based to a great extent on the sublimation of sexual energies.[1] On these products of sublimation depend our social life and our entire civiliza-tion. There is not one among them which is not weakened or removed through the effect of alcohol.

In normal individuals the homosexual component of the sexual instinct undergoes sublimation. Between men, feelings of unity and friendship become divested of all conscious sexuality. The man of normal feelings is repelled by any physical contact implying tenderness with another of his own sex. And a number of similar feelings of repugnance or disgust originating in the same source could be mentioned. Alcohol suspends these feelings. When they are drinking, men will fall upon one another's necks and kiss one another; they feel that they are united by specially close bonds, and are easily moved to tears by this thought and very quick to use the intimate *Du* ('thou') in speaking. When sober, the same men will term such conduct 'effeminate'. Recent events have caused a lot of talk about 'abnormal friendship' between men. The

[1] Cf. Freud, *Drei Abhandlungen zur Sexualtheorie*, and Rank, *Der Künstler, Ansätze zu einer Sexualpsychologie* (1907).

presence of such feelings, which are stigmatized as morbid or immoral in that connection, can be observed by anyone during a drinking bout. In every public-house there is an element of homosexuality. The homosexual components which have been repressed and sublimated by the influence of education become unmistakably evident under the influence of alcohol.

Freud was the first to give due importance to the pair of component-instincts which are manifested in *scoptophilia* and *exhibitionism* respectively. They are closely associated with sexual curiosity, and their sublimation produces the feelings of shame. In the first years of its life the child has no such feelings; it has first to learn to feel 'embarrassment'. If sublimation does not take place then a perversion (*voyeurism* and exhibitionism) arises. Now the feeling of shame is not confined to the naked body only, but sets up important barriers in regard to social relations, conversation, etc. It is precisely these barriers which fall before alcohol. Obscene wit, which according to Freud's [1] brilliant analysis represents an exposure in a psychological sense, is inseparably associated with the enjoyment of alcohol. Forel [2] has described in a masterly manner how 'flirting' assumes coarse and repugnant forms under the influence of alcohol.

There is another pair of component-instincts which also represent active and passive counterparts of each other. The one impels the individual to dominate his sexual object, the other to submit to its will. Feelings of pity, horror, etc., originate from the sublimation of these tendencies. If sublimation does not take place we get the perversions called *sadism* and *masochism* respectively. It is hardly necessary to mention that many brutal crimes are perpetrated in states of alcoholic intoxication. Nevertheless, the repressed component-instincts need not necessarily be expressed in such a crude way; we can recognize them in more disguised forms. Drinking customs and laws have existed since primitive times; the 'drink king' at a carousal is absolute master. I might point to the German students'

---

[1] Freud, *Der Witz und seine Beziehungen zum Unbewussten* (1905).
[2] Forel, *Die sexuelle Frage*.

Komment of to-day with its rigorous obligation to drink, the proud satisfaction with which the older students compel the younger ones to do so, and the blind submission of the latter to the commands of their elders. I know that my view of these customs will meet with opposition. Let me therefore remark that these students' drinking laws have gradually developed their present more civilized forms out of incredibly gross customs in the past.

We have still to mention one more important limitation of the sexual instinct. As it grows up the normal child first transfers its libido on to the persons of the opposite sex in its immediate environment,—the boy on to his mother or sister, the girl on to her father or brother. A long period of cultural development was required before the nearest blood relations were excluded as eligible objects. The repudiation of incest led to the sublimation of the child's love for his parents, which became converted into filial respect. Every child has to repeat this process of development. At a certain period it transfers its awakening sexual wishes on to the parent of the opposite sex. These impulses become repressed, in the same way as our moral code condemns an unsublimated inclination on the part of a father for his daughter. But alcohol does not spare even these sublimations. Lot's daughters knew that wine would break down the incest barriers, and they attained their object by making their father drunk.

It is generally said that alcohol removes mental inhibitions. We have now recognized the nature of these inhibitions: they are the products of the sublimation of sexual energy.

The re-emergence of repressed sexual impulses increases the individual's normal sexual activity so that he gets a feeling of increased sexual capacity. Alcohol acts as a stimulus to the 'complex' of manliness.[1] We are familiar with the arrogance of the male from many examples in the

[1] In accordance with the nomenclature of the Psychiatric Clinic at Zürich, I use the shortened expression ' complex ' to denote a complex of images and ideas together with the feelings accompanying them, that is repressed into unconsciousness in certain circumstances, but can, in others, force its way back into consciousness once more.

animal kingdom. And we meet with the same phenomenon, *mutatis mutandis*, in human beings. The man feels
proud of being the begetter, the giver; the woman ' receives '.[1] Analysis of the myths of Creation shows in a
surprising manner how deeply rooted this grandiose complex is in the male. In a work I have in preparation [2] I
hope to bring forward detailed evidence to show that the
myths of Creation among different peoples originally represented a deification of the male power of procreation,
thereby proclaiming it as the principle of all life. In myths
the male power of reproduction and the divine power of
creation are identified and the two are often used inter-
changeably. We meet here a psychological process of
extraordinary importance, whose effects we can recognize
in all forms of imaginative activity, whether normal or
morbid, whether of the individual or of the group; and we
term this process *identification*.

A question which has occupied mankind from the beginning, but which we are still unable to answer satisfactorily, is how ' sexual excitement' arises. The assumption
that in the male the stimulus proceeds from the semen was
a very natural one; and, because intoxicating beverages
are sexually exciting, the naïve mind of the common people
went on to identify such beverages with semen or with
that unknown substance which (in the absence of artificial
stimulants) causes sexual excitement. This popular idea
finds expression in the German word *Liebesrausch* (' intoxication of love ').

The sphere of influence of this particular identification is very wide. Tales of the nectar of the gods and
of its origin are found throughout the whole of Indo-
Germanic mythology. This nectar, which is represented as
an invigorating and inspiring drink, is identified with the
intoxicating beverages of ordinary men. But the identification goes still further. In the above-mentioned work I
have quoted the old Indian myths to show that the drink of
the gods is considered equivalent to semen. This is because

[1] [German, *empfängt* also=' conceives '.—*Trans.*]
[2] *Traum und Mythus* (1909).

of the life-giving properties of semen.   It is worth noting that stories about the begetting (Creation) of the first man, as found in the Prometheus Saga, etc., stand in the closest possible relation to stories about the drink of the gods.   It is not possible to make a deeper psychological analysis of these myths here.   I will only mention that the Greek tales of the birth of the god of wine, Dionysus, show the same identification.

Love potions play a great part everywhere in myths. Undoubtedly the idea of their erotic effect is borrowed from the effect of alcoholic beverages.   Here also intoxication and sexual excitement are identified.   We meet the same idea in numerous customs.   The banquets dedicated to the god of wine are always at the same time erotic in character. In many customs wine is used as a symbol of procreation or fertilization.   Riklin [1] relates that in a certain locality it is customary at the Spring Festival to pour wine into girls' laps.   Here the symbolic representation of semen by wine is quite manifest.   Drinking healths in wine is a universal custom.   The alcoholic beverage represents the vital force on account of its stimulating effect.   If one drinks the health of another person it is equivalent to saying : ' May the invigorating effect of the wine benefit you '.

This identification must be an exceedingly firmly established one.   There is a close association between the deference paid to prowess in drinking and prowess in the sexual field.   He who does not drink is looked upon as a weakling. A man begins to take alcohol at puberty, at the time when he wishes to be looked upon as a man; and if he does not drink with his companions he is regarded as immature. Boasting about drinking is never so pronounced as in the period of commencing manhood.   If in later years he loses his potency, a man will eagerly seize upon pleasure-bringing alcohol; and it becomes a surrogate for his diminishing power of procreation.

Men turn to alcohol because it gives them an increased feeling of manliness and flatters their complex of masculinity. The nature of her psychosexual constitution urges a woman

[1] Riklin, *Wunscherfüllung und Symbolik im Märchen* (1908).

far less to take alcohol. Her sexual instinct is less active and her resistance against its impulses greater. We traced this difference in her attitude to the new onset of repression at puberty. A woman stimulates a man through her psychical resistances, just as a man pleases her by his energetic initiative. The girl at puberty has no motive to turn to alcohol, for it would remove the effects of repression—the resistances—and if she relinquished these she would no longer attract the man. We should expect to find on closer observation that women who show a strong inclination for alcohol always have a marked homosexual component in them.

The results of alcohol—*i.e.* the facilitating of sexual transference and the removal of the effects of repression—are not merely temporary, but, as is well known, chronic as well. Chronic drinkers exhibit a characteristic excess of feelings; they are coarsely familiar, look upon every one as an old friend, indulge in unmanly sentimentality, and lose the feeling of shame. I need scarcely refer to the scenes that children of drinkers have to witness. In short, all the finer feelings which owe their origin to sublimation are destroyed in the habitual drunkard.

And it is not the sublimations alone of the sexual impulse that are destroyed. An acute alcoholic intoxication will, as we know, reduce a man's actual sexual capacity. And we are acquainted with the poisonous effect of alcohol on the embryonic cells (blastophthoria).[1] We know that a great number of drinkers become impotent. Alcohol has proved a false friend. They imagined that it increased their virility, because it gave them a feeling of sexual power; and instead, it has robbed them of that power. But even so they fail to recognize the fraud. They will not give up alcohol, and they continue to identify it with their sexuality and to use it as a surrogate of the latter. I see in this an analogy to certain sexual perversions in which a sexual stimulus, which might normally have served as an introduction to the sexual act, is put in the place of that act. Freud terms this 'fixation of a temporary sexual aim'. For

---

[1] Cf. Forel and Juliusburger, ' Über Blastophthorie ' (1908), p. 346.

instance, looking at the sexual object is under normal conditions a source of fore-pleasure merely, while the sexual act itself alone gives rise to satisfaction-pleasure. Certain perverts, however, are content with looking alone. And the alcoholic behaves in a similar manner. Alcohol excites the sexual feelings; this excitement the drinker seeks to capture and thereby loses his capacity for normal sexual activity.

There are yet other analogies between alcoholism and sexual perversions. The investigations of Freud have shown us the intimate relations that exist between the perversions and the neuroses, and that many neurotic symptoms are the expression of repressed perverse sexual phantasies,[1] and are therefore a kind of sexual activity on the part of the patient. The patient always opposes an extraordinary resistance to the analysis of his symptoms; this is connected with his repression of his sexual complexes. In attempting to discover and resolve the patient's symptoms by psychoanalytic means the only reply which the physician obtains is a 'no', however much his inquiry may be justified. Instead of the real causes the patient brings forward cover-motives. In the same way the alcoholic will deny with his last breath facts which cannot possibly be disputed. He has a plentiful choice of cover-motives for his alcoholism and uses them to parry every attempt to get to the bottom of the matter. I think we must conclude that for the same reason that the neurotic protects his symptoms the drinker fights in defence of his alcoholism. It represents his sexual activity.

There is yet another point that seems to me worth mentioning. Certain ideas of an undoubtedly sexual nature play a prominent part in the morbid changes that take place in the mentality of the alcoholic. I refer to the well-known jealousy of the drinker—a jealousy which may increase until it becomes a delusion. The cause of this jealousy is, I believe, a feeling of diminishing potency on the subject's part (I base my conclusion on a wide range of experience which I cannot quote here in detail). The drinker makes use of alcohol as a means of obtaining pleasure without trouble. He gives up women and turns to alcohol. This

[1] Freud, 'Hysterical Phantasies and their Relation to Bisexuality' (1908).

state of affairs is exceedingly painful to his self-esteem; and he represses it, just like the neurotic, and at the same time effects a displacement such as we are accustomed to find in the mechanism of the neuroses and psychoses. He displaces his feelings of guilt on to his wife and accuses her of being unfaithful.

We see, therefore, that alcoholism, sexuality and neurosis are connected in many ways. It seems to me necessary to employ the psycho-analytic procedure developed by Freud, which enables us to penetrate into the structure of the neuroses, for the analysis of alcoholism as well. From the oral communications of colleagues, I know that in cases of morphinism psycho-analysis has demonstrated the existence of unexpected relations between sexuality and the use of narcotics. I may also mention the inexplicable behaviour of many nervous persons in regard to narcotics. Hysterical patients often beg their physician not to prescribe morphia or opium for them whatever he does, because they cannot stand it; and they go on to tell of the unpleasant experiences they have had with it. It looks very much as though the drug evokes sexual excitement in certain hysterical persons—an excitement which, in consequence of the hysteric's peculiar psychosexual constitution, is converted into physical symptoms and feelings of anxiety. Perhaps the intolerance of alcohol so frequently met with in nervous people has a similar cause. Finally, I might mention a remarkable fact which I have repeatedly observed in insane patients. When they are given a hypodermic injection of morphia, etc., they regard it as a sexual assault, and they interpret the injection syringe and the fluid in a symbolic way.

As we see, the psychological investigation of alcoholism still offers many unsolved problems. External factors such as social influences, faulty education, hereditary taint, etc., are not by themselves sufficient to explain drunkenness. An individual factor must be present. Our first task is to investigate that factor; and it seems to me only possible to succeed in this if the connections between alcoholism and sexuality are constantly borne in mind.

CHAPTER IV

HYSTERICAL DREAM-STATES [1] (1910)

IN a recently published paper,[2] Löwenfeld has dealt with certain peculiar disturbances in neurotics which have not previously been given sufficient consideration in the literature of the subject. As an introduction to my subject I will quote Löwenfeld's general description of these states. He says: 'The external world does not make the usual impression on the patient. Familiar and every-day things seem changed, as though they were unknown, new and strange; or the whole surroundings give the impression of being the product of a phantasy, an illusion, a vision. In the latter case in particular it seems to the patients as though they were in a dream, or half asleep, or were hypnotized or somnambulic; and they generally speak of these conditions as their *dream-states*.' The author also says that these states differ greatly in degree, exhibit considerable variations in their duration, are often associated with the affect of anxiety and are, as a rule, accompanied by other nervous symptoms.

Löwenfeld bases his description on a considerable number of medical histories. I myself have come across these states in a number of patients whom I have treated by psycho-analysis. Since these dream-states have not been dealt with from a psycho-analytical point of view up to the present, I will give the main results of my observations in the following pages. They form a further addition to the knowledge derived from psycho-analysis concerning the nature of episodic phenomena in the clinical picture of hysteria.

[1] [No. 17, A. B.]
[2] ' Über traumartige und verwandte Zustände ' (1910).

Case A [1]

The first example, a simple case, will show how far we can explain the nature of dream-states without making use of psycho-analysis. I was only able to give the patient in question one consultation. In it I examined him in the usual way and elicited the following relevant facts: The patient, still a young man, was prone to very vivid day-dreaming. According to his account his waking dreams were mainly stimulated by actual occurrences. For example, the account of the discovery of the North Pole gave rise to the phantasy that he was taking part in a great expedition. He imagined this with great minuteness of detail, especially as regards the part he himself played. Phantasies of this type had almost completely absorbed him for some considerable time past. He had only to catch a word said in the street—for example, the word 'zeppelin'—for his imaginative faculties to be set in motion. As soon as his day-dreaming had attained a certain intensity he would begin to feel himself more and more removed from reality. A dream-like stupefaction would come over him. Next, there was a mental blankness lasting a short time; and after that there followed rapidly a strong sensation of giddiness associated with anxiety and palpitation of the heart. He described the state up to the onset of the giddiness as a pleasurable one. He also had the following symptoms: nervous vomiting, nervous diarrhœa, headaches, irritability, timidity, etc.

This case, and, as will be seen, all those that follow, plainly demonstrate the connection of dream-states with day-dreaming. I emphasize this fact, because Löwenfeld has paid no special attention to it.

A state of *phantastic exaltation* forms the typical introduction of the dream-state, the content of which varies altogether in character according to the individual. This

---

[1] I have named the following cases A, B, C, etc., arranging them in alphabetical order. All details about their age, occupation, and personal relations which it is not necessary for us to know have been omitted.

is followed by a condition of dream-like ' removal from reality ' (*Entrückung* [1]). In this state, as Löwenfeld has well described, the person's familiar surroundings appear changed, unreal, and strange to him. He feels ' as if he were in a dream '. The word ' dream-state ', which is spontaneously used by many patients, describes the phantastical trend of thought belonging to the first stage and the alteration of consciousness belonging to the second one. I recognize, however, yet a third stage, that of mental blankness. This is described by patients thus: ' My thoughts stop ', ' an emptiness in my head ', and similar phrases. Finally a state of depression occurs, the most important characteristic of which is a feeling of anxiety with its usual accompanying phenomena of giddiness, palpitation of the heart, etc. Most patients also complain of phantasies of a depressive type.

There is no sharp line of demarcation between the different stages. On the contrary, it is possible to observe transitions from one to the other. The practical utility and importance of differentiating between these states is only apparent when we come to discuss cases which have been thoroughly analysed; and I shall then be able to add considerably to the above brief and superficial description of those stages.

The third stage undoubtedly forms the culminating point of the dream-state. It is its turning-point, as it were, not only because its appearance puts a sudden end to the production of the phantasy, but also because it is the line of demarcation between two affects of an opposite character. It is not unusual to find the dream-state, as in the present case, described as pleasurable up to its third stage and a high degree of displeasurable affect assigned to its later stages.

By this kind of examination of the patient we are able to obtain much information about the ideas and feelings contained in the dream-states, the circumstances that give rise to them, and the fluctuations in consciousness that are

---

[1] The term *Entrückung* is borrowed from Breuer (cf. Breuer und Freud, *Studien über Hysterie*, Zweite Auflage, S. 191).

involved in them. By investigating a further series of cases in a similar manner we should discover the individual variations in those respects, and we should also be able to confirm Löwenfeld's account of their differences in intensity and duration. So long, however, as we restrict ourselves to the consciousness of the patient, this is as far as we can go. The causes of the appearance of dream-states will remain unexplained. For as a rule the neurotic contents himself with ordinary day-dreams, and it remains obscure why this condition should occasionally undergo an aggravation of such a kind as to develop into an acute quasi-paroxysmal state accompanied by mild disturbances of consciousness. The state of ' removal from reality ' is altogether unintelligible to us, especially the feelings of strangeness and unreality, the temporary mental blankness, and finally the appearance of anxiety with its accompanying manifestations. All these phenomena are subject, besides, to individual variations; each case presents its own particular problem. In particular, the phantasies of the initial stage and those of the final one are only intelligible to a limited extent in the absence of a thorough analysis.

The knowledge of the phantasy-life of neurotics gained by psycho-analytic investigation gives us the key to the solution of the problem. Freud has shown us that our instinctual desires are revealed in our phantasies. When our desires are prevented from being fulfilled we endeavour to imagine them as fulfilled, or as about to be fulfilled. In the neurotic the whole instinctual life and all the component-instincts are originally of abnormal strength. At the same time there is a special tendency in him towards a repression of instincts. The neurosis develops from the conflict between instinct and repression. The neurotic is a maker of phantasies because of the great variety and intensity of his instinctual life and the wealth of his repressed desires; and therefore, as observation shows, he is very prone to day-dreaming. He has frequent and vivid dreams in his sleep as well. The dynamic power of his repressed wishes is, however, so strong that he finds those means of expression which he has in common with the normal individual inadequate. His neurosis itself subserves those tendencies exclusively. The neurotic dream-state, as I shall presently show, is only one of a variety of phenomena by means of which the multitude of his repressed wishes finds expression.

I shall now proceed to give such details from an extensive analysis of a case as are relevant to the problem of dream-states. This case gives us some insight into the confusion of instinctual tendencies that co-exist in the mind, either reinforcing or opposing one another. The analysis enables us to recognize the dominating significance of sexual phantasies. It will become quite clear that the conscious phantasies which, on the surface, appear to be non-sexual, have arisen from sexual wishes through the process of sublimation. The phantasies which are admitted to consciousness by the censorship serve as a medium for the representation of repressed wishes and derive their energy from the latter source.

CASE B

This patient suffered from an unusually severe hysteria accompanied by phobias and compulsions. His morbid anxiety about going out of the house alone had rendered him incapable of following his calling or of participating in any form of social life for the last five years. Besides his severe attacks of anxiety he was very liable to dream-states.

He could remember that the first attack of this kind had occurred when he was ten years old, on an occasion when he had felt slighted. He had been overcome by a feeling of *Weltschmerz*, which had been instantly succeeded by the counteracting idea, ' Later on, when I'm grown-up, I'll show you ', and he had fallen into a state of ecstatic exaltation and had experienced a dream-like alteration of consciousness. Since that time he used to be overcome by a dream-state whenever he had to recognize the superiority of others and his own inactivity. His present situation was naturally constantly exposing him to such states. For example, it was only necessary for someone to refer to the ability or success of any person of his own age for him to

react in this way at once.   As time went on the occasions
giving rise to these states became more varied.   The sight
of women, the theatre, music, reading, etc., had this effect
on him, since they induced phantasies of an ambitious or
erotic nature.   It is less easy to understand why such states
were induced by vigorous bodily movement, such as walking
in the street, or by hearing loud noises, such as that of a
train passing over a bridge.   They used to come on most
frequently when he was in the street.

Occasions of this kind would begin by producing a
marked activity of his imagination, together with the resolve
to work most energetically for the realization of his
imaginary desires.   He would, as he put it, summon up
the whole of his will-power.   First and foremost would
be the thought that some day he would emerge from his
seclusion and impress the whole world.   He would imagine
how he would cause a sensation on account of his great
learning, or would be called before the curtain as the author
of a drama and so be the centre of universal attention; or
how he would become a master-player at chess and go
from table to table in a café, playing simultaneous games,
and would make his moves under the admiring gaze of
the onlookers.   At other times he would create the image
of a great general, behind whom his own ambitions were
concealed.   His energetic resolutions would be outwardly
manifested by his walking hurriedly about the room, or
going at a tremendous pace along the streets.

The patient himself described the process as an ever-
increasing state of ' enthusiasm '.   This condition would
merge rapidly and almost imperceptibly into the second
stage.   His description of the latter was very characteristic:
it was that there occurred a complete ' turning into oneself ',
a shutting out of all external impressions, and that in making
phantasies ' one loses the ground under one's feet '.   That
is to say, he was no longer able to control his train of thought
and left the solid ground of reality.   At this point he would
seem to himself to be in a dream; his entire surroundings,
even his own body, would appear strange to him, and
he would even doubt the reality of their existence.   The

typical third stage—that of 'cessation of thoughts'—
would follow.   Morbid anxiety would develop immediately
and usher in the fourth stage, in which he would be seized
with giddiness and have the feeling that he was no longer
going forward, that he could not lift his legs, that he was
sliding, falling, sinking down.   These sensations would
be associated with the most intense anxiety.   People and
surrounding objects would appear to him remarkably
big.   He himself would feel small and want to be so in
order not to be seen; he would like to be 'as nothing', 'to
sink entirely into the earth'.   He also described a feeling
that he must crawl on all-fours in order to reach home.

The patient described the first stage as pleasurable.
Nevertheless even during his 'enthusiasm' there would
come, as he expressed it, a current of an opposite character
which was at first perceived as a sensation of coldness.   We
find here paræsthesias and vaso-motor symptoms as accompanying phenomena of the dream-state, to which we have
as yet not given sufficient consideration.   During the
stage of mental blankness the feeling of coldness was intense.   A sudden 'heat wave' would then sometimes set
in with the anxiety, accompanied by a feeling of congestion
in the head.   When his anxiety used finally to give way to a
feeling of weakness the sensation of coldness would always
become very strong; and at the same time he would have
the feeling that parts of his body had 'died off'.

The patient used to welcome the commencement of
the dream-state on account of its accompanying pleasure.
Nevertheless, he often used to attempt to interrupt it before
it had reached its culminating point, i.e. the stage of mental
blankness.   He said, 'I try to tear myself away from my
"enthusiasm"; I attempt to come out of it as from a
cloud'.   The expression 'cloud' should be noted; it
indicates the feeling of a clouding of consciousness, that is,
the dream-like quality of his state.   If that state was
prematurely interrupted he used to experience anxiety and
a feeling of weakness.

The last stage was very protracted in this patient.   In
order to free himself from his anxiety which he could not

overcome he used to adopt a peculiar method: he lit a cigar. Incidentally, the desire to smoke used to come on as early as in the stage of 'enthusiasm'.

During the analysis of his dream-states the patient told me spontaneously that for a long time he had considered these states as a kind of translation of his sexual impulse into a mental form. My investigations fully confirmed this view.

The patient was one of those neurotics who had been addicted to masturbation in early childhood and had later on maintained a continual struggle against that habit. He had frequently attempted, and as often failed, to renounce it; and this had given rise to the usual disappointments, self-reproaches, and hypochondriacal troubles. A number of his symptoms, which cannot be discussed here, had arisen in this connection. The conflict between wish and repression had found its solution in a compromise, as is so often the case in the neuroses. The patient had often given up onanism for long periods at a time, during which he had avoided physical self-excitation together with its final aim, ejaculation. Thus from a superficial point of view he had given up his sexual habits. But his unconscious required a substitutive gratification the nature and purpose of which should elude consciousness so that it could be carried out free from inhibiting influences.

Freud [1] has conclusively shown that certain episodic phenomena of hysteria are a substitutive gratification for masturbation when this has been given up. (We shall later have to consider this point.) Now the dream-state is also a substitutive gratification of this kind. Before I bring forward evidence for this, I must mention that more recently the patient used also to have dream-states at a time when he did not resist the impulse to masturbate. However, this fact is only in appearance incompatible with the idea that the dream-state was a substitutive gratification, because at such times the patient was subject to counteracting ideas which prevented him from yielding to his impulse quite freely. Besides, the strength of his impulse

[1] 'General Remarks on Hysterical Attacks' (1909).

was so great that it was difficult to obtain a complete gratification of it; so that even the frequent practice of masturbation did not render surrogates superfluous. Finally, these surrogates themselves became a source of pleasure, and we know how difficult it is, especially for the neurotic, to give up anything that is a source of pleasure.

The patient had been accustomed in early youth to indulge in day-dreaming, and when the activity of a vivid phantasy was at its height, to make use of masturbation as an outlet for the accumulated excitement. When he tried to abandon the practice of masturbation his day-dreaming had to find a different end. It now formed an introduction to a dream-state, just as earlier it had been an introduction to masturbation. The second and third stages—that of removal from reality and of mental blankness—corresponded to the increasing sexual excitement and to its culminating point, the moment of ejaculation. The final stage of anxiety and weakness was transposed unaltered from the act of masturbation. Those symptoms are familiar to us as the regular consequence of masturbation in neurotics.

The comparison we have made requires further confirmation as regards the second and third stages. A stage similar to the removal from reality in the dream-state is also found in masturbation, in which the increasing sexual excitement leads to an exclusion of all external impressions. In the dream-state this effect is chiefly evident on the mental plane. The patient was aware of his attention being entirely 'turned inwards'. This auto-erotic occlusion from the outer world gave him a feeling of isolation. He 'withdrew from the world'. His ideas transplanted him into another world which was founded on the model of his repressed wishes. So great was the power of his repressed wishes when once they emerged from the unconscious that he accepted their fulfilment in phantasy as reality and perceived reality as the empty fabric of a dream. His entire surroundings, and even his own body, seemed strange and unreal to him.

The feeling of being isolated is peculiar to many neurotics who retire from the world in order to indulge in sexual practices in solitude. The patient remembered a favourite phantasy from his early youth which related to a secret underground room, hidden away somewhere in a forest, to which he wished to escape in order to be alone with his phantasies. Later on, anxiety appeared in the place of this wish. And anxiety of being alone in a closed room still dominated him as a grown-up man.

The disappearance of thought—the mental blankness —that characterizes the third stage corresponds roughly to the marked 'loss of consciousness'[1] which takes place, especially in neurotics, at the climax of each sexual excitation; and there then occurs a marked sensation of giddiness or of something akin to giddiness but difficult to describe. The patient definitely stated that he had the same sensation during masturbation at the moment of ejaculation. This short suspension of consciousness corresponding to the moment of emission is also met with in hysterical attacks.

It need no longer surprise us to find that the dream-state is pleasurable up to the stage of mental blankness; for this would tend to confirm its derivation from masturbation, which is also pleasurable up to the corresponding stage, and afterwards often produces the liveliest feelings of distress in neurotics. It is also very interesting to remember that the patient under discussion used frequently to interrupt his dream-state prematurely, *i.e.* before the onset of mental blankness. This is a kind of attempt to renounce the habit of having dream-states. Neurotics frequently do exactly the same when they wish to give up masturbation.[2] In their opinion it is the loss of semen which is the harmful thing in masturbation, and they content themselves with breaking off the act before emission. They then indulge in the consoling idea that they have not *really* masturbated. One frequently meets with this sophism in neurotic persons. They endeavour to compensate for the renunciation of the end-pleasure by very greatly increasing the fore-pleasure. The anxiety they feel at the

---

[1] Freud, 'General Remarks on Hysterical Attacks' (1909).
[2] See Rohleder, 'Über Masturbatio interrupta' (1908).

end, however, is something they cannot escape. The sexual excitement that has accumulated finds no discharge and is changed into anxiety.

In regarding the patient's dream-states as a substitutive gratification for a form of sexual practice which has been relinquished, we are still far from fully understanding all the characteristics of those states. The phantasies of the first and fourth stages are of such an individual nature that they can only be understood after we have gained an intimate knowledge of the patient's instinctual life.

In the present instance the patient's infantile tendencies had, in the regular way known to psycho-analysis, been fixated to such a degree upon the people in closest relation to him that at puberty he had been unable to detach them in the normal way. His fixation was of a marked bisexual character. The heterosexual components of his libido had his mother as their object, in relation to whom he identified himself with his father who was dead. His homosexual components were attached to his father, and in relation to him he identified himself with his mother. Thus in his neurosis he sometimes played the father, sometimes the mother. His behaviour in general could be described as markedly passive. He had resigned himself to the misfortune of his neurosis. His love for his father, who had been a very energetic person, took the form of an unconditional subjection to a superior person. He showed the typical jealousy of the neurotic, which he had preserved from childhood. As a boy he had regarded his father as his rival in regard to his mother, while his mother had stood in the way of his attachment to his father. As a result, there had arisen hostile wishes in him which—as is so often the case in neurotic children—had culminated in the phantasy of killing his father or mother. These sadistic impulses had been subjected to very strong repression. A great number of his dreams, in which he witnessed the death of his father or mother, bore witness to the persistence of those unconscious wishes. He also had frequent waking phantasies of the same kind, as well as sudden aggressive impulses. These repressed impulses, and certain instances of aggressive conduct during childhood and puberty, were responsible for the idea he had that he was a criminal, as well as for a number of obsessive symptoms from which he suffered.

The patient's aggressive tendencies had been extensively sublimated so that he could employ their impulsive force in planning high achievements outside the sphere of sexuality. However, this had not sufficed to stem the full force of his instincts. In order to be neutralized effectually those tendencies had had to be turned into their direct opposite. His aggressive feelings towards his mother had been replaced by complete passivity, by an absolute dependence upon her, which still persisted although he was long since a grown man. He now became wholly tied to her and to the house, just like a little child. This was the chief source of the anxiety which prevented him from going out alone. This dependence upon a particular person (or persons) is present in every case of street anxiety. The attempt to leave home alone represented to the patient a forbidden activity; it would have symbolized a loosening of the tie between himself and his mother, and also, as the analysis showed, a homosexual approach towards his father. As soon as he attempted to tear himself away from his heterosexual incestuous phantasies he fell a prey to his homosexual ones, which were likewise energetically rejected by his conscious. A very extensive suppression of his instinctual tendencies had therefore taken place, and this accounted for the peculiar intensity of his nervous anxiety.

Like other neurotics, the patient endeavoured to correct the unsatisfying reality with the help of phantasies. He used this means in especial whenever some external occurrence made him realize how greatly he differed from his more healthy contemporaries owing to his childish dependence and passive conduct, and above all, his propensity for masturbation. Even in boyhood he had suffered from this feeling. It had been his ardent desire to become 'like the others'. He used to torture himself with self-reproaches because he was singled out among the 'others' on account of his tendencies, and because those tendencies made him incapable of competing with them. He used to be especially tormented by the fear of appearing ridiculous or despicable in their eyes. This was the reason of his excessive sensitiveness to the idea of being slighted in favour of ' others '. He considered that such a slight would show that he was not respected, and all his suppressed activity would rise in revolt. Originally his aggressive tendencies would have moved him to react to a slight with an act of violence, but they had been rendered harmless early on by ' reaction-formation ', and now only ventured forth in the shape of secret phantasies. When he thought himself slighted he reacted with sublimated desires to be active and with phantasies of grandeur whose fulfilment he placed in the future: ' When I am grown up . . .'

The older the patient became, the more pronounced became his feeling that he had remained a child. He failed to recognize that it was the strongest wish of his unconscious to preserve this childish state. His consciousness reacted with the opposite tendency. Every dream-state subserved a wish to be grown up. Being grown up signified many things to him—it meant being independent, self-supporting, energetic (like his father), free from his besetting habit and, above all, capable of sexual activity. For he was dominated by a fear of being impotent, like every neurotic who is unable to relinquish his infantile sexual practices and the objects of his infantile sexual phantasies. The phantasies of grandeur which we have traced back to sublimated sadistic impulses were always connected in this patient with the idea of excelling before others and of drawing all eyes upon himself. This idea may be explained as a sublimation of repressed ' exhibitionistic ' wishes. In neurotics who show morbidly pronounced ambition I have always been able to demonstrate that that feature of their character provides a kind of common outlet for their repressed sadistic and exhibitionistic wishes. In the present case it could be established that the patient had actually carried out actions of a sadistic-exhibitionistic character in his youth, and that he felt severe self-reproaches on that account. The constantly recurring necessity of repressing those impulses was a continual source of anxiety to him. For example, he was not able to travel by tram because he would suddenly feel the impulse to expose himself before the people present or to make a sexual assault upon a woman. Similar impulses used to occur on other occasions, as, for instance, when he was in conversation with women. The process of sublimation led to a partial or total renunciation of the original aim of his instinct to exhibit, *i.e.* to expose himself in a sexual way. The forbidden exhibitionism was replaced by phantasies which contented themselves with a much more innocent aim; in them the patient drew attention to himself, not on grounds of sexual desire or sexual curiosity, but merely in admiration.

We have heard of various kinds of occasions which used to bring on the patient's dream-states. We can now say that they had this effect because they stimulated wishes of sexual aggression or exhibition in him which found expression in a sublimated form. It can now be easily understood why the sight of women was able to provoke a dream-state. Moreover, whenever he became too much aware of his passivity by contrast with other, energetic people, he used to correct reality with the help of his imagination and picture himself as a very active man and the object of everyone's interest. Vigorous movements of the body could also act as exciting causes by giving him a feeling of activity. The jolting and clatter of a train would stimulate in him the wish to be strong. And all his other phantasies belonged to the same category. As a player of chess in cafés, going from table to table and playing simultaneous games, he certainly had a good opportunity of exhibiting himself before the gaze of others. Moreover, chess itself, as his analysis showed, offered him ample opportunity for the employment of sublimated instincts. In chess there is a struggle between two parties, each of which attacks, takes pieces, overthrows the enemy's position, etc.—a set of ideas which, according to the patient's own testimony, had a great fascination for him. He revelled in the technical expressions employed, and used to gratify his instinct of aggression by playing games by himself.

Whereas the fulfilment in phantasy of his ambitious wishes, *i.e.* the gratification of his sublimated instincts, was associated with feelings of pleasure, the concluding stage of his dream-state exhibited the opposite affect of anxiety. And it can be demonstrated that in the concluding stage his phantasies had a quite different content from the earlier ones. The beginning of the dream-state lifted him out of his habitual passivity into activity. The concluding stage put him back into his former state. In place of his ambitious plans we find want of courage and a dispirited mind; and whereas a short while ago he was filled with feelings of power and strode along the streets he now felt weak and inhibited in his movements. He felt as if he could no longer go forward—a striking symbolical representation of his actual situation! He was once more a small child who could not walk by himself.[1] The unconscious tendency which preserved the infantile state in him had carried the day. It was because of this that the patient seemed to himself so diminutive, and people and things appeared to him to be so large.[2] He wanted to crawl home on all-fours to his mother like a child who has not learned to walk. A few moments before, he wished to draw all eyes upon him, but now he would have liked to disappear, to sink into the ground in order not to be noticed.

The patient's intense feeling of weakness in the fourth stage had several determining factors. In the first place, it signified the dreaded sexual weakness. Whereas he had begun to feel strong and active at the commencement of his dream-state, he ended once more by relapsing into passivity. He lacked masculine vigour. His sensation of being too weak to stand up contained a symbolic allusion to impotence. A further determinant of his weakness was furnished by his death phantasies, which are never missing in cases where aggressive intentions against relatives have

[1] I shall not in this place discuss the further determinations of 'slipping' and 'falling'.

[2] This is the most important cause of the symptom described as 'macropsy'. I have also observed its presence in the anxiety-attacks of a female patient.

had to be suppressed. These death phantasies of the concluding stage stood in marked contrast to the energy and animation of his phantasies in the first stage.

In the last stage of his dream-state his impulses of aggression and exhibition were once again suppressed; and, as we have already said, he would seek to obtain relief from the state of depression in which he was left by smoking a cigar. It was, however, not so much the nicotine itself that gradually removed his depression. It was rather that smoking had the significance of a substitute gratification. It was a mark of that masculinity which he lacked,[1] and was a consolation to him in his state of weakness.

The accompanying vaso-motor and paræsthetic symptoms require separate consideration. The sensation of heat described by this patient, and, as will be shown, by others, too, is a normal accompaniment of sexual excitation. It had been transferred in his case from masturbation to the dream-state. It is worth noting that he blushed very easily. As soon as he came among people his extraordinarily excitable sexual phantasy became active, and expressed itself physically as a wave of heat. It should not surprise us to find that this increased flow of blood also accompanied his phantasies of activity, since, as we know, they represented his unconscious sexual phantasies. Even in the early stage of his 'exalted' phantasies he used to notice an 'under-current' of coldness and anxiety besides the rising heat; and in the final stage the feeling of coldness dominated. In general, therefore, the feeling of heat used to appear when he wished to push forward to sexual activity, while the feeling of coldness used to come on when his instinctual emotions had changed into anxiety and the tendency to repression had obtained the upper hand once more. His blood was now no longer being impelled to the periphery with the same force. But the oncoming feeling of coldness was determined by still other causes. The patient used to feel as if parts of his body had died off, and as if he was going to collapse and vanish away in the

---

[1] Space does not permit me to go into the other determinants of smoking (such as utilization of the mouth zone, identification with the father, etc.).

next minute.   Thus the fourth stage was a symbolic death which was also expressed by the sensation of coldness. Further analysis showed that this dying also had a double significance: the impotence he feared gave it a second, more special meaning—that the essential energy of life was lacking in him.

Just as the first stage of his dream-state subserved his phantasies of vigour and masculinity, so the final stage exhibited a condensation of two sets of ideas which were opposed to those phantasies, namely, (1) to remain a child; (2) to die.   The adult man, filled with vital energy, stands midway between childhood and death.

The patient's dream-states give us an insight into the conflict between impulse and repression as it is fought out in every neurosis.   Repressed impulses, originally of abnormal strength, succeed in struggling free from the unconscious, only once more to succumb swiftly to the forces of repression.   Each of these dream-states represented a revolt against his neurosis, but one foredoomed to failure.

The next case, however, will show that not all dream-states contain the same tendencies.

Case C

In this patient (a woman) dream-states used to appear in the same way when she felt worried, depressed, or humiliated by a present situation which she could not avoid.   Conversation of a painful nature, or a physical indisposition, particularly menstruation, would induce these states.   As she said, ' During menstruation I lose all sense of reality '. In her case, too, the dream-state brought on a feeling of isolation from the external world; and so we might expect to find that it served in the same way to remove her from the painfulness of reality.   But the opposite was the case. Her phantasies used to induce a state of still greater suffering in her and one of absolute passivity; and from this she obtained masochistic pleasure.   She gave interesting details from her childhood concerning actual masochistic practices. These masochistic impulses were still clearly recognizable

at the present day.   For she was able to induce a dream-
state at will.   (I may say that I have met with this phenomenon in other cases.)   As she said herself, ' Something
often impels me to bring on a dream-state '.   To do this
she used to recite from memory a passage out of Hebbel's
Maria Magdalena (Act 3, Scene 2), where Clara makes the
following declaration:

' I will serve you and I will work for you, and you shall
give me nothing to eat.   I will earn my own livelihood.   I
will sew and spin at night for other people.   I will go
hungry if I have nothing to do.   I would rather bite into
my own arm than go to my father, lest he should observe
anything.   If you should strike me because your dog is
not at hand, or because you have put him away, I would
sooner swallow my tongue than utter a single cry that
might betray to the neighbours what is happening.   I
cannot promise that my flesh will not show the marks of
your whip, for I cannot help that.   But I will lie; I will
say that I knocked my head against the cupboard, or that
I fell down on the floor because it was slippery.   And I
will say all this before anyone has had time to ask what
has caused my bruises.—Marry me.   I shall not live long.
And if even so you should tire of me and not be willing
to bear the expense of a divorce in order to free yourself
of me, buy poison and put it somewhere as though it were
meant for the rats and say nothing.   I will take it, and
when I am dying I will say to the neighbours that I
thought it was powdered sugar! '

When the patient had sunk herself into these typically
masochistic ideas she used to fall into a state of dream-like
' removal from reality '.   She felt the masochistic subjection
of Clara, with whom she identified herself, and her own
isolation from the world as pleasurable.   She laid great
stress on the pleasurable character of that seclusion, and
used to experience similar situations in her dreams.   In
them the world was remote; her body seemed changed, and
her own voice was unfamiliar to her.   As she said, ' The
person ' (meaning herself) ' who is speaking is quite strange
to me '.   To add to her torment, everything would assume

absurd and distorted forms which recalled drawings by
Kubin. 'Everything is more cruel and gloomy than
reality', she used to say. Her masochistic phantasies used
to culminate in thoughts of death, in the idea that she must
jump out of the window, etc. After the crisis had passed
extreme anxiety used to set in, accompanied by anxiety-
ideas which varied with the situation of the moment. For
example, if the patient happened to be in the street she
would have the feeling that she must fall, that she could not
get home alone, that she must go up to some man or other
and accost him. 'To fall' and 'to accost a man' are
equivocal expressions. They not only indicate a state of
helplessness and need for assistance, but they point to those
prostitution phantasies which are so often met with in
hysterical women, but are kept so strictly secret by them.[1]
The patient used to have an impulse to give herself to the
first man that came her way, and at times, when she was
suffering from frequent attacks of the kind described, she
used actually to do so. Her prostitution desires appeared
as a special form of masochism, and represented to her, who
had in general a high opinion of herself and was even somewhat masterful, the deepest form of humiliation.

In this patient we meet furthermore with the occurrence
of very protracted dream-states, such as Löwenfeld has also
described. In many neurotics the feeling of being in a
dream and uncertain about the reality of their surroundings
can last for some months or even longer. The present
patient was for a long time under the impression that everything around her was only make-believe, and that her body
was dead and she was only a spirit looking on at the real
world without having anything to do with it. She said
that this protracted state was particularly tormenting, but
that, for that very reason, it procured her access to things
which otherwise would have been hidden from her. These
states enabled her to find refuge in a world of dreams
from the world of reality in which her wishes found no
gratification.

[1] These phantasies came to expression very clearly in many of the patient's
dreams, and were also betrayed in her symptomatic actions.

Case D

The patient, quite a young man, had suffered since childhood from severe hysteria which rendered him almost incapable of associating with other people. For example, he would scarcely speak to anyone at all, and would avoid eating in the presence of strangers, because on such occasions he always used to suffer from severe anxiety. His manner of living in itself, therefore, cut him off from the external world. And his dream-states reinforced this tendency.

Such an eccentric mode of living in so young a man was due to a quite exceptionally strong fixation of his libido on his nearest relatives, to whose narrow circle he was almost entirely confined. Every time he overstepped those boundaries he used to be overcome by anxiety. If he wished to leave the house or pay a call or speak to a superior, he would always be seized with anxiety. His unusually strong sexual phantasies centred about his family; and not only did he have heterosexual wishes fixated upon his mother and sister, but he was very much interested in his father from a homosexual and masochistic point of view. As soon as he approached a strange person he would begin to have sexual phantasies about him; but his attempt at a ' transference ' would be as rapidly suppressed. He had wanted for a moment to leave his narrow confines, but the fixation of his libido was too strong, and so every attempt he made in that direction resulted in anxiety.

The patient's above-mentioned sexual phantasies always led up to masturbation, an act which he performed in a refined manner, never making a direct use of his hands, but applying long-continued and quite gentle stimulation such as gentle pressure of the thighs together and manipulations through his clothes. This physical stimulation and the accompanying phantasies used to bring on the dream-like ' removal from reality '. Ejaculation never occurred, but he used to have a very pronounced period of mental blankness. In the present case we can see the dream-states still in their direct and original association with masturbation.

Yet they were also able to appear quite spontaneously. This was especially the case when the patient's father was present. For then those phantasies would be activated to which the patient was addicted when alone, and in this situation they would induce a dream-state, just as at other times they would lead to masturbation.

For many years the patient had enjoyed these highly pleasurable states during school-hours. His teachers had noticed that he was inattentive at his lessons and usually absent-minded. He was preoccupied with phantasies which were quite remote from his studies; and if he was startled out of a reverie by a question from his teacher severe anxiety would occur. As the years passed this propensity persisted unchanged; and the dream-state still served him to this day as a means of completely secluding himself. He was wholly sunk in himself, and it was difficult for him to concentrate upon anything which lay outside the circle of his phantasies. If he found himself in some unwelcome situation he would often evoke a dream-state deliberately by a simple method which symbolized in the clearest manner an exclusion of external impressions: he would close his eyes. During psycho-analysis he always used to shut his eyes when he came to a subject which he did not want to talk about. Then it was quite impossible to get a single word out of him. He would sit there motionless and absent-minded. When I explained to him that his dream-states required a careful psycho-analytical investigation, he immediately reacted with a dream-state, which naturally made it impossible to institute such an investigation for the time being. He was also able to interrupt the dream-state at will; this he did by giving a sudden jerk of his head.

The patient used to employ his dream-state in one other way besides, and that was when he had to suffer a particular pain of psychological origin. He would then evoke a dream-state by means of certain sexually exciting manipulations, and his pain would become gradually transformed into a sensation of pleasure.

CASE E

This patient, too, exhibited an excessively strong infantile sexual transference on to both parents, together with those death wishes which regularly accompany it and which are rigidly rejected by consciousness. These latter were especially directed upon his mother, but had been transformed through reaction-formation into an excessive attachment to her of a thoroughly childish character. Though he was long since grown up, it seemed strange to him that he was no longer the child he still felt himself to be. It is worth noting that it was the death of his mother which had brought on his first dream-state. This state had been a very protracted one, and for many months he had had the feeling of going about in a dream. But the intensity of this feeling showed great variations. He said quite spontaneously, ' I cannot think that anything is real if I am not at her ' (his mother's) ' side '. In place of the repressed phantasies which had once been directed against his mother's life, therefore, the idea appeared in consciousness that his own life depended on hers and would end with it. His death phantasies had become turned back upon himself. To quote his own words: ' Hand in hand with this goes the idea that all existence is futile '. When his mother had died the world had ceased to have any value for him. His libido had been temporarily withdrawn from the objects around him; and, as was the case with the other patients, everything seemed strange to him now, as though he had not seen it before. People to whom he was actually speaking did not seem to exist at all. All early events, *i.e.* those which had taken place in the lifetime of his mother, seemed remote. He said: ' All the past has a dream-like character, as if it had happened an eternity ago.' The patient used often to have these states without particularly noticing them. He was generally quite able to carry on his work, which necessitated great intellectual concentration. But more recently there had appeared dream-states which were of shorter duration and more acute. The history of their origin is very peculiar, and is as follows:

The patient used to suffer periodically from violent headaches which caused him great agony. (We shall say something about their origin later.) About three years ago he decided to consult a nerve specialist, who specialized in hypnotic treatment. After a number of unsuccessful attempts had been made to produce hypnosis, he gave up the treatment. But he then began to try to put himself into a mental state which differed from his usual one, in the hope of getting rid of his headache in that way. He succeeded a number of times in inducing a state of this kind, which was highly pleasurable and which he regarded as an 'auto-hypnosis'. But his headaches persisted. During his treatment with me, too, he repeatedly and earnestly expressed the wish to be hypnotized. To subordinate himself to the will of another fitted in with his masochistic tendencies. As he himself said, his ideal was to be able to be completely passive, and it was torture to him to have to exert all his energy to go on with his life.

His sexual life showed a great number of unmistakable masochistic traits. For a long time he used to masturbate to the accompaniment of masochistic phantasies, but after a severe struggle he succeeded in partly giving up the practice. The symptom of his sexual passivity which threw most light on his dream-states was his psychological impotence, which had begun at the same time as he had started bringing on his dream-states. Moreover, he spontaneously told me that he had already had the wish to be sexually passive before. He wanted to be able to yield to sexual pleasure in a passive way like a woman.

His dream-state brought about the realization of that ideal together with a high degree of pleasure. And it was quite in accordance with this desire to give up all activity that his method of inducing such a state should have been to concentrate all his will on thinking of nothing. His life in general necessitated great intellectual effort, but his desire was for the opposite. As we have seen in the other patients, a 'mental blankness' sets in at the height of the dream-state.   In the present case the patient had a conscious intention of bringing on this stage, which, as we know, corresponds to the moment of greatest pleasure.

I will quote his description of this state in his own words.   He gave it of his own accord and with every sign of strong emotion; and it is quite intelligible to us after what has been said.   He said: 'At first it is an effort, as in sexual intercourse.   If I wanted to do it I should have to lie down and work at it.   I have to concentrate with all my might upon thinking of nothing.   I close my eyes. Nothing must be allowed to reach me from the outer world. Then comes a short stage of bliss in which all my sensations are reversed.   It is the greatest physical change that I know, and I cannot find words strong enough to describe it.   That short stage of pleasure is nevertheless like an infinity.'   At the climax of the process of excitation—for such we must term it—his thoughts used to stop.

The patient completed his description as follows: ' One has the idea that in life everything is moving forward; I mean, for example, the circulation of the blood.   But suddenly everything is changed: everything ebbs away, as though it were no longer going forward but backwards. It is as though some magic had begun to work.   While at other times everything tends to leave the body, now everything is driven back into it.   I no longer radiate things out but absorb them.'   After a short pause he continued: ' There is an absolute, harmonious peace about it, a comforting passivity, in contrast to my real life.   Waves flow over me.   Something is done to me.   If the state did not pass I would not move till the end of time.'

These dream-states enabled the patient to obtain unlimited pleasure in imagination out of his sexual passivity. He wanted to be a woman, and in his dream-states he experienced the fulfilment of that wish.   He was perfectly right when he spoke of the ' greatest conceivable change', for a more radical alteration than a change of sex cannot be conceived.   And to the patient it signified not only a change of sex, but a reversal of his whole mode of life.

His wish to be a woman draws our attention to the

H

homosexual components in him.   We already know about
his intense transference of infantile libido on to his father,
so that we can assume that in wishing to be a woman he
was identifying himself with his mother in order to occupy
her place with his father.   Such an assumption is confirmed
by the ætiology of his headaches to which we have already
referred, and which plainly served to identify him with his
mother.   For in his childhood she had suffered from
headaches to which his own bore a striking resemblance.
She always used to get them when her periods came on.
At those times she used to be very irritable and have to
take great care of herself.   The patient's headaches used
also to recur at intervals of four weeks and to last from
three to four days on each occasion.   During that time he
would become extremely sensitive to every external stimulus,
and be obliged to stop work and spend one or two days in
bed.   His headaches, therefore, served to identify him with
his mother.   That he had some inkling of this connection
was shown by the fact that once in the early part of his
treatment he jokingly said: 'I have got my period just now'.

His attacks of headache and his dream-states served
to transform him into a woman.   The monthly period and
sexual passivity are two very important features in the
sexual life of women.   The patient was following a perfectly correct instinct when he sought to expel, or as we
should now more correctly say, to replace, his headache by
a dream-state, since both served the same aim of sexual
passivity.   If his plan had succeeded he would have
replaced a displeasurable symptom by an equivalent but
pleasurable one.   That he was disappointed in this expectation is also quite explicable.   For his headaches did not
depend upon that one motive we have mentioned alone,
but subserved other repressed wishes as well which would
not have found adequate expression in his dream-states;
so that the dream-states could only appear side by side
with his headaches but not in place of them.

The patient's attempt to ward off displeasure had
miscarried, but he had obtained a new source of pleasure.
Although his dream-states did not relieve him of his pain,

they nevertheless offered him a compensatory pleasure which enabled him to put up with the pain he was obliged to endure.

Case F

Intermediate States between Day-dreams and True Dream-states

I will give an extract from an analysis of a case which did not exhibit marked dream-states in the sense we have described, but which showed a kind of introductory stage to these. It demonstrates in a particularly clear manner the origin of dream-states from day-dreams, and also the close relationship that exists between neurotic dream-states and dreams during sleep.

The patient, F, was dominated to such an extent by certain recurring phantasies that he called them ' obsessive ideas '. Reading, in particular, used to furnish a stimulus for these phantasies. He used immediately to identify himself with the hero of the tale. He said: ' When I read a love romance I imagine myself to be the hero with whom all the women are infatuated '. Actually the patient's sexual activity was very limited. Besides these erotic day-dreams he used to be occupied with phantasies of greatness. In reading about a historical figure he would have the idea that he was that person, and he would live his life in imagination. As he said: ' I like reading about Napoleon, for instance. For then I, too, seem to hear myself receive the acclamations which he received.' In fact, he had only to think of shouts of joy, fame, and acclamation to feel a shudder run over him. Music, chiefly military music, also had an exhilarating effect upon him and used to provoke this ' shudder '. In the day-dream which used to result from such occurrences the patient, who was a business man, used to imagine himself becoming an important or wealthy man, ' perhaps a manufacturer like Krupp '. He then used to imagine how he would completely disregard the feelings of his staff, and force his will upon them (cf. his idea of being Napoleon). It was difficult for him to free himself from these ideas. He said: ' When I have these obsessive ideas ' (day-dreams) ' I recite a poem in order to divert my thoughts—generally the " Loreley ", or "Hail to the Victor", or any poem from my school-days '. He had, however, to repeat such poems many times before they had the desired effect.

The central figure of the patient's phantasies was either a doughty lover or a brutal despot or a military hero. It was not difficult to see that in his day-dreams he sought to gratify those wishes which proceeded from the confluence of his sexual instinct and his instinct of aggression, *i.e.* his sadistic feelings. He had the feeling in general that he did not give an impression of manliness, and that he was being treated like a child. This feeling resulted from the suppression of his sadism. In his dreamings he was the energetic, despotic man, but afterwards he changed back into the weak and dependent ' child '. The poems of his schooldays formed a suitable interruption of his phantasies, because they took him back into his childhood. One is immediately struck by the similarity in the content of this patient's phantasies with those of Case B, which have been fully described. This similarity extended to a particular symptom. We found in the patient B a striking tendency to blushing; and the patient F also suffered from blushing and marked erythrophobia.

In the present case the dream-states did not have the same character as those previously described, for the stages of removal from reality, mental blankness, and subsequent anxiety were absent. Moreover, his states ran a different course. Nevertheless they went beyond the ordinary day-dream in their great intensity, and they had one characteristic in common with the dream-state proper. This was that the patient lost control over his own thoughts during his phantasies and could not interrupt them at will. Like the others, he had to discover a method by which he could break off his phantasies, and to make liberal use of it before it was effective. His extremely vivid visualization of his phantasies requires special notice; and we shall presently give closer consideration to this feature.

This case also shows very well how waking phantasies are the precursors of dreams in sleep. The patient told some dreams which had often recurred since his childhood. In one of them he was being attacked in bed by a man with a beard. The man stabbed him with a dagger, while he himself lay still as though his hands were paralyzed. He would awake from this dream in great anxiety. He used still more frequently to dream that he was being pursued by a lion, and that finally, in great anxiety, he slipped through a cleft in the wall through which the lion could not follow him.[1] The man with the (symbolic) dagger was his father, whose (sexual) ' attacks ' on his mother he had observed as a little boy. The dream betrayed his repressed wish to occupy his mother's place with his father. His dream about the lion belonged to the same complex.

When the patient, who was only under treatment for a short time, was asked to say what occurred to his mind, as is the rule in analytic procedure, he used usually to close his eyes and describe mental pictures which appeared before him. Concerning the dream of being stabbed with a dagger he said:[2] ' I see a man being stabbed by another man. The first one is lying on a couch, and the second one is kneeling on him and stabbing him in the breast. The one who is lying down is grasping his opponent's right hand tightly with his left. The kneeling man appears to be about thirty years of age. He looks very wild and has a dark beard. The other looks well-bred and aristocratic. He has on a silk doublet with a lace collar.'

It is obvious that these mental pictures have the same content as the perennial dreams mentioned above. The lying man was the patient himself. (Incidentally, he was lying on the couch in my consulting-room at the time of having them.) It is particularly worth noticing that in his description he used the passive voice—' a man is being stabbed by another man '—for he was the subject

---

[1] The patient B also had constantly recurring dreams of this kind. But I have not given the analysis of these dreams here, in order to avoid unnecessary complication.

[2] The interpretation given above of the dream was unknown to the patient at the time when he related his visions.

himself.   At the time when he had slept in his parents'
bedroom as a child his father had been approximately thirty
years old and had worn a beard.   The fact that the patient
endowed the recumbent figure with an aristocratic appearance is explained by the typical parentage phantasies [1]
which occur with great intensity in neurotic children.   The
silk doublet with the lace collar was taken from a picture
hanging over my sofa (' The Laughing Cavalier ', by Franz
Hals).   He had regarded it attentively before shutting his
eyes, because it had touched his infantile ' aristocratic '
complex.   As he looked at it a second time he remarked
that the dress reminded him of aristocratic ladies' clothes.
The picture, therefore, had touched a further complex—
the homosexual one.   A day or two afterwards the patient,
again lying on the couch, had the following visions:

' A centaur—now a little child appears . . . he is a
little centaur too.'   (These were his father and himself.
Note the sexual symbolism of the comparison with a wild
centaur or a stallion.)

' A race . . . the riders jumping over the hurdles.'
(This represented his rivalry with his father.   The patient
had in general that character-trait which the patient B
termed in himself a ' competitive feeling').

' A horse that has fallen down.'   (The patient said that
on the way to my house he had seen a horse that had fallen
down.   A deeper determinant of this picture is to be found
in typical phantasies of his father's death.) [2]

' The man in the helmet, the picture by Rembrandt.'
(This picture did not hang in my room, but it was a favourite
of the patient's.   The patient's father was a big, powerful
man.   He had been in the Guards and had taken part in
two wars.   The patient wanted to be a soldier like his
father, who was, moreover, the prototype of his Napoleon
phantasy.)

The patient had other visions of a similar character.

[1] Cf. my *Traum und Mythus* (1909), S. 40 [No. 14, A. B.] ; also Rank, *Der
Mythus von der Geburt des Helden* (1909).

[2] I have recently found the same phantasy of the fallen horse in another case.
And a similar phantasy has been analysed by Freud in his 'Analysis of a Phobia in
a Five-year-old Boy ' (1909).

Both the patient's waking dreams and his night dreams derived their content from his childhood phantasies. They even had in common hallucinatory pictures. In his dream-states, too, there was a psychological process analogous to the ' dream-work ' which formed the manifest content out of the repressed (latent) thought-material. I need only refer to the abundant use of symbolism, as well as to the very marked degree of condensation. We have met with numerous examples which show that some particular detail of the dream-state (and also the dream-state itself considered as a whole) served to express very different, even opposite, phantasies.

Dreams and neurotic dream-states are not the only derivatives of day-dreaming. There are two more such derivative states, characterized by a deeper disturbance of consciousness. Out of the dream proceeds the somnambulistic dream in which the neurotic converts his phantasies into more or less complicated actions of which later he has no remembrance. Similarly, dream-states can give rise to ' hypnoid states ' and ' twilight states '. In these latter we find elements which are familiar to us from the dream-states, such as ' remoteness ', ' fading away of surrounding reality ', and ' affective cessation of thought '.[1] In these twilight states quite complicated actions can be carried out. The extent of the amnesia that follows on them is in proportion to the degree of disturbance of consciousness that has taken place during them. Such an amnesia is not characteristic of the dream-states we have been discussing.

To these episodic phenomena of the clinical picture of hysteria there can be added other closely connected phenomena whose relation to day-dreams has already been demonstrated in earlier investigations. I may mention in the first place hysterical attacks. Freud[2] has recently summed up his view of their nature in a very concise form. I will quote a few passages from his discussion of the subject to which I have already referred.

---

[1] I make use of Breuer's terminology. Cf. Breuer and Freud, *Studien über Hysterie* (1895). [2] See reference, p. 97.

' Investigation of the childhood history of hysterical patients shows that the hysterical attack is a substitute for an auto-erotic gratification previously practised by them and since given up.' Our analysis of dream-states has led to analogous results.

' The anamnesis of the patient established the following stages: (*a*) Auto-erotic gratification without ideational content. (*b*) The same in connection with a phantasy, which culminates in the act of gratification. (*c*) Renunciation of the act with retention of the phantasy. (*d*) Repression of this phantasy, which then breaks through in the hysterical attack either unchanged or else modified and adapted to new experiences, and (*e*) which may even restore the act of gratification which belongs to the phantasy and has apparently been given up. This is a typical cycle of infantile sexual activity: repression, failure of the repression, and return of the repressed.' Thus the first three stages are common to dream-states and hysterical attacks.

' The loss of consciousness, the mental vacancy of the hysterical attack, is derived from that transient but unmistakable disappearance of consciousness which is experienced at the height of every intense sexual gratification, including auto-erotic gratification. . . . The mechanism of this mental vacancy is a relatively simple one. At first all attention is fixed on the course of development of the gratificatory process; then with the actual appearance of the gratification itself the whole of this concentration of attention is suddenly arrested, so that a momentary blankness of consciousness takes place. These physiological gaps in consciousness, as we may call them, are then extended in the service of repression until they can absorb everything which the repressing faculty repudiates.'

Thus dream-states and hysterical attacks start from the same initial stages and subserve the same ends; but they differ in their methods of expression, and usually also in the part played by consciousness. Whereas the mental vacancy in dream-states is nearly always of short duration, especially in comparison with the protracted duration of the other stages, the ' gap in consciousness ' of the hysterical attack lasts according to the requirements of the case. The hysterical attack makes use of the 'reflex mechanism of the action of coitus' in order to express the repressed phantasies, and thus brings about a 'motor discharge of the repressed libido'. In the dream-state the process expresses itself on the level of phantasy, if we except certain motor expressions (as, for example, alteration of bodily position or movement) which have no relation to the action of coitus.

Next to the motor attacks of hysteria, anxiety-attacks stand in close genetic relation to dream-states. In this kind of episodic hysterical phenomenon, too, we have to recognize sexual excitatory processes that have undergone transformation.[1] I may mention that the patients whose dream-states I have reported in detail all suffered from more or less frequent anxiety-attacks, but not, on the other hand, from hysterical motor attacks. There are evidently individual differences in the clinical picture here, but we have not yet obtained sufficient insight into them.

I might mention that dream-states of a quite analogous type occur in insanity (dementia præcox). In the case of a young hebephrenic I have recently been able definitely to establish their origin from day-dreams. In this case the condition of 'remoteness' was particularly marked. In his dream-states it seemed to the patient 'as if everything were only a theatre'. I may point out that twilight states also occur in dementia præcox and that they have important characteristics in common with hysterical states. Dream-like states which have a protracted course and are accompanied by especially pronounced feelings of strangeness have been described by Wernicke, Juliusburger, and other writers.[2]

The cases that have been analyzed above were without exception severe psychoneuroses. But it does not follow from this that dream-states do not occur in slight cases. Undoubtedly a great number of people who are only slightly

---

[1] Cf. Stekel, *Nervöse Angstzustände und ihre Behandlung* (1908).

[2] I have recently been able to observe a number of catatonic attacks in a female patient. They began by violent kissing movements of the mouth, and went on to represent a sexual act in a quite unmistakable fashion. We have here also, therefore, an analogy with a hysterical attack.

ill suffer from such states as well as those who are more severely affected. All of them have a tendency to indulge in day-dreaming, and none have succeeded in overcoming their craving for the auto-erotic activities of childhood. Their simple waking dreams, or the more complicated mental structures derived from them, serve as a temporary means of fleeing from reality into the realms of childhood. If a person is disposed to dream-states a very slight stimulus touching upon his repressed complexes will be sufficient to evoke such a state.

In the case of only slightly neurotic people dream-states often elude medical observation, or their particular significance is not recognized. Female patients, for example, frequently complain to the physician—and not by any means only in psycho-analytic treatment—that they feel themselves hypnotized by him. This is a transparent example of 'transference'. The patient is unconsciously prepared to subordinate herself to the physician's will, *i.e.* is ready to adopt a passive attitude towards an unconsciously desired assault on the part of the physician. Her phantasy is working hard on the subject of the fulfilment of this wish, until the stage of 'remoteness' is brought on, followed by the further stages with which we are acquainted. In fact, the patient goes through a dream-state during her visit to the physician. With some hysterical women the presence of any man suffices to make them feel that they are being hypnotized. I once treated a patient who always had anxiety in trams. She would have the feeling that she was being 'bored through' by the glance of any man sitting opposite her. This feeling immediately induced a state which she called a kind of hypnosis and which ended in anxiety.

Other neurotic girls state that in the middle of a conversation with a man they will suddenly feel themselves 'removed from reality', and their own voice will appear strange to them as if someone else were speaking. Then will come the 'mental blankness', and finally anxiety and a feeling of shame. Analysis shows that such persons are in the habit of indulging very liberally in day-dreaming.

They are especially fond of having phantasies as they lie in bed in the morning. The thread of these day-dreamings is taken up again as soon as a suitable occasion arises, and there then follow the other typical stages of the dream-state.

In the discussion previously referred to, Freud has given a condensed description of the exciting causes and the purpose of hysterical attacks. A hysterical attack is evoked *associatively* whenever the complex is stimulated through a connecting link with conscious life. It is evoked *organically* whenever the libido is increased from external or internal causes, and has no outlet. It is quite obvious that as a rule both situations arise together. The same stimuli are also operative in the production of dream-states.

According to Freud hysterical attacks serve in the first place to assist the primary purpose of the illness (flight into illness), and are therefore a kind of consolation for the patient. In the second place they serve the secondary purpose of the illness, whenever the illness is of practical benefit. The same is true in every respect of dream-states. The patient E, who fell into a dream-state of long duration after the death of his mother, furnishes an excellent example of a ' flight into illness '. That dream-states also have a present and practical purpose has been evident in every case we have considered. In many patients the dream-state will appear as if at call in distressing situations. Not only this, but it must be particularly mentioned that many patients will call up a dream-state consciously and intentionally in order to avoid displeasure or to obtain pleasure. We are once more reminded of the genetic relation of dream-states to onanism. The neurotic often has recourse to onanism as a consolation—to remove depression of spirits, for instance.

Both dreams and neurotic dream-states have as their function the avoidance of displeasure.[1] But the dream-states also serve to provide a positive pleasure-gain. The patient B, whose dream-state used to remove him from his condition of passivity, used not only to escape displeasure

[1] See Freud, *Der Witz*, 1905, S. 154.

by this means; in the first stages of the process he used also to derive positive pleasure from his phantasied activity.

A change in the sexual aim such as occurred in the dream-states of the patient E is not the rule. There is another type, that represented by the patient C. In his case the phantasies developed along the lines of that passivity which was already his dominating attitude, and thus served to intensify his masochistic feelings to an extraordinary degree.

Dream-states offer the neurotic patient, just as other neurotic phenomena do, a substitute for a sexual activity which is denied him. His unconscious makes use of this surrogate so long as he cannot obtain the gratification of certain desires. But if the libido experiences sufficient gratification, then the dream-states will diminish and even subside altogether. I saw this actually happen in the case of a slightly neurotic lady as soon as she obtained sufficient sexual gratification in her married life. And a young man who came to me for treatment on account of psychical impotence, found that the restless activity of his sexual phantasies subsided and attained a normal degree when he once more became potent and could obtain adequate gratification.

The analysis of dream-states demonstrates once more the extraordinary fruitfulness of Freud's theories. Since the introduction of the psycho-analytical method of investigation we are no longer limited to a mere description of the symptoms of the neurosis without understanding their meaning or being able to explain their individual character in each case. We are able to comprehend the conditions that give rise to the neurosis and its motives, and to ascertain its hidden purpose and the instinctual forces at work in it. We are able to understand the individual peculiarities of each case, since we not only consider the present-day instinctual life of the neurotic, but investigate the repressed wishes of his childhood as well. For in the innermost recesses of his mind he is continually striving to repeat those infantile situations of gratification the memory of which he still retains in his unconscious.

Chapter V

REMARKS ON THE PSYCHO-ANALYSIS OF A CASE OF FOOT AND CORSET FETISHISM [1]
(1910)

IT is only latterly that special attention has been paid to the problems of fetishism by psycho-analysis. In the first edition of his *Drei Abhandlungen zur Sexualtheorie* Freud assigned to it a unique position among the other sexual aberrations and among the neuroses. Further observation has shown, however, that in many cases fetishism and neurosis are both present in the same individual. In the second edition of his above-mentioned book Freud has made a short reference to this fact, and has traced the phenomena of fetishism back to a special variety of repression which he has called 'partial repression'. In consequence of this the once emphasized contrast between neurosis and fetishism has been done away with.

The analysis of a case of shoe and corset fetishism which I am going to discuss has led me to certain conclusions regarding the psychogenesis of this form of fetishism; and other cases have confirmed that view.

We must assume that as the basis of such an abnormality there is a specific sexual constitution which is characterized by the abnormal strength of certain component-instincts. Given this, the complex of fetishistic phenomena is formed by the co-operation of two factors, namely, the partial repression mentioned above, and a process of displacement [2] which we shall discuss in greater detail.

[1] [No. 18, A. B.]
[2] Concerning the idea of *displacement* see Freud, *Traumdeutung*, S. 209.

I will give as brief an account of the case as possible: At the time of his analysis the patient was twenty-two years old and a student at a technical college. At the commencement of the treatment he handed me an autobiography which dwelt in detail on his sexual life. The first thing to be noticed in it was that at the age of puberty he differed from other persons of his own age in that he did not share their sexual interest in women. He experienced no feelings of love in the usual sense towards male persons either. His conscious knowledge of the most important facts of sexuality was acquired very late. As soon as he did obtain such knowledge he had the idea that he would be impotent. He had a strong antipathy to manual self-gratification as carried out by young men of his own age.

His sexual interests turned in another direction. At the age of fourteen he began to tie himself up, and he repeated this performance whenever he was undisturbed at home. He derived pleasure from books whose theme was chaining or binding — for instance, in stories about Red Indians in which the prisoners are tied to a stake and tortured. But he never attempted to bind another person, nor did he like to suffer such treatment at the hands of others.

When he was about fifteen, while staying at a health resort, he saw a boy of eight or ten years of age who immediately attracted his attention on account of the elegant shoes he wore. He wrote in his autobiography: 'Each time I looked at his shoes I felt great pleasure and longed for this opportunity to recur'. On his return home he began to take an interest in elegant shoes, especially those worn by his school-fellows. This interest soon became transferred to women's shoes, and grew into a passion. ' My eyes were attracted to women's shoes as though by magic force. . . . Ugly shoes repelled me and filled me with feelings of disgust.' Henceforth, the sight of dainty shoes on women induced in him an ' inward joy '. This feeling of pleasure used often to change into violent excitement, especially when he saw patent-leather boots with high heels like those worn by *demi-mondaines*. It was not only the appearance of the shoes that excited him, however, but his vivid mental picture of the discomfort it must cause the person to walk in them.   In order to have a direct experience of the feeling of having one's feet painfully compressed he would often wear his own shoes on the wrong foot, forcing his right foot into his left boot, and *vice versa*.

His interest in corsets began soon after his interest in footwear.   When he was sixteen he got hold of an old pair of his mother's stays, and used to lace himself tightly in them, and sometimes wear them under his ordinary clothes out of doors.   The following description in his autobiography is characteristic: 'If I see women and girls tightly laced and picture to myself the pressure of their corsets on their breasts and body I can get an erection.   On those occasions I have often wished I was a woman, for then I could tight-lace myself, wear women's boots and high heels, and stand in front of corset-shops without attracting notice. This is impossible, but I often long to wear women's clothes, stays, and shoes.'   Looking out for elegant shoes or tightly-laced waists became his most important sexual activity. This interest occupied the chief place in his vivid daydreams.   At night he had frequent erotic dreams about stays, tight-lacing, etc.   And, as we have already said, he had a preference for reading stories of a sadistic nature. He had kept everything that related to these propensities strictly secret until he sought the advice of a specialist, who referred him to me for psycho-analysis.   From the beginning I was sceptical of a therapeutic result.

Accidental causes, to which in the older literature on the subject great significance in the ætiology of fetishistic tendencies is ascribed, could not be discovered in his case. The fact that the patient had as a boy frequently seen his mother put on her stays cannot have had the effect of a psychic trauma.   His interest in his mother's corsets or later in boy's shoes was doubtless the expression of a perversion which was already in existence.   An ætiological significance cannot be ascribed to these circumstances.

What stands out most distinctly in this case and in every one of its kind is the extraordinary reduction in the person's sexual activity.   In fact, we can hardly speak of a sexual activity at all in the case of this patient, apart from his earlier attempts at lacing and tying himself up. He had never put into practice any sadistic or other desires towards other people; he gratified his wishes in this direction entirely in phantasy. In practice he had never moved outside the field of auto-erotism.

If, on the one hand, we have found very little evidence of sexual activity in the patient, we have seen, on the other, that his sexual instinct to look was very pronounced. But even that instinct had been diverted from its real sphere of interest. It was not directed to other people's bodies as a whole, nor to their primary and secondary sexual characteristics, but to certain portions of their clothing. It was directed, therefore, not to the naked body but to its covering. And here again the patient had specialized on the footwear and on the constricting garments of the upper part of a woman's body. His sexual desire did not go beyond the viewing of these objects. It is therefore a question of fixation upon a preliminary sexual aim.[1] Nevertheless the sight of women's shoes only excited pleasure in him when they were elegant in form and design; clumsy, ugly footwear made him feel disgusted. We find, therefore, side by side with a sexual overestimation of the fetish, a pronounced tendency towards an emotional rejection of it, just as is the case with neurotics. The high æsthetic standard that the shoe-fetishist demands of his sexual object indicates a strong need to idealize it.

Although the patient's sexual activity had been so much reduced, and although his instincts found gratification in the attainment of preliminary sexual aims, it by no means follows that there was a fundamental, primary weakness of the libido in him. Analysis of the neuroses has shown quite clearly that instincts which have originally been excessively strong can be paralyzed through repression. And the analysis of the present case disclosed a similar state of affairs. Numerous facts, only a few of which can be brought forward in this place, showed that the patient's active sadistic component-instincts and his sexual pleasure

[1] Cf. Freud, *Drei Abhandlungen zur Sexualtheorie.*

in looking had originally been abnormally strong. Both instincts, which were in the closest 'confluence' (Adler), had been overtaken by repression.

It appeared, however, that other component instincts had been included in this process of repression. The particular need felt by the fetishist for æsthetic value in his sexual object indicates that his libido originally sought certain aims which seem particularly unæsthetic to the generality of normal adults and give rise to feelings of disgust in them. Before taking up this analysis I had had my attention drawn to a definite sphere of instinctual life. Professor Freud had told me in a private communication that according to his experience repression of the coprophilic pleasure in smell played a peculiar part in the psychogenesis of foot-fetishism. My own investigations have fully confirmed this view. In the present case of fetishism I found that the patient's pleasure in 'disgusting' bodily odours had been unusually strong originally. Repression of his co-prophilic pleasure in smell, his scoptophilia and his sexual activity had led to the building up of compromise-formations. And it is precisely these compromise-formations that constitute the characteristic peculiarities of foot-fetishism.

There are cases of fetishism in which the sexual anomaly shows itself in an unrepressed, i.e. a fully conscious, pleasure in disgusting odours. In this so-called smell-fetishism pleasure is very frequently obtained from the odour of perspiring and unclean feet; and these attract the patient's scoptophilic instincts at the same time. In the present case it turned out that the patient had passed through a stage which corresponded to smell-fetishism, and that after this a peculiar modification had taken place by which his osphresiolagnia had been repressed and his pleasure in looking had been sublimated to pleasure in seeing foot-wear which had an æsthetic value.

But how was it that his scoptophilic and osphresiolagnic instincts could turn so markedly to the feet, instead of being directed to the sexual organs and their secretions? Certain observations led me to suspect that both instincts

I

had originally been concerned with the genital zone, but that other erotogenic zones had prematurely entered into competition with it.   An ascendancy of this kind of other erotogenic zones (mouth, anus, etc.) is quite familiar to us from the theory of the sexual aberrations as well as from analyses of neuroses and dreams.

And in fact the analysis of the patient showed that the genital zone had quite early been exposed to strong competition from the side of the anal zone.   The purely sexual interest of his first period of childhood had given place to an interest in the processes of excretion; and at puberty he had been overtaken by another wave of repression with a similar (feminine) aim.   He had retained for an unusually long time those infantile ideas according to which the processes of excretion have the significance of a sexual function.   The symbolism of his dreams was of a corresponding character.   His scoptophilia and his osphresiolagnia—in so far as they were not displaced on to the feet—were chiefly directed to the function and products of urination and defæcation.

The patient's memories of early childhood were chiefly connected with impressions of smell, and only secondarily with impressions of sight.   If his attention was directed back to that time certain obsessive ideas would frequently come into his mind.   One of these was the smell of iodoform and pyroxylic acid, two substances used by his mother in his younger days.   Another was a scene at a seaside resort, in which he saw his mother wading into the water.   The real significance of this scene was only explained through his associations, and was this: he had once or twice soiled himself at that time and his mother had taken him into the sea to clean him.

Many memories connected with smell occurred to him out of his later childhood, too.   For instance, he remembered finding in his mother's room a packet of hair the odour of which was agreeable to him; and he remembered hugging his mother in order to smell her armpits.   He had one more recollection dating from his early childhood in which his younger sister was at his mother's breast and he had touched the other breast with his mouth and had liked the smell of his mother's body.

The patient's fondness for his mother lasted until he was about ten years old, and up to that time he had frequently got into her bed. But at ten his affection gave place to dislike. He became very intolerant of the bodily smell of women. At the same time as his pleasure in smell became repressed his sexual interest turned away from women and attached itself to the nearest male object —his father. In this transference his interest in bodily evacuations came to the fore. His attention was undoubtedly especially directed to these processes through certain peculiarities of his father, who would, for example, often make water before his children. His phantasies were occupied to a great extent with everything that concerned this function in himself and in his father.[1]

Intimately related to his transference on to his father was his wish to be a woman, a wish that persisted, as we know, after puberty. As far as he was conscious, however, this wish was not directed towards fulfilling the sexual function of a woman. What he desired was ' to wear laced shoes and corsets like a woman and be able to look at them in shop-windows without attracting notice '. Once or twice at the age of puberty, as has already been said, he had actually worn corsets under his clothes. His wish to be a woman was expressed unconsciously in various ways which have still to be mentioned.

His infantile impulses of rebellion and jealousy were necessarily directed against his father and mother alternately. This attitude was associated in the customary way with death and castration phantasies, the latter being sometimes of an active and sometimes of a passive nature. His active castration phantasies also had as their object his mother, to whom his infantile imagination attributed a male sexual organ. His passive castration phantasies corresponded to his desire to be a woman. They originated in a period in

[1] In connection with this there developed a horse and giraffe symbolism absolutely identical with that described by Freud in his 'Analysis of a Phobia in a Five-year-old Boy' (1909).

which he held the view that the female sex had originally possessed a penis but had been deprived of it by castration. All these ideas played a large part in his dreams.   He used to dream that he had to amputate the finger of a woman, or that he had to carry out an operation on a man (his father), and that afterwards his mother helped him to sew up the wound.   In other dreams a child would have to be beheaded.   A recurrent dream of his worth mentioning was one in which a man was pursuing him with a knife in his hand.   The exceptional development of his castration complex testifies to the original strength of his sado-masochistic impulses.

In the patient's phantasies castration not only had the obvious significance of emasculation, but also had reference to a certain idea that had always interested him particularly, namely, that of being unable to urinate owing to castration. From this point there are connections which lead to another complex of ideas.

All neurotics in whom the anal and urethral zones are especially erotogenic have a tendency to retain their excreta. This tendency was unusually strong in the patient in question.   His childhood memories mostly concerned the pleasurable practices he used to indulge in in this direction. A nervous symptom of his—a 'urinary stammer'—was also connected with those practices.

The patient had all his life-long indulged in phantasies in which he was forced to refrain from relieving his needs. For instance, he would like to imagine that he was tied to a stake by Indians and compelled to hold back the contents of his bladder and bowels.   A strong masochistic element was present in this phantasy as well.   Another of his favourite ideas was that he was an Arctic explorer and was prevented by the terrible cold from opening his clothes even for a short time in order to relieve the calls of Nature. His experiments in tying himself up were also determined, among other things, by the same motives; and it is significant that those practices took place in the w.c.   This tying-up, which plays a large part in the phantasies of sadists and masochists, acquired its significance in his case through its association with the functions of evacuation. Tight-lacing caused a pressure on the bowels and bladder which was pleasurable to him; and when he had put on corsets for the first time he had had an erection and had then passed water. One important determinant of this whole lacing-up *motif* was to be found in certain auto-erotic habits of his connected with squeezing-in the genitals.

In this patient the anal zone greatly predominated. In his childhood it had subserved a peculiar auto-erotic practice in which he used to sit down so that the heel of his boot was pressed against the anal region. And in his memories we find a direct connection between foot and anus, in which the heel corresponded more or less to the male organ and the anus to the female organ. This connection was strengthened by his coprophilic pleasure in smell. His auto-erotism found abundant gratification in the odours of his own excretions and secretions. Such odours arising from the skin, the genital region, and the feet were pleasurable to him at an early age. In this way the foot was able to acquire genital significance in his unconscious phantasies. It may be mentioned with regard to his coprophilic pleasure in smell that many of his dreams had their setting in the w.c. or fulfilled anal-erotic desires by means of a transparent symbolism. A characteristic type of dream was one in which he put his nose between two big hemispheres.

It has already been said that the patient's scoptophilic instinct was also chiefly directed on to excrement. He often used to dream of his father and brother in situations of this kind; and water occurred as a symbol in the majority of his dreams, of which the following is an interesting example. He was in a boat with his brother, going through a harbour. In order to get out of the harbour they had to pass through a peculiarly built passage, like a house on the water. Then they got into open water, but suddenly they were on dry land and the boat was passing down a street without touching the ground. Then they were floating along in the air, and a policeman was looking on at them. I will only say a few words about the interpretation of the dream. The word 'harbour' (*Hafen*) contains a double meaning, since in certain dialects *Hafen* means chamber utensil. And the word 'boat' ['*Schiff*'] is very similar to a word vulgarly used for making water ['*Schiffen*']. The passage out of the harbour reminded the dreamer of the tapering columns of the temple at Philæ. Another association was 'Colossus of Rhodes'. The Colossus represents a man standing with his legs apart over the entrance to the harbour of Rhodes. It reminded the patient of his father, whom he had seen urinating in a similar attitude. His subsequent voyage in the boat in company with his brother, and the part about the boat going through the air, were connected with a childhood memory which concerned a certain not infrequent contest among boys with respect to making water. The exhibitionistic factor in this dream was also of some importance; for the urinating was done in front of a policeman, and we know from experience that in dreams persons in authority signify the father.

The extraordinarily rich dream-material which the patient supplied in the course of his analysis contained a great number of dreams with a similar theme. One can conclude from the amazing variety of these dreams that his phantasies were occupied in quite an unusual degree with a coprophilic pleasure in looking. It may be mentioned that he exhibited the typical character-traits of sublimated anal-erotism; pedantic economy and love of orderliness were especially prominent features.

The degree to which the foot replaced the penis in the patient's mind was clearly seen in certain dreams of his, two of which I will briefly relate. In the one dream he was wearing slippers which were trodden down behind so that his heels were visible. This dream turned out to be an exhibitionistic dream. The heel was exposed to view as the sexual organs are in the ordinary exhibitionistic dream. The affect was the same as in typical exhibition dreams that are accompanied by anxiety. In the other dream he touched a woman with his foot and in this way dirtied her. This dream can be understood without further comment.

It is now clear why the patient took particular interest in the high heels of women's shoes. The heel of the shoe corresponded to the heel of the foot—a part of the body which, in virtue of the displacement referred to, had taken on the significance of a male genital. Thus the patient's predilection for women's feet and their covering, and more especially the heels, prolonged his infantile sexual interest in the supposed penis of the female.

The facts brought forward here only represent a small part of those which his analysis furnished, but they seem to me sufficient to show that the foot can be a substitute for the genitals. The patient's scoptophilic and osphresiophilic instincts, which had been particularly directed to excreta from the first, had undergone far-reaching though certainly very dissimilar alterations. His osphresiophilic instinct had been repressed to a great extent, whereas his scopto-philic instinct had been very much accentuated but at the same time diverted from its original sphere of interest and idealized. To this latter process, which only affected the second of the two instincts in question, we can apply Freud's term of 'partial repression'.

Since having had this case I have more than once had an opportunity of analysing fetishistic traits in neurotics where such traits have formed secondary symptoms; and in every case I have come to the same conclusions concern-ing the importance of those instincts which formed the basis of the fetishistic symptoms in the present case. On account of this uniformity in my results I do not propose to bring forward new material from these later cases.

A few words must be said about the therapeutic effect of psycho-analysis in the present case and in other cases of fetishism. I did not succeed in removing the fetishistic symptoms in this particular case; but the analytic interpreta-tion succeeded in very greatly diminishing the power which the patient's sexual abnormality had hitherto exercised over him. His power of resistance against the attraction of women's shoes, etc., was considerably increased, and normal sexual instincts often emerged during his analysis. I do not think it impossible that if the treatment had been persevered with, a gradual strengthening of the normal libido would have been achieved.

The therapeutic outlook seems to me more favourable in less pronounced cases, as, for instance, when certain fetishistic symptoms accompany a neurosis. A case of this kind which I analysed recently seemed to show that psycho-analysis can remove both the neurotic and the fetishistic symptoms and can bring about a normal sexual attitude in the patient.

CHAPTER VI

NOTES ON THE PSYCHO-ANALYTICAL IN-VESTIGATION AND TREATMENT OF MANIC-DEPRESSIVE INSANITY AND ALLIED CONDITIONS[1] (1911)

WHEREAS states of morbid anxiety have been dealt with in detail in the literature of psycho-analysis, depressive states have hitherto received less atten-tion. Nevertheless the affect of depression is as widely spread among all forms of neuroses and psychoses as is that of anxiety. The two affects are often present together or successively in one individual; so that a patient suffering from an anxiety-neurosis will be subject to states of mental depression, and a melancholic will complain of having anxiety.

One of the earliest results of Freud's investigation of the neuroses was the discovery that neurotic anxiety origi-nated from sexual repression; and this origin served to differentiate it from ordinary fear. In the same way we can distinguish between the affect of sadness or grief and neurotic depression, the latter being unconsciously moti-vated and a consequence of repression.

Anxiety and depression are related to each other in the same way as are fear and grief. We fear a coming evil; we grieve over one that has occurred. A neurotic will be attacked with anxiety when his instinct strives for a grati-fication which repression prevents him from attaining; depression sets in when he has to give up his sexual aim

---

[1] [No. 26, A. B.]

without having obtained gratification. He feels himself unloved and incapable of loving, and therefore he despairs of his life and his future. This affect lasts until the cause of it ceases to operate, either through an actual change in his situation or through a psychological modification of the displeasurable ideas with which he is faced. Every neurotic state of depression, just like every anxiety-state, to which it is closely related, contains a tendency to deny life.

These remarks contain very little that is new to those who regard the neuroses from the Freudian point of view, although surprisingly little has been written in the literature of psycho-analysis concerning the psychology of neurotic depression. But the affect of depression in the sphere of the psychoses awaits more precise investigation. This task is complicated by the fact that a good part of the diseases in question run a ' cyclical ' course in which there is an alteration between melancholic and manic states. The few preliminary studies [1] which have hitherto been published have only dealt with one of these two phases at a time.

During the last few years I have met with six undoubted cases of this kind in my practice. Two of these were light manic-depressive cases (so-called cyclothymia), one of whom I treated only for a short time. The third, a female patient, suffered from short but rapidly recurring states of depression accompanied by typical melancholic symptoms. Two more had succumbed to a depressive psychosis for the first time, but had previously shown a tendency to slight changes of mood in a manic or depressive direction. The last patient had been overtaken by a severe and obstinate psychosis at the age of forty-five.

Most psychiatrists, following Kraepelin, do not consider states of depression as belonging to manic-depressive insanity if they come on after the patient's fortieth year. Nevertheless, as the analysis proceeded this last case disclosed such a marked similarity in its psychic structure to those cases which did undoubtedly belong to the manic-

[1] Maeder, ' Psychoanalyse bei einer melancholischen Depression ' (1910). Brill, ' Ein Fall von periodischer Depression psychogenen Ursprungs ' (1911). Jones, ' Psycho-Analytic Notes on a Case of Hypomania ' (1910).

depressive insanities that I should certainly class it in that group.   I do not, however, intend this as a statement of opinion concerning the line of demarcation between the two psychoses.   And I do not wish to discuss states of depression occurring in dementia præcox.

Even in my first analysis of a depressive psychosis I was immediately struck by its structural similarity with an obsessional neurosis.   In obsessional neurotics [1]—I refer to severe cases—the libido cannot develop in a normal manner, because two different tendencies—hatred and love —are always interfering with each other.   The tendency such a person has to adopt a hostile attitude towards the external world is so great that his capacity for love is reduced to a minimum.   At the same time he is weakened and deprived of his energy through the repression of his hatred or, to be more correct, through repression of the originally over-strong sadistic component of his libido. There is a similar uncertainty in his choice of object as regards its sex.   His inability to establish his libido in a definite position causes him to have a general feeling of uncertainty and leads to doubting mania.   He is neither able to form a resolution nor to make a clear judgement; in every situation he suffers from feelings of inadequacy and stands helpless before the problems of life.

I will now give as briefly as possible the history of a case of cyclothymia as it appeared after a successful analysis had been made.

The patient remembered that his sexual instinct had shown itself very precociously—before he was in his sixth year—and had set in with great violence.   His first sexual object at that time had been a governess whose presence had excited him.   She still figured very vividly in his phantasies.   His emotional excitement had led him to practise onanism, which he had done by lying on his stomach and making rubbing movements.   He had been discovered doing this by his nurse (formerly his wet-nurse), who expressly forbade him to do it, and whipped him when-

---

[1] The following brief description adheres closely to Freud's characterization in his paper, ' Notes upon a Case of Obsessional Neurosis ' (1909).

ever he disobeyed her.   She also impressed upon him the fact that he would suffer for it all his life.   Later, when he was at school he had been attracted in an erotic way by a school-fellow for a period of several years.

In his childhood and later he had never felt satisfied at home.   He always had the impression that his parents favoured his elder brother, who was unusually clever, while he had only an average intelligence.   He also believed that his younger brother, who was delicate, received greater attention from his mother than he did.   The result of this was that he had a hostile attitude towards his parents, and one of jealousy and hatred towards his brothers.   The intensity of this hate can be seen from a couple of impulsive acts which he carried out in his childhood.   On two occasions when quarrelling over trifles he had become very violent towards his younger brother, and had knocked him down and seriously hurt him.   Such violence is particularly remarkable when we learn that at school he was always the smallest and weakest among his contemporaries.   He never made any real companions, but generally kept to himself. He was industrious, but had little to show for it.   At puberty it became evident that his sexual instinct, which at first had shown itself so strongly, had become paralysed through repression.   In contrast to his attitude in childhood he did not feel attracted to the female sex.   His sexual activity was the same that he had carried out in childhood; but he did not perform it in the waking state but only in his sleep or half-asleep.   He had no friends. He was quite aware of his lack of real energy when he compared himself with others.   He found no encouragement at home; on the contrary, his father used to say contemptuous things about him in his presence.   Added to all these depressing factors he suffered a definite psychic trauma: a teacher had the brutality to call him a physical and mental cripple in front of the whole class.   His first attack of depression appeared soon after this.

Even later on he made no companions.   He kept away from them intentionally, too, because he was afraid of being thought an inferior sort of person.   Children were the only human beings he got on well with and liked, because with them he did not have his usual feeling of inadequacy. His life was a solitary one. He was positively afraid of women. He was capable of normal sexual intercourse, but had no inclination for it and failed to obtain gratification from it. His onanistic practices in his sleep were his chief sexual activity even in later years. He showed little energy in practical life; it was always difficult for him to form a resolution or to come to a decision in difficult situations.

Up to this point the patient's history coincided in all its details with what we find in obsessional neurotics. Nevertheless, we do not find obsessional symptoms in him but a circular parathymia that had recurred many times during the last twenty years.

In his depressive phase the patient's frame of mind was ' depressed ' or ' apathetic ' (I reproduce his own words) according to the severity of his condition. He was inhibited, had to force himself to do the simplest things, and spoke slowly and softly. He wished he was dead, and entertained thoughts of suicide. His thoughts had a depressive content. He would often say to himself, ' I am an outcast ', ' I am accursed ', ' I am branded ', ' I do not belong to the world '. He had an indefinite feeling that his state of depression was a punishment. He felt non-existent and would often imagine himself disappearing from the world without leaving a trace. During these states of mind he suffered from exhaustion, anxiety and feelings of pressure in the head. The depressive phase generally lasted some weeks, though it was of shorter duration at times. The intensity of the depression varied in different attacks; he would have perhaps two or three marked states of melancholy and probably six or more slighter ones in the course of a year. His depression gradually increased during the course of an attack until it reached a certain height, where it remained for a time, and then gradually diminished. This process was conscious to him and perceptible to other people.

When the patient was about twenty-eight years old a

condition of hypomania appeared, and this now alternated with his depressive attacks. At the commencement of this manic phase he would be roused out of his apathy and would become mentally active and gradually even over-active. He used to do a great deal, knew no fatigue, woke early in the morning, and concerned himself with plans connected with his career. He became enterprising and believed himself capable of performing great things, was talkative and inclined to laugh and joke and make puns. He noticed himself that his thoughts had something volatile in them; a slight degree of 'flight of ideas' could be observed. He spoke more quickly, more forcibly and louder than usual. His frame of mind was cheerful and a little elevated. At the height of his manic phase his euphoria tended to pass over into irritability and impulsive violence. If, for example, some one disturbed him in his work, or stepped in his way, or drove a motor-car quickly past him, he responded with a violent affect of anger and felt inclined to knock the offender down on the spot. While in this state he used often to become involved in real quarrels in which he behaved very unfeelingly. In the periods of depression he slept well but during the manic phase he was very restless, especially during the second half of the night. Nearly every night a sexual excitement used to overtake him with sudden violence.

Although his libido had appeared very early and with great force in his childhood, the patient had for the most part lost the capacity for loving or hating. He had become incapable of loving, in the same manner as the obsessional neurotic. Although he was not impotent, he did not obtain actual sexual enjoyment, and he used to get greater satisfaction from a pollution than coitus. His sexual activities were in the main restricted to his sleep. In this, like the neurotic, he showed an auto-erotic tendency to isolate himself from the external world. People of this kind can only enjoy pleasure in complete seclusion; every living being, every inanimate object, is a disturbing element. It is only when they have achieved the complete exclusion of every external impression—as is the case when they are asleep—that they can enjoy a gratification of their sexual wishes, by dreaming them.   Our patient expressed this in the following words : 'I feel happiest in bed; then I feel as though I were in my own house '.[1]

At puberty in especial the patient was made aware that he was behind his companions of the same age in many important respects.   He had never felt their equal physically.   He had also been afraid of being inferior mentally, especially in comparison with his elder brother.   And now the feeling of sexual inadequacy was added.   It was precisely at this time that his teacher's criticism ' (a mental and physical cripple ') struck him like a blow.   Its great effect was explained by the fact that it recalled to his memory the prophecy of his wet-nurse, when she had threatened him with lifelong unhappiness because of his masturbation.   Just when he was entering upon manhood therefore, and ought to have had masculine feelings like his companions, his old feelings of inadequacy received a powerful reinforcement.   It was in this connection that he had had the first state of depression he could recollect.

As we so often see in the obsessional neuroses, the outbreak of the real illness occurred when the patient had to make a final decision about his attitude towards the external world and the future application of his libido.   In my other analyses a similar conflict had brought on the first state of depression.   For example, one of my patients had become engaged to be married ; soon afterwards a feeling of incapacity to love overcame him, and he fell into a severe melancholic depression.

In every one of these cases it could be discovered that the disease proceeded from an attitude of hate which was paralysing the patient's capacity to love.   As in the obsessional neuroses, other conflicts in the instinctual life of the patients as well can be shown to be factors in the psychogenesis of the illness.   I should like to mention especially the patient's uncertainty as to his sexual rôle in

---

[1] I might remark that the other male patients whose depressive psychoses I was able to analyse behaved in the same way.   None of them were impotent, but they had all derived more pleasure from auto-erotic behaviour all along, and to have any relations with women was a difficult and troublesome business for them.

this connection. In Maeder's case [1] a conflict of this kind between a male and female attitude was particularly pronounced; and in two of my patients I found a condition surprisingly similar to that described by him.

In their further development, however, the two diseases diverge from each other. The obsessional neurosis creates substitutive aims in place of the original unattainable sexual aims; and the symptoms of mental compulsion are connected with the carrying out of such substitutive aims. The development of the depressive psychoses is different. In this case repression is followed by a process of 'projection' with which we are familiar from our knowledge of the psychogenesis of certain mental disturbances.

In his 'Psycho-Analytic Notes upon an Autobiographical Account of a Case of Paranoia (Dementia Paranoides)' Freud gives a definite formulation of the psychogenesis of paranoia. He sets out in short formulæ the stages which lead up to the final construction of the paranoic delusion. I will here attempt to give a similar formulation of the genesis of the depressive psychoses, on the basis of my analyses of depressive mental disturbances.

Freud considers that in a large portion at least of cases of paranoic delusions the nucleus of the conflict lies in homosexual wish-phantasies, i.e. in the patient's love of a person of the same sex. The formula for this is: 'I (a man) love him (a man)'. This attitude raises objections in the patient and is loudly contradicted, so that the statement runs: 'I do not love him, I hate him'. Since internal perceptions are replaced by external ones in paranoia, this hatred is represented as a result of the hatred endured by the patient from without, and the third formula is: 'I do not love him—I hate him—because he persecutes me'.

In the psychoses with which we are here concerned a different conflict lies concealed. It is derived from an attitude of the libido in which hatred predominates. This attitude is first directed against the person's nearest relatives and becomes generalized later on. It can be expressed in

[1] [See footnote, p. 138.]

the following formula: ' I cannot love people; I have to hate them '.

The pronounced feelings of inadequacy from which such patients suffer arise from this discomforting internal perception. If the content of the perception is repressed and projected externally, the patient gets the idea that he is not loved by his environment but hated by it (again first of all by his parents, etc., and then by a wider circle of people). This idea is detached from its primary causal connection with his own attitude of hate, and is brought into association with other—psychical and physical— deficiencies.[1] It seems as though a great quantity of such feelings of inferiority favoured the formation of depressive states.

Thus we obtain the second formula: ' People do not love me, they hate me . . . because of my inborn defects.[2] Therefore I am unhappy and depressed.'

The repressed sadistic impulses do not remain quiescent, however. They show a tendency to return into consciousness and appear again in various forms—in dreams and symptomatic acts, but especially in an inclination to annoy other people, in violent desires for revenge or in criminal impulses. These symptomatic states are not usually apparent to direct observation, because for the most part they are not put into action; but a deeper insight into the patient's mind—as afforded in the catamnesis, for instance —will bring a great deal of this kind of thing to light. And if they are overlooked in the depressive phase there is more opportunity for observing them in the manic one. I shall have more to say about this subject later on.

It is more especially in regard to such desires to commit acts of violence or revenge that the patients have a tendency to ascribe their feelings to the torturing consciousness of their own physical or psychical defects, instead of to their imperfectly repressed sadism. Every patient who belongs to the manic-depressive group inclines to draw the same

---

[1] In many cases, and particularly in the slighter ones, the original connection is only partly lost; but even so the tendency to displacement is clearly recognizable.

[2] Cf. with this the etymology of the German word *hässlich* (' ugly ') = ' that which arouses hate '.

K

conclusion as Richard III., who enumerates all his own failings with pitiless self-cruelty and then sums up:

> And therefore, since I cannot prove a lover . . .
> I am determinèd to prove a villain.

Richard cannot love by reason of his defects which make him hateful to others; and he wants to be revenged for this. Each of our patients wishes to do the same, but cannot, because his instinctual activity is paralysed by repression.

New and morbid states, such as feelings of guilt, result from the suppression of these frequent impulses of hatred and revenge. Experience so far seems to show that the more violent were the person's unconscious impulses of revenge the more marked is his tendency to form delusional ideas of guilt. Such delusions, as is well known, may attain enormous proportions, so that the patient declares that he alone has been guilty of all sins since the world began, or that all wickedness originates from him alone. In these persons an insatiable sadism directed towards all persons and all things has been repressed in the unconscious. The idea of such an enormous guilt is of course extremely painful to their consciousness; for where there is a great degree of repressed sadism there will be a corresponding severity in the depressive affect. Nevertheless the idea of guilt contains the fulfilment of a wish— of the repressed wish to be a criminal of the deepest dye, to have incurred more guilt than everyone else put together. This, too, reminds us of certain psychic processes in obsessional neurotics, as, for instance, their belief in the ' omnipotence ' of their thoughts. They frequently suffer from anxiety lest they have been guilty of the death of a certain person by having thought about his death. The sadistic impulses are repressed in the obsessional neurotic also: because he cannot *act* in conformity with his original instincts he unconsciously gives himself up to phantasies of being able to kill by means of *thoughts*. This wish does not appear as such in consciousness but it takes the form of a tormenting anxiety.

As a result of the repression of sadism, depression, anxiety, and self-reproach arise. But if such an important source of pleasure from which the active instincts flow is obstructed there is bound to be a reinforcement of the masochistic tendencies. The patient will adopt a passive attitude, and will obtain pleasure from his suffering and from continually thinking about himself. Thus even the deepest melancholic distress contains a hidden source of pleasure.

Before the actual state of depression sets in many patients are more than usually energetic in their pursuits and manner of life. They often sublimate in a forced manner libido which they cannot direct to its true purpose. They do this so as to shut their eyes to the conflict within them, and to ward off the depressive frame of mind which is tending to break into consciousness. This attitude often succeeds for long periods, but never completely. The person who has to combat disturbing influences for a long time can never enjoy peace or security within himself. Any situation which requires a definite decision in the field of the libido will cause a sudden collapse of his psychic equilibrium which he has so laboriously kept up. When the state of depression breaks out his previous interests (sublimations) suddenly cease; and this leads to a narrowing of his mental outlook which may become so pronounced as to attain to monoideism.

When the depressive psychosis has become manifest its cardinal feature seems to be a mental inhibition which renders a *rapport* between the patient and the external world more difficult. Incapable of making a lasting and positive application of his libido, the patient unconsciously seeks seclusion from the world, and his auto-erotic trend manifests itself in his inhibition. There are other means, it is true, by which neuroses and psychoses can give symptomatic expression to an auto-erotic tendency. That it should be inhibition rather than some other symptom that appears in this case is fully explained from the fact that the inhibition is able to serve other unconscious tendencies at the same time. I refer in particular to the tendency towards a 'negation of life'. The higher degrees of inhibition in especial—*i.e.* depressive stupor—represent a symbolic dying. The patient does not react even to the application of strong external stimuli, just as though he were no longer alive. It is to be expressly noted that in the foregoing remarks only two causes of the inhibition have been considered. In every case analysis revealed still further determinants, connected with the individual circumstances of the patient.

Certain features commonly present in states of depression become comprehensible if we accept the well-founded conclusions of psycho-analytic experience. Take, for instance, the frequent ideas of impoverishment. The patient complains, let us say, that he and his family are exposed to starvation. If a pecuniary loss has actually preceded the onset of his illness, he will assert that he cannot possibly endure the blow and that he is completely ruined. These strange ideas, which often entirely dominate the patient's thoughts, are explicable from the identification of libido and money—of sexual and pecuniary 'power'[1]—with which we are so familiar. The patient's libido has disappeared from the world, as it were. Whereas other people can invest their libido in the objects of the external world he has no such capital to expend. His feeling of poverty springs from a repressed perception of his own incapacity to love.

We very frequently meet with fears or pronounced delusions centering round the same idea in states of depression connected with the period of involution. As far as my not very extensive psycho-analytical experience of these conditions goes, I have reason to believe that it is people whose erotic life has been without gratification who are liable to such delusions. In the preceding decade of their life they had repressed this fact and had taken refuge in all kinds of compensations. But their repressions are not able to cope with the upheaval of the climacteric. They now pass in review, as it were, their wasted life, and

---

[1] [The German word used, *Vermögen*, means both 'wealth' and 'capacity' in the sense of sexual potency.—*Trans.*]

at the same time feel that it is too late to alter it.   Their
consciousness strongly resists all ideas connected with this
fact; but not being strong enough to banish them completely, it has to allow them entrance in a disguised form.
They are still painful in the form of a delusion of impoverishment, but not as intolerable as before.

Viewed externally, the manic phase of the cyclical disturbances is the complete opposite of the depressive one.
A manic psychotic appears very cheerful on the surface;
and unless a deeper investigation is carried out by psycho-
analytic methods it might appear that the two phases are
the opposite of each other even as regards their content.
Psycho-analysis shows, however, that both phases are
dominated by the same complexes, and that it is only the
patient's attitude towards those complexes which is different.
In the depressive state he allows himself to be weighed down
by his complex, and sees no other way out of his misery but
death;[1] in the manic state he treats the complex with
indifference.

The onset of the mania occurs when repression is no
longer able to resist the assaults of the repressed instincts.
The patient, especially in cases of severe maniacal excitation, is as if swept off his feet by them.   It is especially
important to notice that positive and negative libido (love
and hate, erotic desires and agressive hostility) surge up
into consciousness with equal force.

This manic state, in which libidinal impulses of both
kinds have access to consciousness, once more establishes a
condition which the patient has experienced before—in his
early childhood, that is.   Whereas in the depressive patient
everything tends to the negation of life, to death, in the
manic patient life begins anew.   The manic patient returns
to a stage in which his impulses had not succumbed to
repression, in which he foresaw nothing of the approaching
conflict.   It is characteristic that such patients often say
that they feel themselves ' as though new-born '.   Mania
contains the fulfilment of Faust's wish :

[1] Some patients cling to the idea that they can be cured by the fulfilment of
some external condition—usually one, however, which never can be fulfilled.

> Bring back my passion's unquenched fires,
> The heavenly smart of bliss restore;
> Hate's strength—the steel of love's desires—
> Bring back the youth I was once more.

The maniac's frame of mind differs both from normal and from depressive states, partly in its care-free and unrestrained cheerfulness, partly in its increased irritability and feeling of self-importance. The one or the other alteration can predominate according to the individuality of the patient or the different stages of the disease.

The affect of pleasure in mania is derived from the same source as is that of pleasure in wit. What I have to say about this is therefore in close agreement with Freud's theory of wit.[1]

Whereas the melancholiac exhibits a state of general inhibition, in the manic patient even normal inhibitions of the instincts are partly or wholly abolished. The saving of expenditure in inhibition thus effected becomes a source of pleasure, and moreover a lasting one, while wit only causes a transitory suspension of the inhibitions.

Economy of inhibition is, however, by no means the only source of manic pleasure. The removal of inhibitions renders accessible once more old sources of pleasure which had been suppressed; and this shows how deeply mania is rooted in the infantile.

The technique of the manic production of thoughts may be regarded as a third source of pleasure. Abolition of logical control and playing with words—two essential features of manic ideational processes—indicate an extensive 'return to infantile freedom'.

Melancholic inhibition of thought finds its reverse in the manic flight of ideas. In the melancholic phase there is a narrowing of the circle of ideas, in the manic phase a rapid change of the content of consciousness. The essential difference between flight of ideas and normal thinking is that whereas in thinking or speaking the healthy person consistently keeps in view the aim of his mental processes

---

[1] *Der Witz und seine Beziehung zum Unbewussten*, 1905.

the manic patient very easily loses sight of that aim.[1]   This differentiation serves to characterize the external aspect of the flight of ideas, but not its significance for the manic subject.   It is especially to be noted that the flight of ideas offers the patient considerable possibilities for obtaining pleasure.   As has already been said, psychic work is economized where the abolition of logical control is removed and where the sound instead of the sense has to be considered.   But the flight of ideas has yet another function, and a double one: it makes it possible to glide by means of light allusions over those ideas that are painful to consciousness, for example, ideas of inadequacy; that is to say, it favours—like wit—transition to another circle of ideas. And it also permits of playful allusion to pleasurable things which are as a rule suppressed.

The similarity between the mind of the maniac and that of the child is characterized in a number of ways of which only one need be mentioned in this place.   In the slighter states of manic exaltation the patient has a kind of careless gaiety which bears an obviously childish character.   The psychiatrist who has had much to do with such patients can clearly see that his *rapport* with them is the same as with a child of about five years of age.

The severer forms of mania resemble a frenzy of freedom.   The sadistic component-instinct is freed from its fetters.   All reserve disappears, and a tendency to reckless and aggressive conduct takes its place.   In this stage the maniac reacts to trifling occurrences with violent outbursts of anger and with excessive feelings of revenge. In the same way, when his exaltation had reached a certain height, the cyclothymic patient mentioned above used to feel an impulse to strike down anyone who did not at once make way for him in the street.   The patients often have an excessive feeling of power, measuring it not by actual performance but by the violence of their instincts, which they are now able to perceive in an unusual degree.   Fairly frequently there appear grandiose ideas which are very similar to children's boasts about their knowledge and power.

[1] Liepmann, *Über Ideenflucht* (1904).

Arising from the case of cyclothymia already described at length, there is one important question which I cannot attempt to answer definitely. It remains to be explained why, when the patient was about twenty-eight, states of manic exaltation should have appeared in addition to the depressive state which had already existed for a long time. It may be that it was a case where psychosexual puberty followed a long time after physical maturity. We often see the development of instinctual life delayed in a similar manner in neurotics. On this hypothesis the patient would not have experienced an increase of his instinctual life at puberty but have been overtaken, like a woman, by a wave of repression; and it would only have been towards the end of his third decade that a certain awakening of his instincts would have occurred in the form of the first manic state. And in fact it was at that age that his sexual interests turned more to the female sex and less towards auto-erotism than before.

I must now say a few words about the therapeutic effects of psycho-analysis.

The case I have most fully reported in these pages was so far analysed at the time when I read my paper at Weimar[1] that its structure was apparent in general. But there still remained a great deal of work to be done on it; and therapeutic results were only just beginning to be discernible. These have become more clearly visible during the last two and a half months. Naturally a definite opinion as regards a cure cannot yet be given, for after twenty years of illness, interrupted by free intervals of varying length, an improvement of two months' duration signifies very little. But I should like to record the result up to the present. In the period mentioned, no further state of depression has appeared, and the last one passed off very easily. In consequence of this the patient has been able to do continuous work. During the same period there did twice occur a changed frame of mind in a manic direction, which could not escape a careful observation; but it was of a far milder character than his previous states of exaltation. And,

[1] [See No. 26, A. B.]

besides this, certain hitherto regularly observed phenomena were absent. Between these last two manic phases there has been no depressive one, as was usually the case, but a state which could be called normal, since no cyclothymic phenomena were present. For the rest we shall have to follow the further course of the case. There is only one more thing I should like to add: If the patient succeeds in permanently maintaining a state similar to that of the last two months, even this partial improvement will be of great value to him. In the other case of cyclothymia the period of observation has been too short to permit of an opinion regarding therapeutic results. But its pathological structure was found to be remarkably similar to that of the first case.

The third case described at the beginning of this paper showed the effectiveness of analysis in a striking manner, in spite of the fact that external circumstances obliged the treatment to cease after about forty sittings. Even in the early part of the treatment I was able to cut short a melancholic depression which had just developed in the patient, a thing which had never happened before; and as treatment proceeded its effect became more lasting and expressed itself in a distinct amelioration in the patient's frame of mind, and in a considerable increase of his capacity for work. In the months following the cessation of his analysis his state of mind did not sink back to its former level. It may be noted that in this case the preponderating attitude of hatred, the feeling of incapacity to love and the association of depression with feelings of inadequacy were clearly to be seen.

In the two above-mentioned cases of a melancholic depression occurring for the first time, a consistent analysis could not be carried out on account of external difficulties. Nevertheless, its effect was unmistakable. By the help of a psycho-analytical interpretation of certain facts and connections I succeeded in attaining a greater psychic *rapport* with the patients than I had ever previously achieved. It is usually extraordinarily difficult to establish a transference in these patients who have turned away from all the world in their depression. Psycho-analysis, which has hitherto enabled us to overcome this obstacle, seems to me for this reason to be the only rational therapy to apply to the manic-depressive psychoses.

The sixth case confirms this view with greater certainty, since I was able to carry the treatment through to the end. It had a remarkably good result. The patient came to me for treatment fifteen months after the onset of his trouble. Before this, treatment in various sanatoria had had only a palliative effect in relieving one or two symptoms. A few weeks after the commencement of psycho-analytic treatment the patient felt occasional relief. His severe depression began to subside after four weeks. He said that at moments he had a feeling of hope that he would once again be capable of work. He attained a certain degree of insight and said: ' I am so egoistic now that I consider my fate the most tragic in the world'. In the third month of treatment his frame of mind was freer on the whole; his various forms of mental expression were not all so greatly inhibited, and there were whole days on which he used to feel well and occupy himself with plans for the future. At this time he once said with reference to his frame of mind: ' When it is all right I am happier and more care-free than I have ever been before'. In the fourth month he said that he had no more actual feelings of depression. During the fifth month, in which the sittings no longer took place daily, distinct variations in his condition were noticeable, but the tendency to improvement was unmistakable. In the sixth month he was able to discontinue the treatment; and the change for the better in him was noticeable to his acquaintances. Since then six months have passed without his having had a relapse.

From a diagnostic point of view the case was quite clearly a depressive psychosis and not a neurosis of the climacteric period. I am unfortunately unable to publish details of the case; they are of such a peculiar kind that the *incognito* of the patient could not be preserved if I did. There are also other considerations which necessitate a quite special discretion—a fact which is greatly to be regretted from a scientific point of view.

There is one objection that might be raised regarding the therapeutic results obtained in this case, and that is that I had begun treating it precisely at that period when the melancholia was passing off, and that it would have been cured without my doing anything; and from this it would follow that psycho-analysis did not possess that therapeutic value which I attribute to it. In answer to this I may say that I have all along been careful to avoid falling into an error of this kind. When I undertook the treatment I had before me a patient who was to all appearances unsusceptible to external influence and who had quite broken down under his illness; and I was very sceptical as to the result of the treatment. I was the more astonished when, after overcoming considerable resistances, I succeeded in explaining certain ideas that completely dominated the patient, and observed the effect of this interpretative work. This initial improvement and every subsequent one followed directly upon the removal of definite products of repression. During the whole course of the analysis I could most distinctly observe that the patient's improvement went hand in hand with the progress of his analysis.

In thus communicating the scientific and practical results of my psycho-analyses of psychoses showing exaltation and depression I am quite aware of their incompleteness, and I hasten to point out these defects myself. I am not in a position to give as much weight to my observations as I could have wished, since I cannot submit a detailed report of the cases analysed. I have already mentioned the reasons for this in one of the cases. In three other very instructive cases motives of discretion likewise prevented me from communicating any details. Nor will intelligent criticism reproach me for adopting this course. Those who take a serious interest in psycho-analysis will make good the deficiencies in my work by their own independent investigations. That further investigations are very greatly needed I am fully aware. Certain questions have not been considered at all or only barely touched upon in this paper. For instance, although we have been able to recognize up to what point the psychogenesis of obsessional neuroses and cyclical psychoses resemble each other, we have not the least idea why at this point one group of individuals should take one path and the other group another.

One thing more may be said concerning the therapeutic aspect of the question. In those patients who have prolonged free intervals between their manic or depressive attacks, psycho-analysis should be begun during that free period. The advantage is obvious, for analysis cannot be carried out on severely inhibited melancholic patients or on inattentive maniacal ones.

Although our results at present are incomplete, it is only psycho-analysis that will reveal the hidden structure of this large group of mental diseases. And moreover, its first therapeutic results in this sphere justify us in the expectation that it may be reserved for psycho-analysis to lead psychiatry out of the *impasse* of therapeutic nihilism.

Chapter VII

A COMPLICATED CEREMONIAL FOUND IN NEUROTIC WOMEN[1] (1912)

SEVERAL years ago Freud published a short paper[2] in which he discussed the relation between obsessional neurosis and religious practices. Ordinary observation shows us that very many neurotics—and not only obsessional ones—carry on in private a cult which in its various forms reminds us of religious rites and ceremonies, and that they repeat some of these practices day by day with the same regularity and fixed procedure with which a religious community will repeat its prayers every morning and evening.

Although there is a very wide scope for individual difference in a private cult of this kind, we often find persons making use of the same or of very similar neurotic ceremonials, notwithstanding that they come from entirely different social circles, and differ completely in their way of life, the circumstances in which they are placed, their intellectual abilities, and their opinions. This applies particularly to the simplest forms of ceremonial. For example, there is the very prevalent compulsion of having to step in a certain way on the flagstones of the pavement; and there is the equally frequent compulsion to count one's steps in walking or going upstairs and to end up with an even number. This compulsion has to do with ideas of fairness, and is also an over-compensation for certain forbidden impulses. But this is a subject we cannot enter into any further in this place.

[1] [No. 32, A. B.] [2] 'Obsessive Acts and Religious Practices' (1907).

The coincidence is far more striking, however, when we meet a really complicated ceremonial in one neurotic woman, and soon afterwards find an almost identical one in another female patient of quite a different character and unacquainted with the first patient.   In this paper I shall discuss a coinciding ceremonial of this kind that has not as yet been described.   I shall relate from the analysis of the first case as much as is necessary for an understanding of it, and shall only refer to those features of the second case which deviate in a characteristic way from the first.

For certain reasons, which I shall give later, the patient, Frau Z., spontaneously told me the following facts in the course of her psycho-analysis.   She said that whenever she went to bed she used to get herself ready with extreme care and in a most methodical fashion.   She used to be especially careful about her hair being tidy; she used to undo it and then bind it up with a white ribbon.   She gave as a reason for her ceremonial (this first description of which was an incomplete one) that she might happen to die suddenly in the night and that she would not like to be found in an untidy or unprepossessing condition.

At the next sitting she supplemented the above description, and said that she did her hair at night in the same way as she had worn it when quite a young girl.   After overcoming perceptible resistances she went on to say that when she lay down she was careful that her bed should be in as perfect order as possible.   She would often wake up in the night and straighten her nightdress and bedclothes if they had become disarranged.   She would then be able to go to sleep again, but would always wake up after a little while and go through the same performance.   Up to the present it had been impossible for her to forego any part of this procedure.

The motives for her peculiar behaviour were for the most part unconscious, and they are not comprehensible on the face of them.   So far we are only able to translate some part of this symbolic mode of expression into our own language.   It is clear that Frau Z. expected her death every night, and that at the same time she put herself back into the period of her childhood. The white ribbon she used to put in her hair points to bridal innocence and also to death. She was anxious that no signs of disorder should be found about her or her bed when she was dead—that is, that no doubt could arise as to her bridal chastity.

Further light was thrown on the meaning of the ceremonial from the circumstances in which the patient first mentioned it. After having told me of a very pronounced phobia of snakes that she had, she one day related a dream in which she had seen a little girl playing with a snake. From certain things about the girl she concluded on waking that the girl represented herself. Soon after, she said that latterly almost every night she had started up from sleep in great anxiety fearing that there was a big snake in her bed. During the analysis of this anxiety she always spoke of the 'big snake'.

Her associations to the above dream led first of all to her elder brother who was dead and of whom she had been extraordinarily fond. She mentioned that as children they had daily seen each other naked while dressing, undressing, and in the bath; and that they had slept in the same room and had often got into each other's beds. Further associations led to the subject of her later disgust of the male body.

She related about her brother that he had been very imaginative as a boy and used to be quite absorbed in stories about Red Indians. He used to sleep on a shield he had made himself, and had adopted the name of a certain young Indian. After she told me this a 'blank' occurred, and she could not remember the name of the 'last of the Mohicans' (it was 'Uncas'). This disturbance of memory could only have had the purpose of preventing her thoughts from going any further in that direction. In this case, however, it was not difficult to establish the associations against whose recovery her resistance was directed. In Fennimore Cooper's story the father of Uncas is called 'Chingach-gook', which means 'Big Snake'.

The interpretation of the dream in which the patient was a little girl and played with a snake now presents no difficulties: she was playing with the genital organ of her brother, which was still small and infantile. A question in which boys and girls alike are much interested is whether the penis is very much bigger in the adult man (above all in the father) than in the boy. Children tend to have an exaggerated idea of its size. Stekel has alluded to this tendency in his monograph on nervous anxiety-states. In Freud's 'Analysis of a Phobia in a Five-year-old Boy', the child's idea of the immense size of a man's penis plays a significant part.

The 'big' snake, in contrast to the still infantile penis of her brother, can now be understood to refer to the penis of an adult man. In the patient's fear of finding a 'big snake' in her bed we recognize in the first place the typical anxiety of neurotic women regarding the male organ. But the constant recurrence of the term 'big snake' points quite definitely towards her father. The patient's analysis had already furnished material in this sense which could now be added to. It appeared that she had been intensely fixated upon her father from early childhood, and more especially since the early death of her mother. He was the chief object of her repressed sexual phantasies. In her eyes he was the only real man; no one else, she was convinced, could ever satisfy her. She had watched his behaviour to other people with great jealousy. Strong affects appeared when she related how after her mother's death she had slept for a short time near her father, and how he occasionally used to pass through her bedroom. Her father died when she reached the age of puberty. And it was in the same manner that she used to wear her hair at that period that she now dressed it with such painstaking care every evening.

We can now understand her ceremonial to a great extent. In it she took herself back to a time when her father was still alive. It was he whom she was expecting every night. When she used to wake out of her sleep and imagine that the 'big snake' was in her bed, she was experiencing the fulfilment of her incestuous wishes directed to her father—a fulfilment which, of course, could only take place to the accompaniment of violent anxiety. Her repressed wish to have a child by her father, moreover, came to light as well, but in another connection.

The patient was in fact married, but in her unconscious mind she rejected marriage with any other man but her father. She exhibited every imaginable sign of sexual aversion in evidence of this. Her phantasies removed her so far from reality that every evening she was able to attire herself as a young girl and a bride and thus give proof of her loyalty to the dead father whom she awaited. In her unconscious she was attached to him alone.

It is true that consciously she expected, not her father, but death. But her analysis showed that the two ideas were identical. Assaults and acts of violence played a large part in her phantasies, and especially in her dreams. Her attitude in them was a masochistic one. She expected to be killed by a sexual attack on the part of a man, *i.e.* her father. She experienced in phantasy the fate of the Asra, ' who die when they love '. Thus bridal garment and shroud, bridal bed and death-bed, were identified in her mind and were able to represent each other in the creations of her unconscious phantasy.

It is to be noted that the repressing forces as well as the repressed incestuous wishes had participated in the formation of her ceremonial. At the same time as she was continually expecting a sexual attack in her unconscious she yet had always to keep her bed and night attire properly arranged so as to prove that her death had been preceded by no sexual act.

Although the symbol of the snake did not come into the ceremonial itself, it occupied an important place in the ideational material belonging to it and had a manifold determination. It was not merely a symbolic substitute for the male genital. A snake is able to kill by means of its poisonous bite, hence as a symbol it can give expression both to coitus and to death phantasies. In connection with this it is to be noted that a snake enfolds and crushes its victim. Death from a snake is thus death in an embrace. Moreover, the ideas of ' snake ' and ' worm ' are closely associated in unconscious thought. A worm is also a male

L

sexual symbol [1] and a death symbol as well.   In the present case the patient's anxiety contained a childhood memory. When she was nine years old she and a boy had moved away a stone in a churchyard, and she had been terrified to see a quantity of worms under the stone.   The thought of this scene still caused her the greatest anxiety.

Her fear of the snake had yet another exceedingly important basis.   The snake was for her the totem animal of her dead father.   Her childhood fear of her father was transferred to this symbol.   This was also connected with a definite memory of childhood.   When she was about nine years old she had been very much afraid of her father's eye.   We know from many instances that in folk-psychology the glance of a snake is considered especially dreadful. Thus her identification of father and snake is seen to be still further determined.

The statements of the second patient showed that she too had observed a strict ceremonial each night for many years.   After taking off her clothes, she would arrange them with the greatest possible neatness.   Then she would lie down on her back, smooth the bedclothes and her night attire in an exceedingly careful manner, cross her arms over her breasts and force herself to lie as motionless as possible so that her position and clothes should remain undisturbed.   As an explanation of this procedure she gave exactly the same reason as the first patient, viz. that she might die in the night, and nothing must be found in an untidy or slovenly condition about her.   The reason for crossing her arms was that that was the way people's arms were placed when they were dead.   She used also to arrange her hair in a particular way.   This latter procedure she quite consciously explained by saying that she wanted to be certain what arrangement of her hair would best please a man if she were to be married later.   This explanation was a satisfactory one in so far as it betrayed the erotic substratum of the ceremonial.   But she put off her erotic expectation and placed it in an indefinite future, whereas she fixed her expectation of death in the next few hours.

[1] In neurotics worm phobias are usually found as well as snake phobias.

The process of displacement was quite obvious in this case. Unfortunately, it was not possible to carry out a full psycho-analysis of this patient, so that I can say nothing definite concerning the connection of her ceremonial with her father complex. But the situation seemed to be very similar to the one in the first case.

Complicated actions of a similar character to the ones described here will presumably be found in neurotics quite frequently once attention has been directed to them. I refer particularly to those persons who before going to sleep are compelled to arrange their clothes in an absolutely fixed way which must never be departed from.

As a name for the form of ceremonial analysed above I would suggest 'The Bride of Death Ceremonial'.

Chapter VIII

MENTAL AFTER-EFFECTS PRODUCED IN A NINE-YEAR-OLD CHILD BY THE OBSERVATION OF SEXUAL INTERCOURSE BETWEEN ITS PARENTS [1] (1913)

THE editor of this Journal has asked for accounts of dreams occurring in childhood the interpretation of which would justify the conclusion that the dreamer had witnessed sexual intercourse at an early age. The following contribution only in part satisfies this request, in that in this case the observation of parental sexual intercourse did not take place in the earliest years of childhood, but in all probability took place immediately before the occurrence of the dream which I am about to relate and of the concomitant neurotic anxiety. Nevertheless, I consider it worth publishing, because the case shows with more than usual clearness how a child disposed to neurosis reacts to an event of this nature.

Some time ago I was called in to see a little girl of nine and three-quarters who had recently begun to suffer from anxiety states.

Ten days before the consultation the child had been put to bed as usual in the evening. After having slept for a good hour she called for her mother with screams of fear. Her mother, who was in the next room, went to her, and the little girl told her a dream with every sign of terror. She said: ' A man wanted to murder you in bed, but I saved you'. While relating this she still could not distinguish

[1] [No. 42, A. B.]

between dream and reality. When her mother tried to soothe her she said with a horrified expression, ' Oh, you aren't my mother at all '. She then showed fear of objects in the room, mistaking them for animals. It was some time before she could be pacified; but she then slept till morning. On waking she declared that she had slept well and undisturbed during the night, and that she felt quite well. When her parents questioned her cautiously (and hence only superficially) it appeared that she did not remember the episode.

Thus in this case there had been a severe anxiety-dream followed by a twilight state. There was no family history of epilepsy, nor did the child show any symptoms that pointed directly to the existence of mental disorder in the narrower sense of the word. As a result of the further development of her condition and of my examination of her I was able to diagnose a hysterical twilight state.

During the next few days the patient showed various symptoms of illness. She was very nervous and inclined to start. In speaking with her mother she often used to talk in a way which resembled the paralalia of Ganser. She used to have pronounced anxiety in the evening. Once or twice she had visions of animals. On the occasion of my visit, for instance, she told me that she had been terrified by a snake which had crawled into her bed and tried to bite her leg; and she was afraid to go to the w.c. because there were black men there who threatened her with their fingers. She also exhibited a marked astasia abasia and fear of falling as an accompanying phenomenon. This disturbance reacted to the influence of suggestion to the extent that I was able to conduct her across the room only lightly holding her sleeve. In the end she was able to return to the bed alone without falling, although she staggered. No symptoms of an organic paralysis were present.

In answer to my inquiries the patient told me that latterly she had often had anxiety-dreams. When I asked her to relate one of these dreams she immediately gave the one quoted above, although she had not been previously

reminded of it by her parents.   Her amnesia in regard to
the evening on which her illness had begun was therefore
only a partial one.

As I had only been called in for a consultation with the
patient, I had to content myself with making a diagnosis of
the state in which I found her, and with applying some
therapeutic measures to calm her.

With the help of the child's father I endeavoured to
gain further knowledge regarding the ætiology of her
illness.   Her anxiety-dream had at once led me to suspect
that she had witnessed sexual intercourse between her
parents, and that she had re-modelled the impression in a
typical childish manner, in accordance with a sadistic theory
of coitus, and had then re-enacted the scene in her dream.
(It is to be noted that she slept in her parents' bedroom.)
I accordingly told her father my suspicions, and briefly
gave my reasons for them.   He at once took my point and
said that he quite agreed with my view, adding that the
little girl would also in recent times have heard occasional
quarrels going on between her parents after they had gone
to bed.   Thus those quarrels would furnish a further
determinant besides the sexual one for her idea that her
mother was being murdered.

The foregoing case clearly shows an attitude in the
girl which is analogous to the Oedipus complex of the boy.
The daughter dreams of an attempt upon her mother's
life.   The meaning of the phantasy is not altered by the
fact that the dreamer ' saves ' her mother.   Even if this
was not made clear from the well-known meaning of rescue-
phantasies, it is only necessary to point out that the patient
disowned her mother immediately after the dream ; she
got rid of her in a way with which we are familiar in
' phantasies of descent '.

In a waking hallucination, furthermore, she saw a
snake, a male symbol obviously representing her father,
approaching her.[1]   Her statement that ' the snake wanted
to bite her leg ' was made with distinct hesitation and an
altered expression of countenance.   She seemed to be con-

---

[1] Cf. the preceding chapter.

cealing something.   Probably she named her leg in place of her genitals, in the same way that the stork is said to bite a woman's leg.

When, as is the case here, the parental complex appears in so acute and intense a form and, for the psycho-analyst, beneath so transparent a disguise, it justifies us in the conclusion that some affective experience connected with the parents has influenced the child.   Both the external circumstances and her father's account tended to show that immediately before the appearance of her symptoms the child had observed parental intercourse.   Of course it was not possible to question her directly in the first and only consultation.

This episode, however, could not be a sufficient cause in itself for such a serious state of illness.   Moreover, the connection between certain symptoms and that particular psychic trauma was, to say the least, uncertain.[1]   Conversation with the father brought further material to light. It appeared that the child was accustomed to associate with a neighbour's daughter who was said to practise mutual masturbation with other girls.   It is probable, therefore, that, excited by sexual acts and conversations with this friend, she had reacted much more violently to the incident in her parents' room than she might otherwise have done. Her dread of figures making threatening gestures at once suggests a sense of guilt; and as far as our experience goes we can say that in all probability this could be traced to the practice of forbidden sexual acts.   That she should have seen these figures in the w.c. is a fact of some interest, for this place is the most frequent scene of children's secret and forbidden acts.

This fragmentary analysis is particularly disappointing in one respect.   The patient's associations usually direct our attention to early infantile wishes and impressions from which the neurotic symptoms develop.   In this case, however, it was not possible to investigate the deeper strata of the patient's unconscious.   I am inclined to think that

---

[1] I have purposely omitted an interpretation of certain symptoms because sufficient evidence was not forthcoming.

such an investigation would have shown that the recent experience from which she was suffering had received its most important reinforcement from her unconscious, *i.e.* from repressed memories of a like nature belonging to the first period of childhood. But as I have said, satisfactory proof of this was not obtainable.

I think we may come to the conclusion that in this case the child's observation of parental coitus had been the exciting cause of her psycho-neurotic attack, the first noticeable symptom of which was a severe anxiety-dream followed by a twilight state.

CHAPTER IX

RESTRICTIONS AND TRANSFORMATIONS OF SCOPTOPHILIA IN PSYCHO-NEUROTICS; WITH REMARKS ON ANALOGOUS PHENOMENA IN FOLK-PSYCHOLOGY [1] (1913)

THE sexual component-instinct of scoptophilia, or pleasure in looking, is—like its counterpart, exhibitionism, or pleasure in displaying—subject to numerous restrictions and transformations. Under normal conditions both instincts, which are allowed free expression in early childhood, are subjected to a considerable measure of repression and sublimation later on. In psycho-neurotics these instincts are inhibited and transformed to a very much greater degree than in normal people; while at the same time they carry on a continual struggle against the forces of repression.

In a short paper [2] Freud has laid down certain lines of thought which open the way to a deeper insight into the neurotic inhibitions and transformations of the scoptophilic instinct. He makes use of his theory of the erotogenic zones and component-instincts, and speaks as follows concerning the scoptophilic instinct and its erotogenic zone, the eyes: ' The eyes perceive not only those modifications in the external world which are of import for the preservation of life, but also the attributes of objects by means of which these may be exalted as objects of erotic selection,

---

[1] [No. 43, A. B.]
[2] ' Psychogenic Visual Disturbance according to Psycho-Analytical Conceptions ' (1910).

their "charms". We now perceive the truth of the saying that it is never easy to serve two masters at the same time. The more intimate the relation of an organ possessing such a duality of function with one of the great instincts, the more will it refuse itself to the other.'

If this scoptophilic impulse has become too strong, or is directed on to forbidden objects, then a conflict in the subject's instinctual life results. In the same paper Freud says: ' If the sexual component-instinct which makes use of sight—the sexual " lust of the eye "—has drawn down upon itself, through its exorbitant demands, some re-taliatory measure from the side of the ego-instincts, so that the ideas which represent the content of its strivings are subjected to repression and withheld from consciousness, the general relation of the eye and the faculty of vision to the ego and to consciousness is radically disturbed. The ego has lost control of the organ, which now becomes solely the instrument of the repressed sexual impulse. It would appear as though repression on the part of the ego had gone too far and poured away the baby with the bath-water, for the ego now flatly refuses to see anything at all, since the sexual interests in looking have so deeply involved the faculty of vision. The other representation of the situation, however, is probably closer to the facts, the aspect in which we see the *active* part in the process played by the repressed scoptophilia. It is the revenge, the indemnification of the repressed impulse, thus withheld from further psychical development, that it can succeed in so boldly asserting its mastery over the organ which serves it. The loss of conscious control over the organ is a detrimental substitute-formation for the miscarried repression, which was only possible at this cost.'

Freud brings forward as the motive for such a far-reaching repression of scoptophilia the law of talion, *i.e.* self-punishment for the pleasure got from looking at a forbidden object.

This is the first advance made by psycho-analysis into a large though little explored region. And it is the object of this paper to penetrate further into that region, where a great mass of material awaits careful investigation. Hysterical blindness, which Freud has chosen as the standard of neurotic disturbances of vision, is only one form—though a particularly striking one—of neurotic disturbance associated with the instinct of looking. It is not very often met with in medical practice. During the last six years I have not come across a single unmistakable example of it, though I have observed that certain other disturbances—some of which have not been written about at all—occur comparatively often.

From the clinical point of view these latter disturbances consist partly of a transformation of scoptophilia into a specific fear of exercising the instinct, partly of disturbances of vision and partly of neurotic symptoms which occur in the eye without being directly related to the sense of sight. In the following pages I shall not endeavour merely to add to our knowledge of the symptomatology of this affection on the basis of psycho-analytical investigation. I shall go beyond this purely medical interest and attempt to explain certain phenomena of folk psychology in the light of the results obtained in the field of individual psychology.

For the sake of conciseness and clarity I shall limit my inquiry to the manifestations of scoptophilia and leave aside the consideration of exhibitionism. I am well aware that it would be more correct to treat the two instincts and their effects together, in the same way that Rank has done in his excellent work.[1] But since the neurotic symptoms which I am about to consider arise for the most part from repressed scoptophilic instincts, I feel justified in confining my investigation to this one side of the question.

1. *Neurotic Photophobia*

The analysis of a disturbance which I should like to call ' neurotic photophobia ' affords information of a particularly instructive nature. This is by no means a rare affection, and it has received some attention in non-analytic

[1] ' *Die Nacktheit in Sage und Dichtung* ' (1913).

literature. I have had the opportunity of observing several clear cases of this kind and of making a thorough analysis of most of them. These patients showed other symptoms which also originated in the repression of their scopto-philia, and I will include a psycho-analytical explanation of these as well in my discussion of their major symptom of photophobia.

Persons who suffer from a photophobia of this kind find sunlight, daylight, and usually artificial light disagree-able. They even feel dazzled by a feeble light. Some of them complain of a more or less violent pain in the eyes as soon as they are exposed to light, even if it is only for a short time. They will protect their eyes from light by all sorts of means. But they not only show a sensitiveness of the eyes to a light-stimulus but react to it with an aversion which has all the characteristics of neurotic anxiety. In pronounced cases they will protect their eyes from every ray of light in just as careful a manner as a neurotic person who suffers from fear of touching will preserve his hands from contact with an object. The ideational content of their anxiety is the danger that they may be blinded.

Psycho-analytic literature has hitherto given no special consideration to the disturbances which I have thus briefly described, and yet it contains an important clue to our understanding of them. In his postscript to his ' Psycho-Analytic Notes upon an Autobiographical Account of a Case of Paranoia ' Freud has given a psycho-analytical interpreta-tion of a delusion of a psychotic patient, Dr. Schreber,[1] who declared that he could bear the light of the sun for several minutes without being dazzled.[2] It could be gathered from the patient's attitude to the sun—an attitude which he de-scribed in all its remarkable details—that it signified for him a ' sublimated father-symbol '. With reference to the ordeals imposed as tests of parentage among so many peoples, Freud concludes: ' When Schreber boasts that he can look into the sun without being punished and without being dazzled, he has rediscovered the mythological

---

[1] Cf. his *Denkwürdigkeiten eines Nervenkranken*, S. 139, Anm.

[2] I have also met with the same delusion in other psychotic persons.

method of expressing his filial relation to the sun, and has confirmed us once again in our view that the sun is a symbol of the father '.

Schreber's delusion is the exact psychotic counterpart to a neurotic photophobia. The healthy individual reacts, within certain limits, without any special sensitiveness to light falling on his eyes, and nevertheless instinctively protects himself efficiently from a glaring light; the mentally affected person fancies he will not succumb to the blinding effect of the brightest sunlight; while the neurotic person is alarmed to an exaggerated degree at the risk of being blinded, so that he may truly be said to suffer from sun phobia.

I should now like to give certain details from the psychoanalysis of a young man which may help to explain this aversion to light as well as certain phenomena closely related to it.

The patient, whom I will call A, came to consult me about a disturbance of his sexual potency and a profound depression of spirits. At the commencement of the treatment he was in a state of great dejection. He had formerly been very much engaged in all that was going on around him, but he had now lost all interest in the people about him, in his vocation, his amusements, etc. His mental activity was becoming more and more restricted to neurotic brooding. On further investigation it transpired that the eye and the function of vision played a striking part in his mental life, that certain ideas in this connection caused him anxiety, that a sexual perversion from which he suffered likewise referred to the eye, and finally, that he was troubled with a pronounced photophobia.

The severity of such a disturbance can be judged from the protective measures which the patients adopt against the object of their anxiety. In this case the patient protected himself against broad daylight by tightly screwing up his eyes and by similar methods which he carried to far greater lengths than any normal person would do. He protected himself in a similar manner against artificial light in the evening. But the method he adopted to exclude any ray of light from reaching him at night after he had gone to bed was more striking still and decidedly pathological. He had hung up three thicknesses of curtain over his bedroom window so that no ray of light could penetrate in the morning; and to prevent any artificial light from coming in he had not only blocked up the keyhole of his bedroom door, but had carefully filled up the minutest cracks in the panels.

At the beginning of his analysis other material came to the surface, and it was not until a month had passed that I was able to obtain any information about his numerous thoughts connected with the eye. This delay in itself tended to show that the thoughts relating to that subject were particularly painful to him. And the further course of his analysis proved this to be so, for it appeared that those thoughts were very closely associated with repressed incestuous wishes.

In connection with this aversion to light the patient told me some more things. He said that he had a kind of obsessional anxiety that either he or one of his relatives might lose an eye. He was extremely sensitive to anything coming near his eyes. He was also very interested in affections of the eye in other people. He said: 'People who have something wrong with their eyes compel my interest'. Girls who wore pince-nez were a source of great interest to him, and he was always on the look-out for girls who were blind in one eye. When he met women whose eyes were quite normal he 'persuaded himself that they were blind in one eye'. Once he had a dream about a girl with whom he was acquainted and who was blind in one eye, in which he thought that her eye had been knocked out by her father, so that the latter had been responsible for her partial blindness.

It soon transpired that the patient's anxiety concerning the eyesight of other persons referred in the first instance to his father, towards whom, as had already become clear, he had a distinctly ambivalent attitude. He had first expressed this attitude by speaking of his 'ardent respect' for his father; but no sooner had he said this than there occurred a sudden ' breaking off ' of his thoughts and a short suspension of consciousness. Soon after, ideas of an opposite character occurred to him, such as phantasies of the death and burial of his father. He next complained about his failure in life, and said that his father literally weighed him down. He could not help recognizing the superior intellectual capacities of his father, who occupied a high position in his native town. He felt it was impossible for him ever to be his father's equal or superior. He had often wished to do or to know something better than his father, yet he had always had to acknowledge the latter's superiority. This made him feel that he was in his father's power. It had always been impossible for him to conceal anything from him, for he had seen everything. The patient's anxiety about his father's eyesight is now no longer entirely incomprehensible to us. It is in the first place a distorted expression of his wish to be removed from the observant eye of his father.

At this point the patient produced one or two free associations between ' father ' and ' sun ' without being himself aware of the connection. He identified his father's watchful eye with the sun, an identification which was confirmed later on by numerous examples, one of which I will give here. It was the following recollection, which occurred to him accompanied with strong affect: When he had been at school he had regarded a certain poem as ' disgusting '. In this poem, which was about a wicked man whose crime was unexpectedly brought home to him in the end, each verse ended with the words, ' The sun will bring the deed to light '. [1]

But the sun had yet a second meaning as the representative of his father. For his attitude towards his father was not solely traceable to the latter's rôle of ' watcher ', to his ' omniscience ', one might almost say. This second determinant was his enthusiastic appreciation of his father's ' greatness '—his intelligence, his knowledge, his

---

[1] The patient had also transferred to the sun his ambivalent attitude towards his father in a remarkable way. He disliked the light of the sun but he loved its warmth.

'ability'.[1]   Burdened as he was with a sense of insufficiency, he compared his father's power and superiority with the splendour of the sun.   He felt that his father's light would always outshine his own importance, just as the sun outshines the other stars.   Yet in spite of his excessive praise of his father, his jealousy of him was unmistakable.[2] When the patient's unconscious fused the idea of the paternal eye with that of paternal splendour, in order to give both a common symbolic expression in the sun, it did no more than primitive peoples have done from time immemorial.

The function of watching over things has been frequently ascribed to the sun-god.   In the Homeric poems, for example, Helios is constantly called ' he who sees and hears all things '.[3]

In Psalm xix, which clearly contains the remains of an old hymn to the sun, we find the following verse: ' His [*i.e.* the sun's, originally the sun-god's] going forth is from the end of the heaven, and his circuit unto the ends of it: and there is nothing hid from the heat thereof'.

The material of folk-psychology provides a great many parallels to such an identification of the eye of the father with the splendour or light of the sun.   I will take a few examples from language.   Although such examples are widely found in different languages, I will limit myself to those that occur in German.

The most obvious example is the word *Augenlicht* [' eyesight'.   *Augen* = ' eyes';   *Licht* = ' light'].   In reality the eyes perceive the light; language, however, makes it appear as though the light belonged to or originated in the eyes.   The use of the word *blind* [' blind '] is interesting.

---

[1] I need only allude to the disturbance of potency mentioned at the beginning in order to render the patient's jealousy regarding his father's ' ability ' comprehensible.   I was able to substantiate the fact more clearly in other cases (cf. case B) than in this, that the sun represented not only the greatness, in other words, the potency, of the father, but that it was a symbol of the father's phallus.   Aversion to the sight of the latter is also known to us as a phenomenon of folk psychology (cf. the Biblical tale of Noah's sons).

[2] As will be shown later, the elevation of his father to the sun signified not only an increase but at the same time a reduction of his power.

[3] We may especially notice the passage in the *Odyssey* (viii. 266) where Helios observes the forbidden meeting of Ares and Aphrodite.

It refers not only to a person who has lost the power of sight, who cannot see, but frequently also to a person or thing that is not seen. For instance, we speak of a *blinde Passagier* [' stowaway ']. It is also customary to denote as *blind* an object that has lost its lustre. This shows that our language identifies *sehend* [' seeing '] and *glänzend* [' shining ']. There is no doubt that these peculiarities of speech have originated in the ' antithetical meaning of primal words ' (Abel). In a short paper [1] Freud has shown that antithetical ideas are paired off in the unconscious of the individual in the same way as they are in the primitive stages of language, traces of which still persist in its later stages.

The patient's dread of his father's observing eye found an important extension in his avoidance of looking at his mother. He had in fact consciously imposed upon himself a prohibition of looking at her. From adolescence onwards he had refused—as he expressed it—to think that his mother was beautiful. At the time of the treatment he still shrank from seeing any portion of his mother's body uncovered except her face and hands. Even seeing her in a blouse with an open-work neck used to cause him great distress.

It then came out that the sun whose sight the patient shrank from was a bisexual symbol for him. It not only represented his father (*i.e.* his watchful eye or his shining splendour) but also his mother, whom he must not look at for fear of calling down upon himself his father's anger. In this as other cases the prohibition of looking at his mother originated in the more particular prohibition of seeing her naked, and in especial of seeing her genitals. The idea of not being allowed to look at her was changed into the fear of not being able to look at the light of the sun.

This bisexuality of the sun symbol appears in Schreber's case, too. In his *Denkwürdigkeiten* there is one place in which he shouts at the sun, reviling it in the words, ' The sun is a whore '. Here there can be no doubt of the female character of the sun symbol.

Without going deeper into the prohibition of looking

[1] ' The Antithetical Sense of Primal Words ' (1910).

M

at the mother's body in this place, I will only say that according to my experience a particular avoidance of seeing even unimportant parts of the mother's body proceeds from a repressed pleasure in looking, which was originally directed in an excessive degree towards the mother, and especially towards her genitals.

The patient's pleasure in looking at other women was inclined to be more than ordinarily great, but was not directed to those parts of their body which normally act as stimuli. He had a pronounced aversion to their genitals. His scoptophilia was directed in the first instance to two parts of the body far removed from the genitals, namely, to the eyes and the feet. Even these parts of the body were not themselves permitted to play the rôle assigned to them through the process of displacement, but had to yield it to accessory parts that did not belong to the body itself. Thus girls who wore glasses or who had a false leg would attract him most of all; and a lame gait which suggested a stiff leg or an artificial limb would have the same effect on him. Yet his horror of the female genitals was most clearly seen in the fact that he never in reality touched a girl who was lame or who had an artificial leg.

The patient's aversion to the female body, or, to be more correct, to the female genitals, was found to have many determinants, chief among which was his fear of castration. Of special interest was an associative chain which disclosed a close relation between the following affective states of mind:

1. His astonishment as a little child on discovering the absence of a penis in his small sister.

2. His anxious avoidance of touching his own penis.

3. The deflection of his interest from the female genitals.

4. His interest in women who had had an amputation.

This last interest in particular showed the extraordinary strength of his castration images, for it represented the woman ' who has had a member cut off '. We find here, as is so often the case in our psycho-analyses, that the unconscious has retained the infantile idea that the woman possesses a penis, too. When this is so, the fear of being castrated is often present in conjunction with an idea of an

active nature—that of castrating women. I have alluded
to this phenomenon in a paper concerned with the analysis
of foot fetishism.[1] In the present case, too, there was
pronounced fetishism. Considerations of space make it
impossible for me to go into this in detail; but I should
like to say a few words about the connection of foot and
eye-glass fetishism with the sadistic component-instinct.

One of the patient's most pleasurable phantasies was the
idea of taking away her glasses from a short-sighted girl, or,
better still, a one-eyed girl, or of depriving a young woman
of her artificial leg, thereby making her helpless.[2] His
associations made it more and more evident that these ideas
concerned displaced castration phantasies. Particularly
important in this connection was the dream described above
about a girl he knew by sight who could only see with one
eye. His idea in the dream was that her missing eye had
been knocked out by her father. From here his associations
led to his own fear of losing an eye. This anxiety arose
from two sources, namely, the idea of punishment for forbidden looking, and the displacement of castration anxiety
from the genitals to the eye. This displacement is quite
analogous to the one mentioned above from the female
genitals to the eye. Both ideas clearly bear the significance of a talion. I have the satisfaction of knowing that
my conclusions in this respect agree with Freud's views,
and also with those of other analysts.

Ferenczi[3] has recognized in the self-blinding of Oedipus
a symbolic substitute for self-emasculation, i.e. self-punishment proportionate to incest. Rank[4] and other authors[5]

[1] Cf. Chapter V.
[2] It may be mentioned that these sadistic instincts were limited to phantasies;
in actual life the patient was extremely kind-hearted.
[3] 'Symbolic Representation of the Pleasure and Reality Principles in the
Oedipus Myth' (1912).
[4] Rank, Inzestmotiv (1912), S. 271, A. 2. Cf. also: Storfer, 'Jungfrau und
Dirne.'
[5] Eder, 'Augenträume'. Gebsattel (Zeitschrift für Pathopsychologie, 1912).
The significance of the eye as a female genital symbol has been considered by Jung
in the Indra-Mythus. I myself, following Kleinpaul, have likewise recognized in
the eye, especially the pupil, a female genital significance (Traum und Mythus,
1909). Bleuler (Dementia præcox oder Gruppe der Schizophrenien) likewise mentions
the eye as a female genital symbol in the delusions of the insane. Jones ('Einige
Fälle von Zwangsneurose', 1913) shows the male genital significance of the eye.

supply abundant material from dream analyses to show that
the eye can have sometimes a male and sometimes a female
genital significance; and Eder has shown that in dreams
things done to the eyes signify—as with the teeth—
castration.[1]

The correctness of this assumption was confirmed by
further dreams of the patient in which castration was
expressed by means of other symbols of less doubtful
significance. For instance, in one of his dreams a person
appeared and cut off his pubic hair.

The ' punishment ' of blinding proved to be a reprisal
for the patient's unlawful desire to look at his mother and
for his active castration or blinding phantasy directed against
his father. Analysis showed that this latter assault played
a direct part in the patient's phantasies. In this connection
I shall mention only one obsessive idea which he used to
have. When he was a schoolboy and was having lessons
with a particular master he constantly had to imagine how
he would shoot him through the middle of the forehead.
It was easily discovered that this master was a substitute
for his father.

Shooting through the forehead would in itself certainly
not be an obvious castration symbol; and indeed it would
not be necessary to devote any special attention to it here
did there not exist many unmistakable proofs that the forehead is frequently used as a substitute for the eye. In the
first instance I may refer to the myth of the blinding of
the Cyclops by Odysseus. Beings who possess only one eye
which is situated in the centre of the forehead are everywhere
found in myths. It is interesting to note that at times something similar to the myth of Polyphemus occurs in dreams.
Eder has published a dream of this kind.[2] I have fairly
often had the opportunity of corroborating this fact, and I
can confirm from experience Eder's observation that the
Cyclops corresponds to the father of the dreamer, and that
the blinding of the giant represents a castration of the father.

[1] In the dreams of women something done to the eye can have the significance
of coitus. A young girl, for example, dreamed that someone was opening her eye
with a long instrument.
[2] Eder, ' Augenträume '.

It seems to me a particularly interesting fact that the middle of the forehead, which in phantasy primarily represents the eye, can stand either for the male or the female genitals. With regard to its significance as the male organ, I should like to refer to an observation of Reitler's; [1] and with regard to its female significance to an example taken from my own experience.

Reitler discusses certain wooden figures made by the peasants in the Salzkammergut that are used for obscene jokes, and he gives reproductions of them. The joke is that when the head of the figure is pressed a big penis appears. On the forehead of the figure a third eye is roughly sketched. Reitler ascertained that among the people of that district this eye is directly recognized as a penis symbol.

As a parallel to this curious fact of folk psychology I may mention the following observation I have made myself: One of my patients suffered from a compulsion to wrinkle her forehead in the middle, thus making a vertical crease. She used then to violently to rub this crease with the forefinger of her right hand. Certain associations, which I am unfortunately unable to reproduce here, suddenly made it clear to her that the procedure was simply an act of masturbation displaced upwards, and that the vertical crease on her forehead corresponded to the vulva. This idea was confirmed by the fact that when rubbing the crease she used to experience a ' feeling of pressure in the lower part of her body '.[2]

It seems to me that whenever the genital symbolism of the eye has been discussed its significance as a female organ has so far alone been considered. It is only quite recently that I have come across the male significance of the eye. It was in a dream analysis, and the dreamer, a woman, said that the glans penis seemed to her like an eye.

I return to the subject of the patient A's fear about his eyesight. We have recognized in his fears of castration

[1] Reitler, ' Zur Augensymbolik ', 1913.
[2] I might here refer to a statement of Sadger's that the temples have a genital significance. Cf. ' Über sexualsymbolische Verwertung des Kopfschmerzes ' (1912).

an important determinant of his anxiety; and in this connection it is worth while mentioning a further detail which
at first sight might seem quite unimportant.   I have noticed,
not only in the case before us but also in others, that the
patients always speak of their anxiety regarding the *eye* of
their father, and of their avoidance of touching their own
eye.   They never spoke of their *eyes* but, with a regularity
which excluded all chance, only of *an eye*, as though only
one eye existed.   This is quite intelligible if we keep
in view the mechanism of 'displacement upwards'.
'The' eye is a substitute for an organ which only exists in
the singular.[1]

Anxiety about the eye of the father therefore corresponds
to the repressed castration phantasy directed against him.
Having established the identity of the eye and sun, however,
there can be little doubt that the sun has the same phallic
significance as the eye of the father.   Avoidance of the
sight of the sun has therefore the further significance of
shunning the sight of the father's penis.   This meaning is
borne out, incidentally, in folk psychology.

It is not possible to enter further into the subject of
castration-anxiety in this place; but I will add a few remarks
in order to render more intelligible certain facts that appeared in the present case.   We have learnt that the boy's
desire to see his mother's genitals, and also his castration
phantasy directed against his father, belong to those offences
for which he is threatened with castration by someone or
fears it in his own mind.   Masturbation should also be
included in them, since the phantasies that accompany it
make it a deeply guilty act.   We know from our psycho-
analytic work that there are also certain other experiences
of childhood which frequently give rise to a great deal of
self-reproach.   I refer in especial to the child's observation
of sexual intercourse between its parents.   With regard to

[1] I might remark that there are still further determinants to be considered.
I need only refer to the above-discussed identification of the eye of the father with
the sun, which is only a single thing.   We may assume that there is a special form
of condensation, a unification, at work which renders possible a number of parallels:
one genital, one father, one sun, and also one eye.   (One might add one God.   The
reader is referred to later parts of this paper.)

all these ' sins ' the boy is often very fearful lest he should be discovered by his father's watchful eye.[1]

It is precisely on account of such forbidden observations that many neurotic persons suffer from the fear of going blind. But this kind of neurotic reaction does not concern us at the moment. What I want to bring forward here is the fact that in quite a number of instances the pleasure the child has derived at night from watching its parents and listening to them has led to an over-sensitiveness both to light and to sound.[2] In the present case there was a definite sensitiveness to sound as well as to light. Both symptoms are especially liable to occur at night, and the reason for this is now readily understood. We see why the patient in question was afraid of artificial illumination and of the slightest ray of light which might happen to penetrate through a crack in the door. The extreme precautions he adopted so as to exclude any light from without are of the nature of prohibitory measures. The careful blocking up of the tiniest crevice had also a further purpose. This was to prevent the patient from being observed by other people. It is quite obvious that here again the compelling motive was the avoidance of his father's watchful eye. Nevertheless, his procedures for darkening the room are not fully explained by his negative desire to exclude light and avoid every possibility of being observed. Being in complete darkness has a positive value for the patient as well. But I will exemplify this point in another case.

For the present I will pass over certain of the transformations the patient's scoptophilia had undergone and only mention certain psychological peculiarities which he showed. These were, a compulsive curiosity, a propensity to brooding, and an exaggerated inclination for everything that was problematical. I shall return later to these characteristics. Finally, the following signs show us that the eye had an important erotogenic significance for this

[1] The child's pleasure in observing adults urinate also gives rise to neurotic self-reproaches. Cf. footnote on p. 188.

[2] I have been able to get some knowledge of the genesis of neurotic sensitiveness through a number of psycho-analyses, the results of which I shall publish later.

patient, not only as an organ of sight: he derived pleasure from touching his eyes, he had a great tendency to rub them and to draw down the upper lids, and he had often cut off his eyebrows in the past.[1]

In regard to the therapeutic results of the analysis I may say that the patient was completely restored to health. His horror of light and his sensitiveness to noise entirely disappeared. His attitude towards his parents became like that of any healthy person of his age, as was seen when he returned to his home after the termination of his analysis. He developed normal sexual interests in place of his abnormal ones, and his fetishistic interest in particular disappeared, except for certain slight and unimportant traces. As he was getting better he had dreams in which he felt pleasure in looking at the female body, especially the genitals; and soon afterwards he was able to have a normally directed scoptophilia in his waking life. At the same time his unfruitful inquisitiveness and pathological brooding gave way to a keen desire for knowledge, which manifested itself in most varied directions. In other words, the sublimation of his scoptophilic instinct had completely succeeded. Social adaptation (capacity for work in his calling, etc.) went hand in hand with the establishment of a thoroughly normal sexual function. It is now a year and a half since his treatment was ended, and there has been no recurrence of the trouble so far.

The psycho-analysis of neurotic photophobia in other patients has fully confirmed the above results and theories. I will briefly indicate the essential points in another of my cases. This was an undoubted case of dementia præcox (schizophrenia), which I had the opportunity of treating by psycho-analysis only because the patient was sent to me as a neurotic case. It was only on going thoroughly into his symptoms that I discovered the nature of his illness. It has often been our experience that the secrets of the unconscious are much less disguised

---

[1] We may recall the dream previously mentioned in which someone cut off the patient's pubic hair. Cutting off the eyebrows obviously signified a symbolic castration, too.

in the psychoses than in the neuroses. And so it was in this case. The patient would produce associations, frequently without much resistance, in connection with the most extraordinary things, and associations of such a nature that the required connection was surprisingly quickly revealed.

This patient, whom we will call B, drew attention to himself at the very first consultation by requesting that he might sit with his back to the light. In addition he kept his eyes closed most of the time and covered them with his hands as well.[1] He steadily continued to keep his eyes thus closed during the analytical sittings, although his face was turned away from the window; and this lasted until the amelioration of this symptom made such a proceeding unnecessary.

The history of this patient was very similar to that of the first case. He too was the son of a remarkably intelligent and efficient man. In his own view his father's attainments were absolutely unrivalled. In speaking about him he made use of almost the same words as the first patient. He said that for a long time he had vainly hoped to surpass his father in some attainment or other. His ambivalent attitude towards his father, too, was similar to that of the other patient, except that it was less disguised on account of the nature of his illness, as has been pointed out.

His father had always seemed to him a ' powerful and benevolent being '. This expression sounds a religious note, and had it not referred to a human being, one would have supposed that it was being used of God, or some other being held in religious awe. We have only to recall the all-seeing eye of God to notice that there is here a tendency to elevate the father into a higher being. Free associations brought to light with extraordinary rapidity one of the causes which had convinced the son that his father saw all things. His father's watchful eye had discovered that the boy masturbated; and he had obtained a

---

[1] I might add that this attitude is fairly frequent in neurotic persons and betrays the existence of neurotic dread of light.

promise from him to give up this practice in future. At a later period the patient felt as though the eye of his father was watching him every time he relapsed into that habit. That this feeling of being observed had other and probably still more important sources will be shown later. Consciously, however, the patient attached the greatest importance to his father's discovery of his masturbatory activities.

When the patient was about twenty years old his father died. Soon after this he had the idea that his father was standing in heaven next to the sun and looking down upon him in order to observe what he did. This was not a fixed delusion as yet. But a little later undoubted delusions did develop. The significance of placing his father in heaven is quite obvious. His position immediately next to the sun shows that he was being likened to the sun without as yet having been united with it into a single being.

To this veneration and deification of his father which persisted after the latter's death there was opposed an extremely powerful affect of hostility, which was kept from consciousness for a long time. It was expressed during the treatment in a dream in which the patient slew his father in single combat and took possession symbolically of his mother. The killing of the father in single combat and the final taking possession of the mother are the two great events in the Oedipus myth and many related stories.

The patient's castration anxiety found a similar expression to that of patient A. I need therefore only bring out one or two details in connection with it. He too had anxiety regarding his father's eye, the meaning of which we already know. A childhood memory in connection with this anxiety is of some interest. When he was nine years old he had once seen his father naked and had inspected his genitals with great interest. His phantasies, which at this age turned towards male persons, often reverted to that scene. And yet the thoughts associated with it were by no means purely pleasurable; on the contrary, he was continually worried by the question whether his genitals would attain the size of his father's. When he became grown up he fell a prey to the tormenting belief, so very common in neurotic persons, that his penis was too small.

We once more meet, therefore, with a jealousy of the father's capacities. In the present case the son's awe of his father referred to his genital organ and his eye.[1] In this case, therefore, there was not such a far-reaching repression of the sexual character of the boy's dread of his father. All that was repressed was his pleasure in looking at his father's genitals. The patient used occasionally to have a kind of ' lightning ' hallucinations, which for a moment showed him the object of his interest.

Patient B also very closely resembled A in his relation to his mother. He had a most pronounced aversion to looking at her and also at his sister, even when they were fully dressed. When conversing with his mother he used to cover his eyes with his hands. He betrayed the incestuous direction of his wishes in the first hour of psychoanalytic treatment through a peculiar choice of expression. He was saying that after the death of his father he had remained at home with his mother and sister, and was emphasizing the fact that in a certain measure he had to consider himself as his father's successor; for, he went on to say, he was now ' the only male member ' in the family. The wish-phantasies that had determined the choice of this expression soon appeared. The patient suffered from anxiety lest he should unintentionally impregnate his mother and sister. In especial, when he had taken a bath after having had a pollution, he used to be very much afraid that remains of the semen might adhere to the sides of the bath and impregnate his mother or sister when they used the bath after him. From this fear we may infer the existence of a repressed wish of the same nature—*i.e.* to possess all his female relations.

The patient's libidinal wishes directed towards his mother were also transferred to other, mainly older women; but here, too, they were prevented from showing themselves in their real character, and were expressed in a dread of

---

[1] I refer here to the designation '*das Gemächt*' (' might ') for the male genitals; language has here transferred the strength of a man to his genitals.

looking at women of this description.[1]   This aversion was associated with a very troublesome neurotic symptom.   At the sight of mature women, who often consciously reminded him of his mother, a blackness would come before his eyes.   This symptom expresses an inhibition of scoptophilic tendencies, though it has, as far as I know, hitherto not been regarded in this sense.   The 'blackness' arising before the eyes, so often described by neurotics, more especially as a phenomenon accompanying attacks of giddiness, should regularly be the outcome of a suppression of a libidinal tendency.   The increased circulation of the blood associated with every sexual excitation often leads in neurotic persons to an increased flow of blood to the head, and especially to the eyes, and has as one of its effects an obscuration of the field of vision.

In this way the patient was prevented in real life from seeing women who were attractive to him.   That he should have found a substitute along hallucinatory paths for this imposed privation is in complete agreement with the psychology of dementia præcox.   He would, for instance, see lying naked before him a middle-aged woman who, according to his own account, bore a great resemblance to his mother.   He furthermore admitted in a way which carried conviction that his avoidance of the sight of female persons was in effect an avoidance of the female, or more correctly of the maternal, genitals.

At the time when distinct signs of a return to health were already noticeable, the patient once visited his mother. He told me afterwards that he had once again had to cover his eyes with his hands in her presence, although his sensitiveness to light had already become distinctly less. As I was about to comment on this he put his hands to his eyes, and said spontaneously: 'I didn't want to look at the plate with the wire down the middle at all'.   These words were spoken in a self-justificatory tone as though he was afraid I might put a wrong construction on his behaviour.

---

[1] I am indebted to Dr. de Bruine of Leyden for the interesting information that according to a Dutch popular belief anyone who looks at an old woman relieving the calls of nature will become blind.

This remark was at first quite unintelligible to me; but the explanation immediately followed. The patient, who was reclining on a couch during the treatment, had directed his glance to the ceiling on which a round polished brass disc was fixed, through the centre of which there ran a wire connected with the electric lights. This visual impression, occurring at the moment when the conversation touched on his avoidance of the sight of his mother, had been sufficient to call forth the associations of vulva (disc) and penis (wire in the disc).

His original hostility and jealousy towards his father had gradually changed to admiration and acknowledgement of his greatness and power. Nevertheless, his suppressed hostile feelings sometimes produced disturbances of the contrary feeling which had obtained control. In an ecstatic moment the patient had once wanted to write an ode to the sun, but he had only been able to produce a few words. They ran:

> Oh sun, endow us with thy might!

At this point so strong a disturbance (blocking) of his thoughts occurred that he could not get beyond the first words. It is characteristic that this ' blocking ' should have happened at the moment when he wished to give expression to his veneration for the power of the sun, *i.e.* his father. It will be remembered that a similar ' blocking ' occurred in patient A when he began speaking of his ardent admiration for his father.

On one occasion the patient's wish to be his father's equal found utterance in a form which clearly showed the symbolic equivalence of father and sun. He had the sensation that both his eyes became one. He saw this eye before him in a hallucination as though it was ' outside ', *i.e.* not part of his body. It then became a shining sun. In this way he raised himself to the level of his father. That it was precisely the eye and not any other part of the body to which this happened is explicable partly from what has already been said about the eye and sun, and partly as a symbolic substitution of the eye for the penis. This hallucination furthermore enables us to recognize a tendency in the patient to liken his own power of procreation to the fructifying power of the sun.

In psycho-analysing an obsessional neurotic I have met with a process that was similar in content, though different from a symptomatological point of view. After his father's death this patient had a great fear of his father's watching eye. He always localized that observing eye in the sky, as was also apparent from certain of his dreams. This acknowledgement and glorification of his father was nevertheless only one side of his ambivalent attitude towards him. At times he used to have an extremely defiant attitude towards his dead father. On such occasions he suffered from a compulsion to look at the sun in a bold and challenging fashion. At the same time there would arise the obsessional idea: ' Perhaps I am God '.

In my essay on Amenhotep IV.[1] I have analysed a remarkable episode in the history of Egypt in which its ruler attempted to identify himself with the sun. The ambivalent attitude of the king towards his dead father was the principal cause of the introduction of the Aton cult in which the power of the sun was worshipped.

As in the case of patient A, B's dread of being blinded by the sun becomes fully explicable only when it is realized that the sun symbol had not only a paternal but a maternal significance. The polished brass disc on the ceiling above referred to from which hung the electric light on the ceiling represented a kind of sun in the sky.[2]

His tendency to transplant a female symbol, that is in his case a maternal one, into the sky was expressed in a phantasy which he told me of his own accord. During one sitting when the sky became considerably overcast, he said, ' It would give me great pleasure to push my head into a cloud '. This phantasy corresponds to certain mythological ideas.[3] In the most ancient forms of the Prometheus

---

[1] [No. 34, A. B.]

[2] The identification of ceiling and sky bears a genuine infantile character. Quite recently I heard a boy of three and a half call the ceiling of the bathroom the ' bath sky '.

[3] Cf. my analysis of the Prometheus legend in *Traum und Mythus* (1909).

myth, boring into a cloud so as to create heavenly fire is identified with the sexual act.

As regards case B, I have only to add that the therapeutic results were very satisfactory and that the patient's aversion to light entirely disappeared.[1]

I shall not give any more examples from analyses of this particular symptom of aversion to light, concerning which I have a good deal more material at my disposal; for according to my experience neurotic dread of light is not a rare affection. A mild degree of such increased sensitiveness, as, for instance, towards glaring sunlight, is often found in the slighter neuroses.

There is, however, one more point I should like to mention, in connection with a case of severe obsessional neurosis I once treated. The patient also suffered from a slight degree of photophobia; and once when his associations brought him to certain prohibitions proceeding from the father-imago he suddenly covered his eyes with his hands. His behaviour was explained by his subsequent associations. He had always had a guilty conscience with respect to his father—he had never been able to look at him properly. His antagonism against his father had, among other things, found expression in the phantasy of blinding his father. In this case covering the eyes had a further, special significance. It represented, besides the meaning we have already considered, a self-punishment, *i.e.* a blinding of himself. It was an application of the law of talion [2] for his designs against his father.

II. *Other Forms of Neurotic Disturbances in Connection with the Scoptophilic Instinct*

As soon as a more detailed investigation of the neurotic inhibitions and transformations of scoptophilic tendencies is made, it is surprising to find what a variety of disturbances

---

[1] In explanation of the satisfactory result of psycho-analysis in this case of dementia præcox, I may remark that the patient soon proved himself capable of making a sufficient ' transference '. His psychosis was but little advanced in the direction of the formation of delusions, whilst hallucinations played a predominating rôle.   [2] Cf. Oedipus's blinding of himself.

are based on these processes.   Such disturbances sometimes appear in people who suffer from an aversion to light, sometimes as an isolated symptom.

In my description of case B I only very briefly mentioned a disturbance of this kind which existed in addition to his aversion to light; and I should now like to add just a few more words about it.

The patient complained of want of *sharpness* of vision and said that objects appeared blurred and indistinct.   No defect of the eyes was discoverable.[1]   The neurotic character of his affection was confirmed by the fact that it disappeared during his analysis at the same time as his aversion to light did.   In order to avoid repetition I will describe in this place a similar disorder in another case about whose psycho-analysis I have something to say.

This patient, C, a woman, was an artist.   Although very keen on her work, she said that at times of strong neurotic excitability it was difficult for her to appreciate correctly the forms of objects and also to impress them on her memory.   She began to speak of this trouble when certain motor attacks from which she suffered became the subject of interest in her psycho-analysis.   The trouble proved to be mainly determined by a repressed and incestuously fixated pleasure in looking which was directed on to her father and his body.   The analysis of certain special attacks which she had, and which I once or twice had an opportunity of witnessing, brought to light a specific determinant.   While lying on the couch she would begin to show signs of marked psychical excitement and to stretch and raise herself in an *arc de cercle* of a not very pronounced kind.   Her whole body, and especially the extremities, would then vibrate and twitch convulsively, and she would make groaning noises, until a general relaxation set in.   Once during each attack she would suddenly sit upright, twist her head sideways for a moment, and then sink back again.

---

[1] I may remark that the affections described in this paper occurred in persons whose visual apparatus was perfectly normal.   A single exception will be mentioned later.

The analysis of these attacks was carried out in the teeth of a very strong resistance; and it was not till the end of her treatment that, after having been several times begun and several times given up, it was finally successful. The attacks proved to be a mimic representation of an occurrence in her early childhood, which had been associated with extremely violent affects and whose authenticity certain facts made it impossible to doubt. It was this: One morning she had woken up earlier than usual and, since she shared her parents' bedroom, had witnessed sexual intercourse between them. As her associations bit by bit revealed, she had sat up in bed for a moment, and then, terrified, had lain down again. This, her own active share in what took place at that time, expressed itself in her later attacks in the sudden raising up of the upper part of her body. Her memory of the agitating event itself was repressed, but it showed itself in a disguised form on certain occasions which need not be gone into here. The really serious after-effects of the occurrence, however, were expressed in violent self-reproaches and in certain inhibitions of her instinctual life, of which only the limitation of the scoptophilic instinct interests us here. This limitation first appeared as an avoidance of all sexual looking and knowledge; for example, in an anxious avoidance of reading anything that might give her any enlightenment on love and sexual passion. Psycho-analysis showed that her aversion had extended to seeing in general, and that it more particularly referred to seeing the shapes of objects.

This case shows very clearly the effect of witnessing parental sexual intercourse on a neurotically disposed child. Such impressions fixate the scoptophilic instinct on the parents in an unusual degree, so that later efforts to detach it from them are doomed to failure. At the same time they cause a restriction of the instinct, which extends far beyond the actual sphere of sexuality. The law of talion can be carried to very different lengths in different cases. It can go as far as neurotic blindness, or can content itself with certain restrictions of vision; or it can give rise to the formation of phobias. In this case the patient suffered from

N

occasional compulsive thoughts of having to put out her own eyes.

Although I did not treat them psycho-analytically, the next two cases are worth mentioning as showing the great diversity found in neurotic disturbances of vision.

The first was that of a neurotic woman who used at times to suffer from a disturbance of vision which prevented her from reading a book without glasses. She, moreover, had a marked dislike of illustrations in books, and used to avoid them as far as possible.

The second was that of a young man who had been affected since childhood by a dread of darkness and by an obstinate phobia of becoming blind. Later on he had a disturbance of vision which was at once diagnosed by an eye specialist as neurotic. The patient described his trouble as follows in a letter to me: ' For the last ten to fourteen days I have been seeing badly, *i.e.* there is a kind of flickering before my eyes, as though I were constantly dizzy, and I see as through a veil. It began one afternoon; I saw zigzag lines flickering in front of my eyes, just as though I had looked at the sun or at a dazzling light for a long time. This lasted about half an hour. The same thing happened three days later, and since then I have had it almost continually. The flickering effect is less now, but my vision is dimmed and I have a strong feeling of fear, of course. At first I was afraid that I might be going blind.' As I have said, I was not able to analyse this patient, but I was able to find out that he was at this time involved in a sexual conflict which was an exact replica of his infantile Oedipus situation.

There is a rarer disturbance connected with the scopto-philic instinct which is entirely opposed in its external signs to the disturbances of perception described above, yet which has the same origin and serves the same purposes. This consists in an exaggerated concentration of attention on objects and processes in the external world, and associated with it, a surprisingly faithful memory for the minutest details. This constant visual tension, this noticing of things which seem unimportant to other persons and are rightly overlooked by them, gives an erroneous impression that the person takes a keen pleasure in looking. Such a person will be extraordinarily well-informed about a thousand trifling things that come within his field of vision. But that field is sadly circumscribed. It is limited to interests connected with his childhood, his family, or his home. There is, on the other hand, an aversion to getting to know what lies outside this sphere. Such a person will in especial avoid sexual looking and every kind of sexual activity. As is evident, a process of displacement has taken place. Whatever is likely to stimulate the person's scoptophilic instinct strongly is avoided as something illicit, and his interest is displaced on to indifferent and permissible things.

In one of my cases such a process could be traced back to early childhood. Before coming for treatment the patient had vaguely heard something to the effect that infantile events had to be reproduced in psycho-analysis, and he told me during the first sitting that he had exceptionally detailed and accurate memories of his earliest childhood. He then told me one or two such recollections, and added many more later on. They had taken place when he was between four and seven years of age. The minuteness of his recollections at two points in his childhood—when he was three and when he was six—was the most astounding of all. In the second of these two periods he had been staying at a health resort with his parents. He remembered a great number of names from that short time, described minutely the appearance of his playfellows, remembered what this and that person had said, and recollected each piece of furniture in the house in which he lived. His memories were so vivid and gave such an impression of freshness that one could rightly speak of a regular hypermnesia.

This phenomenon was puzzling to me at first. I was unable to believe in such a marked exception to the general rule of amnesia for early childhood years; and there were no grounds for thinking that the patient's recollections were paramnesic. His statements had nothing of the phantastic about them, for they dealt with the most ordinary matters of everyday life. It was impossible to conceive from what motives this perfectly reasonable man should have chosen to embellish his childhood with such a mass of uninteresting details which contained no strongly affective impressions and no memories that might have flattered a desire for greatness either in the child or in the adult.

His hypermnesia, however, was explained as soon as I was able to discover an apparently unimportant concealed amnesia in its neighbourhood. In connection with his stay at the health resort the patient remembered only one thing with which a strong affect was associated. This was that he had begun to have lively feelings of self-reproach. But he had completely forgotten what these self-reproaches had been about. It then transpired that he had already passed through a period of violent self-reproach in his fourth year. The cause of this was also unknown.

In trying to remove an amnesia of this kind existing since childhood we usually meet with strong resistances in the patient; and it was so in this case, too. But gradually, to a great extent by means of his dreams, the essential points were brought to light, and it became evident that in his case also observation of parental sexual intercourse in his early childhood had given rise to severe repression. This must have happened just before the first appearance of his self-reproaches. His sexual curiosity became repressed, and there appeared in its place an exaggerated attention to unimportant details of daily life.

The investigation of the patient's early childhood brought to light material which showed that his interest had quite early on been directed in an unusual degree towards his mother's body. His fixation on his mother had persisted till after puberty and had been expressed in a severe neurosis—an anxiety-hysteria. It is worth noting that he shrank from looking at his mother. The prohibition of looking at his mother's naked body had changed into an avoidance of the sight of her in general. He particularly liked looking into the faces of strange women, especially into their eyes. Doing this had an erotic attraction for him, and was his only sexual practice with the female sex.

If we recall what has already has been said about the genital significance of the eye, it would appear that this greatly restricted sexual activity of his represented a scoptophilic gratification which had been deflected ('displaced upwards') from its original aim, the genitals. In this connection we may remind ourselves that the expression of the eye easily betrays erotic excitement. Men with diminished sexual activity often seek this sign of affection in women; they will sometimes restrict themselves to evoking this sign, and will renounce every other form of approach. These matters will be more fully discussed later on. It is sufficient here to point out this interesting displacement of the scoptophilic instinct.

The same patient, however, also had a disinclination to look at male persons, even intimate friends. His pleasure in looking had therefore become repressed to a considerably greater extent in the homosexual direction than in the heterosexual direction.

A similar suppression of scoptophilia is of considerable significance in the causation of a widely-spread motor symptom in connection with the eyes, namely, a compulsive kind of twitching of the eyelids. As far as my psychoanalytical experience goes, compulsive movements of this kind go back to a sudden closing of the eyes in horror. This is in the first place an expression of fear of castration; for the twitching of the eyelids seems generally to be associated with dread of injury to the eyes, which, as we have already pointed out, is equivalent to anxiety regarding the genitals. The spasmodic closing of the lids corresponds furthermore to a shrinking from certain phantasies which have appeared with the clearness of a vision to the patient and given expression to forbidden desires to look. It appears that these phantasies are concerned partly with erotic ideas, partly with ideas of a sadistic nature (phantasies of the death of relatives, for instance). These ideas impose themselves upon the patient one day in the form of pictures (obsessional hallucinations), are banished by him with a feeling of horror, and become repressed. The compulsive sudden closing of his eyelids, however, shows that these proscribed phantasies still exist in the patient's unconscious, and that a constant expenditure of repressive energy is needed to keep them out of consciousness.[1]

One particular transformation undergone by the scoptophilic instinct is seen in that disturbance which I may call compulsive looking.   I once treated an obsessional neurotic who, besides suffering from a compulsion to brood over the problem of the origin of every object, was obliged to see and examine the back of it.[2]   In front of my house was a small garden, on the railings of which my plate was fixed. On his first visit to me, which took place in the evening, this patient was not content with reading what was on the plate but, after entering the garden, closely examined the reverse side by the light of a match.   He then—I am quoting his wife's account—spent some time talking aloud to himself, pondering over the way in which plates of this kind were made.   When his wife finally got him into my consulting-room his eyes were caught by a little bronze figure, and he took it from the table, turned it round, and examined the back of it with special attention.

His analysis, which was very incomplete, showed that in his childhood he had manifested a very great interest in people's buttocks.   His first compulsive symptoms had appeared after he had unexpectedly seen the buttocks of a woman.   His interest in buttocks had then become displaced on to inanimate and indifferent objects, whose 'backside' he was obliged to inspect in a compulsive way.   Why the scoptophilic instincts in this case and in many other neuroses should have been so strongly directed upon the buttocks instead of the genitals cannot be discussed at length in this place.

One disturbance which occurs especially in neurotic women is the fear of causing sexual excitement in persons of the opposite sex by looking at them.   This fear may

---

[1] I wish to state expressly that I am not proposing to give an exhaustive explanation of the symptom.   The above points are taken from incidental observations, not from a detailed analysis.

[2] Cf. an account of this in my paper ' Eine Deckerinnerung, betreffend ein Kindheitserlebnis von scheinbar ätiologischer Bedeutung ', 1913.   [No. 38, A. B.]

lead to a dread of meeting anyone at all, so that the subject is unable to go into society.

The characteristic feature in this and in certain other cases I shall mention is that the person ascribes some kind of virtue to his eye or his glance as though he were in possession of magic powers. And we find that such people restrict their thoughts in a quite surprising way to a circle of ideas in keeping with their overestimation of the eye and its power. Experience leads me to believe that these cases can be divided into two classes from a diagnostic point of view. In neurotics this fear of evoking sexual excitement in every person through the glance is associated with other phobias or obsessional thoughts. It seems to me to be exactly analogous to the idea of the 'omnipotence of thoughts'. Such an 'omnipotence' is in this case ascribed to the glance. But there are other cases in which the patient fears that his glance will have an effect extending far beyond erotic excitation. Such cases belong to quite another class from a diagnostic point of view. They are psychoses of a paranoid character which often run their course for a long period under the outward form of a neurosis.

A young girl had the fear that her glance would horrify other persons to such a degree that they would become motionless and die on the spot. The identity of her belief with the classical myth is most striking, and she herself likened her glance to the Gorgon's head. Her fear increased more and more in the course of years, and necessitated her withdrawal from all society. In one of her dreams she found herself among thousands of people in a huge room rather like the hall of a railway station. Suddenly a cry of terror resounded that the 'Rigor Mortis' had broken out, whereupon the people fled in a panic before the dreamer.

I found similar phantasies in another young girl. Her idea that she killed innumerable people through her glance was expressed not only in dreams, but also in delusions during the waking state. For example, on one occasion when she went to a ball she noticed to her dismay that the face of every person whom she looked at assumed the greenish-white colour of a corpse.   This gave her the impression that she was among dead people.

Both these patients indulged in extravagant sadistic phantasies.   One of them used to dream that she was breaking every bone in her mother's body; the other had phantasies of assaults by brigands on her family, members of which were murdered or tortured.   Of such dreams and phantasies there was any number, and in them the eye was employed, as it were, as a sadistic weapon.

As far as my experience goes, cases of this kind only occur among women.   In both the last-mentioned cases, analytic treatment had to be carried out under great difficulties associated with the nature of the illness itself.   It is only with the greatest reserve, therefore, that I can say that as far as I could observe in both these patients, who liked to assume the male sexual rôle in their phantasies, the eye seemed to have the significance of a penis with which people could be terrified and killed.   This idea, which at first sounds strange and improbable, is confirmed by the fear not infrequently met with in neurotic women of being ' bored through ' or ' pierced ' by the glance of a man.   Thus one of my patients used to avoid the glance of every man because she felt bored through by it in a literal sense.   As soon as she encountered the glance of a man she felt a stabbing pain in the lower part of her body.

Other neurotic persons experience stabbing or boring pains in the eye.   In many of these it is a case of ' displacement upwards ' of the genital sensation just mentioned. But there are also rare cases of severe neurotic pain in the eyes, which disclose a very complicated psychological structure. I will give a more detailed report from the analysis of such a case below.   In it the pain in the eyes was associated with extreme aversion to light, and the patient, a woman, lived for a long time in complete darkness.   This case is particularly suited to explain the significance of darkness in the mental life of a person suffering from photophobia.   I will begin by reviewing the results obtained in our analysis of this symptom.

III. *On the Significance of Darkness in the Psychology of
the Neuroses*

In our analysis of neurotic dread of light we have shown
that the sun is in the first place a father symbol though it
can also represent the mother. With regard to its second
and decidedly minor significance we can say that the sun,
as a unitary phenomenon, symbolizes the father - imago,
and that the latter has, as it were, absorbed into itself
the mother-imago. We find, for instance, distinct traces
of such a process in the Biblical story of the Creation. If
we carefully analyse this myth, which exhibits signs of
an extraordinary degree of modification and distortion, we
can see that the female and maternal element has been
merged into a male and paternal one. Whereas a 'parental
pair' is found in other cosmogonies with which we are
familiar, in Genesis the single (male) God alone creates the
world, all animals and finally mankind, or to be more
correct, a man. It is from this man that woman originates,
and the two produce sons but no daughters. This far-
reaching elimination of the female element nevertheless
proves to be a quite secondary phenomenon. We shall
take up this point again later.

Considering that it is principally the father-imago that
finds expression in the sun symbol, it might be asked
whether the imago of the mother is not perhaps also
represented by some special symbol in the phantasy-
formations of our patients. For the mother plays a
significant part in their unconscious phantasies, so that
the ideas relating to her have the same claim to adequate
symbolic expression as the phantasies referring to the father.
I found the answer to this problem in an indirect way as
I was attempting to elucidate another unsolved question
connected with neurotic dread of light. The patients'
aversion to light was not entirely comprehensible so long
as the question why they sought the darkness had not been
fully answered. I was inclined at first to see in it merely
an escape from light. But on making a more careful study

of these cases I found that darkness had by no means only a negative significance. A communication by Dr. A. Stegmann of Dresden drew my attention to the positive pleasure-value of darkness. This enabled me for the first time to understand the very complicated measures that these patients sometimes adopt to ensure complete darkness, especially in the evening. I have intentionally omitted this important aspect of the patients' behaviour in the first two psycho-analyses I have considered here in order not to complicate the discussion. I will now supplement my account of these cases in this sense; and in addition I will make reference to the psycho-analysis of a woman who was suffering from an extremely severe photophobia.

The significance of darkness was shown to have several determinants in all three patients. Every time this subject was approached in the analysis certain mental currents came to the surface. It appeared that all these patients suffered from moods of depression and had an unmistakable tendency to flee from the world. In their unconscious the light of day was a symbol of life and darkness a symbol of death. This symbolic use of light and darkness is also found in usages of speech. Neurotic persons in general are more usually afraid of the day (especially on waking in the morning) and feel better in every respect in the evening, because the day is over and night is drawing near; but they do this without special reference to the question of light or darkness. Day is the time for life in general, for activity; night signifies the opposite. But to those neurotics with whom we are dealing here, it in the *light* of day that represents life and the *darkness* of night death. Neurotics in whom repressed pleasure in looking plays a dominant part talk a special ' dialect ' in their symptoms, to use an apt expression of Freud's. This dialect is determined by the patient's prevailing component-instinct and his dominant erotogenic zone.

The neurotic's aversion to light, and particularly his complicated arrangements for excluding any ray of light in the night, thus become more intelligible. He unconsciously longs for darkness, and when the day which he dislikes so much has ended he seeks to make the darkness as absolute as possible. As has already been described, one patient, a woman, actually lived in completely darkened rooms even in the daytime.

Such a flight from the world is, needless to say, not merely a flight—*i.e.* something purely negative—but has a positive pleasure-value as well. The patient withdraws into the depth of the night in order to know nothing of the external world, that is, in order to be alone with himself and his phantasies. In those neurotics who tolerate the light of day, so long as it is not direct sunlight, we meet with a kind of compromise-formation. They keep a contact with the external world to some extent during the day, but at night they remove it completely. If, however, a patient excludes every ray of light during the day it signifies that he has turned away entirely from real life.

I should like to make a reference to a symptom which in its origin and effects is analogous to photophobia. This is a neurotic intolerance of noise. In this affection, too, one of the determinants is the patient's flight from the world. All life involves sound. Sounds are therefore for the neurotic signs of restless, pulsating life from which his repudiation of sexual life excludes him. He hates noise, but he particularly hates noisy people whose behaviour shows that they are free from inhibitions and feelings of uncertainty. It is interesting, too, to find that aversion to light and aversion to noise are often associated with each other. A particularly characteristic symptom of persons who suffer from both conditions is that they not only sleep in carefully darkened rooms at night, but draw the bed-clothes over their heads in order to be entirely isolated from both light and noise.

The free associations of the patients regularly proceed from these ideas of flight into a darkened, occluded room to ideas which we know as 'womb phantasies' and with which we are familiar in other neuroses. This leads us to the view that darkness is to be taken as a symbol of the mother. It is easy to corroborate this meaning of darkness from the data of folk psychology. The facts relating to this are too well known to require repetition in this place. I shall therefore go on to discuss the results gained from a very instructive neurotic case.

At the time when she took up psycho-analytic treatment this patient—a woman, whose case I have already alluded to once or twice in these pages—was living day and night in absolute darkness. Not only did she suffer from an extreme dread of light, as has already been said, but any kind of light caused her severe pain in the eyes. There was nothing the matter with her eyes themselves except a certain degree of astigmatism. A number of well-known eye specialists had agreed that her symptom was not merely the pain which often accompanies astigmatism. The ætiological connection of her trouble with strong emotional excitement was emphasized by the patient herself.

Each visit of the patient's to my house was rendered extremely difficult on account of her neurosis. She could not come in broad daylight, nor in the evening when the streets were lit up. Her only possible time was the hour of dusk. She used to prepare herself for her expedition by putting on a pair of pince-nez with very dark glasses, and over them dark motor goggles which more especially kept ofr the light from the sides. As a further protection she used to put on a thick veil and turn down the very broad brim of her hat. Thus protected she would come in a closed cab for treatment. She used to adopt similar complicated methods for excluding the light in her home.

It soon turned out that in this case, too, light and life were identified, and that the enormously strong accentuation of the wish to live in darkness proved to be a longing for death. In one of her poems the patient, who had formerly had great ambitions in life, compared her existence to a churchyard. In her darkened room, where she for the most part lay in bed, she felt that she was *buried alive*. The element of self-punishment present in this proceeding is quite obvious to the psycho-analyst, who knows how frequently neurotic symptoms arise from repressed phantasies of being buried alive.

But what was of decisive importance was, as we shall see, the phantasy of the return into the womb. The patient, who had great psychological insight, once said with reference to her extraordinarily strong fixation on her mother that, psychologically speaking, the 'umbilical cord' between her and her mother had never been severed! In one of her poems she gave a very graphic representation of this womb-phantasy.

Special considerations make it impossible for me to mention more than a few of the various determinants of the patient's photophobia and pains in the eyes. In her phantasy-life there existed strong motives which caused her to forbid herself every pleasure in looking, and to punish herself with violent pain for every transgression against this self-imposed prohibition. Among her phantasies were some which were directed against a particular person in her immediate environment because that person, a woman, outshone her in every way.

The strange procedures which the patient had to adopt before leaving the house were to a great extent explained by their effect. In consequence of her goggles and her veil she could not 'make eyes' at any man, and she became a forbidding figure to every male person—to her own husband, too, it may be added.

I shall not enter any further into the causes of the patient's symptoms, whose sadistic determinants in especial I have passed over, but I may mention that in the course of a few months an amelioration of her horror of light took place to such an extent that with the help of relatively slight protective measures she was able to go out into society in the evening in brightly-lighted rooms. Once she spent four hours in a brightly-lit drawing-room. This very satisfactory result, which of course rested in part on the effects of transference, was followed by a period of intense resistance. Psycho-analysis had helped the patient to return to ordinary life and had almost severed her 'umbilical cord'. But she was not, as it were, permitted to see the light of the world. The resistance which now set in awakened her womb-phantasies anew. Her severe pains returned, and she retired into the prison she had scarcely left and refused all further treatment, which was in effect never resumed.

The symbolic meaning of darkness is a thoroughly ambivalent one. Darkness signifies at once birth and death, just as earth and water do. In the symbolism of dreams and neuroses this double significance attaches to all cavities into which no light penetrates, and not only those of the human body but every other kind of cavity.

Dark cavities which symbolically represent the womb are often to be interpreted not as the uterus but as the bowels. For those experienced in psycho-analysis it is sufficient to refer to the well-known infantile sexual theory that children are born out of the anus of the mother, and to the frequent over-accentuation of the child's (or the neurotic's) interest in the bowels and their functions. Psycho-analytic experience has drawn my attention more and more to the fact that the interest many neurotics show in being alone in a small dark room discloses still further determinants of an anal-erotic nature. In especial, as may be easily supposed, the room very often signifies the w.c. in their phantasies. What is more surprising, though explicable enough to the initiated, is the not infrequent idea neurotics have of being shut up in a cesspool (*Klosettgrube*).[1] This place is sometimes the scene of their secret pleasurable desires and sometimes that of their haunting fears.

In concluding this section I have referred to the infantile and the neurotic interest in closed dark places because this helps to explain other psychological phenomena which we must now consider. In many neurotics, particularly obsessional ones, the very pronounced interest in all that is 'dark', *i.e.* mysterious, supernatural, mystic, etc., is not solely referable to repressed scoptophilia in general. It has a special determinant in that pleasurable interest in dark cavities which our knowledge of infantile sexuality has rendered intelligible to us.

---

[1] [*Klosettgrube* signifies a large receptacle in the cellar of a block of flats which collects the refuse from the lavatories situated on different floors.—*Trans.*]

IV. *Notes on the Psychology of Doubting and Brooding,*
with Parallels from Folk Psychology

In his 'Notes upon a Case of Obsessional Neurosis'
(1909) Freud has shown that certain symptoms in obsessional
neuroses arise from a process of repression and displacement
to which the scoptophilic instinct has been subjected. In
doing this he has referred in especial to the relation between
pleasure in looking, desire for knowledge, doubting and
brooding.

With the help of the analytical material at my disposal
I intend to investigate more closely the processes discussed
by Freud, and in certain respects to amplify his conclusions.
And in addition I shall consider certain parallel phenomena
of folk psychology.

In neurotics who suffer from a mania for questioning
and brooding we regularly find a diminution of sexual
activity. That activity has in extreme cases succumbed
completely to the brooding mania.[1] These people are as
helpless as children in the face of the important questions
of sexuality. Their interest has been diverted from the
sexual field and displaced on to other interests in a way that
may have momentous consequences for them.

The child's first sexual curiosity is directed to the body,
and especially to the genitals, of its parents, and then to the
processes of fecundation and birth. The fact that boys,
with whose behaviour we are here principally concerned,
direct their interest to a much greater degree upon the
mother than upon the father, is explicable not only on the
ground of difference of sex, but chiefly because of the
child's interest in the origin of children out of the mother's
body.

In its primitive curiosity the child desires to *see* these
organs or processes; a desire to *know* about them implies
that its scoptophilic instinct has already been subjected to

[1] This applies in the majority of cases to male patients. Among women the
mania for brooding is much rarer. But wherever I have found in women symptoms
of questioning mania or similar phenomena, there has regularly been an unusually
marked turning away from sexual interests.

restraint.   In many neurotics this limitation goes a good deal further, and even *knowing* about sexual matters falls under an interdict.   Numerous transformations of their scoptophilia ensue as a result of this, the most important of which have been dealt with by Freud in the paper already mentioned.   Von Winterstein [1] has also furnished valuable contributions to this question.

We will now discuss these transformative processes and their products.

We assume with Freud that a considerable part of the scoptophilia of a healthy person succumbs to repression and sublimation in childhood.   Some of the important psychological phenomena which owe their origin in a great part to this process are the desire for knowledge (in a general sense), the impulse towards investigation, interest in the observation of Nature, pleasure in travel, and the impulse towards artistic treatment of things perceived by the eye (for example, painting).

In many neurotics we have to assume a constitutional intensification of the scoptophilic instinct.   Nevertheless, the pleasure in looking can increase in importance as a result of an inhibition of sexual activity.   In that case, instead of active sexual behaviour there appears a greater tendency to look on inactively at things from a distance. The results of this neurotic pleasure in looking may be very diverse.   It may be in part preserved in its original form, in part altered through sublimation in the sense described above, and finally in part employed to form neurotic symptoms.   The stronger the instinct is, the greater must be the work of sublimation in order to prevent the development of neurotic disturbances, and the more severe will such disturbances be if the formation of symptoms does take place.   The sublimatory process may also take various directions.   I shall first of all discuss those neurotics who show a keen interest in knowledge or investigation of a concrete nature.   In this form of sublimation of scoptophilia the original instinct can sometimes be recognized without any special aids, but in other cases it requires

[1] ' Psychoanalytische Anmerkungen zur Geschichte der Philosophie ' (1913).

psycho-analytical methods to do this. The two following cases are particularly instructive.[1]

A very intelligent and cultivated neurotic man had a pronounced desire for universal scientific knowledge. In regard to his very active mental life he noticed that there was always one single problem which especially attracted him in each science which he took up. When I asked him to give an example he mentioned the following:

What interested him most in chemistry was the *status nascendi*. On going more closely into this it appeared that the moment in which a substance was formed or in which two substances united to form a new one had a positive fascination for him. His interest in procreation (combination of two substances in the formation of a new one) and in birth (*status nascendi*) had been displaced on to scientific problems in a successful way. He unconsciously discovered in each science the problem that was best suited to afford a veiled representation of the interests of his childhood. The field of palæontology supplied another very instructive example of this sublimatory tendency. The geological period termed pliocene—the period in which man first appeared—particularly engrossed his interest. The child's typical question concerning its own origin had been here sublimated to a general interest in the origin of the human race.

It would be easy to go on adding to the number of these examples. Those here quoted show that this form of sublimation has an important advantage for the neurotic, namely, that it brings him into close touch with phenomena of the external world. In other cases the repressed pleasure in looking is changed into an unproductive desire for knowledge which is not applied to real events.[2] This constitutes neurotic brooding, which might be termed a caricature of philosophic thinking.

[1] There is also an unproductive interest in concrete things which is not infrequently found in neurotics and represents nothing else than curiosity of an infantile character. In case A this curiosity became successfully resolved, and in its place there appeared a thoroughly productive and active interest in the phenomena of the external world.

[2] It is worth mentioning that as a rule under such conditions the person's pleasure in the aspects of Nature is very small, as is his interest in the various forms of visual art.

We owe to von Winterstein[1] some very excellent remarks on the unconscious motives of philosophic thinking. According to him the philosopher desires to see his own thoughts. His libido is no longer directed to the forbidden (incestuous) aim, no longer to that which one *must not* see, but to that which one *cannot* see. At the same time it has turned back upon the ego in a way which we can only comprehend as a regression to the position of infantile narcissism. I shall presently quote certain facts from one of my analyses which show clearly that a similar process takes place in the neurotic who is given to brooding. I shall eliminate as far as possible the question of narcissism in this connection so as not to overstep the bounds of my subject; and I shall restrict myself to the task of demonstrating the presence of traces of repressed incestuous scoptophilia in neurotic brooding and doubting.

As an example of neurotic brooding I will take a very common problem which recurs with the persistence of an obsession in some patients. This is the problem of the origin of thoughts. An obsessional neurotic of advanced age whom I was treating brooded over this subject for many years. It transpired that this problem had originally been immediately preceded by another one, namely, the question, ' Where shall I go after death ? ' This question had arisen in his mind during a sea voyage shortly after he had developed certain hypochondriacal fears about his life. He had been seized with the fear: 'If I were to die now during the voyage, will my body be buried at sea according to sailor custom ? ' He had wanted, that is, to be certain where he would go after death. Soon after this the second problem regarding the origin of thought had appeared, but it had not succeeded in entirely removing the earlier one.

The patient had attempted to elude the first problem by taking a practical measure. When his mother had died he had built a mausoleum. He now knew where—provided his burial in the mausoleum was not prevented by

[1] *Loc. cit.*

special circumstances—he was going to lie after his death,—at his mother's side.[1]

Without going into its manifold determinants I should like to say that the question, ' Where shall I go after death ? ' is a typical reversal of another question that is more interesting to the child: ' Where was I before I was born ? '   Moreover, in the present case analysis showed that the patient's chief obsessional thought, that regarding the origin of thoughts, was only another metamorphosis of this primary, infantile question.

The patient was not content with brooding and with abstract forms of thinking alone, but used to endeavour to get a visual image of how thoughts arose in the brain and how they ' come out ' of it.   He desired actually to *see* this process.   A young philosopher whom I treated psycho-analytically volunteered the following astonishingly simple explanation, ' I compare the brain to the womb '.   In the patient's desire to observe the origin of thoughts we can only see a displacement of the typical wish of the child to see with its own eyes the act of fecundation and birth.   I might remark that the comparison of mental and sexual products is not uncommon.   We speak, for instance, of the ' conception ' of a poetical work, etc.   If we advance still deeper in the analysis, we come upon the identification of birth and the act of defæcation, and thus to an equation of the products of the brain (thoughts) and those of the bowels.

It is of interest to note that the patient who was so much occupied in brooding over the origin of thoughts and where his body was to be after his death was surprisingly ignorant of certain important facts connected with the process of birth.   He had never surmounted his ignorance of the latter point and had displaced his desire for knowledge on to those problems over which he brooded.

There is another very common speculation in which

[1] I have had the opportunity of making a number of similar observations in which a son desired to be buried beside his mother, or a daughter beside her father, so that the other parent would be deprived of his or her natural place. An interesting example of this way of possessing the mother is afforded by the ancient Egyptian king, Achnaton.   Cf. my essay on Amenhotep [No. 34, A. B.].

the desire to see how human life begins undergoes another kind of inversion. This is not to ask after the origin but after the purpose of human life. This obsessive question, too, is insoluble in spite of the subject's attempts to answer it from a religious standpoint in a way satisfactory to his feeling. A young man, for instance, whom I was treating had been obsessed by this question for a long time during puberty. It turned out that he had a real terror of learning about the structure of the female body and about the sexual functions. In later years, too, anxiety and disgust had held him back when he had had the opportunity of looking at the female body. These affects referred particularly to looking at the genital region. When the patient came for treatment and found that sexual processes were talked about in psycho-analysis, he expressly begged me to give him for the present no ' explanations ' about what he did not know. The analysis very clearly showed that his scoptophilic instinct, which was inhibited by such strong affects, was directed in his unconscious to his mother.

The problems of the obsessional neurotic are always insoluble. The question which in fact he wants to ask is not *allowed* to be answered; the question which takes its place *cannot* be answered; and thus the secret is kept. There exists in the patient a permanent conflict between two parties, one of which would like to investigate and know the facts while the other strives to remain ignorant of them.

We now see why brooding-mania and sexual ignorance are so regularly found together. But as a further reason for this connection it may be said that for many neurotics the secret itself has more pleasure-value than its disclosure. I have alluded to this already. Occasionally one meets patients who suffer seriously from their ignorance and yet cannot free themselves from it. I had a case of a young man of twenty-eight, for instance, who suffered from severe states of agitation. The content of his thoughts in these states was quite conscious. It was: ' Everybody knows; I alone am kept from knowing '. ' Knowing ' signified to him not only knowledge of sexual matters but, in the first place, ' seeing ' and sexual activity. It is quite evident that he who avoids sexual enlightenment is entirely withdrawn from sexual activity. On one occasion this patient left a piece of paper in my consulting-room; it was covered with a medley of unintelligible and disconnected phrases. In the centre of the paper in large writing were the words, ' I don't know '. It was in this phrase that he used to express the whole torment of his ignorance. In his states of agitation he used to run round the room shouting the same words. And he used to write them on sheets of paper and surround them with all sorts of curses. I was only able to see this patient for a few sittings, but they were sufficient to give me a certain insight into his unconscious mind. It became evident that his libido was fixated in an incestuous way to a degree which was astonishing even to a psycho-analyst. For purposes of comparison I will mention a fact of folk psychology, to which von Winterstein [1] has already referred. In Biblical Hebrew the word to ' know ' is also used for the sexual act. A man is said to ' know ' his wife. The preliminary sexual act of looking at a woman by means of which a man gets to know her is used here in place of the final act itself. The words used in the Mosaic Law in reference to incest are particularly interesting: among all the many prohibitions it is not *intercourse* between blood-relatives which is forbidden, but it is said that the man must not ' uncover the shame ' of this or that woman. The prohibition of uncovering and viewing the object is an extension of the simple prohibition of incestuous intercourse. It corresponds in this respect to the strict prohibition against looking with which many neurotics protect themselves not merely from the sight of the actual prohibited thing but from exercising any kind of sexual activity.

An investigation into the inhibitions of looking and knowing is incomplete without adequate consideration of the phenomenon of doubt. In doing this I shall once more have recourse to Freud's illuminating discussion of the subject. According to him the obsessional neurotic

[1] *Loc. cit.*

feels a *need* for uncertainty. He retreats from reality, from everything palpable or certain, and is unconsciously urged to maintain and cultivate his uncertainty and artificially to create new uncertainties. His doubt proceeds from an inner perception of his own conflict of thought. What he really doubts, therefore, is the trustworthiness of his own feelings, and he has a great tendency to displace this uncertainty on to objects and processes in the external world. In doing this he usually seizes upon those things which are actually subjected to doubt, as, for instance, memory, or the duration of life.

We are here reminded of the phenomena of brooding mania, which are very similar to those of doubting mania. We saw that the man who broods withdraws his interest from the world of concrete things, of things perceptible to the senses, and applies it to insoluble problems. The brooder unconsciously seeks to preserve his ignorance just as the doubter endeavours to maintain his uncertainty. This explains why doubts and brooding usually exist together in the same individual. It is also obvious that every inhibition of scoptophilia and of the desire for knowledge—which we regard as inseparable from scoptophilia—not merely promotes brooding on abstract subjects but also doubt. Doubting mania finds, as it were, increased points of attack if the individual is unable to direct his mind and thoughts towards real things. Again, his feelings of uncertainty urge the neurotic to a constant renewal of his brooding; he has to examine again and again the train of thought which he has already gone over a thousand times.

The neurotic patient has various methods of eluding the tortures of his doubting and brooding mania. Although, as we have seen, he strives unconsciously to preserve the cause of his sufferings, he shows at the same time the opposite tendency to do away with his uncertainty and to banish his doubt and ignorance. But he cannot, of course, succeed in doing this of his own strength and by his own methods. He is obliged to rely on authority and to submit to the knowledge and opinions of others; but in this way he puts the responsibility upon them. Many obsessional neurotics like to burden their physician with a responsibility of this kind. If they are unable to come to a decision on a particular matter, they will try to get the physician to pronounce some judgement and so remove their indecision. In this way they alter the situation in such a manner that it appears as if no doubt existed at all.

In this place I must make a digression and consider certain phenomena of folk psychology which are apparently not directly associated with the scoptophilic instinct, but an understanding of which is indispensable for the further course of our investigation. In folk psychology devices for removing doubt are found which are quite similar in their mechanism to the neurotic behaviour described above.

I will start with the peculiar and, as I believe, almost unremarked fact that in the Hebrew language of the Biblical writings there is no word for 'to doubt'.[1] And it must not be forgotten that those writings originate from very different periods. It is a fact worth noticing that such a word should be missing from the language of the people who first attained to a monotheistic religion; and still more so, when we consider that the languages and dialects of neighbouring peoples possessed a suitable expression, so that borrowing could easily have taken place. The fluctuation between the monotheistic cult and the worship of Baal, Astarte, and other deities of Asia Minor lasted for centuries, until finally the cult of a single male God obtained the victory. It has been pointed out above that in the Biblical myth of the Creation there is a tendency to ascribe everything to the work of the male God and of man, and to put the woman in a very secondary place. This is in complete accordance with the patriarchal system in which the sole power was vested in the male head of the family.[2] The women and children belonged to him just like all his other goods, animate and inanimate.

[1] I shall deal with an exception later.
[2] Von Winterstein deals in his above-quoted work (S. 192) with this question of the suppression of the female element. At the time of its appearance I had already arrived at the above results, which I found fully confirmed by von Winterstein.

I must now refer to Freud's views,[1] which show in a convincing manner the origin of the male god from the attitude of the son towards the father. Originally the son's affection is directed towards his mother, while he has feelings of revolt and hostility towards his father. One of the earliest acts of repression which civilization demands is a renunciation of this hostile attit de. At first the son stood between father and mother; the repression of his Oedipus attitude then caused him to decide in favour of his father and unreservedly to acknowledge his power. Patriarchy in particular makes rigorous demands on the son in this respect. And just as in the patriarchal family the conflict in the son is decided unconditionally in favour of the father, so it is in the monotheistic religion of the Old Testament.

The non-existence of a word for doubt in the Hebrew language might be regarded as an isolated phenomenon without especial interest if the same language did not show a second characteristic defect. A word signifying goddess is also missing, whereas other languages possess such a word. It might almost be said that in the same way as the conflict in the son, conditioned by his original doubtful position between father and mother, has been got rid of, so the question whether a god or a goddess should be venerated has been decided: and that now the language behaves not only as though this doubt no longer existed but as though *all doubt whatever had ceased to exist in the human mind*.

A good deal of light is thrown upon this problem of the psychology of speech if we consider that in a great number of languages the word *zweifeln* [' to doubt '] is connected with the number *zwei* [' two ']. These languages, at any rate, do not deny the existence of doubt. Indeed, many even make use of a special grammatical construction in order to express doubt. We have only to think of the multiplicity of grammatical forms in Latin where the verb ' to doubt ' requires special constructions which are otherwise hardly used.

[1] *Totem und Tabu*, Kap. iv., 1913.

It is only in one of the late Biblical documents, Psalm cxix, that a word is found which can be correctly translated by ' doubter '; strictly speaking, it means ' one who is divided '.   According to the opinion of experts this Psalm belongs to a late period when Hellenistic influences had already begun to be felt.[1]   A second word with the same significance, probably having originally the meaning of ' divided' or ' split ', is found in still later Hebrew literature. It is very remarkable that a language more than two thousand years old should have expressed itself in the same way as the psychology of to-day, which speaks of a ' psychical splitting '.   A ' split ' suggests an internal conflict more clearly even than those designations for doubt which are connected with the word ' two '.[2]   Once having borrowed two words from another language which admitted the existence of doubt, it became necessary to get rid of doubt in another way.   A simple means was found.   If, for example, it was doubtful whether a particular action was permitted or forbidden, the harsher view was regularly taken.   The decision was made in accordance with the prohibition which was laid down in similar cases by the highest (divine) authority.   At bottom this practice is equivalent to a denial of doubt.

I shall now go on to give one or two especially remarkable observations which I have been able to make during the psycho-analysis of a complicated case of brooding and doubting mania.   But I shall only discuss those factors of the case which are connected with the repression of scoptophilia, and shall merely mention in passing other important sources of the symptom-formation, such as narcissism and sadism.

The patient in question had had feelings of uncertainty quite early on in his life.   As a boy he used to torment everybody with his mania for asking questions, and later on had worried himself with doubts on every possible

[1] Cf. Baethgen, *Die Psalmen*, 1897.
[2] This ' inner perception of uncertainty ' (Freud) finds a curious and striking expression in an ancient American language, the Nahuatl.   This language expressed doubt by means of the word *omeyolloa* (' two hearts ').   [Cf. the English expression ' to be in two minds about a thing '.—*Trans.*]

subject. He doubted his intelligence, his 'ability' in every respect, his memory and his judgement. He doubted his manliness, and when he was a child he used to doubt whether he ought to behave like a boy or a girl. His affections had oscillated between his father and mother. When he first became acquainted with two young girls he did not know which of them he was in love with. His whole life was a labyrinth of doubt which he sought in vain to overcome by the power of reason. He too had recourse to the subterfuge of delegating all decisions to an authority. In one instance he tried to kill his doubt in a very curious way. As a university student he came across a man whom he had heard speak in Berlin. This man's lectures and writings had previously aroused in him severe doubts and brooding. He had partly succeeded in getting away from this influence, but he was afraid that if he once again heard the man his influence would be renewed. He endeavoured to save himself from the dilemma by inciting his acquaintances to scoff at the speaker during a meeting. I might incidentally remark that this act was also an expression of a hatred which he felt for every person in authority, as he had originally felt it for his father.

The facts which psycho-analysis elicited regarding the patient's childhood showed that his sexual curiosity and scoptophilia had originally been unusually strong and had only gradually given way to his questioning and brooding mania. Educational influences had been especially active in bringing about this change, and in particular the direct prohibition against asking questions which he had received from his mother at puberty when his desire for sexual knowledge had been re-awakened. This had accentuated the suppression of his desire for knowledge in the years that followed. When his neurosis appeared a whole number of symptoms showed that his incestuous pleasure in looking was striving to break through the repression. His dreams also betrayed the same tendency. At the beginning of treatment the patient, who had occupied himself with philosophical studies, stated that as a schoolboy he had envied Pythagoras. The cause of his envy was that according to his own assertion Pythagoras had witnessed his own birth three times. The patient's most intense interest was still associated with the child's question: ' Where did I come from ? '

As we have said above, what the child really wants is to *see* where it comes from. The neurotic patient who is given to brooding has taken this childish interest along with him into a later period of life; his greatest wish is to see with his own eyes his own birth out of his mother's body.

In the present patient the early forcing away of his scoptophilic instinct from its real objects and aims led not only to a typical brooding, but also to a morbid propensity towards secret and mystical things. The tendency we have already spoken of to cultivate and preserve the mysterious found expression in the eagerness with which he used to devour mystical, theosophical, and spiritual writings at a very youthful age. This tendency came into conflict with an opposing one of wanting to see with his eyes what could only be thought about. The desire to be able to see his thoughts was especially pronounced in him. He pictured mental processes in the most naive fashion, endowing them with physical and spatial properties. He thought of the brain as having compartments and pigeon-holes in which thoughts were deposited, and from which they occasionally emerged; and his brooding was chiefly occupied with these processes. He also of course had a desire to see supernatural things. He would brood endlessly over the problem of what ghosts and spirits looked like and what God looked like. Then inhibitions would arise and forbid him to think of such things.

I need hardly refer to the countless similar phenomena that are to be found in folk psychology—on the one hand, secret cults, mysteries, occultist movements, etc., and on the other, religious prohibitions against inquiring into the most secret things.

Concerning the significance of ghosts, which played a very great part in the patient's thoughts, one of the factors that came out is familiar to us from other psycho-analyses.

His brooding about ghosts was traceable to certain childhood impressions he had received at night. Here, as in
other cases, parents in their white night clothes are the
prototypes of the child's conception of these mysterious
forms. Into however distorted and phantastic a shape the
thing observed had been fashioned by this patient's childish
imagination, we can nevertheless recognize that he was on
the right road to the formation of a correct conclusion.
When later the prohibition against looking and knowing
had obtained a hold over him, his repressed wish for a
repetition of the pleasurable impressions of childhood was
displaced on to ' ghosts '. He longed all the time to see
ghosts. He went still further and transferred on to his
brooding over ghosts all his desire for knowledge concerning
the mystery of procreation.

One of the problems which obsessed him for years was,
' How do ghosts come into a closed room?' I pass over
the highly interesting determinants of the patient's various
attempts to solve this question, and will only mention that
behind that insoluble substitute-problem were concealed
two problems the solution of which was forbidden, namely,
the questions, ' How does the man penetrate the female
body?' and, ' How does the child get into the womb?'
What made the questions forbidden ones was their ultimate
connection with his father and mother, and especially his
originally pleasurable desire to see what was kept secret.

His repressed pleasure in looking, however, not only
sought a substitute-gratification in brooding, but took
other means to this end. Those means are of great interest,
and we must therefore consider them in greater detail,
particularly as in doing so we shall gain valuable insight
into the origin of certain phenomena of folk psychology.

Like many people, the patient was able to visualize
with pictorial clearness persons and processes, etc., about
which he was thinking. In many neurotics simply shutting
the eyes is sufficient to induce these visions, while others
call up these ' pictures ' intentionally and amuse themselves
with them as though they were at a theatre. This capacity
seems to exist in every one in childhood, but disappears in

many as they grow older. It should therefore not necessarily be concluded that a man does not belong to the ' visual ' type if he does not have such pictorial accompaniments of his thought. For it is more probable that there is an inhibition of his scoptophilic instinct resulting from a repression.

Since his wish to see ' ghosts ' could not be fulfilled, the patient attempted to procure a substitute by means of voluntarily evoked visions. And it is highly significant that what he endeavoured to visualize was his parents. But he did not succeed in the way he wished. The picture of his mother did not appear at all, and that of his father only in a distorted form. On the other hand, he easily succeeded in visualizing the appearance of other relatives. Both his attempts to obtain a substitute-gratification for his incestuous pleasure in looking, and the failure of those attempts, are worth noting.

After having observed a similar phenomenon in a number of other cases, I have come to the conclusion that greater importance should be attached to it. Many neurotics attempt to conjure up a vision of their parents, or at least to represent their appearance as distinctly as possible to themselves. One of my female patients, whose fixation on her father was most marked, could not succeed in visualizing him. In another case it was very difficult for the patient, a man, to portray clearly the features of his mother. He succeeded better with those of his father; but as soon as the picture of his father appeared the face became distorted and the eyes took on a fixed stare. In this case it turned out that the patient's scoptophilia directed towards his mother had undergone very intense repression, whereas his death-phantasy directed against his father had not been equally successfully repressed and found utterance in the rigid look of the eyes in his father's image.

It is as though in these persons a prohibition was at work strictly circumscribing their scoptophilic instinct. A dream of a neurotic young girl furnished me with a good illustration of this. The dreamer found herself in a church among many other people who were looking at a picture of the Madonna. She alone could not see the picture. Analysis disclosed the presence of a strong homosexual tendency in her directed towards her mother. This inclination had been changed in general into an intense repugnance, but it used occasionally to appear in its original form with great violence. Her mother was a particularly beautiful woman, and her daughter had to secure herself against those forbidden attractions by means of a regular prohibition against looking.

In a recent publication [1] Freud has drawn our attention to certain phenomena common to the mental life of neurotics and savages. What interests us most in this place is the analogy between certain obsessional prohibitions in neurotics and the so-called taboos of certain peoples. These taboos have the characteristic peculiarity that the people who obey them can give no reason for doing so. In the same way neurotics who succumb to the obsessional prohibition in question are unable to furnish a reason for it. It is interesting to note the agreement between the neurotic looking-prohibition and the second commandment of the Decalogue, which strictly forbids the setting up of an image of the only (paternal) God. Freud has attempted to give a brief explanation of this prohibition on other lines.[1] The explanation given here is not in opposition to his but rather supplements it in accordance with the recognized over-determination of all psychological products. After I had practically completed the present paper I found in a recent publication by Storfer [2] an explanation of the second commandment based on the same view as my own. Storfer endeavours to trace back the prohibition of setting up an image of God to the dread of the paternal phallus, on the grounds that so many images of gods and cultural emblems bear a phallic character. This explanation seems to me to be in agreement with many of the ideas brought forward in this paper. Nevertheless it requires more thorough study and verification by the methods of comparative mythology.

[1] ' Animismus, Magie und Allmacht der Gedanken ' (1913).
[2] *Marias jungfräuliche Mutterschaft*, 1914, S. 32.

This parallel between phenomena of individual and folk psychology can be traced yet further. As has already been said, the patient in question was disturbed by constant doubt and uncertainty which referred among other things to his parents. In his relations to them doubt and prohibitions against looking at their image both played an important rôle. Now if we look more closely at the Decalogue we see that the commandment to recognize only one God and the commandment to make no image of him are in immediate juxtaposition. Psycho-analysis of a great number of mental products of every variety has led us to the conclusion that the immediate proximity of two mental elements points to an internal connection between them. And so it is worth noting that the prohibition against images immediately follows the commandment to recognize only one god, *i.e.* the commandment designed to eliminate all hesitation (doubt) between the father and the mother.

The analysis of individual psychological products throws a new light on this subject. Let us return to the patient who felt that he ought not to make an image of his parents, and see what he did in order to find a substitute for the prohibited act. He endeavoured with the whole power of his imagination to represent to himself the appearance of ghosts which, as we know, stood for his parents in his brooding system. That his ultimate desire was to represent to himself sexual intercourse between his parents was made quite clear from the ideas he had formed as to what ghosts looked like. To quote his own expression, he conceived them as ' big naked beings ', as ' voluptuous forms '.[1]

As we have already said, the patient found abundant material for brooding in a certain class of literature, especially that of a theosophical character. In connection with what he had read there he identified his parents not merely with ghosts but also with ' giants '. He had found in one of these books the statement that the inhabitants of the submerged continent Atlantis had been giants, and that

[1] The evocation of such ideas or visionary appearances subserved other tendencies to which I can only briefly allude here. Among other things they were a gratification of the infantile grandiose idea of being able to procure everything by the power of imagination (omnipotence of thoughts).

they had had a higher form of consciousness than ourselves
—*i.e.* an astral consciousness—and that they had hence
been initiated into secrets which were hidden from us.
The book stated that 'their knowledge was so great that
the earth *resounded* with it'. These giants immediately
assumed the significance of parents to the patient. They
' knew ' more than he did, that is, they were in possession
of the sexual secret. The child, however, had attempted
not only to see that secret with its eyes but to hear it with
its ears. He had obviously made the same equation which
we met with as a linguistic phenomenon: he had identified
' knowledge ' with sexual intercourse.

It was furthermore characteristic that the patient had
attempted to imagine God as a material being. We shall
not be surprised to learn that he thought of God as a giant
also. In phantasy the child ascribes extraordinary power
to the father. It is very apt to compare him to a giant on
account of his great superiority of size, as the dreams of
adults often still show. When a child hears about God
it can only represent him in the likeness of its father; it
does neither more nor less than those religion-forming
peoples who venerate a paternal god. And in pondering
over the appearance of God, our patient was only once
more repeating the attempt to break through the prohibition
against looking at his father.

How well the neurotic prohibition against representing
the father or both parents pictorially and the Biblical
prohibition against portraying God agree in their essence
is evident from the fact that both prohibitions are trans-
gressed in an identical manner. I have in mind here one
of the typical brooding questions so frequently found in
the writings of the Talmud. The prohibition against a
concrete representation of God might not be infringed;
and when for some reason or other men felt themselves
obliged to give their idea of God a more living and material
content, they had to have recourse to brooding. This
need, together with the strict observance of the visual
prohibition, explains the Talmudic question concerning the
bodily dimensions of God. The question could, however,

only be answered by keeping strictly to the statements found in the Scriptures. In them is contained the pronouncement made by God, ' Heaven is my throne and the earth is my footstool ', from which it was inferred that his legs were so long that they reached from heaven to earth. This kind of brooding resembles that of our patient in an astonishing way, not merely because the repressed wish to visualize God, *i.e.* to look at him, recurs in it, but because the infantile idea of the giant form of the father or God is once more found.

It is thus evident that there is an unmistakable analogy between the inhibitions of the scoptophilic instinct in neurotic individuals and in primitive peoples; and I shall now proceed to show that psycho-analysis affords us a yet deeper insight into the nature of this parallel.

v. *The Origin of Sun and Ghost Phobias from Infantile Totemism*

In the course of our present discussion we have met with two symbols to which we have had to ascribe a preponderant father significance—the sun and ghosts. We have seen that certain neurotics are distressed by sunlight or react with affects of rebellion or defiance at the sight of the sun in a manner that differs from the conduct of a healthy person; and we have learned that in each case these neurotic patients had an ambivalent emotional attitude towards the sun. They loved and reverenced the sun, but had at the same time a dread of it. In speaking of the latter condition I have definitely called it a sun phobia. Among neurotic brooders we found a particular interest in spiritistic phenomena. Ghosts or the idea of them also called forth ambivalent reactions—the wish to see them and the dread of their appearance—which we might call a ghost phobia. If we accept the sun and ghosts as symbols of the father, and if we are familiar with the ambivalent attitude of the neurotic towards his father, we shall not be astonished to find this division of feeling transferred to the symbols representing the father. Psycho-analysis, however, cannot be content with this knowledge. As a theory of development which sets out to demonstrate the strict determination of all mental products it must inquire further into the origin of those phenomena. In order to obtain access to the origin of these symbols we must make use of that key which Freud has given us in his paper on *Totem und Tabu*.

We find even at the present time in certain tribes whose civilization is very primitive an organization which regulates their religious and social life. It is called *totemism*, and is a form of ancestor cult. The central point of the cult is the totem, generally an animal, which is regarded as the original ancestor of the clan concerned. Freud has been able to show that these primitive peoples have an ambivalent attitude towards their totem. They will not hunt, kill, eat, or even touch the totem animal, *i.e.* in general they will preserve it; but under special circumstances they will kill and eat it with elaborate ceremonial. The totem is the object both of their love and their fear. Many customs of these people clearly indicate their double attitude towards the totem.

Psycho-analytical investigation [1] has brought to light the remarkable fact that under the conditions of civilization of to-day the totemistic attitude still reappears in the mental life of the child, and leaves behind unmistakable traces in the unconscious of the individual. Certain products of children's phantasy bear an extraordinary resemblance to the totemistic system of primitive peoples. A child who often openly displays an ambivalent attitude towards its father or mother, will frequently displace its feelings from them on to a certain animal or class of animals, or sometimes on to several such classes. It shows interest and love for this animal which is equivalent to a totem. But in its day dreams and night dreams the same object plays the part of an anxiety-animal. If the child develops a phobia, as so often happens, it is this animal which is usually the object of its anxiety. In not a few cases the animal retains its significance even later on, and appears in the phobias of adult neurotics just as it does in children.

[1] Cf. Freud's references to his sources in his work quoted above.

I have made a considerable number of observations relative to this, though I cannot give them in detail in this place. I shall select one or two only on which to base the remarks which follow. In the first place, the ambivalence of their attitude towards their totem (the feared animal) is obvious to many of the patients themselves. One of my cases, a woman who suffered from a slowly progressive hebephrenia, gave me, with that freedom from inhibition which is characteristic of such patients, most precise and instructive information concerning this and other important points of individual totemism. In her case the fly played the main part as an anxiety-animal. On one occasion she volunteered the information that her feelings towards flies were ' full of love ', but that at the same time she had an impulse to kill them.

It is also important to note that especially in dreams a particular animal may often represent not only the father (or mother) but the patient himself. In a dream of this kind which I came across, three generations—the father of the dreamer, the dreamer himself, and his son—were all represented by the same symbolic animal—the dog. This corresponds to the very common hereditary totemism of primitive peoples.

I next refer to another individual parallel to the primitive totemic cult. This is concerned with plant-totemism, which, though rarer than animal-totemism, is occasionally observed. A neurotic who was constantly fleeing from his incestuous desire for his mother, showed in his waking phantasies and in his dreams all the phenomena of tree-totemism. In the garden of a small château where he lived as a boy there was a very large old tree which he regarded with religious awe; he used to pray to it and receive oracles from its rustling sounds.[1] His defence against his incestuous wishes was associated with severe anxiety. He was pursued by continual unrest and could not settle down anywhere. In his waking dreams he seemed to be a tree standing in the parental garden, surrounded by other trees (his relatives) near the big oracle

[1] Cf. in this connection the oracle of Dodona.

tree (his father), and to have taken firm root there. It seems to me that the repression of his incestuous desires demanded extraordinary measures so that his parents could not be symbolized by an animal. They had to be symbolized by a tree, which is sexually undifferentiated. This may throw some light on the totemism of certain primitive tribes, where the totem is not, as in most cases, an animal, but a plant.

When we view infantile animal phobias and neurotic totemic symptoms we are struck by one fact which has hitherto found little or no consideration. In some of these cases the totem is a four-legged animal whose size and strength make it at once clear why it should be identified by the child with the mighty father. But in a considerable number of cases we find that the anxiety-animal is the smallest kind of animal known to the child, such as flies, wasps, butterflies, caterpillars, etc. The same thing occurs in a number of neurotics. The actual dangerousness of such animals is not a sufficient explanation of this form of infantile totemism, for only certain of them are at all injurious; others are quite harmless, and the child is able to kill them without risk. According to the evidence of my psycho-analyses of neurotics there seems to be a simpler and better explanation. These animals have the characteristic of making a sudden appearance. They approach all of a sudden, touch the human body unexpectedly, and disappear with equal rapidity. Of course individual determinants enter into every case. For instance, in one of my patients the wasp had replaced another animal, the tiger. The colour and marking of the wasp reminded the patient of the tiger, and its buzzing could represent the tiger's roar, which latter sound was associated with the child's dread of the deep, threatening voice of his father when he was angry. This patient spontaneously said that the sound of a wasp flying about with its threatening buzz was associated in his mind with feelings of rage. My psycho-analytic experience leads me to believe that small animals have a manifold significance. They represent the father who surprises the child by suddenly appearing near it or by alarming it with a threatening voice. It is also characteristic of these animals that they disappear quickly and can be killed more easily than big ones. Thus these small flying animals [1] indicate on the one hand the dangerous power of the father, but serve on the other as an expression for the child's ideas of getting rid of him. These are the same animals that we meet with in mythology as ' spirit animals '. Patient E, whom we have already often mentioned, gave me quite freely considerable information about the infantilism which still persisted in him, and drew my attention among other things to his ambivalent attitude towards flies. He said that he used to amuse himself with killing flies and wasps in his childhood.

In this place I must give further details from his psycho-analysis. (I may remark that certain phenomena which are also found in other patients were manifested in him in a quite undisguised form.) When he had killed a fly or a wasp he always became a prey to anxiety lest the dead fly should revenge itself upon him. This piece of information, spontaneously given by the patient, is of great importance. It concerns an individual psychological process which fully coincides with the fear of the dead found among primitive people. In his discussion of the taboo of the dead, Freud has analysed this unexplained element and has shown that the hostile impulses which one human being feels towards another while he is alive become repressed after his death through the appearance of opposite impulses of mourning and grief and are projected on to the dead person, who now becomes dangerous to those still alive and able, so to speak, to drag them after him. This patient, too, had 'loving' feelings towards the animal he had killed; at the same time his murderous intentions were projected on to the killed animals, with the result that he was afraid of their revenge.

During the treatment the same patient had a dream in which he was about to attack a tiger with a pole. Then (I pass over a great many details of the dream) the animal

[1] Small crawling animals (caterpillars, etc.) are like flying ones in that they suddenly appear on the child's body and thus excite fear.

was suddenly taken up into heaven, so that the patient did not succeed in killing it.

Here we meet with the important element of translation into heaven. It concerns an object to which the patient's attitude was ambivalent, and the process is one with which we are already familiar. I need only call to mind patient B,[1] who, in a phantasy bordering on a delusion, elevated his dead father to the sky and placed him next the sun. We must conclude, therefore, that symbolization of the father through the sun represents a heavenly translation of this kind, the motivation of which no longer presents any difficulty, since we can ascribe it to the ambivalent attitude of the son towards his father.

I shall again refer to the spontaneous statements of patient E, which he made in the form of free associations. According to them, his father (tiger, wasp) was raised to heaven in order that he (the son) should be removed as far as possible from the dangerous animal. An idea immediately followed which confirmed the correctness of his view. The patient described the method by which, as a boy, he had kept as far away as possible from wasps and flies when he was killing them. Too timid to attack directly, he used to fasten a lighted candle on a long pole and bring it near an insect on the window pane, till the creature fell down dead or helpless.[2] The further away the animal, *i.e.* the totem or father, the less risk he ran from it; and at the same time the totem was exalted from an earthly plane to higher regions. This process must now be investigated in greater detail.

The ambivalent significance of a translation of the totem to heaven is illustrated in a specially instructive manner by the following example from the nursery. Two children with very imaginative minds used often to watch the clouds, and to give them names. These names, which, for professional reasons, I must abstain from quoting, could easily be seen to contain a condensation of two elements—an

[1] Cf. p. 186.
[2] This explains the ' pole ' with which the patient was about to kill the tiger in the sky.

obvious distortion of the words ' papa ' and ' mama ', and the word ' animal '. In this naive way their father and mother were first represented as animals and then taken up into the sky in the shape of unearthly forms (clouds). This example is the more interesting since both children were discovered to have an ambivalent attitude towards their parents; they showed, on the one hand, tenderness and respect towards them, but, on the other, tended to turn them, especially the father, into figures of fun.

A short time ago I was able to analyse a dream of a neurotic woman in which admiration and respect for her father (as a sublimation of a strong erotic fixation) and also death-wishes against him were expressed in a very characteristic manner. He was represented by an enormous chandelier hanging in the sky, composed of innumerable stars and surrounded by a great number of phallic symbols.

In all these products of individual phantasy, whether they are the thoughts of children at play, the dreams of adults, or the fears of neurotics, we perceive the same mental processes that go on in folk psychology and underlie the development of religion. I shall only refer in this place to those mythological products in which traces of the translation of the totem to heaven can be seen in an almost undisguised form, as, for instance, the lightning-bird of the Indians, the sun-cow of the Egyptians and the cloud-tree of the whole Indo-Germanic mythology.

The effects of this elevation of the father or mother to the sky are numerous. I shall begin by discussing the representation of the father by means of the sun symbol. In view of what we know about the ambivalent character of the process, we may separate those effects into two groups.

The first group is connected with the friendly, loving feelings which are turned towards the father, and the acknowledgement of his paternal power. The symbolic representation of the father by the sun obviously signifies a great enhancement of his power. All life around us is dependent on the sun. Through identification with the sun the father is literally raised into the principle of all life, and particular emphasis is laid on the recognition of his procreative powers. Doubt and unbelief can no longer assail his might. Since, however, one of the properties of the sun is that it outlives earthly beings, eternal life and indestructibility are ascribed to him through his identification with it. Placed in the sky as the sun he is able to observe all things, while his dazzling light hides him from his son's view. At the same time he is placed out of reach of the latter's aggressive desires. He is raised above them, as in the saying about the moon which need not be troubled by the baying of the dog.

But all this power is only a seeming one. For, as Freud has convincingly demonstrated in his essay on totemism, it is to the dead, or rather to the murdered, father that translation to heaven and elevation to the level of a deity is accorded. The results of psycho-analysis justify us in coming to the conclusion that it is only when he thinks of him as a dead person, or wishes him to be so, that the son elevates his father to the level of a sun-god. These death phantasies give expression to impulses of hate, hostility, and jealousy on the part of the son. They rob the father of his power, so that he is in reality helpless and harmless. An omnipotent power is then subsequently granted him as a compensation.

I should like to recall the fact that mankind not only transplants his deities and other powerful beings into the sky, but that, according to an idea which is still prevalent, human beings themselves 'go to heaven' after death. The mental life of the individual gives rise to similar products. A dream will illustrate this: During a certain period of his treatment one of my patients had a number of dreams which gave expression to his unconscious incestuous impulses. After having dreamed many times that he had raped his step-mother, he had a dream whose content apparently differed from the previous dreams, but in reality formed a complement to them. In this dream he climbed up a ladder into heaven. There he found God sitting on his throne; but his face was that of his father. Analysis showed among other things that the patient had placed his father in heaven, *i.e.* had removed him from among the living. He had exalted him into a god, but in doing so had only in appearance increased his power. He himself climbed up to the same height as his father in his dream. Climbing up ladders is a frequent coitus symbol, which is used here in the sense of an incest-wish. The patient takes possession symbolically of his step-mother, because his father is no longer living. The divine power of his father is ineffective and cannot hinder him from carrying out his intentions.

With reference to this dream, in which the son contests the right of a father who is elevated into God, it is worth while remarking that any such elevation raises the son as well and makes him powerful like his father. It is sufficient to allude to certain royal dynasties and priestly castes who, in order to enhance their power, style themselves sons of the sun.[1]

Now that we have succeeded in understanding the sun phobia, the ghost phobia can be solved without special difficulty. The ghost is the 'dead' father. If he is represented by the sun, then it becomes unbearable to look at. If he is transformed into a ghost, then he is as a rule invisible; and his unexpected appearance excites violent anxiety. According to my observations, which nevertheless need supplementing in this direction, many neurotics seem at first to have a dread of sunlight or light, and only later acquire a dread of ghosts. With the advance of the repression of their scoptophilia the symbol which represents the father or mother has always to become more and more incorporeal. One of my patients produced within a short period two dreams, in one of which his father appeared as light, while in the other he appeared as a ghost. In the first of these dreams the patient was in school (which he had left several years before). The headmaster, who in other dreams played a pronounced father-rôle, came into the class-room and spoke to him. At first the patient defiantly opposed his orders, but later he had to obey them, while there appeared over the master's head a blinding light,

---

[1] I might briefly mention that in many neurotics the father is not represented by the sun, but by lightning, i.e. by another phenomenon of light in the sky. Lightning here more especially represents the punishing (killing) power of the father.

at the sight of which the patient fainted. Whereas in this dream the paternal power was represented by a blinding light, the same purpose was served by the ghost in the other dream. What was noticeable in this case was that it was the white form of the ghost which dazzled the dreamer. Ghosts are generally thought of as white, but faint and pale in appearance. The phobia of ghosts is most marked among neurotic doubters, who, as we have seen, show a tendency to substitute what is indefinite, indistinct, and non-material for what is clear and solid and perceptible to the senses.

Those who have psycho-analytical experience themselves will easily recognize that these remarks in no way exhaust the extensive field with which they are concerned. No doubt much more could be added to the collection of the phenomena here analyzed, but I have aimed at the greatest possible conciseness in this study. I have omitted to consider many aspects of the question which might have contributed further to the explanation of the symptoms, and have only given others the merest mention. The fragmentary character of my remarks may, however, help to show how much further investigation of the symptoms is still needed. The line that such an inquiry will have to follow will be in the sense of our concepts of the 'component-instincts' and the 'erotogenic zones'—concepts which have become indispensable to our understanding of the subject; and in my present paper I have tried to demonstrate this in the case of one particular component-instinct and one particular erotogenic zone.

CHAPTER X

A CONSTITUTIONAL BASIS OF LOCOMOTOR ANXIETY [1] (1913)

THOSE who have investigated the psychogenesis of locomotor anxiety with the help of Freudian methods have regularly met with certain factors operating in the formation of this trouble, so that they have been bound to regard them as typical for that illness. They were, of course, well aware that the neurotic who needs the constant company of particular persons shows the incestuous fixation of his libido in a particularly marked degree, and that every attempt he makes to separate himself from his love-object signifies in his unconscious an attempt to detach his libido from it. They have recognized, furthermore, that the anxiety such a person feels causes him suffering on the one hand, but, on the other, enables him to exert his power over the persons about him. Further typical determinants of his 'topophobia' are the subject's fear of life—symbolically represented by streets—and in particular, his fear of the temptations which beset him as soon as he leaves the protection of his parental home. There is also his dread of death which might overtake him unawares when he is away from the people he loves.

The knowledge of these determinants—and many others could be added—increases our understanding of street anxiety, but it does not completely solve the problem. It is still obscure why in a fairly large group of neurotics it should be precisely movement away from a place that is

---

[1] [No. 44, A. B.]

rendered difficult through anxiety. The fixation of the patient's libido on particular persons in his immediate vicinity is not in itself a sufficient cause, otherwise we should expect that a much greater number of neurotics would suffer from street anxiety than is actually the case. And the other psychosexual factors mentioned above also operate in the formation of neurotic illnesses which do not exhibit locomotor anxiety.

We are therefore bound to conclude that there must be a specific factor present in the sexual constitution of neurotics who suffer from locomotor anxiety—a factor which does not affect all neurotics alike, and which, combined with other psychosexual factors of the kind described above, favours the appearance of street anxiety and similar affections.

The psycho-analysis of a case of severe street anxiety has enabled me to form a definite opinion on the matter, which I shall proceed to discuss.

My patient, who had suffered from this trouble for many years—since puberty, that is to say—was only able to venture out into the street in the company of his mother or of a few persons whom he knew very well. On one occasion he remarked to me quite unexpectedly that he found walking very pleasant in itself as long as anxiety was prevented by his having a suitable companion. He said that when he was walking in the street he felt as though he were dancing. It further transpired that the patient, who was sexually abstinent, derived great pleasure from dancing; and his pollution dreams were often dreams of dancing. In a poem he had once written he represented prostitution allegorically as a woman who danced with any man she came across.

I do not propose to go into the erotic significance of dancing, or its capacity to represent erotic aims by mimicry. What interests us in this briefly sketched case is not the commonplace fact that the patient derived pleasure from dancing, but that walking and dancing offered him a substitute for sexual gratification which was otherwise denied him by his neurotic inhibitions.

It is not seldom the case in neurotics that the act of

walking is accompanied by sexual excitation, especially a genital one. I have to thank Dr. Eitingon for a very interesting communication of a case which may very fairly be termed a 'walking compulsion'. It was that of a neurotic who, in obedience to a powerful impulse, went for tremendous walks until they brought on an orgasm.

The 'negative' of this peculiar perversion, according to Freud's view in his *Drei Abhandlungen zur Sexualtheorie*, seems to be the neurosis which we know as 'street anxiety'. I have observed a number of cases which support this view. One woman whom I treated by psycho-analysis used to experience a violent excitement which passed into a paralysing anxiety as soon as she left her parents' house. She, too, derived pronounced pleasure from bodily movement. Walking in especial had been particularly pleasurable to her originally. It is very characteristic that this patient used greatly to enjoy dancing alone in her room. On the other hand, if she danced with a man at a ball she would immediately have a feeling of excitement which would start with violent palpitation of the heart and then turn into anxiety associated with a kind of feeling of paralysis. This symptom made it in fact impossible for her to dance with a strange man. Not only could she not do this, but she was also unable to walk with anyone she chose to on account of her anxiety. She could go for walks with her nearest relatives, but not without suffering a certain degree of anxiety. She was only completely free from it when she was walking with her father. When she had no anxiety, however, walking gave her a pleasure which in her unconscious was equivalent to sexual pleasure in the narrower sense. She used to enjoy going walks with her father, for walking with him represented a symbolic fulfilment of her incest-wish—a substitute for real union. It was her fixation on her father that prevented her from walking with anyone else. Any deviation from this law enforced by her neurosis would have signified unfaithfulness to her father.

I may call attention at this point to the fact that in very different languages the sexual act is denoted by an expression which signifies a mutual 'going together' of the two

persons, as, for example, *coire* in Latin.   I imagine that
this meaning of going or walking together will be familiar
to any psycho-analyst who has investigated a case of locomotor anxiety.   Nevertheless, it is not sufficient merely to
point to the symbolic meaning of walking; emphasis must
be laid on the pleasure-value of walking itself.   My
investigation of the present case, together with other observations, have led me to the conclusion that neurotics who
suffer from locomotor anxiety have to begin with a constitutionally over-strong pleasure in movement, and that
neurotic inhibitions of bodily movement have arisen later
from the failure of the repression of this tendency.

Sadger [1] has laid especial emphasis on the significance
of pleasure derived from movement.   He speaks of ' muscle
erotism ' as an independent source of sexual pleasure, and
places it side by side with what he has termed ' skin erotism '
and ' mucous membrane erotism '.   He gives some interesting data concerning positive pleasure derived from bodily
movement.   I can support his observations in many ways,
but I will in this place only discuss the question in so far as
it throws light on street anxiety.

We find that pleasure in movement [2] is not completely
repressed in the patients in question.   The examples
already briefly quoted show that they can enjoy this pleasure
under certain conditions imposed on them by their illness.
Since I have had my attention called to the significance of
this constitutional factor I have reviewed my earlier analysed
cases of street anxiety—and the material they contain is
quite considerable—and I have been astonished to find how
strongly this element comes to the fore.   I found that I had
discovered data of this kind without recognizing that they
were of a typical character.   As a result of my second
inspection I was able to detect this factor as a constantly
recurring theme.   It found expression partly as pleasure
in movement with a directly sexual colouring recognized as
such by the patients themselves, partly as pleasurable motor-

[1] ' Haut-, Schleimhaut- und Muskelerotik ' (1912).
[2] I prefer this expression to the term ' muscle erotism ' because it avoids any
localization of the pleasure.

impulses of an apparently non-sexual character. These phenomena should throw further light on those neurotic symptoms which I have attempted to attribute to a pleasure in movement which is kept out of consciousness.

I have repeatedy been able to observe that the patients in question show a peculiar interest in the rhythm of their movements. This fact seems to me to be of great importance. They will carry out their movements, so far as outward circumstances permit, in some definite rhythm which they specially like. If they think they are unobserved they will walk across the room in this rhythm, and perhaps whistle some tune to their step. One patient stated quite spontaneously that this rhythm reminded him of sexual rhythms. It seems as though it was partly the rhythm of masturbatory acts, partly that of ejaculation, that was concerned. This particular patient noted down his rhythm in the following manner:

$$\angle\cup\cup\angle\cup$$

While a female patient noted down her favourite one thus:

$$\angle\cup\cup\angle\cup\cup\cup\angle\angle$$

She had even composed a prose poem which was entirely about the feet and their movements during dancing.

Many patients who suffer from locomotor anxiety have a pronounced pleasure in taking firm or rapid steps.[1] They also often find pleasure in running downhill quickly, and sometimes feel a pressure in the bladder, accompanied by sexual feelings. On the other hand, one of my female patients, who suffered from street anxiety as an adult, had, as a child, been afraid of going downhill; and her anxiety was certainly not explicable merely as a fear of suddenly falling to the bottom. I have repeatedly observed in neurotics a fear of walking too quickly. This is connected with the repression of pleasurable emotions which might 'run away'[2] with them. (It is significant that language

---

[1] When they are walking very quickly some neurotics feel great anxiety and have a pollution.

[2] [*Durchgehen*, lit. to 'go through'=to 'run away' of a horse. It is also used in the sexual sense of 'running away' or eloping with someone.—*Trans.*]

compares this to the uncurbed energy of a bolting horse.)

Among such patients pleasure in bodily movement is not of course limited to the lower extremities, although, as we have said, walking is especially pleasurable to them. For instance, I observed in a young man suffering from street anxiety that he was continually clenching his fists, contracting the muscles of his arm, and in particular pressing his jaws tightly together, for which latter purpose he strongly contracted the masticatory muscles.[1] Another patient, a woman, was obliged to clench her fists convulsively, to take forced breaths, or to make heaving movements with the upper part of her body. Neurotics of this description often seem to have a feeling of stiffness or rigidity all over their body.

Besides these physical signs I have regularly found in these patients a psychical condition which I am inclined to trace to the same sources. It is worth noting that many patients spontaneously select the same term for both groups of phenomena. They speak of a 'tension' in the body as well as of a state of mental 'tension'.

A person who suffers from severe locomotor anxiety finds himself in an almost permanent state of mental tension. He wakes in the morning with the anxious expectation of having to go out somewhere in the course of the day. As the time for setting out approaches, the tension increases. It continues while he is out. When he arrives home again he begins to worry about what will happen the next day.

Many patients describe this state by a phrase which is familiar to every neurologist. They speak of a 'fear of fear'. It has always struck me that patients make use of this expression with a certain emphasis, as though they are saying something especially profound and as though they are giving the physician a most important clue to their condition. And they are in fact quite right. Superficially the expression 'fear of fear' seems foolish enough. The psycho-analyst, however, cannot fail to recognize that this

---

[1] In his case there was also an unusual erotogenic significance attached to the mucous membrane of the mouth.

tension preceding the real anxiety is analogous in every respect to the fore-pleasure which precedes the satisfaction-pleasure in sexual life.

Many of these neurotics say that they cannot at all imagine what their life would be without a state of permanent expectation of anxiety. A more precise knowledge of the sexuality of these patients shows furthermore that they exhibit an excessive tendency to protract their fore-pleasure and not to leave it. Among patients suffering from street anxiety one finds in particular a remarkably large number who have wholly renounced normal sexual gratification-pleasure in consequence of their neurotic inhibitions. They are pronouncedly auto-erotic, and thus they are inclined to postpone reaching the end-pleasure indefinitely. As a form of protracted enjoyment of fore-pleasure I may mention the so-called 'dream-states' which I have dealt with in detail in a previous paper.[1] Among the patients in whom I studied these states a considerable percentage suffered from street anxiety. The dream-states themselves show in the clearest manner how erotic tendencies pass over into anxiety and other neurotic symptoms.

The psycho-analysis of 'topophobia' shows that we are dealing with patients who dread attaining their libidinal aim. Their anxiety prevents them from becoming free from themselves and from the objects upon which their love was fixed in childhood, and from finding the way to objects belonging to the external world. Every path which leads them away from the charmed circle of those people upon whom they are fixated is closed to them. They may only enjoy their pleasure in movement in the company of those very people. If they act in opposition to the prohibition dictated by the neurosis and go for a walk without their prescribed companion, their pleasure in movement is changed into fear of movement. It is impossible for them to enlist their pleasure in movement in the service of object-love in the same way that in healthy people the originally autonomous component-instincts enter the service of a central tendency.

Now that we have succeeded in tracing back the neurotic's

[1] See Chapter IV,

Q

fear of independent movement to a factor in his sexual constitution which has not yet been sufficiently taken into account hitherto, the question as to the origin of such a ' prohibition ' answers itself.　The fact that the presence of his father or mother releases the patient from anxiety enables us to recognize sufficiently clearly that the source of his inhibition in movement is an incestuous fixation.　I need hardly mention that all my psycho-analyses of topo-phobias agreed in bearing out this view.

The preceding remarks require to be completed in one direction.　In order to simplify matters I have only spoken so far about pleasure derived from active movement and about the change of such pleasure into anxiety.　As a rule, however, the same patients are afraid of movement in a passive sense, too, as soon as it removes them from the neighbourhood of certain persons.　My experience points to the fact that originally travelling also gave a high degree of pleasure to these patients.　Anyone who has studied their dreams will have noticed how frequently they are con-cerned with travelling, and in more recent times especially with travelling in the air.　Many neurotics experience a pro-nounced bodily pleasure in travelling.[1]　As a particularly characteristic example I may mention one patient of mine who used to make long railway journeys and to keep awake all through even the longest of them in order not to lose his pleasure in travelling; and who used to travel chiefly for the sake of that pleasure.　It may be mentioned that in many persons a long railway journey always brings on a pollution during the following night.

The view that such a repression of pleasure in passive movement has occurred in the group of neurotics under discussion was recently confirmed to me by a spontaneous remark made by a female patient.　She had at first only been able to make the journey from her house to mine with the greatest effort.　Psycho-analysis had at first only effected a diminution of her anxiety; until one day she arrived in

---

[1] Reference may also be made to children's pleasure in travelling.　I knew a boy who as soon as he received his pocket-money of one shilling regularly spent it in going for tram rides the whole afternoon.

very high spirits and told me that she had been quite astonished to find that the journey had given her pleasure that day. Her anxiety in connection with the journey had given way to a pronounced pleasure in it. A few years ago I succeeded in obtaining very satisfactory and complete therapeutic results in a case of severe street anxiety. The patient, who had previously only been able to leave her house with the strongest feelings of anxiety, not only got pleasure from travelling after her cure but even put her name down to take part in a balloon trip. She was no longer debarred by neurotic prohibitions from deriving pleasure from movement.

The fact that fear of movement can change into a corresponding pleasure seems to confirm the views advanced above regarding the basis of locomotor anxiety. The derivation of fear of movement from an originally overstrong pleasure in it falls into line with other psycho-analytic results that have been confirmed by experience. As an example I need only mention the fear of touching which we have been able to trace to originally pleasurable impulses to touch things.

Psycho-analysts have been occupied for a long time with the difficult question of what the psychological conditions are which determine the form of the neurotic disease to which the individual will succumb. It is as though he had a choice between different illnesses and—led by unknown impulses—selected one or other of them.

From the most recent investigations (I refer principally to Freud's paper on the origin of the obsessional neurosis,[1] and Jones's [2] contributions on the same subject) we have got a step nearer the problem of the 'choice of neurosis'. I hope that the views put forward in this paper on the psychogenesis of 'locomotor anxiety' may be regarded as a slight contribution to the solution of this problem.

[1] 'The Predisposition to Obsessional Neurosis' (1913).
[2] 'Hate and Anal Erotism in the Obsessional Neurosis' (1913).

CHAPTER XI

THE EAR AND AUDITORY PASSAGE AS EROTOGENIC ZONES [1] (1913)

SEVERAL years ago my attention was drawn by the following observation to the significance of the ear and external auditory meatus as erotogenic zones.

A neurotic patient suffered from peculiar 'attacks' which occurred ten to twenty times a day and even more often. I had ample opportunity of observing these 'attacks' during a long psycho-analytic treatment. In the middle of a conversation the patient would suddenly jump up, turn pale, put his hands up to his ears, and run to the door; then he would stick the forefinger of his right hand into his right ear and move the finger violently about in it with every sign of the most intense excitement. At the same time his face would work as though he were in a towering rage, and he would wriggle about and stamp his feet. The motor inner-vation would finally be discharged in panting breaths, and he would then sink down exhausted. After a few moments he would be able to continue his previous train of thought, though I sometimes had to recall to his memory the words he had been speaking immediately before his attack. Con-sciousness was always clouded during the attacks; and after them the patient had a feeling of returning to reality out of a different state. He knew that quite definite thoughts appeared at the height of his state of excitement, but he was never able to recollect what they were precisely. The analysis, which cannot be given in full here, showed that at the beginning of each attack the patient felt violent itching in the auditory meatus, of which he rid himself with every sign of great excitement. These attacks were a surrogate for certain kinds of sexual activity which were denied him.

[1] [No. 46, A. B.]

It is particularly interesting to note that the attacks, and most of his other symptoms as well, disappeared on one occasion for some months. This was at a time when he had become acquainted with a girl. They did not proceed to sexual intercourse, but found pleasure in tickling each other with feelings of great excitement until they became exhausted.

In this case there was obviously an unusually strong erotogenic state of the skin in general, while the ear and auditory meatus exhibited this characteristic in an extreme degree. It is well known that some neurotics derive an extraordinary pleasure from being tickled. If other ways of sexual gratification are closed to them the neurotic symptom of *pruritus* frequently appears, in which the person is led to perform chafing or scratching movements which sometimes lead to orgasm. For instance, I was able to observe a female patient with pruritus of the left arm who, by scratching the part with increasing violence until it reached a kind of frenzy, could produce a complete orgasm. This method had the advantage over masturbation, which she had practised earlier, in that no self-reproach was attached to it. To scratch oneself on account of a nervous skin irritation or a concomitant eczema would appear as a necessity and not as a moral lapse.

It has long been known that in early childhood the ear is used to obtain auto-erotic pleasure. I need only refer to the frequent habit of children who suck their thumbs, etc., of catching hold of an ear and rhythmically pulling the lobe while sucking for pleasure. Furthermore, it must be remembered that during their childhood, and even later, many people poke their fingers into the auditory meatus, insert things into it, and like to occupy themselves with the auditory secretions. In one case a boy caught a fly and put it into his ear. In consequence of his manipulations the ' foreign body ' passed so deeply into his ear that medical intervention was necessary. Children often put small objects such as peas, etc., into their ears.[1]

---

[1] Mental patients frequently exhibit a tendency to put all kinds of things into their ears.

It is only recently, however, that I have become convinced that a much more general significance attaches to the ear as an erotogenic zone. I have to thank my colleague Dr. H. Hempel, an ear specialist in Berlin, for the following reliable observations which I quote here because observations such as these deserve the attention of psycho-analysts and because their importance has not been sufficiently appreciated up to the present.

Small children often suffer from a moist eczema of the ear and external auditory meatus, accompanied by intense itching. After the physician has treated the ear such children adopt a different behaviour towards his subsequent visits from that usually shown when medical attention is called for. The child who has been crying before on account of the discomfort of the eczematous condition will become extraordinarily quiet at the physician's approach and will not struggle in the least. As long as the physician is doing anything to the itching part the child will remain quiet and will even murmur contentedly; it only starts crying again when his manipulations cease. I may mention that these observations were made without any special knowledge of the Freudian conception of infantile sexuality, and that nevertheless the observer had come to the conclusion that the conduct depicted was very similar to the conduct of the child during masturbatory stimulation. It may be added that adults also exhibit unmistakable signs of agreeable sensations during the treatment of aural eczema. Dr. Hempel mentioned to me that he once saw a man who had scratched both ears till they were raw, but who would not consent to be treated for this affection.

Many products of phantasy show what an important part the ear can play in the sexuality of the child. One patient told me of a tendency she had had from childhood to invent phantastic stories. When she was about nine years old (and probably earlier as well) she often used to imagine that she was being punished for some misdeed. She was particularly fond of picturing a scene in which she was going for a walk with her younger sister, and the Kaiser came driving along in a carriage and had them arrested for some unspecified crime. Punishment followed which consisted in this,—that both children had to have their ears cleaned! The child experienced at once pleasure and fear during this procedure. Her phantasies on this theme not only contained a partly longed-for, partly feared stimulation of an erotogenic zone but also a gratification of masochistic tendencies.

In the same way we can observe children or adults who imagine scenes in which they are being tickled in the most sensitive parts of their body. Various signs point to a fusion of sado-masochistic impulses with pleasure in tickling or being tickled. I will only give as an instance here the signs of a violent affect of rage which were evident in the ' attacks ' of the neurotic described above, and in the patient who scratched her arm so violently.

I have only to refer to a few facts which up to now have been little considered. In the first place there is the reddening of the ears to which many neurotic people incline. I intend later to consider in greater detail the connection between that symptom and processes of sexual excitation. It would appear, furthermore, that in some people the part of the neck adjacent to the ears, especially the angle between the neck and the jaw, has a particular erotogenic significance. The erotogenic significance of the ear should also be considered in relation to neurotic ringing in the ears and other sounds of subjective origin. And finally, reference may be made to the fact, well known to psycho-analysts, that the ear has at all times been frequently employed as a genital symbol.

I am probably right in assuming that every psycho-analyst could produce observations similar to those given here. Sadger [1] has mentioned a number of interesting observations which admirably supplement mine, and in a paper by Jekels [2] there is an allusion to mutual stimulation of the auditory meatus in inverts.

[1] Sadger, ' Haut-, Schleimhaut- und Muskelerotik ' (1912).
[2] Jekels, ' Einige Bemerkungen zur Trieblehre ' (1913).

CHAPTER XII

THE FIRST PREGENITAL STAGE OF THE LIBIDO [1] (1916)

I

IN his *Drei Abhandlungen zur Sexualtheorie*, which first appeared in 1905, Freud gave a comprehensive account of his views concerning the sexuality of the child. In the third edition of the book, published in 1915, he has amplified those views, so that it is still to-day the standard work on the subject.

The advances which have been made in psycho-analytical knowledge have required us to assume the existence of certain stages in the early development of the infantile libido. Freud calls those stages the 'pregenital organizations' of the libido, since they do not as yet show a predominating importance of the genital organs.

The following remarks relate to the earliest of those stages of development. They are supported by extensive observations which were exclusively made before the theoretical views concerning the libidinal stages were put forward. A preconceived theory of the pregenital organizations cannot therefore have influenced the choice of that material. It seems to me necessary to point out this, since each further extension of the sexual theory will probably meet with objections similar to those raised at the first appearance of the *Drei Abhandlungen*. Nevertheless, before presenting my material and the conclusions which I have

[1] [No. 52, A. B.]

248

drawn from them, I shall have to review the fundamental facts upon which the theory of the pregenital stages of the libido is based.

In his remarks on the earliest phenomena of infantile sexuality Freud was able to refer to an authority who long before him had arrived at new and daring, but at the same time convincing, conclusions in this sphere. This important piece of pioneer work had been carried out by Lindner in 1879 in his studies on sucking habits in children. He had not failed to notice the libidinal character of the process; he remarked on the fact that sucking, even when it did not serve the purpose of satisfying hunger, was carried out by children with an intensity which completely absorbed their attention. He had also observed an excitement in the child during the act of sucking which increased to a kind of orgasm, and he considered that the falling asleep of the child after this occurrence was an effect of the gratification it had obtained. Furthermore, he drew special attention to the instinct of grasping which is associated with sucking, and recognized the gradual transition of sucking to masturbation—that is, to an activity of an undoubtedly sexual character.

Freud accepted Lindner's views, and he established definite characteristics for infantile sexuality, as they are most clearly seen in that primitive form of instinctual activity, sucking. These characteristics are, that in the first place the instinct is not directed on to another object, but is manifested auto-erotically. In the second place, this most primitive form of sexual expression is not an independent phenomenon, but is dependent upon a function important for the preservation of life, namely, sucking for nourishment; so that it is the reproduction of a pleasurable stimulus which the child has experienced during feeding. In the third place, the attainment of the pleasure is attached to an 'erotogenic zone'—the mucous membrane of the lips. Gratification of the need for nourishment and gratification of the erotogenic zone cannot be separated from each other in their earliest state. The mucous membrane of the lips must, moreover, possess erotogenic quality, which fluctuates in intensity in different children, for they exhibit the tendency to suck for pleasure in very different degrees.

According to Freud a similar double function attaches to the anal aperture of the alimentary canal as well. He believes that in early childhood this aperture does not have excretory functions alone but also subserves infantile sexuality as an erotogenic zone. The child seeks to re-experience the local sensations necessarily associated with the emptying of the bowel, and, by holding back its contents, is able to intensify those sensations. As with the lip-zone, the erotogenic capacity of the anal zone must be presumed to vary with each individual. The deliberate intensification of this accessory pleasure obtained in defæcation by stimulating an erotogenic zone is, like sucking, similar in nature to genital masturbation, which is also practised in early infancy.

Besides the auto-erotic phenomena of early childhood Freud describes certain component-instincts which are directed from the outset upon other persons as sexual objects (pleasure in looking and exhibiting, active and passive components of cruelty). At first these component-instincts are not organized firmly together, but proceed independently in the obtaining of pleasure. It is only later that the erotogenic zones and component-instincts become united under the primacy of the genital zone. When the sexual instinct enters into the service of procreation its development reaches its normal completion.

As we have said, Freud has called ' pregenital ' those stages of the development of the libido which precede the setting in of the primacy of the genital zone. They relate to antecedent stages of the later ' normal ' sexuality, through which the libido of the child generally passes without anyone being aware of the alterations that are occurring. The same processes, which under normal conditions are not especially noticeable, become ' highly active and able to be detected by superficial observation ' (Freud) in pathological cases.

Up till now the psycho-analysis of neurotic cases has enabled us to infer the existence of two such pregenital organizations. The earliest is the oral stage, which may also be called the cannibalistic stage. As has already been said, in this stage sexual activity is not yet separated from the taking of nourishment. Freud says: ' The object of the one activity is also that of the other. The sexual aim consists in the incorporation of the object ' (p. 60) ; and he adds a remark which is important for the understanding of sucking for pleasure: ' Pleasure-sucking can be considered as being the remains of this hypothetical stage of organization which our pathological material has led us to assume. It can be looked upon as a sexual activity which has become detached from nutritive activity, and which has exchanged its external object for one belonging to its own body.'

From his psycho-analysis of the obsessional neurosis Freud was able to infer the existence of yet another pregenital organization. He says: 'A second pregenital phase is the *sadistic-anal* organization. In this the duality of sexual life which is an integral part of it has already come into existence. But it cannot at this period be called *male* and *female*; it must be termed *active* and *passive*. The *activity* arises from the bodily musculature in virtue of the instinct of possession; the *passivity* is pre-eminently connected with the erotogenic mucous membrane of the intestinal canal. Both impulses are directed to objects, which are not, however, the same. At the same time other component-instincts are functioning in an auto-erotic way. In this phase, therefore, sexual polarity and the external object are already discoverable. But there is as yet no organization of the component-instincts or subordination to the function of procreation.'

I have now roughly indicated the present position of the theory of sexuality as far as it applies to our subject. While the observations which have led to the description of the sadistic-anal organization have found special consideration in psycho-analytic literature—I refer particularly to Jones' important communications—the earliest, ' oral ' stage of development of the libido awaits further investigation. As Freud has stated, it is our pathological material which compels us to assume its existence. This fact indicates that we are concerned with developmental processes which are hardly accessible to direct observation in children. At this early period the child can give no information about the processes of its instinctual life. Besides, in normal conditions development in the first year of life takes place so quietly that generally no obvious manifestations of the changes that are occurring can be observed; and later, when repression has fully set in, the individual is naturally less able than ever to give information about the earliest events of his life.

The facts of normal erotism make it plain that the mouth has by no means given up its significance as an erotogenic zone.   And the study of the sexual perversions shows still more clearly that the mouth can take over the whole significance of a sexual organ, *i.e.* can fulfil a genital rôle.   Furthermore, psycho-analysis of the neuroses shows that very frequently the mouth has lost its significance as an erotogenic zone only as far as consciousness is concerned, and that this significance persists in the unconscious and is manifested in consciousness through substitutive formations, which we know as neurotic symptoms.   We owe to psycho-analysis the knowledge that these phenomena are equivalent to infantilisms.   They represent partly a persistence of infantile instincts in the unconscious, partly a return to libidinal stages which had already been left behind.   That such repressed infantilisms could be rendered unrecognizable through numerous alterations and indeed turned into their exact opposites, has been shown by Freud in 1915, precisely in connection with phenomena related to the mouth zone.   According to him, neurotics in whom the erotogeneity of the oral zone had originally been very marked, and in whom this had perhaps been expressed by a continuance of the sucking habit for many years, are often affected by nervous vomiting in later life.

But even though all these phenomena justify us in inferring the existence of an early 'oral' stage of the libido, we still have no clear picture, no direct view, of this archaic condition which is extraordinarily far removed from the instinctual life of the normal adult.   I should therefore like to bring forward some psychopathological material which has hitherto been almost unknown or at least quite disregarded, and which goes to show that the instinctual life of the infant persists in some adults in a positive and unmistakable fashion, and that the libido of such persons presents a picture which appears to correspond in all its details to the oral or cannibalistic stage set up by Freud. I shall begin by giving the most extreme symptoms of a case of this kind as far as they are of interest in this connection.   They will throw light on a whole series of psychopathological phenomena to which no special investigation has hitherto been devoted.   Finally, I shall consider a question which has arisen out of the recent studies made on the psychogenesis of the obsessional neurosis.   The investigations of Freud[1] and Jones[2] have shown that compulsive symptoms result from a defence against sadistic-anal impulses.   It may be expected that a similar defence against a threatened relapse into the oral organization will also lead to the formation of quite typical symptoms; and the correctness of this expectation seems to be corroborated by certain findings of psycho-analysis.   I should like to attempt, on the basis of our material connected with the earliest pregenital organization, to make two contributions to psycho-analytic theory—namely, to consider the question of the origin of psychic states of depression, and to discuss the problem of the ' choice of neurosis '.

II

The material I shall first bring forward comes from the psycho-analysis of a case of dementia præcox (Bleuler's ' schizophrenia ').   The patient did not present the well-known picture of a psychosis with delusions, hallucinations, etc., but that variety of the illness which has been termed ' simple ' dementia præcox.   Patients of this group, which Bleuler has also recently classified as ' schizophrenia simplex ', do not show the above-mentioned gross symptoms

---

[1] ' The Predisposition to Obsessional Neurosis ' (1913).
[2] ' Hate and Anal Erotism in the Obsessional Neurosis ' (1913).

of mental disturbance.   They rather exhibit definite associative disturbances and, particularly, alterations of feeling and
impulse, such as one finds in severe cases side by side with
delusions.   The associative activity of these patients proceeds so far along organized paths that a psycho-analysis
can be carried out with them just as well as with a psycho-
neurotic.   Indeed the work is even facilitated in such
patients on account of the abolition of many inhibitions.
In the neurotic a great deal of material is prevented from
becoming conscious, and therefore from being spoken about,
on account of the intense repression; whereas in these
patients the material lies quite near consciousness, and in
certain circumstances is expressed without resistance.

My patient came from a family in which cases of severe
catatonic dementia præcox had already occurred.   He was
by no means deficient in intelligence, and had had a secondary
education.   After leaving the routine of school life he had
made but little progress in his academic studies, and certain
peculiarities which he had shown as a scholar had developed
more strongly in him.   When he came to me for treatment
his conduct in many ways resembled that of an intelligent
child.   Neither his special subject nor any events in the
external world were able to excite any serious interest in
him.   He amused himself at most with trifles and purely
superficial things; but he turned his attention chiefly on
to his own ego in a markedly narcissistic manner.   The
slightest fancy, a pun on a word, etc., could occupy him
intensely and for long periods of time.   His own physical
condition absorbed his interest more than anything else.
His genital and anal sensations were of the highest importance to him.   Moreover, he was addicted to anal as well as
to genital masturbation.   During the period of puberty he
derived pleasure from playing with fæces, and later on he
occupied himself with his bodily excretions.   For instance,
he took pleasure in eating his own semen.   But his mouth
played a very special rôle as an erotogenic zone.   As often
happens in this kind of case, he was conscious of the sexual
character of certain of his symptoms, though to an out-
sider they would not at once have appeared in this light.

The patient directed my attention to the erotogenic significance of the mouth when one day he spoke of ' mouth pollutions ' as something quite ordinary and well recognized. On being questioned, he described an occurrence which frequently took place. He would wake up in the night from an exciting dream to find that saliva was dribbling out of his mouth. In his free associations he proceeded to bring forward a great deal of material regarding the erotogenic significance of the mouth. I will give the most instructive facts in this connection.

According to the patient's own statements he had not been able to wean himself from the love of milk as a boy. At school he had never been able to get sufficient milk to drink. This tendency still existed, but had changed in certain respects. Up to the age of fifteen he had not simply drunk milk out of a cup or glass, but had had a particular method of sucking it in. He used to curve his tongue upwards and press it behind the upper teeth on the palate and then suck in the milk. The milk had to be neither hot nor cold, but at body temperature. He obtained a particularly pleasant sensation in doing this. He added spontaneously: ' It is like sucking at the breast '. ' I suck at my own tongue as though it were the nipple.' At fifteen he had given up this kind of sucking and had at the same time begun to take cold beverages. Nevertheless, his desire for milk had by no means been overcome, and indeed its sexual determination had come out very distinctly in the following years through frequent occurrences which the patient reported as though they were something quite ordinary. He used often to wake up at night with violent sexual desires; he then used to drink some milk which he had placed ready in his bedroom. He used often to get up at night and go to the kitchen for milk. If at any time he could not find any he used to put an end to his sexual excitement by masturbating; but otherwise he used to satisfy himself by taking milk. He himself felt that his longing to suck milk was his deepest and most primitive instinct. Genital masturbation, strongly though it dominated him, seemed to him to be a secondary thing.

These facts speak for themselves. There cannot be the slightest doubt of the sexual significance of the patient's sucking of milk or of the rôle played by his mouth as an erotogenic zone. His behaviour at night, as described by himself, can easily be seen to be a continuation of the behaviour which neurotically disposed children show in the first and second years of life. These children find great difficulty in acquiring the habit of an unbroken night's sleep. They wake up in the night once or more often and make known through their crying, or, if they are old enough, through other signs, that they desire the breast or the bottle. If they are given milk to suck they are gratified and become quiet; if not, they are able to obtain a substitutive gratification by putting their thumb or finger in their mouths and thereby stimulating the oral zone, or by giving another erotogenic zone, say the genital one, an adequate masturbatory stimulus.

Our patient's behaviour fully coincided with that of the infant. From the fact that as an adult he still felt most intensely that form of gratification which bore the character of incorporation, it is clear that his libido had experienced a strong fixation in the earliest pregenital stage, i.e. the oral or cannibalistic one. Sucking served him as a method of taking nourishment and of obtaining sexual pleasure, although its first function certainly sank into the background in comparison with the second. I may remind the reader of the so-called 'mouth pollutions' already mentioned by the patient. We generally consider the flow of saliva as a sign of appetite. But in this patient, whose mouth zone was so markedly in the service of his sexuality, such a flow was an accompanying symptom of a sexual excitement occurring during sleep. His libido therefore showed a tendency to discharge itself through the predominant erotogenic zone of the first years of childhood.

What psycho-analysis was able to discover in regard to the patient's further libidinal development is of extreme interest. From the subject of sucking, his associations led on to the historically later developed form of taking nourishment, i.e. to eating. In this connection he brought forward a memory to which other important associations became added. He said that when he was a little boy he had had the idea that loving somebody was exactly the same as the idea of eating something good. Since childhood he had had 'cannibalistic ideas'.[1] These ideas were at first traced back along associative paths to his fourth year. At this age—I was able to check the correctness of his statements as to the date—he had had a nurse to whom he had been very much attached. It was she who was the centre of his cannibalistic phantasies. At a later period the patient still often used to want to bite into her, and ' to swallow her, skin, hair, clothes, and all '.

But psycho-analysis was able to penetrate even deeper. A further association of the patient's showed that the taste of meat reminded him of milk; both were ' greasy and sweet '. He said that just as he many times experienced a sudden longing for milk, so he did for meat. It seemed to him as though he wanted a substitute for human flesh. His associations led from this point to the phantasy of biting into the female breast; and here it was that his ideas of meat and milk had a direct connection. I may add that the period during which he had been nursed at the breast had been unusually full of important occurrences. Various circumstances had rendered it necessary for his wet-nurse to be changed several times and for the period of breast feeding to be considerably prolonged. These events were bound to have an effect on a child in whose sexual constitution the mouth zone was so strongly accentuated. They must have facilitated the fixation of his libido on an earlier stage or its regression to such a stage.

In conclusion, it may be mentioned that the patient also experienced a marked degree of pleasure in eating, of which his tendency to over-eat gave ample proof. But this accentuation of pleasure in eating did not to his mind bear

---

[1] Perhaps it is not superfluous to remark that the expression as well as the idea here quoted came from the patient himself. The expression ' cannibalistic ideas ' is not borrowed from the *Drei Abhandlungen zur Sexualtheorie*. The psycho-analysis from which I am quoting took place in 1912, whereas the third edition of Freud's book, which contains that expression for the first time, did not appear till 1915.

R

the same sexual significance as the sucking did; it appeared to him to have a secondary character. Nevertheless, it showed his tendency to excite his erotogenic zones in every way. Even when his libido found new sources of pleasure the earlier ones showed no diminution of their importance; and this peculiarity persisted in the further development of his instinctual life. It explains the fact that when he was grown up his libido never achieved uniformity of direction. He could not attain a normal emotional attitude towards other persons and could not advance to object-choice; and at the same time his different erotogenic zones maintained their original independent significance. Of these, however, it was the mouth zone whose excitation he found by far the most pleasurable, and about whose importance for him he spoke with most affect.

The characteristics of this case may be summed up as follows:

1. The oral zone was more important than the other erotogenic zones. Pleasure in sucking was particularly strong. Sucking milk produced a state of gratification.

2. The sexual function and the nutritive one were associated in the act of sucking.

3. The patient had the desire to incorporate the object which attracted his wish-phantasies. (He himself called this a cannibalistic impulse.)

These are, however, the same characteristics which Freud has been led to attribute to the earliest stage of libidinal development in infancy. The agreement is complete, and causes no astonishment to anyone who has recognized from his own psycho-analytical work to how great a degree Freud's theories are the result of direct observation, and how far they are removed from idle speculation.

An adult whose libido is found to be in a condition such as that just described deviates to an extraordinary degree from the normal. The extreme nature of the symptoms in such a case renders intelligible to us related phenomena which we meet in other persons in a less marked degree or in a more disguised form.

III

There are considerable differences even in healthy children with regard to the time at which they are weaned. These differences are partly based on external conditions, but they can in part only be explained by variations in the individual. Thus the transition from the taking of nourishment by sucking to drinking in the narrower sense takes place sometimes earlier, sometimes later.

With regard to the external factors, ethnological, social and family conditions have to be taken into consideration. In quite a number of partially civilized peoples the children are not weaned until the fourth or even the sixth year. And even among the people of one country, or even of one district, weaning takes place at very different periods. Among our own lower classes it is fairly frequent for older children to be given the mother's breast from time to time when she has a younger child to suckle. Neurotic mothers will frequently delay the weaning of their child for a long time, because the act of giving suck gives them the strongest physical feelings of pleasure; this is particularly so in women with genital frigidity in whom the breast has obtained an over-great significance as an erotogenic zone.

However, we are more interested in those cases in which the child itself causes difficulties in its weaning. We can recognize these resistances in a child even during the period of sucking, when it has to pass from the mother's or wet-nurse's breast to the bottle; and we observe very remarkable differences in the behaviour of children in this connection. Many become used to the change in the course of a few days; and some children, who in feeding at the breast do not use sufficient energy in sucking, very soon prefer the bottle, because the food flows out from it without trouble to them. There are, however, children who resist with great obstinacy the transition from the breast to the bottle. This resistance becomes quite manifest when the child is expected finally to give up taking nourishment by sucking. It frequently happens that neurotically disposed children react to the attempt at weaning by taking so little food that the mother is compelled to give in to them for the time being.   In pronounced cases difficulties of this kind can continue up to school age.   I might mention, for example, a girl of nine years who could not be induced to take her breakfast with her family before going to school. In order not to allow the little girl to go to school fasting, her mother used to bring a bottle of warm milk to her in bed every morning.   The other meals the obstinate little girl took with the family as usual.   In a case reported by Gött, a thirteen-years-old boy had to be weaned from the bottle. This reminds us of the particularly marked case which I have given above in detail.

Such behaviour on the part of the child can be explained in no other way than as an obstinate adherence to the pleasure which sucking affords him through the agency of the lips as an erotogenic zone.   Now we have learned from observation that persons who cling to infantile pleasure-sucking are invariably seriously hampered in the development of their sexuality.   Their instincts of nutrition and of sexuality remain to a certain extent intermingled.   Their libido does not find the way to a living, human object in a normal manner, but seeks its gratification in the first instance in sucking up a material into the mouth.

The part that sexuality plays in pleasure-sucking which persists into later years appears very clearly in those persons who, as adults, have the impulse to suck at the female breast. This kind of sexual practice stimulates them more strongly than normal cohabitation.   One of my patients explained to me that in such an erotic situation he was in a curious state of divided feelings.   On the one hand he was afraid that milk might come out of the breast, and on the other he was angry and disappointed when none did.   In this case the sexual interest in sucking greatly preponderated; nothing remained of its other significance except an inquisitive, uneasy expectancy as to whether the breast would yield milk.

It is well known that after being weaned children preserve a tendency to suck sweet things.   We frequently find in neurotic men with strongly suppressed libido an intense, impulsive desire for sweet things. They take a particular pleasure in sucking at sweets very slowly. In two very pronounced cases I could establish with certainty that it was the sucking-pleasure originating in infantile auto-erotism which had pushed aside the active impulses of the libido and which procured for the subject the most pleasurable feeling of all. One of these patients used to suck sweets in bed in the evening, and then go off to sleep with a feeling of having been gratified. The similarity of this behaviour with that of the child in the sucking period is very obvious. Normal male erotic behaviour was completely suppressed in this case. The other patient showed infantile traits to an unusual degree. His libido was quite without male activity, and instead made thorough use of every auto-erotic source of pleasure. When he set out to his work in the morning he used to go through a characteristic performance. He used to behave as though he were a little boy, and on going used to say to his wife: ' Sonny is going to school now '. On the way he used to buy sweets just as children do, and take great pleasure in slowly sucking them. The patient spoke of this childish amusement with great animation, while sexuality in the sense of normal male behaviour possessed an unusually small interest for him. In the course of his psycho-analysis it became evident from many signs that the libidinal interest belonging to the normal sex function was entirely attached to auto-erotic processes. We can here clearly see the failure of the separation of the function of taking nourishment from that of sex, from the fact that sucking sweet substances received such a strong libidinal emphasis.

In this briefly outlined case we have an example of a failure to leave the infantile pleasure in sucking. The next example will illustrate a subsequent regression to this source of pleasure.

A neurotic young girl, who had for many years practised masturbation, was one day ' enlightened ' by a book as to the wickedness and danger of her habit. She was seized with anxiety and succumbed to a depression of spirits which

persisted for a long time. She abstained completely from
masturbation. During this period of sexual abstinence
and depression of spirits she was often taken with a violent
longing for sweets. She bought and consumed sweets in
the greatest secrecy and with feelings of pleasure and
gratification the intensity of which surprised her. She
had all along had the most extreme disgust of normal union
with a man; and now she had completely abandoned her
genital sexuality through this strict self-prohibition against
masturbation. It was therefore comprehensible that her
libido should enter upon a regressive path and take possession of the oral zone in the manner described. It may be
added that in her psycho-analysis many facts were produced
which indicated the existence of repressed wishes referring
to sucking the male genital.

Having seen that the sucking of substances into the
mouth is to be looked upon as a sexual act in certain people,
we shall find that new light is thrown upon certain other
phenomena that appear very frequently in neurotics.

IV

Many neurotics suffer from abnormal feelings of hunger.
Women in particular are affected with this symptom.
Specialists in nervous diseases are very well acquainted with
those female patients who are suddenly seized with hunger
in the street or other places, and must therefore take care
always to have something to eat with them. Such persons
habitually wake up with a gnawing hunger, and they prepare for this before going to bed by putting some food
beside them. Certain characteristics of this neurotic hunger
are to be noted, namely, that it has no relation to whether
the stomach is full or empty, that it comes on at irregular
intervals, and that it sets in like an attack with accompaniments of a harassing nature which do not belong to the
normal need for nourishment, the most important of which
are feelings of anxiety.

The patients complain of their ' attacks of ravenous
hunger '. They recognize the difference between normal

hunger and this ' ravenous hunger ', but nevertheless are inclined to confuse the two conditions with one another. They show the most violent resistances when psycho-analysis discloses the connection of their neurotic ravenous hunger with repressed libido. However, certain signs betray the fact that we are on the right path. For example, the great frequency of these hunger attacks in frigid women is very striking. And one of my male patients, who showed the symptom of neurotic hunger in a pronounced degree, laid emphasis on the sensation that his hunger was pulling at his testicles.

Strong libidinal impulses, against the undisguised appearance of which consciousness protects itself, can be unusually well masked by a feeling of hunger. For hunger is a sensation that can be admitted to oneself and to others, even if it is excessive. No one, not even the patient himself, suspects from what source the neurotic symptom obtains its power. In some cases this impulse can be so strong that the patient is forced to adapt and subordinate his whole way of life to his morbid craving for food. The power that such a neurotic hunger obtains over the patient enables us to estimate the enormous strength of the repressed impulses which gain expression by this means. As examples I will bring forward some facts of a really amazing nature taken from one of my psycho-analyses.

A female patient of mine used to suffer from severe attacks of ravenous hunger as soon as she had gone a few steps from home. She never left her house without taking some food with her, and when she had eaten this she used to have to go into a confectioner's or some such place in order to appease her hunger. But it was in the night that this need for food used to overcome her most strongly. In the course of years her condition had got to such a pitch that she used to take two or three big meals during the night. Although her dinner was not enough and she used to eat another big meal before going to bed, she used to wake up in the night with a gnawing hunger to which she always had to yield. The result of this constant eating was naturally a marked increase in her weight. She used to eat chiefly vegetables at night, ostensibly because they were less fattening.   At the time of her psycho-analytic treatment she was living in a boarding-house.   She had accumulated large supplies of preserved vegetables, and each evening she used to prepare the meals she was going to take at night. She used to go to sleep at about ten o'clock and wake up at one, three, and five A.M., and eat a large meal each time. Between six and seven in the morning she would hurry down to the kitchen and beg for her breakfast.   Her behaviour was very reminiscent of the 'spoilt' baby who repeatedly wakes up in the night and will only be quietened when its mother gives it something to drink.   This patient was, it may be remarked, an only child.   On the other hand, the behaviour of patients of this kind, who crave for food at short intervals and undergo tortures if their desires are not gratified, is extraordinarily similar to that of morphinists and a good many dipsomaniacs.   Regarding those conditions, psycho-analysis has succeeded in showing that the intoxicating poison affords the patient a substitutive gratification for that activity of his libido which is denied him.   The symptom of excessive and compulsive eating may be regarded in the same light.

The case just described differs from those discussed earlier in that the patient did not desire to suck milk or to indulge in other sucking activities, but had a morbid craving for taking solid food very frequently.   The patient's whole behaviour becomes intelligible to us only when we recognise the pleasure-value—conscious or unconscious— which eating had for her.   Although she never enjoyed a night of peaceful, uninterrupted sleep, she offered the greatest resistance to an analysis of her attacks of hunger and to giving up her meals during the night.   It was, moreover, not merely the eating itself that was charged with so much affect; for she enjoyed a certain fore-pleasure in the purchase of her provisions, the preparation of her meals, etc.[1]

---

[1] In order to supplement the above very incomplete abstract of a psycho-analysis, I may refer to the patient's preference for vegetarian meals at night. The rational explanation she herself gave was insufficient and not really correct as to facts.   If we see in her whole behaviour a form of auto-erotic gratification, then her avoidance of flesh at night is quite intelligible.

V

Neurotics whose sexuality is stunted to such an extent that they remain in a greater or lesser degree attached to nutritional sucking or to eating, show as adults no special tendency to thumb-sucking, at least as far as my experience goes. And again, those adult neurotics who have remained pronounced thumb-suckers show as a rule no particular libidinal accentuation of the function of taking food. On the contrary, such persons often have a dislike of food, especially milk and meat, and suffer from nausea and vomiting.

It may sound a strange assertion, but we can nevertheless say that compared with that group of neurotics which we have just discussed, adult thumb-suckers represent a more advanced stage of libidinal development. Their libido has achieved a certain independence of the nutritive instinct, in so far as the obtaining of pleasure is no longer associated with sucking for nutriment. Their oral zone has certainly retained its predominant rôle, and they, too, are still far removed from having made a successful transference of their libido on to objects. In real life they show many signs of the strongest repudiation of sexuality, whereas in their phantasies the use of the mouth for sexual purposes (such as fellatio and cunnilinctus) plays a prominent rôle—for the most part, if not always, it is true, with the negative affect of nausea and horror.

The tenacity with which these neurotics cling to the auto-erotic stimulation of the mucous membrane of the lips and to the erotic use of the mouth—at any rate in their abundant store of phantasies—is easily comprehensible if we look back at the behaviour of the small child. We need only call to mind the intensity with which the child even from its earliest days indulges in ' pleasure-sucking '. The zest with which it pushes both hands into its mouth, the impetuous way in which it catches at its fingers with its lips, its complete abandonment to the rhythmical motion of sucking and the final gratificatory effect of the whole process—all this shows what power is exercised by those early instinctual impulses. This power is clearly perceptible from the fact that many people remain subservient to it even in adult life.

The behaviour of such persons resembles that of the infant in another respect also. According to my experience, neurotics who have not overcome the sucking habit tend to indulge in a very high degree of auto-erotic stimulation of other zones, especially the genitals. We also find that the small child, besides having pleasure in sucking, tends to take hold of some part of its own body and to carry out on it rhythmical plucking movements. We may call to mind the child's habit of pulling at the lobe of its ear with one hand while sucking the thumb of the other. And very often that hand will seek the genital region in order to stimulate it by means of similar movements.

The thumb-sucking of adults which appears so strange to us is more explicable when we remember that in normal adults the mouth has not quite lost its rôle of an erotogenic zone. We look upon kissing as a thoroughly normal expression of the libido, although it is true that the erotogenic zone in this case serves the purpose of object-love. The kiss does not claim the significance of a final sexual aim, but only represents a preparatory act. And yet here, too, the boundaries are ill-defined; certain forms of kissing can constitute the essential aim of the person's sexual desire. The lip zone in particular takes over real genital functions with a frequency that must not be underestimated.

I shall give some further details from two of my psychoanalyses. They show the course taken by the childish propensity for the sucking habit in a particularly instructive manner, and supplement one another in many ways.

The first patient, a middle-aged man, was suffering from a chronic neurosis, the most troublesome symptom of which was an intractable insomnia. In tracing the psychosexual causes of this trouble, we discovered certain things concerning the vicissitudes of his libido (or, what comes to the same, the development of his neurosis), some of which I give below.

In his earliest childhood the patient had been addicted in an unusual degree to sucking his thumb. When he grew older and nevertheless kept up the habit, the usual nursery methods were applied. His fingers were smeared with a bitter-tasting fluid; and the boy did in fact leave off sucking them. Nevertheless the success of this device was only apparent. The little boy made use of a corner of his pillow or bedclothes instead and used to fall asleep sucking or chewing at them. His parents interposed to stop this new practice, with the result that he submitted to all outward appearance, only to seek a fresh pleasure-substitute. Presently traces of his teeth were discovered in his wooden bedstead. He had adopted the habit of gnawing it as he lay in bed.

During the years before puberty the patient's need of giving his mouth pleasurable stimulus before going to sleep became more and more imperative, and some such stimulus became the indispensable condition of his falling asleep. For many years masturbation played an important part in his auto-erotic methods of getting to sleep. After puberty, especially when he was about twenty years old, he had severe struggles about giving up the habit, struggles in which old prohibitions out of his childhood became operative once more. He used often to succeed for long periods in giving up masturbation, but he had to purchase this success at the expense of an intractable insomnia which used to last for the same length of time. He resorted to medical advice and took sleeping-draughts. But he soon got so dependent on these that he had to carry out another struggle to give them up in their turn. And this struggle, alternating with the struggle against masturbation, had recurred several times in the course of years. When the patient had begun treatment with me and was feeling slightly better, he abstained from the use of sleeping-draughts on two successive nights. On the day after the second night he came to me in an obvious state of annoyance, and when he had lain down in the usual manner for treatment and had told me about the previous night, I observed that he placed his right thumb in his mouth, and instead of going on speaking, sucked his thumb. His resistance could scarcely have been expressed more clearly. This resistance, originally directed against his parents and teachers, and now against the physician through the transference, was as much as to say: 'If gnawing at the sheets, masturbation, and all other means of sleep are forbidden me by you, then I shall turn again to my oldest gratification. So now you see that you can do nothing with me.' The fact that he should have sucked his thumb under the very eyes of his physician was an obvious sign of defiance.

Just as this observation allows us to see very clearly the relations of thumb-sucking to sexuality, so the following abstract from another psycho-analysis shows what complicated phenomena are derived from infantile sucking for pleasure.

A large group of neurotics have an abnormally strongly accentuated pleasure in sucking from the beginning, and tend in adult life to make perverse use of the mouth, yet they nevertheless produce the strongest resistances against acts of this kind. They also present nervous symptoms which occur in the region of the mouth zone. The patient of whom I am about to speak belongs to this group.

The patient, a seventeen-year-old boy who came to me on the advice of his medical attendant, was extremely taciturn and reserved during the first consultation. As I was with difficulty succeeding in getting single short answers out of him, I noticed that he was continually doing something with his mouth and the surrounding parts. Sometimes he would bite his upper or his lower lip, or lick them with his tongue; sometimes he could be seen to suck in his cheeks; then he would clench his jaws so tightly together that the muscles of mastication stood out visibly; or he would open his mouth wide and close it again; then again he would obviously be sucking at his teeth or gums.

When the treatment had succeeded in removing his inhibition in speaking, for a time at least, he told me of a great many more practices associated with the oral cavity, all of which were of a pleasurable nature. An ungovernable

impulse to suck was the especial feature of those habits.
He needed to make continual sucking movements, no
matter whether he was alone or with other people, whether
he was occupied or idle.   When he was about thirteen
years old he had had to wear a regulating plate on account
of the irregularity of his teeth.   The pressure of the plate
on his gums had been painful to him.   But he had made
no complaint and had preferred to react to the stimulus
with a continual sucking at the part of the gums concerned.
He further admitted that he could obtain pleasurable
feelings in yet other ways.   He used to use his tongue in
order to make stroking and tickling movements against
his palate; and these movements gave him voluptuous
sensations.   He was quite aware of the sexual nature of all
these acts.   We may well speak of an *oral masturbation* in
a case of this kind.

Certain symptoms of the patient stood in the closest
relation to the erotogeneity of his oral cavity.   In the first
place his compulsive habit, already mentioned, of opening
his mouth wide certainly had such an origin.   For as soon
as he was with a male person he had a compulsive phantasy
of taking the other man's penis into his mouth.   And while
he was half giving way to this phantasy with feelings of
terror, and half attempting to ward it off, he would make
that gasping movement of his mouth whose meaning could
not be a matter of doubt for a moment.

Now we regularly observe that an organ from which
too much is demanded as an erotogenic zone is no longer
able to carry out successfully its other functions.[1]   In the
present case the mouth could not carry out those functions
which were of a non-sexual nature.   As soon as the patient
was in the company of other persons it was almost impossible
for him to speak or eat.   For instance, he was unable to
carry on a conversation with his colleagues in the common
workroom.   And if in the course of the morning they took
out some lunch which they had brought with them and

[1] Freud has dealt with this process more especially in the case of the eye in
his paper on 'Psychogenic Visual Disturbance according to Psycho-Analytical
Conceptions' (1910).

began to eat it, it was impossible for him to do the same. He used to bring back his sandwich uneaten in the middle of the day, and throw it away in the street, so as not to be questioned about it at home. The effect of the psycho-analytic treatment in this connection is worth noting. His compulsive homosexual attitude, associated with constant anxiety, had scarcely given way to normal sexual interests when he became capable of eating and speaking with his colleagues.

We can see in both these cases what a dominating influence the pleasure in sucking obtains when it persists into adult life, and how it can affect a person's whole conduct. Apart from the few extreme cases of this nature, there are a great many people who have to pay a certain permanent tribute to their oral zone without actually forming any severe neurotic symptoms. The conflict between their auto-erotism and other interests in life is settled by means of compromise-formations. For instance, such people may be efficient and capable in their work— they may have been able to sublimate successfully a part of their libido—but their auto-erotism dictates the condi-tions on the fulfilment of which their capacity to work depends. I once treated a neurotic who could only con-centrate on mental work if he had previously masturbated. In a similar manner many people can only concentrate their thoughts if they at the same time put a finger in their mouth or bite their finger nails or gnaw a pen-holder. Others have to bite or lick their lips while they are doing hard work. Their auto-erotism only permits them to work consecutively so long as it receives a certain measure of gratification at the same time. And the necessity many men are under of smoking while they work may be to some extent accounted for in the same way. But there are more complicated factors at work here.

It is not possible to make a sharp distinction between normal inclination and habit on the one hand, and patho-logical compulsion on the other in this matter. For practical purposes, however, we can in general set up one criterion, viz. the manner in which the individual tolerates

temporary abstinence from the accustomed stimulus.   The
reaction of a person to the frustration of a source of pleasure
on which he is morbidly fixated will bear a pathological
stamp.   He will form neurotic symptoms.

VI

There is no doubt that in the normal person the gratification of his sexual needs exercises a marked influence
on his disposition.   Yet the healthy person is capable of
tolerating a temporary lack of his accustomed gratification
within certain limits.   He is, moreover, able to procure
certain substitutive gratifications along the line of sublimation.   The same thing can be said of a great number of
neurotics.   But others are extremely intolerant of every
diminution of their accustomed pleasure, and the more
so the less their instinctual life is removed from the infantile
level.   They are very like ' spoilt ' children.   Their libido
incessantly craves for its accustomed gratification.   In
consequence they become completely dependent on it and
react with great displeasure if they have to dispense with
their usual pleasure.   And this displeasure passes over into
a marked depression of spirits.

This origin of neurotic depression of spirits does not
seem to me to have been sufficiently highly estimated.
The neurotic person's auto-erotic gratification has two
uses: it prevents a depression of spirits when it is threatened
and removes it when it is there.   Its use in the first sense
is illustrated by the fact that many neurotics immediately
turn to their usual method of gratification early in the
morning in order to prevent a depression of spirits.   This
refers to those people who have difficulty in the morning
in shaking off sleep.   Every new day, every return to
waking life, fills them with lively displeasure.   This displeasure would last and spoil the whole day for them if
they did not have recourse to their usual form of gratification as to a prophylactic against their neurotic depression.   And the various kinds of excitation of the oral
zone, which have already been discussed in detail, are of

particular significance in this respect.   Neurotic behaviour
of this kind cannot be better exemplified than in the case
mentioned above of the nine-year-old child who could not
be got to leave her bed in the morning until she had been
given her beloved bottle of milk.

I should like to discuss in greater detail those neurotics
who employ a pleasurable oral stimulus to dispel their
depression.   I shall purposely leave aside the question of
alcohol as a corrective for depression, because its effect as
a narcotic complicates the matter.

The case of a young cyclothymic female patient whom
I had under observation is particularly instructive.   She
was scarcely able to get mental contact with other people
at all, and had tended to withdraw from them and yield
entirely to her auto-erotic inclinations.   When she became
depressed she used to employ various means to relieve her
condition, of which the chief one interests us here.   This
was to buy some food.   Even while she was eating it she
would feel her spirits rise.   Another method which acted
beneficially on her frame of mind was characteristic of her
auto-erotic tendencies.   She used to ride in a tram for hours
together and obtain from this a very marked pleasure in
movement.[1]   If she felt depressed she used to spend the
greater part of the day in taking tram rides and eating food
which she carried about with her.

How deeply rooted in the infantile all things of this kind
are was demonstrated to me very clearly in the psycho-
analysis of a young man whom I treated for a neurotic
depression.   He was unable for many years after puberty
to transfer his libido on to other women on account of being
very strongly fixated on his mother.   For a long time he
had found a substitutive gratification in his profession,
until certain circumstances brought on an internal conflict
of which he was not conscious.   His fixation on his mother
and his contrary tendency to detach himself from her came
into violent conflict.   His work ceased to gratify him.   The
first result was a depression of spirits, at the beginning
of which something surprising happened.   One day, filled

[1] See Chapter X.

with an intense dissatisfaction with life, feeling without energy and wanting nothing to eat, he went to bed. His mother brought him a cup of milk. As he put the cup to his mouth and his lips came in contact with the fluid, he had, as he expressed it, ' a mingled sensation of warmth, softness, and sweetness '. This sensation surprised him, and yet seemed to be something known to him in the distant past; and at the same time it had an inexplicably soothing effect on him. Psycho-analysis soon solved the puzzle. The patient had been nursed by his mother during the whole first year of his life, and had sucked with great intensity (a fact which was told me by his own parents). During the following years he had often grasped at his mother's breast, and had used fond expressions for it in his childish language. When now his attempt to get rid of his fixation had failed, as I have described, and he began to suffer from a severe depression, he unconsciously turned again to his earliest source of pleasure. The milk brought him by his mother awakened the earliest traces of pleasurable memories, and he was able to alleviate his depression for the time being.

A phenomenon well known to the specialist in nervous diseases now becomes intelligible. Depressed or excited neurotics are often favourably influenced, though only for a time, by merely swallowing medicines, even when they have no sedative action. To explain this fact we are accustomed to fall back upon the suggestive effect of the medical prescription; but experience goes to show that neurotics can feel soothed for the moment by taking anything into the mouth, without a medical prescription. An important factor is here easily overlooked. In the life of every person there was a time when he was freed from all excitement by taking a fluid. The ' suggestive ' effect of a bottle of medicine does not lie only in the physician's treatment by any means, but at least as much in its function of supplying something to the patient's mouth which arouses echoes in him of his earliest pleasurable memories.

The tendency of nervous people to want first one diet and then another prescribed for them, and to prefer as far as possible a fluid *régime*, is also partly explicable in this way. We may call to mind more especially that class of patients who like to be fed by a nurse in bed.

We must, however, not forget the very frequent refusal of food by such patients. This symptom appears in neurotic diseases in numerous and often disguised forms. I will only mention loss of appetite, nausea in regard to eating, sickness and vomiting. Concerning the origin of these symptoms there is nothing of importance to be added to what has already been said.

We often find in people who are mentally depressed a conscious and openly expressed tendency to reject food. This tendency is observable in its most pronounced form in those depressions which are met with in the psychoses. Hence we may expect that the psycho-analysis of these diseases will give us information about the deeper causes of such a refusal of food.

VII

Among the most important and striking manifestations of depressive mental disturbances are found two symptoms which have an immediate relation to the taking of food. These are the refusal to take food and the fear of dying of starvation.

When, some years ago, I made a first attempt[1] to explain the structure of depressive mental disturbances on psycho-analytical lines, I did not give those two symptoms the consideration which they now appear to me to merit. I believe that I am now in a position to give further information concerning the psycho-genesis of depressive states, but I am well aware how far I am from being able to furnish a comprehensive and conclusive solution of the problem.

Anyone who observes a melancholic depressed person at all attentively will at once receive the impression that the patient has no desire to live; and he will be inclined to see in his refusal of food the expression of a suicidal tendency. There is nothing to object against the correctness of this

[1] [No. 26, A. B.]

explanation in itself. Nevertheless, the psycho-analyst cannot be satisfied with it, because it is incomplete and one-sided. The question arises why, if the patient has decided to die, he should choose the lengthy and uncertain way of starvation. Moreover, psycho-analytical experience puts one on one's guard against accepting too readily an idea which seeks to trace back a psycho-pathological phenomenon to conscious and logical causes.

In the same way the origin of the second of the two symptoms mentioned above—the fear of dying of hunger— cannot be accounted for by a few simple causes. This fear of starvation is found most frequently in states of depression belonging to the period of involution. A primitive psychological view of this condition would perhaps be as follows: When a man feels that he is ageing he inclines to worry about the future; and, since the tendency to nervous and psychic disturbances is especially great in the period of involution, this worry is expressed in a morbid anxiety or in a depressive delusion, according to the disposition of the individual.

Such an explanation does not deal with the essence of the condition. It only views the idea as it is formulated —its manifest content. It discloses neither the impelling forces of the psychosis, nor the deeper meaning of the symptoms. In psycho-analysis the latent content of the morbid ideas is looked for. Already in my earlier paper [1] I was able to point out that depressed, low-spirited patients mourn for their lost capacity to love. Now the period of involution, in which states of depression break out most frequently, brings with it a decrease of genital erotism. Among women the feeling of being no longer the object of male desire is of especial significance. But psycho-analysis of depressive mental disturbances occurring in earlier life shows that the same situation obtains. The sick person rejects from consciousness the perception of this internal alteration. At the same time his libido undergoes a regressive change of a particularly far-reaching nature.

A deeper insight into the structure of depressive psy-

[1] [No. 26, A. B.]

choses has led me to conclude that in these patients the libido has regressed to the most primitive stage of its development known to us, to that stage which we have learned to know as the oral or cannibalistic stage.

Even under normal conditions traces of a regressive change of the libido can be seen in the age of involution; and in neurotic persons the signs of this process stand out with unmistakable clearness. But as a rule the regression is not such an extensive one, and it pursues a quiet and even course. The certain signs of this process are so well known to the psycho-analyst that a slight reference to them will be sufficient.

In the climacteric many persons give more attention to the question of nutrition than they used to do. Parallel with the retrogression of the sexual functions (in the strict sense of the word) there appears an increased interest in the matter of food. The regressive tendency of this process is clearly shown from the fact that such persons frequently revert to a childish partiality for sweets. It is also worth noting that at the same time increased attention is given to the functions of the bowels. The more the genital zone retires into the background as a source of pleasure, the more many individuals turn back to oral and anal erotism. It can be frequently noticed that people of this age have an increasing tendency to make oral and anal matters the subject of their conversation.

As we have said, the same kind of thing is found in neurotics to a marked extent. In them ideas concerned with the taking of food assume a hypochondriacal [1] character.

In melancholic states of depression the libido seems to regress to the earliest stage of development known to us. That is to say, in his unconscious the melancholic depressed person directs upon his sexual object the wish to incorporate it. In the depth of his unconscious there is a tendency to devour and demolish his object.

In my earlier paper I pointed out certain striking agree-

---

[1] I refer the reader to Freud's discussion of the psychogenesis of hypochondria. According to him this affection is based on a regression to narcissism; in other words, to one of the early stages of the libido. (Cf. Freud, ' On Narcissism: an Introduction ' (1914).

ments in the structure of melancholia and obsessional neurosis, and in this connection I called special attention to the ambivalence of feelings and the original predominance of sadism in the affective life of both classes of patients. I see now the necessity of emphasizing what seems to me to be an essential difference between those two disorders. I still think that in each case the libido is predominantly hostile towards the object of its desires and endeavours to destroy it; but it seems to me that in contrast to the sadistic desires of the obsessional neurotic, the unconscious wish of the melancholic is to destroy his love-object by eating it up.

Some of the self-accusations of melancholics draw the attention of the psycho-analyst to impulses of this kind, although the patients themselves are entirely unconscious of the connection. These self-reproaches have much that is typical in them. Many patients assert that they are the greatest criminals of all times and insist that they alone have brought all misfortune, all sin, into the world. Anyone who is acquainted with the methods of expression used by neurotics and psychotics will understand without difficulty the deeper meaning of such hyperbolic self-accusations. The patient is warding off from consciousness quite different ideas which would otherwise be particularly terrible and intolerable to him; and I think I am able to say that these ideas relate to his cannibalistic impulses. In certain cases this is quite obvious. For instance, Kraepelin in his text-book of psychiatry quotes among other examples the following: 'According to himself the patient had plunged the whole world into misfortune, had eaten his children and drunk up the springs of grace'. Most often, however, those self-accusations undergo a peculiar distortion.

We see the cannibalistic wish-phantasies very clearly expressed in one particular form of depressive delusion. This delusion was extraordinarily widespread among people in the past and has not wholly disappeared even at present. It is that of being transformed into a wild, man-eating animal—a were-wolf. The older psychiatry was so familiar with this delusional self-accusation that it gave to this particular form of 'possession' the name of *lycanthropy*.

More frequently, however, a peculiar distortion of the patient's self-accusations takes place. Whereas he consciously denies the *quality* of the desired act, he accuses himself of a *quantity* of crimes which he cannot possibly have committed in reality.

If we assume that the deepest repressed wishes of the melancholic are of a cannibalistic nature, that his ' sins ' in their essence refer to a forbidden, even detested, act of eating, then we understand the great frequency with which he refuses to take food. He behaves as though complete abstention from food could alone keep him from carrying out his repressed impulses. At the same time he threatens himself with that punishment which is alone fitting for his unconscious cannibalistic impulses—death by starvation.

The patient's anxiety lest he should die from hunger is now quite easy to understand too. His desire to ' incorporate ', to devour the desired object, meets with powerful internal resistances. Just like other desires the cannibalistic desire becomes changed into neurotic anxiety when its realization meets with too great a resistance. It is threatened with the fate of never being realized. The edict has gone forth that the mouth zone shall never experience that satisfaction which it longs for; and the result is a fear of dying of starvation.

I cannot leave the subject of the melancholic disturbances without pointing out that in the above discussion I have attempted only to explain the wish-content of certain depressive delusional ideas and the unconscious strivings that underlie certain characteristics in the conduct of the melancholic, and not the causes of melancholic depression in general. To attempt to solve this far-reaching problem does not come within the scope of the present investigation.

VIII

The unconscious cannibalistic impulses which appear to me to underlie definite symptoms of depressive mental disturbances also exist in normal adult people. They occasionally come to light in their dreams.

An acquaintance once reported to me the following dream: He saw before him a dish of food which his wife had prepared for him. The food looked like vegetables, but upon it lay the legs of a child, as though they had been cooked in the vegetables. They reminded him in his dream of the limbs of his little son. He awoke in great horror and, starting up out of sleep, realized quite clearly that he had been about to devour parts of his own child in his dream.

The horror which this man experienced at the mere thought of such an act is the same with which we are all filled when we think of the customs of cannibals. Even at the present time it occurs among certain peoples that a chief will kill his rebellious son, or cause him to be killed, and then eat him up.

In many legends of civilized people we meet with the god who devours his own children. This is not the place to enter into mythological and ethnological details. I can only refer the reader to the wealth of material which Rank has collected in his work on the *Inzestmotiv*, particularly the chapter which is devoted to the '*motif* of dismemberment'.

The numerous facts which I have brought together compel us to accept Freud's theory of an early cannibalistic stage in the development of the libido. This phase of the individual instinctual life corresponds exactly to the cannibalistic stage of civilization which has persisted up to the present day among certain peoples and which has also been traversed by the so-called 'cultural' races on the long road of their development. And just as certain psychic products of the healthy and sick individual are reminiscent of that early stage of his childhood, so in its legends and fairy-tales does the race as a whole preserve the traces of its remotest past.

CHAPTER XIII

EJACULATIO PRÆCOX [1] (1917)

No disturbance of male potency is so frequently observed by the nerve-specialist as that of *ejaculatio præcox*. This affection is well known not only to the medical profession but to the laity. In it there is a premature emission of semen immediately after or even before the intromission of the penis during sexual intercourse, and the erection comes to an end. This description is of course a very rough one. But although it has been the subject of special investigation its real nature has not been explained, still less its origin.

Up to the present this disorder has not been given a separate and thorough examination in the literature of psycho-analysis. It has only been treated in conjunction with other disturbances of potency. Steiner has made a condensed survey of psycho-analytical knowledge regarding impotence, while Ferenczi has gone more deeply into the origin of disturbances of potency, and has discussed its unconscious causes; but he has made no special inquiry into ejaculatio præcox.

Nevertheless, psycho-analytic literature already contains certain data which can form the basis of a more exact investigation of the subject. Besides Freud's works, I have in mind Sadger's [2] important contributions; and in the course of this paper I shall frequently refer to both those sources of information.

I have had the opportunity of treating quite a number

[1] [No. 54, A. B.]   [2] 'Über Urethralerotik' (1910).

of cases of ejaculatio præcox in neurotic persons. It is not my intention to report in detail any one analysis of such a case, but to give a brief account of the general conclusions I have gained from them in so far as they have a bearing on the subject.

1. *The Urethra as a leading Erotogenic Zone*

As has been said, the usual description of ejaculatio præcox is incomplete in various ways. If we follow attentively the accounts and free associations of patients—and if they are good self-observers—we shall discover a fact which has not hitherto received sufficient consideration. This is that in their case emission does not take place as a rhythmical expulsion but as a simple outflow of the semen. If the emission is not accompanied by active bodily movements or a maximum erection or even rhythmical contractions of the perineum, and if it actually takes place *ante portas*, then the presence of the semen as a substance is all that is left to remind us of a normal emission of the sex products. On the other hand, the similarity of ejaculatio præcox to another physiological process, namely, micturition, becomes very striking. This latter process takes place with the body at rest and the penis flaccid, and to the accompaniment of constant (not rhythmical) muscular contractions. Ejaculatio præcox can thus be looked upon as a combination of two processes: it is an ejaculation with regard to the *substance* of the emission, and a micturition with regard to the *manner* of it.

It is astonishing with what regularity the associations of the patients lead to this view sooner or later. And on the way to it a number of facts are discovered which indicate that in this group of neurotic persons there is a particular pleasure-value attached to micturition, and a strongly accentuated erotogeneity of the urethra.[1]

Nevertheless, the associations of the patients also point to an important difference between ejaculatio præcox and micturition which must not be overlooked. After infancy,

---

[1] Cf. Sadger's work quoted above.

although urination takes place under the compulsion of a
stimulus which sooner or later cannot be resisted, the child
has yet some free choice as to the moment it shall pass
water. And up to a certain point the same is true of normal
ejaculation. Premature ejaculation is, on the other hand,
independent of the patient's will in general. Consciously he
wishes to perform the sexual act normally, and he is each
time surprised at the premature occurrence of the emission,
as if it was something that was happening in too great haste.
Many patients say that at the moment of premature emission
they experience a feeling of shame with which anxiety and
palpitation of the heart are associated.

Ejaculatio præcox therefore takes place against the
person's conscious will. The process reminded us at first
of normal micturition, but now we shall have to modify this
view to some extent. We shall compare it with the manner
in which urine is passed in infancy. The passive outflow
of semen in ejaculatio præcox corresponds to the involuntary
passing of urine by the infant—a type of behaviour which,
as is well known, may be prolonged in certain neurotics
into adult age to a greater or less extent.

The free associations of the patients furnish material
which points unmistakably to this solution. If we follow
those associations without prejudice we come upon anam-
nesic data which are astonishingly similar in each case.
We learn—apart from those reminiscences relating to the
strongly accentuated pleasure connected with the voluntary
passing of urine in childhood—that it had been a difficult
task to train these patients in habits of cleanliness, that even
in adult age they often passed urine involuntarily in smaller
or larger quantities, that they were bed-wetters up to a late
period of childhood, and that they easily react to excitement
of any kind with an irresistible desire to urinate. The
same persons who have gained control only late on or
imperfectly over the functions of the bladder also tend to
have a premature and precipitate emission of semen.
According to their own account, the physical sensation of
premature emission is identical with that of urinary incon-
tinence. We shall consider later on certain very important

memories of childhood connected with exhibitionistic pleasure in passing urine in the sight of another person and with the assistance rendered by that person in such a situation.

It is now evident that these neurotic persons have remained behind at a definite stage in the development of their libido, and derive infantile pleasure from the outflow of their bodily products. Nevertheless, ejaculatio præcox has at the same time a pleasure and a displeasure value for them. Unable to attain the highest pleasure through a full masculine activity, they have turned to what is to them the most intense pleasure—to the passive one of allowing bodily products to flow out. On the other hand, the ejaculatio præcox is itself a source of severe displeasure for them. They suffer from tormenting feelings of insufficiency, experience nervous anxiety when premature ejaculation occurs, and are not infrequently sensible of something resembling self-reproach. This state of ambivalence is particularly to be noted in the same way as the pleasurable character of ejaculatio præcox, which is as a rule overlooked. In some patients the pleasurable side is emphasized, while in others the displeasure predominates.

It is clear from what has already been said that the libido of persons suffering from ejaculatio præcox has not attained full masculine activity. And this introduces us to a new peculiarity in the sexual life of these neurotics. But first we will turn again for a moment to the question of the pleasure in excretion exhibited by these patients.

If urethral pleasure is excessively marked we shall find that the ' too much ' in this place corresponds to a ' too little ' in another. Investigation of a number of such cases has shown—in spite of many individual variations, which will be mentioned later—that in all the patients the genital zone in the strict sense of the word has not become the leading zone. We must here call to mind Freud's classical theory, as it appeared in the first edition of his *Drei Abhandlungen zur Sexualtheorie*. According to it, the primacy of the genital zone is established in the male child with the advent of puberty, and the remaining erotogenic zones become subordinated to it. They supply the fore-pleasure, while the excitation of the genital zone (in particular the glans penis) leads to the final, satisfaction-pleasure. In the female sex the chief erotogenic state should pass to the vagina at puberty, but this transition often does not take place, because the girl retains from her childhood the predominant excitability of the clitoris—the organ which represents the female analogue to the penis. As Freud says, female sexuality gives up a male characteristic when it transfers the leading erotogenic rôle from the clitoris to the vaginal orifice. But if the pre-eminence of the clitoris persists, a lack of excitability in the woman during the sex act—frigidity—is the result.

In very many cases of ejaculatio præcox it is in fact found that the surface of the glans penis is deficient in excitability. Very frequently these patients cannot tolerate the use of condoms, since the covering sheath removes what little remains of the irritability of the nerve-endings of the mucous membrane.

In some cases, however, this statement seems to be completely contradicted. I refer to those neurotic individuals in whom the slightest genital contact with the female body—and especially the slightest manual contact on the part of the woman—is sufficient to cause a precipitate flow of semen. But such an over-excitability of the genital zone is no indication of its primacy; on the contrary, it is an expression of its weakness. The specific male genital functions—erection, intromission, friction of the female parts—are completely absent. Even before erection has begun to take place a flow of semen occurs, which we have already recognized as equivalent to micturition. We shall later obtain a better understanding of this process.

Whereas in female frigidity the glans clitoridis has, so to speak, taken over all the irritability, the reverse has happened in the ejaculatio præcox of the male. In this the glans penis has lost its normal excitability, so that the person's sexuality has lost its specific male character.

Ejaculatio præcox and female frigidity have still further corresponding characteristics. Besides a deficiency of genital sensitiveness there frequently exists in the male patients a particular erotogenic state of the perineum and posterior part of the scrotum. These parts correspond developmentally to the introitus vaginæ and its surrounding parts. The relation between ejaculatio præcox and female frigidity might now be stated as follows: The leading zone in each sex has surrendered its natural importance to those parts of the body which are the equivalent of the leading zone in the opposite sex. It is the perineal portion of the male urethra in which the pleasurable sensations of ejaculatio præcox are localized. The muscles in the perineum which act in the expulsion of semen deserve particular notice. They normally carry out their function by making rhythmical contractions. In ejaculatio præcox, on the other hand, a relaxation of those muscles occurs, exactly as in micturition. Now it is worth noting that in some patients the muscles of the perineum occasionally contract spontaneously. But this process is equivalent to a neurotic symptom acting independently of consciousness. I refer to those perineal spasms which patients so often describe.

So far our conception of ejaculatio præcox, based on psycho-analytical investigations, seems to be contradicted by one fact. In by far the greater majority of cases premature ejaculation only occurs when the person attempts to carry out the sex act, and not in masturbatory excitation. It may be asked why in the latter case the compromise which we have spoken of between ejaculation and micturition does not take place. We can meet this objection provisionally by conjecturing that it is precisely the presence of the woman which occasions the neurotic disturbance. And this brings us to the problem of the attitude of the patients in question to the female sex.

II. *The Masculine-Active Impulses and their Modifications*

Persons who suffer from premature ejaculation can be divided into two groups, which, however, are not sharply separated from each other. In the first place, the condition is met with in those men whose entire individuality seems inert, without energy and passive,—in short, 'unmanly'. In the second place, it is met with in erethistic, over-lively men who seem to be in a constant state of haste. This apparent contradiction is easily explicable to the psycho-analyst. Every activity which can only attain its object in a hurried and precipitate way is threatened with resistances. The neurotic who does everything in haste is fleeing from the unconscious resistances within him; he has to carry out his projects in feverish haste before his resistances break through and compel him to renounce all. The inert neurotic has given up the struggle against these forces; the erethistic man is still fighting against them.

We may say that premature ejaculation occurs in those men who are burdened with strong—partly unconscious, partly conscious—resistances against activities of a specific-ally masculine character.

The neurotic type who is without energy usually ex-presses a conscious antipathy towards exercising any activity in sexual matters; he even has an open desire to assume the female role. One of my patients liked to play the part of the succubus, and gave as a reason for this that if he paid a girl he did not want to have to exert himself as well—that she ought to 'work' for her money. Naturally, neurotic persons with this degree of displeasure in move-ment are not favourable subjects for medical treatment, particularly if they consciously defend their abnormality. Their chief desire is to attain sexual gratification without taking any active part in it.

The erethistic neurotic type who lives in perpetual haste generally looks upon coitus as a troublesome task to be got through as quickly as possible. His nervous haste does not leave him even when he is with his female partner. Under the influence of unconscious factors the sexual act reaches its end precipitately before it has actually begun.

The antipathy felt by the first group of neurotics to any active motor performance extends to other things. I shall take as an example their attitude towards sport. Many of them have a pronounced antipathy to all physical exertion, whereas others go in for sport with excessive enthusiasm and in an over-zealous and precipitate manner; but as soon as they fail in any way they give the whole thing up.

The inertness and passivity exhibited by these neurotics is, however, a reactive manifestation. It can be found that such an attitude has taken the place of a too forcible sadistic impulse. The tendency to be quarrelsome, to have fits of anger, and to commit violent acts, is extraordinarily marked in such people, in so far as it is not paralyzed by another character-trait which distinguishes them—namely, cowardice. Excessive irascibility and a paralysis of the normal male pleasure in attack are found here in close proximity. The frequent juxtaposition of excessive ambition and severe resistance against work is also met with in this group of neurotic persons.

In this description we have touched upon a number of important manifestations which are usually found in neurotic persons side by side with their ejaculatio præcox, but we have not penetrated beneath the surface of this condition. If we allow ourselves to be guided by the free associations of the patients, we learn that originally their libido was not lacking in a sadistic component. Psychoanalysis teaches us that in most of the cases, besides the unmanly and passive or precipitate and over-active attitude, there exists in the unconscious an aggressive and cruel attitude towards the female. In their dreams and other products of phantasy these patients often produce the idea of killing the woman by copulating with her. In these phantasies the penis is the sadistic weapon.

The reactive transformation of these impulses leads to a result which we can observe often enough in such patients. The male genital is robbed of its dangers. It may no longer get into that condition in which it might be employed in a sadistic way against the woman. Premature flaccidity and ejaculation removes that danger. In addition to this, many of the patients have a pronounced anxiety before carrying out the sexual act about causing the woman pain. There remains to them a remnant of potency only if they are certain of the complete consent of the woman; and their aggressive impulses are so suppressed that all sexual initiative, in the strict sense of the term, is absent. Many of them are quite unable to establish any relations with women on their own initiative; others are capable of beginning such a relationship, but lose their activity at the moment when it ought to pass over into physical action.

One of my patients was, in general, impotent at the commencement of his marriage. He was conscious of a hostile and aggressive attitude towards his wife. The slightest quarrel with her used to result in complete impotence on his part. On the other hand, he noticed that immediately after having had a reconciliation with her he used to have a relatively good potency. Thus whenever the external reason for hostility and a desire for revenge had temporarily disappeared he used to attain a transitory sexual activity.

The associations of the patients indicate in addition, moreover, that in their unconscious ejaculatio præcox signifies the extreme opposite of killing. It is very frequently associated with the unconscious, or even conscious, idea of the subject's own death as a kind of effortless expiring. Many patients make use of the expression that they feel themselves vanishing or melting away. It is typical that a feeling of faintness is sometimes connected with premature ejaculation.

The element of loss of male activity is further shown in the affect of anxiety that so frequently accompanies ejaculatio præcox. Such an anxiety is found more especially in those patients whose lives are spent in a state of perpetual haste. Now, haste and anxiety again remind us of the behaviour of frigid women who according to our experience are constantly in a state of hurry. The peculiar fear such women have of never ' getting a thing done ', which is shown in all their daily tasks, is also found in these male neurotics. They execute their sexual functions in haste, as though they expected to be disturbed every moment. This fear of being disturbed is closely associated in their unconscious with their attitude towards their father. They dread his all-seeing eye and his chastising hand. We find ourselves on familiar ground here, namely, that of castration anxiety.   This fear, whose importance Freud has recognized in the mental life of the small boy and in the unconscious of the growing man, also exerts its influence on the psycho-genesis of ejaculatio præcox.

The same patients exhibit marked dread of the female genital.   It seems to them to be something uncanny. Psycho-analysis repeatedly confirms the fact that it was the lack of the penis in women which originally called out their castration anxiety.   And physical proximity with a woman always re-awakens this horror in them.

Closely related to this anxiety is another one—that of losing the penis through the sexual act itself.   It is not rare for patients to tell the physician of a fear which they have had since puberty that they may not be able to withdraw their penis from the body of the woman, and have to leave it behind.   This fear is founded on one of the infantile sexual theories which are re-vivified at puberty.   According to it there is only one union between the woman and the man, and in it she robs him of his genital organ by tearing it off or pinching it in.   The fear of such an event furnishes a further explanation of the fact that libidinal desire and erection are frequently present in the patients to begin with, but that immediately after intromission or just before bodily contact erection disappears.   These unconscious ideas force the patient to seek safety at the last moment.   In conscious-ness he reacts to this unmanly retreat with lively and tormenting feelings of insufficiency.

In some cases the patients' associations made it clear that the ejaculatio præcox was a kind of castration in the presence of the woman.   We shall later on discover the explanation of phantasies of this kind.

The lack of sexual activity in our patients is expressed in yet another form.   As we know, neurotic resistances against the carrying out of an action are often expressed by clumsiness in its execution.   Persons who suffer from premature ejaculation regularly exhibit a marked clumsiness in the performance of the sexual act.   Their incapacity to introduce the penis without the help of the female partner

T

is a typical instance of this. It is chiefly on this ground that they fear to have intercourse with a sexually inexperienced woman who cannot come to their aid in this way, and from whom they cannot ask any such assistance. I shall give a further explanation of this behaviour later on.

III. *Narcissism as a Source of Sexual Resistances*

So far our investigations have definitely shown that in the patients in question there has been an inhibition in the development of the libido. The patient has not reached the normal attitude of a man towards a woman, and his sexuality shows a number of infantile traits. To put this more accurately: the patients have normal feelings in so far as their libido is consciously directed, if not exclusively yet in its essentials, towards having normal sexual intercourse with women. It is true that in some even getting on to terms of intimacy with women is difficult; but they share this difficulty with other neurotic persons. They only react in an abnormal and specific manner when they have to prove their sexual activity in the strict sense of the word. At that moment a disturbance makes itself evident which is opposed to their conscious wish and which proceeds from unconscious libidinal counter-impulses. We have already learned that these impulses are infantile in their nature. Their tendency is to prevent the sexual act (in its strict sense) from taking place. Instead of it there occurs a passive emission of semen, similar to the involuntary flow of urine in the child. The active motor behaviour of the male is replaced by complete passivity.

What is the nature and origin of the unconscious resistances which prevent the individual from adopting a normal attitude towards the opposite sex? My psychoanalyses invariably pointed to the factor of narcissism, not in the sense of a complete regression of the libido to that infantile stage, as Freud has shown to be the case in paranoia, but as a disturbing influence emanating from repressed narcissistic tendencies that have not succeeded in obtaining complete control. But they nevertheless manifest their power in that they compel the individual to make certain compromises, one of which is that disturbance of potency with which we are here concerned.

A cursory observation of some of the persons suffering from ejaculatio præcox will make this idea clear. These people display an unusual amount of vanity as regards their clothing and appearance The slightest criticism will make them fly into a rage. They want to be admired by their *entourage*, and are filled with a pathological desire to excel. Psycho-analysis brings to light the narcissism of these patients, and never fails to reveal the fact that their object-love is very imperfect. Their true love-object is themselves. In accordance with Freud's view,[1] we find in all our patients a particularly high and abnormally emotional estimation of the penis. An excessive fear of loss or damage to that organ is one of the results of such an over-valuation of it. The psycho-analysis of every case of ejaculatio præcox reveals an abundance of other manifestations of narcissism as well. In order to estimate these at their true value it is necessary to glance briefly at related manifestations in childhood.

The child experiences the first gratifications of its libido from its bodily functions, such as the taking of nourishment and the excretory processes. It directs its first feelings of love to those persons who feed it and take care of it. And since in doing this they have to touch its body, those persons evoke in it pleasurable sensations through the stimulation of erotogenic zones. The child accepts these pleasurable sensations as gifts. This stage of the development of the libido, in which the child itself is the central point of its still limited world, and in which it accepts demonstrations of love from other persons without giving anything in return, we term narcissism.

The child's relations to its love-object develop a step further when it begins to give to other persons something of its own. The products of its own body—which according to the child's idea are a part of its own body—are the first coinage which it makes use of. These products

---

[1] Freud, 'On Narcissism : an Introduction' (1914).

are subjected to a narcissistic over-estimation.   I will quote the common instance of a child who when it is handed round the family circle will always elect, for some unknown reason, to wet a particular person with its urine.   This act is one of the most primitive marks of love, and is far more primary than kissing or embracing, which the child learns only through imitation.   In this connection we are reminded of the forms of greeting of many primitive peoples.   When one man gives another a part of his own bodily products, for example, saliva, it signifies: ' I am giving you a part of myself, something that is very precious to me; therefore I mean well by you '.

The history of our patients enabled us to establish the fact that they had taken particular pleasure in micturition in childhood, and had set a higher value on the penis than is usually found in childish narcissism.   As regards micturition, it seems as though a constitutional peculiarity underlay the pleasure taken in that function.   If we realize what a high value is normally assigned to the penis in the stage of childish narcissism—a value which is based both on pleasure in touching and pleasure in excretion— then we begin to see what are the possible consequences of a constitutionally reinforced urethral pleasure.   At a time when he should long since have turned to normal object-love, the individual will still retain a strong tendency to linger behind in his narcissism.   Furthermore, an over-estimation of the penis as an organ of micturition will be firmly implanted in his mind; so that when later on the organ has to fulfil its true sexual function it refuses to do so.   The result is that compromise which we have already recognized in ejaculatio præcox.

We are now at last able to comprehend the unconscious sexual aim of that symptom.   The normal sexual aim is a physical union with the woman.   In this the man has to accomplish a motor act which should produce gratification in him and at the same time in the woman.   The tendency of ejaculatio præcox is quite different.

As we have said, the patient's libido has remained to a great extent in the stage of narcissism.   Just in the same way as the small child wets his mother with his urine which he cannot as yet contain, the patient wets his partner in his premature ejaculation, thus making evident that she is a substitutue for his mother.   Moreover, the mother or nurse is compelled to touch the little boy's genitals when she assists him in making water or in washing and drying his body.   The pleasure got by the child from being touched in this way is evident from the patient's associations, coming as they do from his unconscious.   One of his unconscious sexual aims is to have his genitals touched by the woman,[1] and then to ejaculate as though he was passing urine.   The significance of the woman as mother is obvious in this connection too.   And, in especial, one peculiarity of our patients which we have already mentioned now becomes intelligible.   This is their tendency to require manual help from the woman in effecting intro-mission.   Pleasurable touching of the penis was one of the early and very significant proofs of love on the part of the mother.   As we know, the person suffering from premature ejaculation is not able to give love, but only to receive it. And in order to do this his unconscious endeavours once more to restore the ways of life of early childhood.

One of these ways has not yet been considered, but the ideas expressed by the patients bring it into prominence. Giving away the products of its own body is not the child's only expression of love in the stage of narcissism.   Another method of conferring love and asking for it is found in exhibitionism.   In the second half of their third year and the first half of their fourth year more especially, small boys are very prone to exhibit themselves before their mother, particularly when micturating, for which function they no longer need their mother's help as they did before. A boy of about four years of age whose urethral erotism was well within the normal limits often used to ask his mother if he should show her his penis.   He, moreover, used a self-invented term for this part of his body.   When he had passed water he often used to ask if it was 'a lot'. His narcissism appears very clearly here—his desire to be

[1] Cf. once more Sadger's work mentioned above.

admired for his performance. On one occasion when he was with his parents at the seaside he used to take pleasure in passing water whenever a wave approached him. On being asked why he did this, he replied, ' so that there shall be a whole lot of water '. The child's narcissism evidently found particular gratification in the idea that the whole sea was his own product.

This narcissistic vanity in regard to the quantity of the emitted substance finds many forms of expression in neurotic persons and is a factor in ejaculatio præcox. As we have already said, some patients are proud of the ejaculation which does not take place inside the body of the female but as it were before her eyes. It is clear therefore that there is an exhibitionistic tendency in ejaculatio præcox. Premature ejaculation carries on the theory of infantile narcissism, according to which the child's own attraction —and particularly his penis and his urinary activities— exercise an irresistible charm over the woman (the mother).

We have already mentioned one form of self-deception which can be explained as a result of narcissism. Some patients delude themselves with the belief that ejaculatio præcox is a sign of an unusually passionate temperament. With this piece of self-deception there is occasionally associated another one, which is that ejaculatio præcox is a sign of a more refined and exalted nature in contrast to the coarse aggressiveness of other men. The symptom which has arisen from repressed narcissism is thus given a secondary justification of a narcissistic kind whose purpose is easy to see. The patient would like to show himself more delicate than his father, whom he considers as a violent and brutal man, and so to supplant him in his mother's affections. The idea of his father's brutality originates in certain childhood experiences. As a child the patient had witnessed sexual intercourse between the parents, and had pictured it as an act of violence on the man's part. This ' sadistic ' theory of coitus becomes active at the time of his own sexual maturity, and normal sexual intercourse appears to him to be an act of brutality. Ejaculatio præcox appeals, as it were, to the feminine delicacy of his mother.

It says in effect: 'Look, I am treating you more gently than my father does'.

It must, however, be borne in mind that this exhibiting before the woman (the mother) bears an ambivalent character. It is not only a proof of the person's love and of his desire to be admired and touched, but at the same time a rejection of the woman. My psycho-analytical experience has regularly shown that this exhibitionism contains a strongly affective hostile attitude which is more especially expressed in a feeling of contempt for the woman. The hostility is derived from infantile sources, especially from childish jealousy. The contempt finds its natural explanation in the person's over-estimation of the penis. He looks upon the woman as inferior and contemptible because she lacks this part of the body. Quite a number of those who suffer from ejaculatio præcox have a disdain for women in general; they cannot cease scoffing at their 'imperfections'. In many cases this attitude is expressed in a violently affective antagonism to the present-day feminist movement.

We have thus arrived at the rather curious conclusion that ejaculatio præcox is also an expression of hostility and contempt which the patient evidences towards women in general as well as to a particular one. Several of my psycho-analyses have given me information about this tendency which I had not at once recognized. From this point of view ejaculatio præcox—and especially when it occurs *ante portas*—is a soiling of the woman with a substance representing urine. We must here have regard to the ambivalent character which attaches to the giving of one's own excreta to another person. Up till now we have recognized it as a means of expression of childish love. A parallel from folk psychology will make this ambivalence clearer. Spitting at another person, which among certain peoples represents a friendly form of greeting, becomes, as repression advances (*i.e.* with the development of civilization) an expression of the strongest contempt. Every child passes through a stage which corresponds to the point of view of these most primitive people—the point of view belonging to the stage of narcissism. On one occasion a little girl of four years called her saliva 'beautiful, clean tongue-water', thus showing a narcissistic appreciation of it which was quite contrary to the canons of polite behaviour. What is later looked upon as nasty and unclean appears in this stage of development in an entirely opposite light. We may also note that neither the small child nor the primitive man feel any disgust of urine. We need only call to mind the fact that among certain negro tribes the cooking utensils are cleaned with urine. Among such people a narcissistic estimation of the bodily products is still very prevalent.

There is another motive which is very closely associated with the unconscious purpose of soiling the woman. My psycho-analyses have again and again demonstrated the fact that wetting the woman in this way represents an act of defiance. The mother has the task of educating the child in habits of cleanliness and in the control of its sphincters. If the mother becomes an object of hostility and contempt, the child opposes her endeavours with a marked defiance—an attitude which we very often meet with in the character of adult neurotics. Thus we must also see in ejaculatio præcox a defiant relapse into that uncontrolled emptying of the bladder which is a characteristic of infancy.

We began by saying that the soiling of the love-object with urine or other bodily products is an infantile narcissistic expression of fondness; but deeper analysis now shows that we have here an example of most marked ambivalence, and once again teaches us that premature ejaculation has the character of a compromise. For when the neurotic person with an ambivalent attitude towards women gives the woman something of his bodily possessions by means of ejaculatio præcox, he is only giving something in appearance. In reality his hostile attitude causes him to guard these possessions jealously. His partner receives nothing, for he keeps his physical energy, and gives her no sensation of pleasure. It is true that he pours out his semen, but he does not give it to her; and, incidentally, he gives her no child. On the contrary, he excites expectation in her and then disappoints her.

As we have already said, every patient of this kind has a passive attitude towards women. He is permanently dependent on his mother, and struggles against this dependence which is lodged in his unconscious. This defensive struggle appears on the surface as a struggle against women. But in it he does not have the advantage of possessing a powerful male activity. He has to content himself with disappointing them, and in this way he takes revenge on every woman for the disappointments of love to which as a child his mother subjected him, and which he finds repeated again in later years.

A hint may be given here regarding other symptoms that are often found in conjunction with ejaculatio præcox, and that arise from the same sources and manifest themselves in the entire social attitude of the patients. In agreement with the narcissism and ambivalence of their feelings, they oscillate between a precipitate transference and a too timid reserve. Many of these patients react to a difference of opinion, to criticism by others, etc., either with a sudden outburst of anger or with a cold withdrawal into themselves. A certain combination of character-traits is so typical of this kind of neurotic that whenever it is met with the presence of ejaculatio præcox can be inferred with some degree of certainty. At a meeting of the Berlin Psycho-Analytical Society on one occasion, certain abnormal affective states in a neurotic patient were being discussed. During the discussion I expressed the opinion, based on the description of the patient's social attitude, that he suffered from ejaculatio præcox; and this surmise proved to be quite correct.

In conclusion, I might mention a rarer neurotic disturbance which is not so well known in medical circles, yet which, although the reverse of ejaculatio præcox, is intimately related to it. I refer to the symptom of impotentia ejaculandi. In many neurotic persons no ejaculation occurs during the sexual act. In this case also there is a sexual disinclination arising from narcissism. In these patients the 'keeping to themselves' is the predominant motive. The effect is the same as in ejaculatio præcox: narcissism gains the upper hand and the woman is disappointed. It need hardly be mentioned here that there is every kind of gradation from normal ejaculation to premature emission on the one hand and to its entire absence on the other. Retarded ejaculation is a not infrequent symptom of many neuroses.

It is the task of psycho-analytical treatment to free the patient from his narcissistic attitude, and to point out to him the path to a normal transference of feelings. If we can succeed in removing his narcissistic rejection of the female, the path is made free for him to carry out the normal sexual functions. Psycho-analysis acts in a similar manner in removing the female counterpart to ejaculatio præcox—frigidity.

Naturally, different cases present various degrees of severity of the illness. The milder disturbances of this nature can appear at times in men disposed to them and disappear without any treatment, though there is a constant risk of relapse. A cure, or at least a distinct amelioration of the symptoms, can be obtained by psycho-analysis even in severe and obstinate cases.[1] From the point of view of prognosis those cases are least favourable in which the ejaculatio præcox set in immediately on the attainment of sexual maturity, and has reappeared again and again for a number of years. These are the cases which exhibit an exceptionally marked urethral erotism as opposed to a genital erotism, and in which the pleasure-value of ejaculatio præcox outweighs its displeasure-value. The treatment of this condition may be technically one of the most difficult tasks for the psycho-analyst, since he has to contend with the very considerable amount of narcissism present in such patients. Nevertheless, a persevering and consistent use of the psycho-analytic method will enable him to surmount difficulties even as considerable as these.

[1] In two cases of impotentia ejaculandi also I have succeeded in obtaining a permanent cure through psycho-analysis.

CHAPTER XIV

THE SPENDING OF MONEY IN ANXIETY
STATES [1] (1917)

THE attitude of the neurotic to the possession of money
has been the subject of much study in psycho-
analytic literature. Both Freud and other analysts
who have followed him in directing their interest to ' anal '
character-traits have dealt with neurotic avarice and the
anxious retention of money from the point of view of unconscious motives; but the opposite behaviour of many
neurotics, the excessive spending of money, has not received
the same attention, although the psycho-analyst frequently
comes across it. This tendency appears suddenly in
many neurotics, like a kind of attack, and stands in con-
spicuous contrast to their usual parsimony.

From the few cases that I have been able to observe
during my psycho-analytic work, it seems to me that this
condition is found in a definite group of neurotics—in
persons who are in a state of permanent infantile dependence
on the parental home and who are attacked with depression
or anxiety as soon as they are away from it. The patients
themselves say that the spending of money relieves their
depression or anxiety; and they produce rational explanations for this, such as that spending money increases their
self-confidence, or that it distracts them from their condition.
Psycho-analysis takes the unconscious into consideration
and adds a deeper explanation to this purely superficial one.
Every psycho-analysis of a case of this kind shows once

[1] [No. 55, A. B.]

again that the patient, in consequence of the fixation of his libido, is prevented from removing himself physically from his parents or the persons representing them. Leaving the home signifies to his unconscious a detachment of the libido from its object. Two contrary mental currents can always be found to exist in these patients—a conservative one, in the direction of a permanent fixation, and another one, in the direction of turning towards objects of the external world.

Every attempt to transfer the libido on to new subjects is accompanied by severe anxiety, for the very reason that the unconscious desire is so especially violent and impetuous. It is only necessary to call to mind the fact that female patients who suffer from street anxiety are heavily burdened with unconscious, at times even conscious, phantasies of prostitution. Their unconscious wants to yield without restraint to every person they meet; but their conscious anxiety restricts the transference of their libido within the narrowest bounds, so that they become incapable of making free use of it, and this not only in the strict sense of actual sex-relationships.

A far-reaching limitation of genital sexuality leads to a substitutive and increased emphasis of other erotogenic zones. Anal erotism takes the place of genital erotism to a greater or less degree. In many cases it can be very clearly shown that the morbid fixation of the patient on his father or mother is carried on through the agency of the anal zone. A small abstract from an analysis will illustrate this.

The patient, a woman, who suffered from severe street anxiety, was completely attached to her father. Her repeated attempts to loosen the fixation always miscarried. This fixation had been very much reinforced by the patient's father during her childhood by the fact that he had been excessively careful about the activity of her bowels, and had very frequently administered enemas, etc. This mistaken procedure had contributed in a fatal manner to maintaining her childish dependence. To use a nursery expression, she could ' do ' nothing without her father, could only ' leave the room ' under his superintendence.

As her analysis showed, her attempts to free herself also demonstrated her anal fixation. To her unconscious, emptying her bowels without paternal superintendence signified independence. If she went out of the house and was overtaken by anxiety she used as a defence against it to spend money on all sides in a quite needless way. She was giving out *money* instead of *libido*. The explanation of this compensatory significance of money is derived from the unconscious equation of money and fæces. It is worth noting that the patient herself suspected that she frequently intensified her anxiety in order to provide herself with a reason for spending money.

In this patient, and also in two other cases, I noticed the tendency to buy many objects at random, articles that were for the most part valueless and only desired at the moment. In this way they could deceive themselves about the free motility of their libido, which in reality was fixed and inhibited to the last degree. Buying objects which have only a momentary value, and passing quickly from one object to another, are symbolic gratifications of a repressed desire—that of transferring the libido in rapid succession to an unlimited number of objects. The allusion to prostitution is unmistakable in this connection; for there, too, money is the means of obtaining transitory and easily changed relationships.

The patients' idea that they spend money in order to increase their self-reliance now receives corroboration in a certain sense; for the spending of money deceives them as to the want of freedom of their libido and thus relieves them for a short time of the painful feeling of sexual insufficiency. In other words, they are under an abnormally strict prohibition, proceeding from the parental imago, against expending their libido freely. A compromise between instinct and repression is made by which the patient, in a spirit of defiance, does expend—not his sexual libido but an anal currency.

We are here reminded of the attitude of certain neurotics whose libido is also bound in an excessive degree. They are, in part or wholly, incapable of sexual love in the mental and physical sense. They give other people not love but pity and become benefactors, and often give money away too freely. They are for ever doomed to this form of substitutive gratification; and, in the vague feeling that they are not giving the right gift in a qualitative sense, they exaggerate it in a quantitative one. Nevertheless, their spending of money is altruistic in its effect, while in the previously described cases such an effect is entirely absent. What is common to both groups is that the spending of money forms a substitute for the sexual transference which their neurosis forbids and at the same time serves as a bulwark against neurotic disturbances.

CHAPTER XV

A PARTICULAR FORM OF NEUROTIC RESIST-ANCE AGAINST THE PSYCHO-ANALYTIC METHOD [1] (1919)

WHEN we begin to give a patient psycho-analytic treatment we make him acquainted with its fundamental rule to which he has to adhere unconditionally. The behaviour of each patient in regard to that rule varies. In some cases he will easily grasp it and carry it out without particular difficulty; in others he will frequently have to be reminded of the fact that he has to make free associations; and in all cases we meet at times with a failure to associate in this way. Either he will produce the result of his reflected thoughts or say that nothing occurs to him. In such a situation the hour of treatment can sometimes pass without his producing any material whatever in the way of free association. This behaviour indicates a ' resistance ', and our first task is to make its nature clear to the patient. We regularly learn that the resistance is directed against allowing certain things in the mind from becoming conscious. If at the commencement of the treatment we have explained to the patient that his free associations give us an insight into his unconscious, then his refusal to give free associations of this kind is an almost obvious form for his resistance to take.

Whereas in most of our cases we meet with a resistance of this kind which appears and disappears by turns, there is a smaller group of neurotics who keep it up without inter-

[1] [No. 58, A. B.]

ruption during the whole of their treatment. This chronic resistance to the fundamental rule of psycho-analysis may obstruct its progress very much and even preclude a successful result. The question has hitherto received little consideration in our literature, like so many other questions of technique. I have met with this difficulty in a number of cases, and other psycho-analysts tell me that they have had the same experience. There is therefore a practical as well as a theoretical interest in investigating more strictly this kind of neurotic reaction to psycho-analysis.

The patients of whom we are speaking hardly ever say of their own accord that 'nothing occurs' to them. They rather tend to speak in a continuous and unbroken manner, and some of them refuse to be interrupted by a single remark on the part of the physician. But they do not give themselves up to free associations. They speak as though according to programme, and do not bring forward their material freely. Contrary to the fundamental rule of analysis they arrange what they say according to certain lines of thought and subject it to extensive criticism and modification on the part of the ego. The physician's admonition to keep strictly to the method has in itself no influence on their conduct.

It is by no means easy to see through this form of behaviour. To the physician who is not experienced in recognizing this form of resistance the patients seem to show an extraordinarily eager, never-wearying readiness to be psycho-analysed. Their resistance is hidden behind a show of willingness. I must admit that I myself needed long experience before I was able to avoid the danger of being deceived. But once I had correctly recognized this systematic resistance its source also became clear to me. For although neurotics of this type, of whom I have treated a certain number, exhibited great variety as regards illness and symptoms, in their attitude towards psycho-analysis and the physician they all produced a certain number of characteristics with astonishing regularity. And I should like to make those characteristics the subject of discussion in the following pages.

Under the apparent tractability of these patients lies concealed an unusual degree of defiance, which has its prototype in the child's conduct towards its father. Whereas other neurotics will occasionally refuse to produce free ideas, these patients do so continually. Their communications are superabundant in quantity, and, as we have said, it is this fact that blinds the inexperienced physician to their imperfection as regards quality. They only say things which are 'ego-syntonic'. These patients are particularly sensitive to anything which injures their self-love. They are inclined to feel 'humiliated' by every fact that is established in their psycho-analysis, and they are continually on their guard against suffering such humiliations. They furnish any number of dreams, but they adhere to the manifest content and understand how to glean from the dream-analysis only what they already know. And they not only persistently avoid every painful impression but at the same time endeavour to get the greatest possible amount of positive pleasure out of their analysis. This tendency to bring the analysis under the control of the pleasure principle is particularly evident in these patients and is, in common with a number of peculiarities, a clear expression of their narcissism. And it was in fact those among my patients who had the most pronounced narcissism who resisted the fundamental psycho-analytic rule in the way described.

The tendency to regard a curative measure merely as an opportunity for obtaining pleasure and to neglect its real purpose must be regarded as a thoroughly childish characteristic. An example will illustrate this. A boy of eight was ordered to wear spectacles. He was delighted with this, not because he was to be relieved of an unpleasant visual disturbance by their use, but because he was to be allowed to wear spectacles. It soon turned out that he paid no attention to whether the trouble was removed by means of the spectacles or not; the fact of possessing them and being able to show them at school pleased him so much that he forgot all about their therapeutic value. The attitude of the class of patients we are discussing to psycho-analysis is

exactly the same.   One expects from it interesting contributions to the autobiography which he is writing in the
form of a novel; another hopes that psycho-analysis will
advance him to a higher intellectual and ethical level, so
that he will be superior to his brothers and sisters towards
whom he has hitherto had uncomfortable feelings of
inferiority.   The aim of curing their nervous disabilities
retreats into the background in proportion as such narcissistic interests predominate.

The narcissistic attitude such patients adopt towards the
method of treatment also characterizes their relations to
the analyst himself.   Their transference on to him is an
imperfect one.   They grudge him the rôle of father.   If
signs of transference do appear, the wishes directed on to
the physician will be of a particularly exacting nature; thus
they will be very easily disappointed precisely in those
wishes, and they will then quickly react with a complete
withdrawal of their libido.   They are constantly on the
look-out for signs of personal interest on the part of the
physician, and want to feel that he is treating them with
affection.   Since the physician cannot satisfy the claims of
their narcissistic need for love, a true positive transference
does not take place.

In place of making a transference the patients tend to
identify themselves with the physician.   Instead of coming
into closer relation to him they put themselves in his place.
They adopt his interests and like to occupy themselves
with psycho-analysis as a science, instead of allowing it to
act upon them as a method of treatment.   They tend to
exchange parts, just as a child does when it plays at being
father.   They instruct the physician by giving him their
opinion of their own neurosis, which they consider a particularly interesting one, and they imagine that science will be
especially enriched by their analysis.   In this way they
abandon the position of patient and lose sight of the purpose
of their analysis.   In particular, they desire to surpass their
physician, and to depreciate his psycho-analytical talents
and achievements.   They claim to be able to 'do it better'.
It is exceedingly difficult to get them away from precon-

ceived ideas which subserve their narcissism. They are given to contradicting everything, and they know how to turn the psycho-analysis into a discussion with the physician as to who is 'in the right'.

The following are a few examples: A neurotic patient I had not only refused to associate freely but to adopt the requisite position of rest during the treatment. He would often jump up, go to the opposite corner of the room and expound, in a superior and didactic manner, his self-formed opinions about his neurosis. Another of my patients displayed a similar didactic attitude. He actually said straight out that he understood psycho-analysis better than I did because it was he and not I who had the neurosis. After long-continued treatment he once said, ' I am now beginning to see that you know something about obsessional neurosis '. One day a very characteristic fear of his came out. It was that his free associations might bring to light things that were strange to him but familiar to the physician; and the physician would then be the ' cleverer ' and superior person of the two. The same patient, who was much interested in philosophical matters, expected nothing less from his psycho-analysis than that science should gain from it the 'ultimate truth'.

The presence of an element of *envy* is unmistakable in all this. Neurotics of the type under consideration grudge the physician any remark that refers to the external progress of their psycho-analysis or to its data. In their opinion he ought not to have supplied any contribution to the treatment; they want to do everything all by themselves. This brings us to a particularly striking characteristic which all these patients show, which is that they make up at home for their failure to associate freely during the hour of treatment. This procedure, which they very often call ' auto-analysis ', contains an obvious depreciation of the physician's powers. The patients actually see in him a hindrance to progress during the hours of treatment, and are exceedingly proud of what they imagine they have achieved without his assistance. They mix the free associations obtained in this way with the results of considered thought, classify them according to some definite idea, and produce them in this state to the physician next day. In consequence of severe resistances, one of my patients thought that he was making very little progress during a succession of hours, and finally that he was making none at all. The next day he came to me and said he had had to ' work ' for many hours alone at home. Naturally I was meant to infer from this the weakness of my own abilities. One element in such an ' auto-analysis ' is a narcissistic enjoyment of oneself; another is a revolt against the father. The unrestrained occupation with his own ego and the feeling of superiority already described offers the person's narcissism a rich store of pleasure. The necessity of being alone during the process brings it extraordinarily near to onanism and its equivalent, neurotic day-dreaming, both of which were earlier present to a marked degree in all the patients under consideration. ' Auto-analysis ' is for them a form of day-dreaming, a substitute for masturbation, free from reproach, since it is justified and even prescribed on therapeutic grounds.

I may say that the cases to which I refer belong chiefly to the obsessional neuroses. One case was an anxiety-hysteria mixed with obsessional symptoms, and in another there was a paranoid disturbance. In view of the more recent results of psycho-analysis we shall not be surprised to find pronounced sadistic-anal traits in all the cases. Their hostile and negative attitude towards the physician has already been mentioned; and anal-erotic motives explain the rest of their behaviour. I will give a few examples of this. In these as in other neurotics with strong anal erotism, talking in the analysis, by means of which psychic material is discharged, is compared to emptying the bowels. (I may say that some identify free associations with flatus.) They are persons who have only with difficulty been taught in childhood to control their sphincters and to have a regular action of the bowels. They used to refuse to empty their bowels at a specific time, so that they could do this when it suited their convenience; and they now behave towards psycho-analysis and the physician in the same way from unconscious motives. Tausk [1] has recently pointed out the fact that small children like to deceive adults with regard to emptying their bowels. They appear to try very hard to satisfy the demands of their mother or nurse, but they have no motion. Tausk adds that this is perhaps the earliest occasion on which the child becomes aware that it can take grown-up people in. The neurotics under discussion continue this tradition of infantile behaviour. They pride themselves, as it were, upon being able to decide whether, when, or how much they will give out from their unconscious psychic material. Their tendency to bring perfectly arranged material to the analytic hour shows not only an anal-erotic pleasure in systematizing and cataloguing everything but exhibits yet another interesting feature. Freud [2] has recently drawn attention to the unconscious identification of excrement and gifts. Narcissistic neurotics with a strong anal disposition such as we are dealing with here have a tendency to give presents instead of love. [3] Their transference on to the physician is incomplete. They are not able to expend themselves unconstrainedly in free associations. As a substitute they offer their physician gifts ; and these gifts consist of their contributions to psycho-analysis which they have prepared at home and which are subject to the same narcissistic over-estimation as the products of the body. The narcissistic advantage for them is that they keep the power of deciding what they are going to give.

One of my obsessional patients who suffered from brooding and doubting mania contrived to make psycho-analysis itself, its methods and its results, the subject of his brooding and doubts. He was almost entirely dependent on his family, and he used to plague himself among other things with doubts as to whether his mother or Freud was ' in the right '. His mother, he said, had often advised him, in order to improve his constipation, not to dream in

[1] *Internationale Zeitschrift für ärztliche Psychoanalyse*, v. Jahrgang, 1919, S. 15, footnote 1.
[2] ' From the History of an Infantile Neurosis ' (1918).
[3] See Chapter XIV.

the closet but only to think of the process of defæcation itself; whereas Freud, on the contrary, gave exactly the opposite rule, namely, to associate freely and then ' everything comes out of itself '. It was a long time before the patient carried out his psycho-analysis no longer according to his mother's method, but according to that of Freud.

The well-known parsimony of anal-erotics seems to be in contradiction with the fact that these patients readily make material sacrifices for the treatment, which, for the reasons above mentioned, is a protracted one. This behaviour, however, is explicable from what has already been said. The patients are making a sacrifice to their narcissism. They are all too apt to lose sight of the fact that the object of the treatment is to cure their neurosis. It is another consideration which enables them not to pay attention to expense. To paraphrase an old anecdote, it might be said that nothing is too dear for their narcissism.

The character-trait of parsimony is, besides, found elsewhere in them. They save up their unconscious material. They are prone to build on the belief that one day ' everything will come out all at once '. They practise constipation in their psycho-analysis, just as they do in the sphere of bowel activity. Evacuation is to take place on some occasion after a long delay and to give them particular pleasure. This finale is again and again postponed, however.

The analysis of patients of this description presents considerable difficulties. These difficulties reside in part in the pretended compliance with which the patients cloak their resistance. For analysis is an attack on the patient's narcissism, that is, on that instinctual force upon which our therapeutic endeavours are most easily wrecked. Everyone who is acquainted with the situation will therefore understand that none of my cases gave quick results. I must add that in no case did I obtain a complete cure, though I did succeed in effecting an improvement of some practical value, which in a few cases was of a far-reaching character. My experiences perhaps give a too unfavourable picture of the therapeutic prospects. When I treated my first cases I lacked a deeper insight into the peculiar nature of the resistances. It must be remembered that it was not until 1914 that we got our first knowledge of narcissism, thanks to Freud's classical study. I certainly have the impression that it is easier to overcome such narcissistic resistances now that I make known to these patients the nature of their resistances at the very beginning of the treatment. I lay the greatest stress on making an exhaustive analysis of the narcissism of such patients in all the forms it takes, and especially in its relation to the father complex. If it is possible to overcome their narcissistic reserve, and, what amounts to the same thing, to bring about a positive transference, they will one day unexpectedly produce free associations, even in the presence of the physician. At first these associations come singly, but with the advance of the process described they become more abundant. Therefore, though I have to begin with called special attention to the difficulties of the treatment, I should like in conclusion to issue a warning against making an entirely unfavourable prognosis for all such cases.

Chapter XVI

THE APPLICABILITY OF PSYCHO-ANALYTIC TREATMENT TO PATIENTS AT AN ADVANCED AGE [1] (1919)

THE question of what the conditions are under which psycho-analytic treatment promises therapeutic success has hardly been discussed at all up to the present, except for some general remarks by Freud in a paper which appeared many years ago.[2]

Since then psycho-analytic experience has been much increased and its technique greatly developed. It therefore seems an opportune moment to consider more carefully this question, which is of great practical importance. The following remarks are intended as a first attempt to throw light on the subject.

In his paper Freud has expressed the opinion that psycho-analysis loses its effectiveness if the patient is too advanced in years. There is no doubt about the general correctness of this view. It was only to be expected that at the commencement of physical and psychical involution a person should be less inclined to part with a neurosis which he has had most of his life. Daily psycho-analytical experience, however, shows that we must not expect mental processes to be too uniform. It warns us against approaching the investigation or treatment of nervous conditions with a priori theories. For instance, has it not been shown that certain mental diseases which psychiatric medicine has pronounced to be quite intractable are accessible to psycho-

---

[1] [No. 62, A. B.]
[2] ' Sexuality in the Ætiology of the Neuroses ' (1898).

analytic methods? It would seem therefore incorrect to deny *a priori* the possibility of exercising a curative influence upon the neuroses in the period of involution. It is rather the task of psycho-analysis as a scientific procedure to inquire into precisely this question as to whether, and under what conditions, the method of treatment can attain results in patients in the later years of life.

Freud's opinion quoted above is often taken to mean that treatment in the fourth decade of life holds out doubtful prospects of relief, and that in the fifth decade, and particularly in the climacteric, the chances of achieving favourable results are decidedly adverse. Beyond fifty it is often denied that our therapy has any effect at all.

In my psycho-analytical practice I have treated a number of chronic neuroses in persons of over forty and even fifty years of age. At first it was only after some hesitation that I undertook cases of this kind. But I was more than once urged to make the attempt by patients themselves who had been treated unsuccessfully elsewhere. And I was, moreover, confident that if I could not cure the patients I could at least give them a deeper and better understanding of their trouble than a physician untrained in psycho-analysis could. To my surprise a considerable number of them reacted very favourably to the treatment. I might add that I count some of those cures as among my most successful results. I will give a few examples.

The first case of this kind held out the least favourable prospects of all. It was a melancholic depression, and the patient, a man, was in the period of involution and had proved refractory to treatment in institutions both for nervous and insane patients. Psycho-analysis had an exceedingly difficult task before it in this inhibited patient, who was in his fiftieth year. Nevertheless, within five months it succeeded in freeing him from his self-accusations and his negation of life, and in making him able to carry on his work. When treatment was begun, his trouble, which had been preceded by a nervous condition that had lasted many years, had existed in its pronounced form for fifteen months. Although the illness that was cured in this case was not of very long standing, there was no doubt that it promised to become a chronic one. And it was, besides, a very severe illness. After this I was scarcely able to regard as hopeless the treatment of a neurosis in the age of involution.

Later I undertook the psycho-analysis of a patient of nearly fifty years of age who was suffering from an obsessional neurosis; and by a not uncommon coincidence I soon afterwards received a second patient of the same class, aged fifty-three. In both these cases I succeeded in obtaining very good results.

The first patient had exhibited all the marks of what is called the obsessional character from his youth upwards; but until he was thirty-five years old he had only shown obsessional symptoms in a slight degree, and had not greatly suffered from them. After his marriage he had become completely dependent on his wife, and she used to decide everything for him. One day he discovered that she permitted herself an intimacy with a relative. This event awakened his jealousy, and led to the outbreak of his neurosis in its severe form. Now that his wife in whom he had placed absolute trust had proved herself unworthy of it, there was nothing left for him to depend upon. He developed the severest doubting mania imaginable. Among other things, he was constantly in doubt whether he had just committed a crime or not. If he saw a man turn out of the street and disappear into a house he was tortured with the thought that he might have murdered him and done away with the body. After the postman had brought a parcel and gone away again he used to search the whole house in the greatest state of anxiety in order to convince himself that he had not murdered him and hidden away parts of his body. All this was accompanied by torturing doubt as to whether he had written his name on a piece of paper that had been thrown away, so that it might be misused in some way. I only mention these few instances out of a great number in order to give some idea of the severity of the case. This man, who at the beginning of the treatment was filled with apprehensions, utterly helpless and dependent, made a very considerable recovery. Six years have now passed since the conclusion of the treatment without his having had any important relapse. He has had occasional fluctuations in his state of health, but none of any importance.

The other obsessional patient whom I treated at the same time suffered from very severe attacks of anxiety and states of depression. He too had always exhibited the signs of an obsessional character, among which exaggerated kind - heartedness and over - conscientiousness were especially prominent. Certain conflicts connected with his fixations on his family brought about the onset of his neurosis when he was between thirty and thirty-five years old. Psycho-analysis succeeded in removing his severe neurotic symptoms, including his attacks of anxiety and morbid doubt, and made him once more fit to take up the work he had been obliged to give up, and to enjoy his life.

I should also like to refer to the recovery of a female patient of forty-one with pronounced street and travelling anxiety. She had been subject to numerous neurotic symptoms from childhood, and had suffered for the last six years from the two serious disabilities mentioned above. She was completely cured. Eight years have now passed since the treatment and she remains without inhibitions as regards her freedom of movement.

Other cases might be adduced, and also some in which partial results were obtained in very severe and deeply-rooted anxiety-hysterias, states of depression, etc.

Having mentioned these gratifying results I must go on to report the failures. I need only briefly touch on those extremely unfavourable cases which very soon necessitate a discontinuance of the treatment. These are patients who instinctively retreat from every unwished-for discovery in their analysis, and even to the necessity of speaking about their instinctual life. More important for our present discussion are those cases in which we have to be satisfied with a partial improvement in spite of continued treatment. If we survey a certain quantity of successful and unsuccessful treatments in patients of this group, the problem of their varying results is explained in a simple manner. The prognosis in cases even at an advanced age is favourable if the neurosis has set in in its full severity only after a long period has elapsed since puberty, and if the patient has enjoyed for at least several years a sexual attitude approaching the normal and a period of social usefulness. The unfavourable cases are those who have already had a pronounced obsessional neurosis, etc., in childhood, and who have never attained a state approaching the normal in the respects just mentioned. These, however, are also the kind of cases in which psycho-analytic therapy can fail even if the patient is young. In other words, the age at which the neurosis breaks out is of greater importance for the success of psycho-analysis than the age at which treatment is begun. We may say that the age of the neurosis is more important than the age of the patient.

In this connection a comparison suggests itself with the prognosis in mental disorders. Among the psychoses known as dementia præcox (schizophrenia, paraphrenia) the prognosis is most unfavourable in those cases which have broken out at puberty or even in childhood, while those that set in at a more mature age tend more to remissions—and to remissions which are of greater permanence. The course taken by the psychoneuroses follows the same laws.

The question how far psycho-analysis can succeed in tracing out the infantile sexuality of neurotics of an advanced age is of great importance. From my experience I should say that it is by no means impossible to work back to the very earliest period of childhood. In a case of obsessional neurosis that I have recently treated, though the treatment is not yet terminated, I succeeded in this with a thoroughness which one could only have hoped for if the patient had been quite a young person.

In some of the cases psycho-analytic treatment in the age of involution is not conducted in quite the same manner as in younger patients. While in general we leave the conduct of the analysis to the patient, in that he chooses in each hour of treatment the starting-point of his free associations, certain older neurotics need to receive a stimulus from the physician on each occasion. I have repeatedly observed this in a pronounced form in obsessional neurotics of older years. Such patients were persons with a weak initiative in general, who had been dependent and lacking in self-confidence since their youth in definite respects. They now wished to be guided by their physician, who signified to their unconscious the superior father. I have many times met with the same thing in these patients at the beginning of their hour. They could not find the way to the psychic material by themselves; but as soon as a little stimulus was given to them, perhaps in the form of an allusion to what had already been spoken about, they immediately produced associations. This conduct is thoroughly infantile in character. I have met it in the treatment of children as well; for instance, in an intelligent boy of eleven who had adopted a strong positive attitude towards me as a father-substitute. It is significant that in youthful patients this behaviour ceases when opposition towards the father or father-substitute appears in the foreground.

With these remarks I hope to have afforded some guide in the choice of cases suitable for psycho-analytic treatment where the patient's age is somewhat advanced. In conclusion, I should like to call attention to the fact that more precise investigations would be useful as to why certain youthful cases prove refractory to psycho-analysis. A more precise standpoint as regards indication would spare us many failures and lead to a full development of the effectiveness of psycho-analytic therapy.

CHAPTER XVII

THE NARCISSISTIC EVALUATION OF EXCRETORY PROCESSES IN DREAMS AND NEUROSIS [1] (1920)

WHILE undergoing psycho-analytic treatment, a female patient had the following dream:
'I was sitting in a basket-chair near the wall of a house which was at the edge of a big lake. The chair was standing right on the water. There were boats on the lake and many people swimming in it. I saw two men in a boat, a young one and an older one. As the boat was approaching me there came a gust of wind which made a huge wave rise just behind the boat and engulf it and its occupants. The people who were swimming in the lake were drowned as well. Only one person, a woman, kept herself above water. She swam up to me and clutched at my chair. I thought that I could stretch out my leg for her to hold on to; but I had just as little sympathy for her as for the other unfortunate people, and I did nothing to help her.'

The analysis of the dream, as far as it is of interest here, elicited the following facts:

The two men in the boat were the patient's father and brother, upon both of whom her libido was over-strongly fixated. The woman who was swimming was her mother. I shall pass over the psychic constellation which caused the dreamer unconsciously to wish for the death of her whole family, and I shall only consider the method by which it was destroyed in her dream.

[1] [No. 63, A. B.]

In the dreams and neurotic symptoms of this patient, whose genital erotism was unusually strongly repressed, we find a very strong expression of anal and urethral erotism. The dream just quoted is an example of this. ' Stool ',[1] ' wind ', and ' water ' are its principal features. The dreamer's family is exterminated by wind and water. She herself appears, on account of the censorship, to be an uninterested looker-on. The lack of feeling with which she views the catastrophe arouses the suspicion that she herself is the cause of the disaster. And this suspicion becomes a certainty when we see how the dream ends. By refusing to help her mother she becomes the cause of her death.

In the psycho-analyses of neurotics we are accustomed to find that anal and urethral sensations are closely related to infantile impulses of love. And the analysis of the present patient produced a quantity of material in evidence of this. It entirely corresponds to our experience of the ambivalence present in the instinctual life of the neurotic when we find the functions and products of the bowel and bladder used as vehicles of hostile impulses. But it is rare to find those impulses so glaringly exhibited as in the example given above, where the functions of the bladder and the bowel are placed exclusively in the service of sadism, and urine and flatus appear as the instruments of a sadistic attack.

The enormous power which the dreamer ascribes to her excretions deserves special consideration. On the basis of this dream we are able to set beside the primitive idea of the omnipotence of thoughts, with which we are quite familiar, the idea of the omnipotence of the functions of bladder and bowel. Both ideas quite obviously express the same narcissistic over-estimation of the self. But the omnipotence of the functions of the bladder and bowel seems to be the more primitive of the two—to be the preliminary stage of the ' omnipotence of thoughts '. A second example may help to confirm this view:

A neurotic patient, a man, who had constantly imagined

---

[1] [German ' Stuhl '=(1) ' chair '; (2) ' stool ', ' fæces '. Cf. ' basket-chair ', German ' Korbstuhl '.]

he was a 'prince', and had played at being 'Kaiser' during his early years and who had in later childhood revelled in phantasies of dominating the world, experienced a peculiar change when he was eleven years old.   Up till then he had been entirely fixated on his mother, who had systematically prejudiced him against his father.   She had greatly increased his anal erotism by almost elevating to a cult her preoccupation about his motions.   She was constantly concerned about their quality and quantity, and used to give him an enema almost daily.   The boy had on his side developed neurotic pains in his stomach in order to compel his mother to continue the enemas.   When he was eleven years old he went a long journey with his parents.   One night, when they were staying in an hotel, he overheard his parents having sexual intercourse.   This event made all the more impression on him since for many years at home his parents had had separate bedrooms.   He now remembered that this event had seemed unbearable to him, and that he had quite consciously determined to prevent its recurrence.   For the remainder of the journey he managed to arrange things so as to share a room with his father.   Since his observation of parental intercourse he had identified himself with his mother and transferred his phantasies of anal coitus on to his father.   Up to this time he had attributed a penis to his mother, which was represented by the enema tube.   But now he took up a female-passive attitude towards his father.[1]   Soon afterwards he was confined to his bed.   During this time he went a couple of days without having an evacuation, and as a consequence of this he had a feeling of pressure in the abdomen.   That night he dreamed that he had to expel the universe out of his anus.

The idea of the omnipotence of defæcation is very clearly expressed in this dream.   It recalls the myths of the Creation, in which a human being is produced from earth or clay, *i.e.* from a substance similar to excrement.   The

---

[1] In his phantasies the patient retained the idea of a woman with a penis even in later years. He used to conceal his genital organs between his thighs in order to feel like a woman.

Biblical myth of the Creation has two different accounts concerning this. In the ' Elohistic ' version God created the universe and also human beings by means of his command, ' Let there be ', *i.e.* by the omnipotence of his thought, will, or deed. In the ' Jahvistic ' version a human being is created out of a clod of earth into which God breathes; so that here we find expressed the more primitive idea of the omnipotence of the products of the bowel. But we cannot go on to consider other mythological parallels in this place.

Returning to the sadistic significance of defæcation, I may mention that the patient who killed her family in her dream by means of her excretions was severely troubled with nervous diarrhœa. Besides the usual causes, psychoanalysis discovered a sadistic element at the bottom of this symptom. Her diarrhœa proved to be an equivalent of suppressed outbursts of rage. Other analysed cases have confirmed this connection. For instance, I know a neurotic woman who reacts with diarrhœa to any event which excites anger or rage.

It seems a curious thing that an outburst of rage should be represented by precisely this neurotic symptom. To find its explanation we must consider the behaviour of the child in the earliest period of its life. In the affect of rage the infant exhibits the same facial congestion, the same gestures, the same movements of the body as when it is expelling its stool. And it makes the same moaning sounds on both occasions. This identity between the means of expression employed in the two conditions indicates a close association between what are apparently dissimilar impulses. We can thus understand how an explosive evacuation of the bowels can offer to the unconscious of the neurotic a substitute for a discharge of angry affect that has not taken place.

The most fundamental relationship between sadism and anal erotism doubtless lies in the fact that the passive sexual feeling associated with the anal zone becomes coupled with the active-sadistic impulses—a combination of opposites which represents the earlier stage of the polarity of

x

male and female. The very marked ambivalent attitude present in the instinctual life of obsessional neurotics is based on this close connection between the active and passive impulses. The connection of sadistic and anal impulses mentioned above does not contradict this view; on the contrary, it shows that libidinal impulses of an active nature are also associated with activity of the bowels,[1] and shows us the over-determination of that relationship.

The narcissistic over-estimation of the excreta has long been recognized in psycho-analytic literature. As early as 1900, in his *Traumdeutung*, Freud has given examples of it. Dreams in which a flow of urine exercises powerful effects occur in women with a strongly marked ' masculine complex '. In an earlier paper [2] I have mentioned the case of a boy of three years old whose narcissistic megalomania was entirely unrepressed so that its connection with the excretions was easily recognizable. As he stood and urinated into the sea he tried to give the impression that the sea was his own product.

The two dreams I have mentioned are closely connected with this infantile phantasy. Whereas in the excretion dreams with which we are already familiar the products of the body are simply over-estimated in a quantitative sense, in the examples before us it is the functions of excretion that are over-estimated, and in the sense of possessing great and even unlimited power to create or destroy every object.

---

[1] The double—active and passive erotogenic significance of the anal zone has been discussed in detail by Federn in his ' Beiträgen zur Analyse des Sadismus und Masochismus ' (1913).

[2] See Chapter XIII.

CHAPTER XVIII

CONTRIBUTION TO A DISCUSSION ON
TIC [1] (1921)

A NUMBER of different phenomena were originally included under the name 'Tic', as, for instance, *tic
douloureux* (trigeminal neuralgia), facial spasms,
and many compulsive symptoms, as well as the symptoms
still designated as tics to-day. Nowadays it is only the
separation of tics from compulsive actions which raises
difficulties from the point of view of differential diagnosis.
Neither Meige, Feindel, nor Ferenczi solve this difficulty.
The characteristics of a tic as given by the first two authors
apply equally well to compulsive actions. The incapability
of mastering a stimulus, which Ferenczi describes, is very
well observed, but this likewise occurs in the obsessional
neurotic. Again, narcissistic phenomena on which Ferenczi
lays particular stress can be seen in all hysterical and
obsessional patients. Regression to narcissism, however,
certainly never goes so far in the person suffering from a
tic as in the psychotic patient. Ferenczi is quite right
in calling attention to the similarities between tics and
catatonia, but he overlooks the much more fundamental
differences between the two conditions. There can be no
question of a tic ending in dementia. On the other hand,
the assumption of an increased organ libido and the conception of a 'pathoneurotic tic' seem to be very useful.

[1] [No. 72, A. B.]
[NOTE. This is the report of a contribution by Abraham to a discussion at a
meeting of the Berlin Psycho-Analytical Society on June 9, 1921, on the subject of
Ferenczi's paper 'Psycho-Analytical Observations on Tic', which had appeared
earlier in the year.]

As far as I can see, a complete separation of tic and compulsive action is not possible, just as hysterical anxiety and conversion phenomena cannot be completely separated from each other. But the relationship between the two is very similar. The person suffering from a tic gives an ætiology for it; that is to say, he connects his suffering with events in his life, in the way that the hysteric does. But he does not attribute any significance to it in his mental life as the obsessional patient does, who fears disastrous results if he omits a compulsive action. The suppression of a tic is displeasurable; its resumption serves undoubtedly to relieve tension. I cannot agree with the view that the suppression of a tic causes anxiety.

An important objection follows from another consideration. Ferenczi says that a tic does not seem to contain any relation to an object. In my analyses, however, I have found a double relation to the object, namely, a sadistic and an anal one, and herein lies the similarity of a tic to an obsessional neurosis. This similarity seems to me to be a closer one than that to catatonia.

The tic first mentioned in psycho-analytic literature (*Studien über Hysterie*, 1895) was a clicking tic, by means of which the patient wished unconsciously to awaken her sick father who had just fallen asleep. A purpose directed against his life is undoubtedly expressed in this case. One of my patients suffering from *tic général* made snapping movements with his fingers, while at the same time he threw his arm forward with an aggressive gesture. The tic which takes the form of making grimaces has an obvious hostile significance. Many more examples of this kind can be adduced.

Other tics, particularly coprolalia, show their anal origin quite clearly, as Ferenczi has pointed out. Some—for example, the whistling tic—are derived directly from anal processes (flatus). Here the patient carries out his hostile and degrading purposes by anal means. Others again are imitations of sphincter contractions. Certain tics seem to be veritable mimic representations of Götz von Berlichingen's famous challenge.

On the basis of my material, which I cannot quote here in detail, the tic seems to me to be a conversion symptom at the anal-sadistic stage. The following scheme will make this view clear:

Object-love	Genital Organization	Control of organ innervation	Capacity to deal with psychical stimuli
		(NORMAL STATE)	
Object-love	Genital Organization	Conversion Hysteria	Anxiety Hysteria
Object-love	Sadistic-anal Organization	Tic	Obsessional Neurosis
Narcissism to Autoerotism	...	Catatonia	Paranoic states

According to this table tic is placed beside the obsessional neuroses, as conversion hysteria is beside anxiety hysteria.

It represents a regression one stage lower than the hysterical conversion symptom, and is nearer to catatonia than to hysteria. It stands, if one may say so, in the conversion and not in the anxiety series.

The differences between Ferenczi's views and mine as I have mentioned them in no way detract from the merit due to this author, who for the first time has ventured to make a comprehensive and psycho-analytic investigation of tics. And certain of Ferenczi's ideas, although they seem to me erroneous, have guided me in the opinions I have expressed above.

CHAPTER XIX

THE SPIDER AS A DREAM SYMBOL [1] (1922)

As far as I know there has been nothing of any practical value written in psycho-analytic literature about the significance of the spider as a symbol, although every analyst must have come across this symbol in the dreams of patients. Freud has once said that a spider represents one aspect of the mother, namely, the angry mother of whom the child is afraid. But it is not clear why it should be precisely the spider that stands for this side of the mother. One might say that it is because spiders catch and kill small animals, and small animals often represent children in dreams. But there are numbers of other creatures who prey on smaller, defenceless ones; why, then, should the spider be singled out to symbolize the wicked mother? The spider is one of those dream symbols whose meaning we know—at least in one aspect—without knowing the reason why it has that meaning.

In practice, however, we find that this meaning of spiders is not always true—or, at least, is not always their only meaning—as we should expect from our knowledge of the ambiguity of symbols. But we shall search our literature in vain for further information on this point. Stekel [2] mentions the spider as a phallic symbol, it is true, but he interprets the dreams he quotes in such a superficial manner that he throws no further light on the subject. In only one of the dreams quoted are the long legs of a species of spider (Phalangium) interpreted as phallic symbols. But this

---

[1] [No. 80, A. B.]
[2] *Die Sprache des Traumes,* S. 135.

spider does not spin a web, so that it remains uncertain what significance is to be attached to those spiders which do not have long legs and which spin webs.

In these circumstances we ought to make a careful note of each example independently. Several dreams of one of my patients at different periods of the treatment enable me to contribute something to the explanation of dreams about spiders.

The patient's first dream occurred a few days after the beginning of his treatment, one result of which had so far been the discovery of his attitude towards his mother. This had made a very great impression on him. It appeared that his fixation on her expressed itself in an excessive dependence on her will and on her views. There is no doubt that she was the dominant partner in his parents' married life. She had also taken upon herself to some extent the maintenance of the family, and in many respects played the part of the father in the patient's life. The ambivalence of his feelings towards her was expressed in a violent opposition to her which existed side by side with his dependence on her, but which up to the time of treatment had exhausted itself in fruitless outbursts of passion. It came out later that the normal Oedipus attitude of the patient had undergone a reversal. His mother figured in his unconscious as a male being endowed with masculine attributes, and in this layer of his unconscious phantasies his attitude towards her was a female-passive one.

The patient told the first dream as follows. 'I was in a bedroom with two beds in it. Two servants were tidying up the room. I and the maid who was on my left suddenly discovered a horrid spider on the ceiling. She lifted up a long broom and crushed the spider, although I told her it could be removed in a less drastic manner.'

The patient remembered that a spider had fallen into the bath on the day before the dream. His wife had wanted to let it drown, but he had rescued it and put it out of the window. The dream ended in the opposite way—the spider was killed. It is true that according to the manifest content of the dream it was not he himself but the servant on his left who killed the spider. This girl represented the dreamer's wife who had on the previous day wanted to let the spider drown, and who in real life signified to the patient the opposite of his mother. Through his marriage he had become disloyal, as it were, to his mother. We can also recognize in the two girls the two tendencies in him, namely, one hostile to his mother (the girl on his left) and the other friendly to her (the girl on his right). In his dream the first tendency obtains the upper hand. The significance of the spider as a mother symbol now at once becomes clear to us. The particular method of killing the spider in the dream—crushing it—is to be explained by the sadistic theory of coitus. (Incidentally, certain of the patient's day-dreams used to culminate in a number of people being crushed to death.) The associations showed that the long broom was a phallic symbol; so that the patient's latent wish to kill his mother by copulating with her becomes unmistakable.

The second dream occurred about two months later and was this: ' I was standing beside a cupboard in the office with my mother or my wife. As I was taking a pile of deeds out of the cupboard, a big, hairy, long spider fell out at my feet. I felt very glad that it did not touch me. A little later we saw the spider sitting on the floor, looking almost bigger and more horrible than before. It flew up and came whirring at me in a big semicircle. We fled through the door into the next room. Just as I was pulling the door to, the spider reached me on a level with my face. Whether it got into the next room, or was shut out in the office, or was crushed in the door I do not know.'

For some weeks prior to this dream the patient's resistances towards the female sex, or to be more correct, towards the female sex-organs, had come to light, together with his tendency to make himself into a woman by way of castration phantasies, and on the other hand to turn his mother into a man. He brought me a drawing of the spider as it appeared in the dream, and was himself astonished to recognize in his drawing the oval shape of the external female sex-organs, the hair surrounding it, and in the middle, where the body of the spider was, something that was unquestionably very like a penis.

The spider's falling down in the dream represents the fall of his mother's penis, which becomes detached on his going to the cupboard (mother symbol). His relief at not having come in contact with the spider, *i.e.* the maternal genitals, comes from his horror of incest. In real life the sight of the female sex-organs, and still more any manual contact with them, used to horrify him. The subsequent increase in size of the spider, which also rises up and flies in a semicircle through the air, is an obvious symbol of erection: the maternal phallus attacks the dreamer. The doubt at the conclusion of the dream as to whether it was crushed in the door, is significant. We here find a phantasy of crushing the penis such as we meet with in the phantasies of neurotic women with a marked castration complex. This feature also reminds us of the first dream in which the spider was also crushed.

We thus arrive at the conclusion that the spider has a second symbolic meaning. It represents the penis embedded in the female genitals, which is attributed to the mother. In support of this I may quote the dream of another patient, in which the dreamer attempted to enter a certain dark room filled with a number of small animals. From certain allusions in the manifest content of the dream, but particularly from the patient's associations, there was no doubt that the room represented the mother's body. As he entered it a butterfly fluttered towards him. For the sake of brevity I need only mention that, just as in other dreams, the wings of the butterfly had the significance of female genitals; this symbolic use of the wings is based, among other things, on the observation of their opening and closing. The body of the butterfly, which is concealed between the wings, was unmistakably a male genital symbol. The idea of a hidden female penis also came out in this patient's neurotic phantasies.

The 'wicked' mother who, according to Freud's view, is represented by the spider, is clearly a mother formed in the shape of a man, of whose male organ and masculine pleasure in attack the boy is afraid—just as young girls are timid in regard to men. The patient's feeling towards spiders can be best described by the word 'uncanny'.

A third dream which occurred about two months after the second one throws further light on the matter. The patient said: 'I was standing by the side of a bed. A spider was hanging in the air over the bed by one or two threads. It had a tuft of yellow hair on the upper part of each thigh. I was afraid that as it swung to and fro on its thread it might touch me or climb on to me. My wife, who was standing on my left, warned me of this. I hit my right hand against the principal thread on which the spider hung, and this prevented it from coming too near me. I repeated this several times, so that in a way I was playing with the spider or teasing it. I said to my wife proudly: "Now I know how to get the better of the spider!" It then disappeared from the dream. I had finally removed it, and I let my hand fall on the bed. To my horror I discovered that my hand was actually resting on a spider's web lying there. The web was the size of my hand, oval and somewhat convex. It was a spider's nest and perhaps full of little spiders. I pulled away my hand and ran into the passage; whether my hand had come in contact with little spiders, or whether any had settled on it I do not know. I could not examine the nest in my haste, but I called on my wife to do so.'

The hanging spider and the threads again represent the male genital organ of the mother; the swinging movement and the getting nearer to the dreamer signify erection and sexual attack, like certain symbols in the second dream. The tufts of hair also have a phallic significance; their duplication characteristically represents the absence of the thing they represent in reality. During the dream the dreamer becomes actively hostile to the spider; his fear of his mother's imagined penis disappears. We need not go into the other details of this part of the dream.

The dreamer next comes in contact with the spider's web, from whose size and shape we have no difficulty in recognizing the female genitals. He now has anxiety with regard to the real female genitals (that is to say, to the lack of a penis) in place of his previous anxiety regarding that fancied attribute. We again meet with the horror of touching that part of a woman's body. The little spiders which the dreamer imagines are inside it are typical symbols of children.   (The patient is the eldest of the family.)

In conclusion, we can say that these three dreams give an explanation of spider symbolism in three directions. The spider represents in the first place the wicked mother who is formed like a man, and in the second place the male genital attributed to her. In this the spider's web represents the pubic hair and the single thread the male genital.

The fact that each dream contains a special use of spider symbolism indicates that there are probably still further meanings of this symbol. Perhaps this communication of mine will stimulate others to publish similar and supplementary analyses.

The significance of the spider in folk psychology has not been sufficiently considered from the psycho-analytical point of view. The fact that it serves both as a good and a bad omen may be regarded as an expression of a generally widespread ambivalent attitude towards this insect. There is no doubt that it produces a feeling of 'uncanniness'[1] in many people. We feel justified in assuming that those feelings of uncanniness originate in the same unconscious source as that of the neurotics described above.

POSTSCRIPT

My view that the symbolic significance of the spider has not been exhausted in my communication has found speedy confirmation. After I had spoken on this subject at a meeting of the Vienna Psycho-Analytical Society, Dr. Nunberg mentioned some points from his analysis of a phobia of spiders. The spider in this case also represented the dangerous mother, but in a special sense. The patient's unconscious phantasies were concerned with the danger of being killed by his mother during incestuous intercourse.

[1] See Freud, 'The Uncanny' (1919).

Nunberg laid stress on the fact that the spider kills its victim by sucking its blood, and that this sucking served as a castration symbol in the case observed, *i.e.* it gave expression to the typical phantasy of losing the penis during the sexual act.

I might remark that I was on the track of similar connections from the beginning; but they were not supported by the associations of my patient, and I preferred to limit myself to the indisputable material obtained in that way. My patient's treatment had to be broken off for external reasons. If it can be taken up again later I shall probably be able to confirm Nunberg's very interesting findings, which form a necessary and illuminating supplement to my analysis.

During the same discussion Prof. Freud drew my attention to a remarkable biological fact which was unknown to me. Whether my patient—consciously or unconsciously —knew of it I do not know and have no means at present of finding out. It is this: the female spider is far superior in size and power to the male, and during copulation the latter runs a very great risk of being killed and devoured by her. There exists, therefore, a striking agreement between the ideational content of the phobia analyzed by Nunberg and a fact of natural science. I must refrain from attempting to explain this coincidence; but further investigations may perhaps throw some light upon it.

Chapter XX

AN INFANTILE THEORY OF THE ORIGIN OF THE FEMALE SEX [1] (1923)

FROM the psycho-analyses of many patients we become acquainted with the infantile idea, which is retained in the unconscious, that the daughter has been made a girl by castration on the part of the father. Recently a female patient told me a dream in which the determination of her sex was assigned in this way to her father. The process, however, was different from that which I have met before in dreams, and was, besides, located in the period before the patient's birth. The dream was as follows:

' I was lying on the ground under water. I was dead, that is to say, I was lying motionless; but I could still observe everything. I saw a big ship sailing on the water. A man with a long pole was standing on it. He was moving the ship forward with the pole, as they do on our rivers. He now plunged the pole into the water in my direction and made a hole in me with it in the region of my mouth. The next thrust struck me in the breast, and the third one bored a hole in my abdomen.'

The dreamer is inside her mother's body witnessing sexual intercourse between her parents—a situation which occurs in many patients' dreams. The particular point in this dream is, however, that the dreamer is made a woman by the process she is witnessing. The dream, therefore, gives expression to the idea that the vagina of the female child is bored out by the father's penis before her birth.

I need not go into the remaining determinants of the dream, as I merely wish to draw attention to an infantile sexual theory in it which I have not come across before.

[1] [No. 83, A. B.]

CHAPTER XXI

AN INFANTILE SEXUAL THEORY NOT HITHERTO NOTED [1] (1925)

A PATIENT in whose childhood there had been an unusually severe struggle between repression and sexual curiosity recounted to me during psychoanalysis two childish theories of procreation. The first was that the man embraces the woman and kisses her, and when this happens some of his spittle passes into her mouth and produces a child in her. Besides this theory, with which the psycho-analyst is familiar, the patient had constructed a second, according to which the man's breast, when he embraces the woman, excretes milk which passes into her breast.

I had never heard of this infantile theory before. It certainly does not belong to the *primary* theories of sexuality which are formed by all children with a great degree of uniformity. Moreover, it was proved that the theory was constructed when the patient had already passed the age at which the primary theories are formed. Now since the views of children in later years vary greatly according to the different external influences to which they are subjected, there would be little reason to spend time over this secondary sexual theory about which the patient told me. But the analysis of it helped me to understand better one of the common primary theories of reproduction, and this seems to justify me in making the present communication.

The capacity of loving the opposite sex was impaired in this patient owing to a vivid phantasy-life of a homo-

[1] [No. 110, A. B.]

sexual character.   In part it was a question of passive
homosexual phantasies having reference to older men,
these latter being father-substitutes.   In relation to his father
the patient identified himself with his mother in a manner
which we know from other observations to be quite common.
A second group of phantasies was active in character and
concerned boys or, later, young men some years younger
than the patient.   He remembered that in early childhood
he had a strong impulse to put his penis into the mouths of
smaller boys, though he never did any such thing.   Analysis
showed beyond doubt that in these imaginings also he
identified himself with his mother.   The boys or young men
stood for the patient's younger brothers, whom he, as the
eldest, had seen at their mother's breast.   This had roused
in him the most violent envy; his brothers were in possession
of something which he himself had once enjoyed but had
had to give up long ago.   His identification with his
mother was his reaction to the preference shown to his
younger brothers.

At a later period nothing stimulated his libido so much
as the sight of a nursing mother.   In his native country it is
quite customary for women of the lower classes to suckle
their children in the street.   The remarkable sexual excitement which accompanied every such impression in our
patient leads us to conclude that for him the suckling of a
child, *i.e.* the introduction of the nipple into the mouth of
another person, was the essence of sexual gratification.   To
his unconscious this situation was a substitute for coitus,
the active rôle being given to the nursing mother.   He
identified himself with her in the homosexual phantasies
mentioned which had to do with the introduction of his own
organ into the mouth of a boy.

I may mention here that in the patient's mother-tongue
the vulgar expression for semen is ' milk '.   This term
(which is widespread elsewhere) had been heard by him as a
little boy from older persons.

The identification of the male nipple with the penis
throws a light upon another of the sexual theories most
commonly met with.   I refer to the idea that the female has

concealed within her a very large penis into which the smaller male organ of the man must penetrate. I think this infantile theory has hitherto not received an adequate psychological explanation. It has been so natural to explain it from two sources: first, from the familiar idea that the female body possesses a male organ — an idea which is universal at a certain period of childhood and which Freud [1] has recently related to the ' phallic ' phase of libidinal development; and secondly, one was bound to add that, logically, only a smaller object could penetrate into a greater, so that the child had to assume the existence of a larger female organ. But we must not forget that in general rational explanations of this sort have very little psychological value.

A disparity between the male and female organ, in which the latter is the larger, does actually exist as regards the breast. Moreover, in my patient's case there was the additional fact that in his mother-tongue the male nipple is designated by a word which is a diminutive of the term used for the female breast. His idea of the little male nipple discharging some substance into the large female breast thus helps us to understand better the typical theory of a small male organ penetrating into the larger female one.

Neurotic men who are found on analysis to have retained the idea of the large female penis regularly suffer from the fear that they themselves have an abnormally small organ. This was the case with my patient, in whom the idea was an obsession, until it disappeared under analysis. The displacement of coitus-phantasies from the genital region to the breast meant for the patient a considerable saving of displeasure. For the smallness of the nipple in relation to the female breast was a characteristic of all men, so that this disparity did not give him any feeling of personal deficiency.

I think it is possible that the facts which I have only briefly touched on here may be of some importance in regard to infantile sexual investigations. To all appearance the male sex is superior as regards the genital organ and the female as regards the breast. This contrast must force

[1] Freud, ' The Infantile Genital Organization of the Libido ' (1923).

itself upon the child, and we cannot wonder if he carries his discoveries in respect of the one region over to the other. The sexual theories of children would thus contain a deposit of this psychological process, and the idea of the great size and strength of the woman's penis would therefore be largely determined by that organ being equated with the breast.

Y

CHAPTER XXII

MANIFESTATIONS OF THE FEMALE
CASTRATION COMPLEX [1] (1920)

THE psychological phenomena which we ascribe to the so-called castration complex of the female sex are so numerous and multiform that even a detailed description cannot do full justice to them. These questions are made still more complicated by their relations to biological and physiological processes. The following investigation, therefore, does not pretend to present the problem of the female castration complex in all its aspects, but is limited to the purely psychological consideration of material gathered from a wide field of clinical observation.

I

Many women suffer temporarily or permanently, in childhood or in adult age, from the fact that they have been born as females. Psycho-analysis further shows that a great number of women have repressed the wish to be male; we come across this wish in all products of the unconscious, especially in dreams and neurotic symptoms. The extraordinary frequency of these observations suggests that the wish is one common to and occurring in all women. If we incline to this view we place ourselves under the obligation of examining thoroughly and without prejudice the facts to which we attribute such a general significance.

Many women are often quite conscious of the fact that certain phenomena of their mental life arise from an intense

[1] [No. 67, A. B.]

dislike of being a woman; but, on the other hand, many of them are quite in the dark as regards the motives of such an aversion. Certain arguments are again and again brought forward to explain this attitude. For instance, it is said that girls even in childhood are at a disadvantage in comparison to boys because boys are allowed greater freedom; or that in later life men are permitted to choose their profession and can extend their sphere of activity in many directions, and in especial are subjected to far fewer restrictions in their sexual life. Psycho-analysis, however, shows that conscious arguments of this sort are of limited value, and are the result of rationalization — a process which veils the underlying motives. Direct observation of young girls shows unequivocally that at a certain stage of their development they feel at a disadvantage as regards the male sex on account of the inferiority of their external genitals. The results obtained from the psycho-analysis of adults fully agree with this observation. We find that a large proportion of women have not overcome this disadvantage, or, expressed psycho-analytically, that they have not successfully repressed and sublimated it. Ideas belonging to it often impinge with all the force of their strong libidinal cathexis against the barriers which oppose their entry into consciousness. This struggle of repressed material with the censorship can be demonstrated in a great variety of neurotic symptoms, dreams, etc.

This fact that the non-possession of a male organ produces such a serious and lasting effect in the woman's mental life would justify us in denoting all the mental derivatives relating to it by the collective name 'genital complex'. We prefer, however, to make use of an expression taken from the psychology of male neurotics, and to speak of the 'castration complex' in the female sex as well. And we have good reason for this.

The child's high estimation of its own body is closely connected with its narcissism. The girl has primarily no feeling of inferiority in regard to her own body, and does not recognize that it exhibits a defect in comparison with the boy's. Incapable of recognizing a *primary* defect in her body, she later forms the following idea: ' I had a penis once as boys have, but it has been taken away from me ',—a theory which we repeatedly come across. She therefore endeavours to represent the painfully perceived defect as a secondary loss and one resulting from castration.

This idea is closely associated with another which we shall later treat in detail. The female genital is looked upon as a *wound*, and as such it represents an effect of castration.

We also come across phantasies and neurotic symptoms, and occasionally impulses and actions, which indicate a hostile tendency towards the male sex. In many women the idea that they have been damaged gives rise to the wish to revenge themselves on the privileged man. The aim of such an impulse is to castrate the man.

We find therefore in the female sex not only the tendency to represent a painfully perceived and primary defect as a secondary loss, a ' having been robbed ', but also active and passive phantasies of mutilation alongside each other, just as in the male castration complex. These facts justify us in using the same designation in both sexes.

II

As was mentioned above, the girl's discovery of the male genitals acts as an injury to her narcissism. In the narcissistic period of its development the child carefully watches over its possessions and regards those of others with jealousy. It wants to keep what it has and to get what it sees. If anyone has an advantage over it two reactions occur which are closely associated with each other: a hostile feeling against the other person associated with the impulse to deprive him of what he possesses. The union of these two reactions constitutes *envy*, which represents a typical expression of the sadistic-anal developmental phase of the libido.[1]

The child's avaricious-hostile reaction to any additional possession it has noticed in another person may often be

[1] For a more detailed discussion of the character-trait of envy, cf. Chapter XXIII., ' Contributions to the Theory of the Anal Character '.

lessened in a simple manner. It may be told that it will eventually receive what it longs for. Such pacifying promises may be made to a little girl with respect to many things about her body. She can be assured that she will grow as big as her mother, that she will have long hair like her sister, etc., and she will be satisfied with those assurances; but the future possession of a male organ cannot be promised her. However, the little girl herself applies the method that has often been successful to this case, too; for some time she seems to cling to this expectation as to something self-evident, as though the idea of a lifelong defect were quite incomprehensible to her.

The following observation of a little girl of two is particularly instructive in this respect. One day, as her parents were taking coffee at table, she went to a box of cigars that stood on a low cabinet near by, opened it, and took out a cigar and brought it to her father. Then she went back and brought one for her mother. Then she took a third cigar and held it in front of the lower part of her body. Her mother put the three cigars back in the box. The child waited a little while and then played the same game over again.

The fact of the repetition of this game excluded its being due to chance. Its meaning is clear: the child endowed her mother with a male organ like her father's. She represented the possession of the organ not as a privilege of men but of adults in general, and then she could expect to get one herself in the future. A cigar was not only a suitable symbol for her wish on account of its form. She had of course long noticed that only her father smoked cigars and not her mother. Her impulse to put man and woman on an equality is palpably expressed in presenting a cigar to her mother as well.

We are well acquainted with the attempts of little girls to adopt the male position in urination. Their narcissism cannot endure their not being able to do what another can, and therefore they endeavour to arouse the impression that at least their physical form does not prevent them from doing the same as boys do.

When a child sees its brother or sister receive something to eat or play with which it does not possess itself, it turns its eyes to those persons who are the givers, and these in the first instance are its parents. It does not like to be less well off than its rivals. The small girl who compares her body with her brother's, often in phantasy expects that her father will give her that part of the body she so painfully misses; for the child still has a narcissistic confidence that she could not possibly be permanently defective, and she readily ascribes to her father that creative omnipotence which can bestow on her everything she desires.

But all these dreams crumble after a time. The pleasure principle ceases to dominate psychical processes unconditionally, adaptation to reality commences, and with it the child's criticism of its own wishes. The girl has now in the course of her psychosexual development to carry out an adaptation which is not demanded of boys in a similar manner; she has to reconcile herself to the fact of her physical 'defect', and to her female sexual rôle. The undisturbed enjoyment of early genital sensations will be a considerable aid in facilitating the renunciation of masculinity, for by this means the female genitals will regain a narcissistic value.

In reality, however, the process is considerably more complicated. Freud has drawn our attention to the close association of certain ideas in the child. In its eyes a proof of love is almost the same thing as a *gift*. The first proof of love which creates a lasting impression on the child and is repeated many times is being suckled by the mother. This act brings food to the child and therefore increases its material property, and at the same time acts as a pleasurable stimulus to its erotogenic zones. It is interesting to note that in certain districts of Germany (according to my colleague Herr Koerber) the suckling of a child is called *Schenken* (to give, to pour). Within certain limits the child repays its mother's 'gift' by a 'gift' in return—it regulates its bodily evacuations according to her wishes. The motions at an early age are the child's material gift *par excellence* in return for all the proofs of love it receives.

Psycho-analysis, however, has shown that the child in this early psychosexual period of development considers its fæces as a part of its own body. The process of identification further establishes a close relation between the ideas ' fæces ' and ' penis '. The boy's anxiety regarding the loss of his penis is based on this assimilation of the two ideas. He is afraid that his penis may be detached from his body in the same way as his fæces are. In girls, however, the phantasy occurs of obtaining a penis by way of defæcation—to make one themselves, therefore—or of receiving it as a gift, in which case the father as *beatus possidens* is usually the giver. The psychical process is thus dominated by the parallel, motion = gift = penis.

The little girl's narcissism undergoes a severe test of endurance in the subsequent period. Her hope that a penis will grow is just as little fulfilled as her phantasies of making one for herself or of receiving it as a gift. Thus disappointed, the child is likely to direct an intense and lasting hostility towards those from whom she has in vain expected the gift. Nevertheless, the phantasy of the child normally finds a way out of this situation. Freud has shown that besides the idea of motion and penis in the sense of a gift there is still a third idea which is identified with both of them, namely, that of a child. Infantile theories of procreation and birth adequately explain this connection.

The little girl now cherishes the hope of getting a child from her father as a substitute for the penis not granted her, and this again in the sense of a gift. Her wish for a child can be fulfilled, although not till in the future and with the help of a later love-object. It is therefore an approximation to reality. By making her father her love-object, she now enters into that stage of libido development which is characterized by the domination of the female Oedipus complex. At the same time her maternal impulses develop through her identification with her mother. The hoped-for possession of a child is therefore destined to compensate the woman for her physical defect.

We regard it as normal for the libido in a woman to be

narcissistically bound to a greater extent than in a man, but it is not to be inferred from this that it does not experience far-reaching alterations right up to maturity.

The girl's original so-called 'penis envy' is replaced in the first instance by envy of her mother's possession of children, in virtue of her identification with her mother. These hostile impulses need sublimation just as the libidinal tendencies directed towards her father do. A latency period now sets in, as with boys; and similarly when the age of puberty is reached the wishes which were directed to the first love-object are re-awakened. The girl's wish for the gift (child) has now to be detached from the idea of her father, and her libido, thus freed, has to find a new object. If this process of development takes a favourable course, the female libido has from now on an expectant attitude towards the man. Its expression is regulated by certain inhibitions (feelings of shame). The normal adult woman becomes reconciled to her own sexual rôle and to that of the man, and in particular to the facts of male and female genitality; she desires passive gratification and longs for a child. Her castration complex thus gives rise to no disturbing effects.

Daily observation, however, shows us how frequently this normal end of development is not attained. This fact should not astonish us, for a woman's life gives cause enough to render the overcoming of the castration complex difficult. We refer to those factors which keep recalling to her memory the 'castration' of the woman. The primary idea of the 'wound' is re-animated by the impression created by the first and each succeeding menstruation, and then once again by defloration; for both processes are connected with loss of blood and thus resemble an injury. A girl need not have experienced either of these events; as she begins to grow up, the very idea of being subjected to them in the future has the same effect on her. And we can readily understand from the standpoint of the typical infantile sexual theories that delivery (or child-birth) is also conceived of in a similar manner in the phantasies of young girls; we need only call to mind, for example, the 'Cæsarian section theory' which conceives of delivery as a bloody operation.

In these circumstances we must be prepared to find in every female person some traces of the castration complex. The individual differences are only a matter of degree. In normal women we perhaps occasionally come across dreams with male tendencies in them. From these very slight expressions of the castration complex there are transition stages leading up to those severe and complicated phenomena of a pronounced pathological kind, with which this investigation is principally concerned. In this respect also, therefore, we find a similar state of affairs to that obtaining in the male sex.

III

In his essay on 'The Taboo of Virginity' Freud contrasts the normal outcome of the castration complex, which is in accord with the prevailing demand of civilization, with the 'archaic' type. Among many primitive peoples custom forbids a man to deflorate his wife. Defloration has to be carried out by a priest as a sacramental act, or must occur in some other way outside wedlock. Freud shows in his convincing analysis that this peculiar precept has arisen from the psychological risk of an ambivalent reaction on the part of the woman towards the man who has deflorated her, so that living with the woman whom he has deflorated might be dangerous for him.

Psycho-analytical experience shows that an inhibition of the psychosexual development is manifested in phenomena which are closely related to the conduct of primitive peoples. It is by no means rare for us to come across women in our civilization of to-day who react to defloration in a way which is at all events closely related to that archaic form. I know several cases in which women after being deflorated had an outburst of affect and hit or throttled their husband. One of my patients went to sleep beside her husband after the first intercourse, then woke up, attacked him violently and only gradually came to her senses. There is no mistaking the significance of such conduct: the woman revenges herself for the injury done to her physical integrity.   Psycho-analysis, however, enables us to recognize a historical element in the motivation of such an impulse of revenge.   The most recent cause of the woman's desire for retaliation is undoubtedly her defloration; for this experience serves as a convincing proof of male activity, and puts an end to all attempts to obliterate the functional difference between male and female sexuality.   Nevertheless every profound analysis reveals the close connection of these phantasies of revenge with all the earlier events—phantasied or real—which have been equivalent to castration.   The retaliation is found to refer ultimately to the injustice suffered at the hands of the father.   The unconscious of the adult daughter takes a late revenge for the father's omission to bestow upon her a penis, either to begin with or subsequently; she takes it, however, not on her father in person, but on the man who in consequence of her transference of libido has assumed the father's part.   The only adequate revenge for her wrong—for her castration—is the castration of the man.   This can, it is true, be replaced symbolically by other aggressive measures; among these strangling is a typical substitutive action.

The contrast between such cases and the 'normal' end-stage is evident.   The normal attitude of love towards the other sex is both in man and woman indissolubly bound up with the conscious or unconscious desire for genital gratification in conjunction with the love-object; whereas in the cases just described we find in the person a sadistic-hostile attitude with the aim of possession arising from anal motives, in place of an attitude of love with a genital aim. The patient's impulse to take away by force is evident from numerous accompanying psychical conditions; and closely connected with her phantasy of robbery is the idea of trans-ferring the robbed penis to herself.   We shall return to this point later.

As has already been mentioned, the woman's desires to be masculine only occasionally succeed in breaking through in this 'archaic' sense.   On the other hand, a considerable number of women are unable to carry out a full psychical adaptation to the female sexual rôle.   A third possibility is open to them in virtue of the bisexual disposition common to humanity—namely, to become homosexual. Such women tend to adopt the male rôle in erotic relations with other women. They love to exhibit their masculinity in their dress, in their way of doing their hair, and in their general behaviour. In some cases their homosexuality does not break through to consciousness; the repressed wish to be male is here found in a sublimated form in the shape of masculine pursuits of an intellectual and professional character and other allied interests. Such women do not, however, consciously deny their femininity, but usually proclaim that these interests are just as much feminine as masculine ones. They consider that the sex of a person has nothing to do with his or her capacities, especially in the mental field. This type of woman is well represented in the woman's movement of to-day.

It is not because I value their practical significance lightly that I have described these groups so briefly. But both types of women are well known and have been discussed in psycho-analytical literature, so that I need not enlarge on the subject and can rapidly pass on to the consideration of the *neurotic transformations* of the castration complex. Of these there are a great number, and I will endeavour to describe accurately—some of them for the first time—and to render them intelligible from a psycho-analytical point of view.

IV

The neurotic transformations originating in the female castration complex may be divided into two groups. The phenomena of the one group rest on a strong, emotionally-toned, but not conscious desire to adopt the male rôle, *i.e.* on the phantasy of possessing a male organ; those of the other express an unconscious refusal of the female rôle, and a repressed desire for revenge on the privileged man. There is no sharp line of demarcation between these two groups. The phenomena of one group do not exclude those of the other in the same individual; they supplement each other. The preponderance of this or that attitude can nevertheless often be clearly recognized, so that we may speak of the preponderating reaction of a *wish-fulfilment type* or of a *revenge type*.

We have already learned that besides the normal outcome of the female castration complex there are two abnormal forms of conscious reaction, namely, the homosexual type and the archaic (revenge) type. We have only to recall the general relation between perversion and neurosis with which we are familiar from Freud's investigations in order to be able to understand the two neurotic types above described in respect of their psychogenesis. They are the 'negative' of the homosexual and sadistic types described above; for they contain the same motives and tendencies, but in repressed form.

The psychical phenomena which arise from the unconscious wishes for physical masculinity or for revenge on the man are difficult to classify on account of their multiplicity. It has also to be borne in mind that neurotic symptoms are not the sole expressions of unconscious origin which have to concern us here; we need only refer to the different forms in which the same repressed tendencies appear in dreams. As I have said at the beginning, therefore, this investigation cannot pretend to give an exhaustive account of the phenomena arising from the repressed castration complex, but rather lays stress on certain frequent and instructive forms of it, and especially some which have not hitherto been considered.

The *wish fulfilment* which goes farthest in the sense of the female castration complex comprises those symptoms or dreams of neurotics which convert the fact of femininity into its opposite. In such a case the unconscious phantasies of the woman make the assertion: 'I am the fortunate possessor of a penis and exercise the male function'. Van Ophuijsen gives an example of this kind in his article on the 'masculine complex' of women.[1] It concerns a conscious phantasy from the youth of one of his patients, and gives us therefore at first only an insight into the patient's still unrepressed active-homosexual wishes; but at the same

---

[1] 'Beiträge zum Männlichkeitskomplex der Frau' (1917).

time therefore it clearly demonstrates the foundation of those neurotic symptoms which give expression to the same tendencies after they have become repressed. The patient used to place herself in the evening between the lamp and the wall and then hold her finger against the lower part of her body in such a manner that her shadow appeared to have a penis. She thus did something very similar to what the two-year-old child did with the cigar.

In conjunction with this instructive example I may mention the dream of a neurotic woman. She was an only child. Her parents had ardently desired a son and had in consequence cultivated the narcissism, and particularly the masculinity wishes, of their daughter. According to an expression of theirs she was to become 'quite a celebrated man'. In her youthful day-dreams she saw herself as a 'female Napoleon', in which she began a glorious career as a female officer, advanced to the highest positions, and saw all the countries of Europe lying at her feet. After having thus shown herself superior to all the men in the world, a man was to appear at last who surpassed not only all men but also herself; and she was to subject herself to him. In her marital relations in real life she had the most extreme resistance against assuming the feminine rôle; I shall mention symptoms relating to this later. I quote here one of my patient's dreams.

' My husband seizes a woman, lifts up her clothes, finds a peculiar pocket and pulls out from it a hypodermic morphia syringe. She gives him an injection with this syringe and he is carried away in a weak and wretched state.'

The woman in this dream is the patient herself, who takes over the active rôle from the man. She is able to do this by means of a concealed penis (syringe) with which she practises coitus on him. The weakened condition of the man signifies that he is killed by her assault.

Pulling out the syringe from the pocket suggests the male method of urinating, which seemed enviable to the patient in her childhood. It has, however, a further significance. At a meeting of the Berlin Psycho-Analytical Society Boehm has drawn attention to a common infantile sexual theory according to which the penis originally ascribed to both sexes is concealed in a cleft from which it can temporarily emerge.

Another patient, whose neurosis brought to expression the permanent discord between masculinity and femininity in most manifold forms, stated that during sexual excitation she often had the feeling that something on her body was swelling to an enormous size. The purpose of this sensation was obviously to give her the illusion that she possessed a penis.

In other patients the symptoms do not represent the wish to be masculine as fulfilled, but show an expectation of such an event in the near or distant future. While the unconscious in the cases just described expresses the idea, ' I am a male ', it here conceives the wish in the formula, ' I shall receive the " gift " one day; I absolutely insist upon that! '

The following conscious phantasy from the youth of a neurotic girl is perfectly typical of the unconscious content of many neurotic symptoms. When the girl's elder sister menstruated for the first time she noticed that her mother and sister conversed together secretly. The thought flashed across her, ' Now my sister is certainly getting a penis ', and that therefore she herself would get one in due course. This reversal of the real state of affairs is highly characteristic: the acquisition of that longed-for part of the body is precisely what is put in place of the renewed 'castration' which the first menstruation signifies.

A neurotic patient in whom psycho-analysis revealed an extraordinary degree of narcissism one day showed the greatest resistance to treatment, and manifested many signs of defiance towards me which really referred to her deceased father. She left my consulting room in a state of violent negative transference. When she stepped into the street she caught herself saying impulsively: ' I *will not* be well until I have got a penis '. She thus expected this gift from me, as a substitute for her father, and made the effect of the treatment dependent upon receiving it. Certain dreams of the patient had the same content as this idea which suddenly appeared from her unconscious. In these dreams, being presented with something occurred in the double sense of getting a child or a penis.

Compromises between impulse and repression occur in the sphere of the castration complex as elsewhere in the realm of psychopathology. In many cases the unconscious is content with a substitute-gratification in place of a complete fulfilment of the wish for a penis in the present or the future.

A condition in neurotic women which owes one of its most important determinants to the castration complex is *enuresis nocturna*. The analogy between the determination of this symptom in female and male neurotics is striking. I may refer to a dream of a male patient of fourteen who suffered from this complaint. He dreamt that he was in a closet and urinating with manifest feelings of pleasure, when he suddenly noticed that his sister was looking at him through the window. As a little boy he had actually exhibited with pride before his sister his masculine way of urinating. This dream, which ended in enuresis, shows the boy's pride in his penis; and enuresis in the female frequently rests on the wish to urinate in the male way. The dream represented this process in a disguised form and ended with a pleasurable emptying of the bladder.

Women who are prone to *enuresis nocturna* are regularly burdened with strong resistances against the female sexual functions. The infantile desire to urinate in the male position is associated with the well-known assimilation of the ideas of urine and sperma, and of micturition and ejaculation. The unconscious tendency to wet the man with urine during sexual intercourse has its origin in this.

Other substitute formations show a still greater displacement of the libido in that they are removed some distance from the genital region. When the libido for some reason or other has to turn away from the genital zone it is attracted to certain other erotogenic zones, the particular ones chosen being a result of individual determinations. In some neurotic women the nose acquires the significance of a surrogate of the male genital. The not infrequent neurotic attacks of redness and swelling of the nose in women represents in their unconscious phantasy an erection in the sense of their desire to be masculine.

In other cases the eyes take over a similar rôle. Some neurotic women get an abnormally marked congestion of the eyes with every sexual excitation. In a certain measure this congestion is a normal and common accompaniment of sexual excitation. However, in those women of whom we are speaking it is not simply a case of a quantitative increase of the condition, lasting for a short period; but they exhibit a redness of the sclerotics accompanied by a burning sensation, while swelling persists for several days after each sexual excitation, so that in such cases we are justified in speaking of a *conjunctivitis neurotica.*

I have seen several women patients, troubled by many neurotic consequences of the castration complex, who thought of this condition of the eyes, which was often associated with a feeling of having a fixed stare, as an expression of their masculinity. In the unconscious the ' fixed stare ' is often equivalent to an erection. I have already alluded to this symptom in an earlier article dealing with neurotic disturbances of the eyes.[1] In some cases the person has the idea that her fixed stare will terrify people. If we pursue the unconscious train of thought of these patients who identify their fixed stare with erection, we can understand the meaning of their anxiety. Just as male exhibitionists seek among other things to terrify women by the sight of the phallus, so these women unconsciously endeavour to attain the same effect by means of their fixed stare.

Some years ago a very neurotic young girl consulted me. The very first thing she did on entering my consulting-room was to ask me straight out whether she had beautiful eyes. I was startled for a moment by this very unusual way of introducing oneself to a physician. She noticed my hesitation, and then gave vent to a violent outburst of affect on my suggesting that she should first of all answer *my* questions. The general behaviour of the patient,

[1] Cf. Chapter IX.

whom I only saw a few times, made a methodical psycho-analysis impossible. I did not succeed even in coming to a clear diagnosis of the case, for certain characteristics of the clinical picture suggested a paranoid condition. Nevertheless, I was able to obtain a few facts concerning the origin of her most striking symptom, and these, in spite of their incompleteness, offered a certain insight into the structure of her condition.

The patient told me that she had experienced a great fright as a child. In the small town where she was living at that time a boa constrictor had broken out from a menagerie and could not be found; and as she was passing through a park with her governess she believed that she suddenly saw the snake in front of her. She became quite rigid with terror, and ever since was afraid that she might have a fixed stare.

It could not be decided whether this experience was a real one or whether it was wholly or partially a phantasy. The association, snake = rigidity, is familiar and comprehensible to us. We also recognize the snake as a male genital symbol. Fixity of the eye is then explicable from the identification, fixed eye = snake = phallus. The patient, however, protected herself against this wish for masculinity, and put in its place the compulsion to get every man to assure her that her eyes were beautiful, *i.e,* had feminine charms. If anyone hesitated to answer her question in the affirmative it is probable that she became exposed to the danger of being overwhelmed by her male-sadistic impulse which she repressed with difficulty, and fell into a state of anxiety at the rising force of her masculine feelings.

I should like to point out here that these various observations by no means do justice to the great multiplicity of the symptoms belonging to this group. Besides these examples which illustrate the vicarious assumption by various parts of the body of the male genital rôle, there are others which show that objects which do not belong to the body can also be made use of for the same purpose, provided their form and use permits in any way of a symbolic interpretation as a genital organ. We may call to mind the tendency of neurotic women to use a syringe and to give themselves or relatives enemas.

There are numerous points of contact here with the normal expressions of the female castration complex, especially with typical female symptomatic acts. Thrusting the end of an umbrella into the ground may be mentioned as an example. The great enjoyment many women obtain from using a hose for watering the garden is also characteristic, for here the unconscious experiences the ideal fulfilment of a childhood wish.

Other women are less able or less inclined to find a substitutive gratification of their masculinity wishes in neurotic surrogates. Their symptoms give expression to a completely different attitude. They represent the male organ as something of secondary importance and unnecessary. To this attitude belong all the symptoms and phantasies of *immaculate conception*. It is as though these women want to declare by means of their neurosis: 'I can do it by myself'. One of my patients experienced an immaculate conception of this kind while in a dream-like, hazy state of consciousness. She had had a dream once before in which she held a box with a crucifix in her hands; the identification with the Virgin Mary is here quite clear. I invariably found that neurotic women who showed these phenomena exhibited especially pronounced anal character-traits. The idea of being 'able to do it alone', expresses a high degree of obstinacy, and this is also prominent in these patients. They want, for example, to find out everything in their psychoanalysis by themselves without the help of the physician. They are as a rule women who through their obstinacy, envy, and self-overestimation destroy all their relationships with their environment, and indeed their whole life.

V

The symptoms we have so far described bear the character of a positive wish-fulfilment in the sense of the infantile desire to be physically equal to the man. But the last-mentioned forms of reaction already begin to approximate to the *revenge type*. For in the refusal to acknowledge the significance of the male organ there is implied, although in a very mitigated form, an emasculation of the man. We therefore approach by easy stages to the phenomena of the second group.

We regularly meet two tendencies in repressed form in the patients of this second group: a desire to take revenge on the man, and a desire to seize by force the longed-for organ, *i.e.* to rob him of it.

One of my patients dreamed that she and other women were carrying round a gigantic penis which they had stolen from an animal. This reminds us of the neurotic impulse to steal. So-called kleptomania is often traceable to the fact that a child feels injured or neglected in respect of proofs of love—which we have equated with gifts—or in some way disturbed in the gratification of its libido. It procures a substitute pleasure for the lost pleasure, and at the same time takes revenge on those who have caused it the supposed injustice. Psycho-analysis shows that in the unconscious of our patients there exist the same impulses to take forcible possession of the 'gift' which has not been received.

Vaginismus is from a practical point of view the most important of the neurotic symptoms which subserve repressed phantasies of castrating the man. The purpose of vaginismus is not only to prevent intromission of the penis, but also, in the case of its intromission, not to let it escape again, *i.e.* to retain it and thereby to castrate the man. The phantasy therefore is to rob the man of his penis and to appropriate it.

The patient who had produced the previously-mentioned dream of the morphia syringe showed a rare and complicated form of rejection of the male at the beginning of her marriage. She suffered from an hysterical adduction of her thighs whenever her husband approached her. After this had been overcome in the course of a few weeks there developed as a fresh symptom of refusal a high degree of vaginismus which only completely disappeared under psycho-analytic treatment.

This patient, whose libido was very strongly fixated on her father, once had a short dream before her marriage, which she related to me in very remarkable words. She said that in the dream her father had been run over and had ' lost some leg or other and his money '.[1] The castration idea is here not only expressed by means of the leg but also by the money. Being run over is one of the most frequent castration symbols. One of my patients whose ' totem ' was a dog dreamed that a dog was run over and lost a leg. The same symbol is found in phobias that some particular male person may be run over and lose an arm or a leg. One of my patients was the victim of this anxiety with reference to various male members of her family.

For many years, and especially during the late war, I have come across women who take particular erotic interest in men who have lost an arm or a leg by amputation or accident. These are women with particularly strong feelings of inferiority; their libido prefers a mutilated man rather than one who is physically intact. For the mutilated man has also lost a limb, like themselves. It is obvious that such women feel an affinity to the mutilated man; they consider him a companion in distress and do not need to reject him with hate like the sound man. The interest some women have in Jewish men is explicable on the same grounds; they regard circumcision as at any rate a partial castration, and so they can transfer their libido on to them. I know cases in which a mixed marriage of this kind was contracted by women chiefly as a result of an unconscious motive of this nature. They also show an interest in men who are crippled in other ways and have thereby lost their masculine ' superiority '.

It was the psycho-analysis of a girl seventeen years old that gave me the strongest impression of the power of the castration complex. In this case there was an abundance of neurotic conversions, phobias, and obsessive impulses, all of which were connected with her disappointment at being a female and with revenge phantasies against the

---

[1] [' *Vermögen* ' (' money ') also means ' capacity ' and ' sexual potency '.— *Trans.*]

male sex. The patient had been operated on for appendicitis some years previously.[1] The surgeon had given her the removed appendix preserved in a bottle of spirit, and this she now treasured as something sacred. Her ideas of being castrated centred round this specimen, and it also appeared in her dreams with the significance of the once possessed but now lost penis.[2] As the surgeon happened to be a relative it was easy for her to connect the ' castration ' performed by him with her father.

Among the patient's symptoms which rested on the repression of active castration wishes was a phobia which can be called *dread of marriage*. This anxiety was expressed in the strongest opposition to the idea of a future marriage, because the patient was afraid ' that she would have to do something terrible to her husband '. The most difficult part of the analysis was to uncover an extremely strong rejection of genital erotism, and an intense accentuation of mouth erotism in the form of phantasies which appeared compulsively. Her idea of oral intercourse was firmly united with that of biting off the penis. This phantasy, which is frequently expressed in anxiety and phenomena of the most varied kinds, was in the present case accompanied by a number of other ideas of a terrifying nature. Psycho-analysis succeeded in stopping this abundant production of a morbid imagination.

These kinds of anxiety prevent the subject from having intimate union with the other sex, and thereby from carrying out her unconsciously intended ' crime '. The patient is then the only person who has to suffer from those impulses, in the form of permanent sexual abstinence and neurotic anxiety. The case is altered as soon as the active castration phantasy has become somewhat distorted and thereby unrecognizable to consciousness. Such a modification of the manifest content of the phantasies makes it possible for the tendencies in question actually to have stronger external effects. It can, for instance, cause the idea of robbing the

[1] The removal of the vermiform appendix often stimulates the castration complex in men as well.

[2] Another patient imagined she had a brother and had to remove his appendix.

man of his genital to be abolished and the hostile purpose to be displaced from the organ to its function, so that the aim is to destroy his potency. The wife's neurotic sexual aversion will now often have a repelling effect on the man's libido so that a disturbance of his potency does actually occur.

A further modification of the aggressive impulse is seen in an attitude of the woman to the man that is fairly frequent and that can be exceedingly painful to him; it is the impulse to *disappoint* him. To disappoint a person is to excite expectations in him and not fulfil them. In her relations with the man the woman can do this by responding to his advances up to a certain point and then refusing to give herself to him. Such behaviour is most frequently and significantly expressed in *frigidity* on the part of the woman. Disappointing other persons is a piece of unconscious tactics which we frequently find in the psychology of the neuroses and which is especially pronounced in obsessional neurotics. These neurotics are unconsciously impelled towards violence and revenge, but on account of the contrary play of ambivalent forces these impulses are incapable of effectually breaking through. Since their hostility cannot express itself in actions, these patients excite expectations of a pleasant nature in their environment and then do not fulfil them. In the sphere of the female castration complex the tendency to disappoint can be formulated in respect of its origin as follows:

First stage: I rob you of what you have because I lack it.

Second stage: I rob you of nothing. I even promise you what I have to give.

Third stage: I will not give you what I have promised.

In very many cases frigidity is associated with a conscious readiness on the part of the woman to assume the female rôle and to acknowledge that of the man. Her unconscious striving has in part as its object the disappointment of the man, who is inclined to infer from her conscious willingness the possibility of mutual enjoyment. Besides this, she has the desire to demonstrate to herself and her partner that his sexual ability is of no importance.

If we penetrate to the deeper psychic layers we recognize how strongly the desire of the frigid woman to be male dominates her unconscious. In a previous article I have attempted to show in accordance with Freud's well-known observations on frigidity [1] that this condition in the female sex is the exact analogue of a disturbance of potency in the man, namely, ' ejaculatio præcox '.[2] In both conditions the libido is attached to that erotogenic zone which has normally a similar significance in the opposite sex. In cases of frigidity the pleasurable sensation is as a rule situated in the clitoris and the vaginal zone has none. The clitoris, however, corresponds developmentally with the penis.

Frigidity is such an exceedingly widespread disturbance that it hardly needs to be described or exemplified. On the other hand, it is less well known that the condition has varying degrees of intensity. The highest degree, that of actual anæsthesia, is rare. In these cases the vaginal mucous membrane has lost all sensitiveness to touch, so that the male organ is not perceived in sexual intercourse. Its existence is therefore actually denied. The common condition is a relative disturbance of sensitivity, in which contact is perceived but is not pleasurable. In other cases a sensation of pleasure is felt but does not go on to orgasm, or, what is the same thing, the contractions of the female organ corresponding with the climax of pleasure are absent. It is these contractions that signify the complete and positive reaction of the woman to the male activity, the absolute affirmation of the normal relation between the sexes.

Some women do obtain gratification along normal paths but endeavour to make the act as brief and prosaic as possible. They refuse all enjoyment of any preliminary pleasure; and in especial they behave after gratification as if nothing had happened that could make any impression on them, and turn quickly to some other subject of conversation, a book or occupation. These women thus give themselves up to the full physical function of the woman

[1] *Drei Abhandlungen zur Sexualtheorie*, 4. Aufl., S. 83f.   [2] Cf. Chap. XIII.

for a few fleeting moments only to disown it immediately afterwards.

It is an old and well-known medical fact that many women only obtain normal sexual sensation after they have had a child. They become, so to speak, only female in the full sense by the way of maternal feelings. The deeper connection of this is only to be comprehended in the light of the castration complex. As we know, a child was at an early period the ' gift ' which was to compensate the little girl for the missed penis. She receives it now in reality, and thus the ' wound ' is at last healed. It is to be noted that in some women there exists a wish to get a child from a man against his will; we cannot fail to see in this the unconscious tendency to take the penis from the male and appropriate it in the form of a child. The other extreme in this group is represented by those women who wish to remain childless at all costs. They decline any kind of ' substitute ', and would be constantly reminded of their femininity in the most disturbing manner if they became mothers.

A relative frigidity exists not only in the sense of the degree of capacity for sensation, but also in the sense that some women are frigid with certain men and capable of sensation with others.

It will probably be expected that a marked activity on the part of the man is the most favourable condition to call forth sexual sensations in women who are frigid in this second sense. This, however, is not always the case; on the contrary, there are many women in whom a debasement of the man is just as essential a condition of love as is the debasement of the woman to many neurotic men.[1] A single example may be given in illustration of this by no means rare attitude. I analyzed a woman whose love-life was markedly polyandrous, and who was invariably anæsthetic if she had to acknowledge that the man was superior to her in any way. If, however, she had a quarrel with the man and succeeded in forcing him to give in to her, her frigidity disappeared completely. Such cases show very

[1] See Freud, ' Beiträge zur Psychologie des Liebeslebens ', sections I. and II.

clearly how necessary is the acknowledgement of the male genital function as a condition of a normal love-life on the part of the woman. We also meet here with one source of the conscious and unconscious impulses of prostitution in women.

Frigidity is practically a *sine qua non* of prostitution. The experiencing of full sexual sensation binds the woman to the man, and only where this is lacking does she go from man to man, just like the continually ungratified Don Juan type of man who has constantly to change his love-object. Just as the Don Juan avenges himself on all women for the disappointment which he once received from the first woman who entered into his life, so the prostitute avenges herself on every man for the gift she had expected from her father and did not receive. Her frigidity signifies a humiliation of all men and therefore a mass castration to her unconscious; and her whole life is given up to this purpose.[1]

While the frigid woman unconsciously strives to diminish the importance of that part of the body which is denied her, there is another form of refusal of the man which achieves the same aim with opposite means. In this form of refusal the man is nothing else than a sex organ and therefore consists only of coarse sensuality. Every other mental or physical quality is denied him. The effect is that the neurotic woman imagines that the man is an inferior being on account of his possession of a penis. Her self-esteem is actually enhanced, and indeed she can rejoice at being free from such a mark of inferiority. One of my patients who showed a very marked aversion to men had the obsessing hallucination of a very big penis whenever she saw a man. This vision continually brought to her mind the fact that there was nothing else in men than their genital organ, from which she turned away in disgust, but which at the same time represented something that greatly interested her unconscious. She had certain phantasies connected with this vision which were of a

[1] The remarks of Dr. Theodor Reik in a discussion at the Berlin Psycho-Analytical Society have suggested this idea to me.

complementary nature. In these she represented herself as though every opening in her body, even her body as a whole, was nothing else than a receptive female organ. The vision therefore contained a mixture of over-estimation and depreciation of the male organ.

VI

We have already shown that the woman's tendency to depreciate the importance of the male genital undergoes a progressive sexual repression, and often appears outwardly as a general desire to humiliate men. This tendency is often shown in an instinctive avoidance of men who have pronounced masculine characteristics. The woman directs her love-choice towards the passive and effeminate man, by living with whom she can daily renew the proof that her own activity is superior to his. Just like manifest homosexual women, she likes to represent the mental and physical differences between man and woman as insignificant. When she was six years old one of my patients had begged her mother to send her to a boys' school in boy's clothes because ' then no one would know that she was a girl '.

Besides the inclination to depreciate men there is also found a marked sensitiveness of the castration complex towards any situation which can awaken a feeling of inferiority, even in the remotest way. Women with this attitude refuse to accept any kind of help from a man, and show the greatest disinclination to follow any man's lead. A young woman betrayed her claims to masculinity, repressed with difficulty, by declining to walk along a street covered in deep snow in her husband's footsteps. A further very significant characteristic of this patient may be mentioned here. As a child she had had a strong desire for independence, and in adolescence she used to be very envious of the calling of two women in particular— the cashier in her father's office, and the woman who swept the street in her native town. The cause of this attitude is obvious to the psycho-analyst. The cashier sweeps money together and the crossing-sweeper sweeps dirt, and both things have the same significance in the unconscious. There is here a marked turning away from genital sexuality in favour of the formation of anal character traits, a process which I shall mention in another connection.

How strong a person's disinclination to be reminded of her femininity in any way can be is already well shown in the behaviour of children. It not infrequently happens that little girls give up knowledge they have already obtained of procreation and birth in favour of the stork fable. They dislike the rôle bestowed upon them by Nature, and the stork tale has the advantage that in it children originate without the man's part being a more privileged one than theirs in respect of activity.

The most extreme degree of sensitiveness in regard to the castration complex is found in the rarer case of psychical depression. Here the woman's feeling of unhappiness on account of her femininity is wholly unrepressed; she does not even succeed in working it off in a modified form. One of my patients complained about the utter uselessness of her life because she had been born a girl. She considered the superiority of men in all respects as obvious, and just for this reason felt it so painfully. She refused to compete with men in any sphere, and also rejected every feminine act. In particular she declined to play the female rôle in sexual life, and equally so the male one. In consequence of this attitude all conscious eroticism was entirely foreign to her; she even said that she was unable to imagine any erotic pleasure at all. Her resistance against female sexual functions assumed grotesque forms. She transferred her rejection of them to everything that reminded her, if only remotely, of bearing fruit, propagation, birth, etc. She hated flowers and green trees, and found fruit disgusting. A mistake which she made many times was easily explicable from this attitude; she would read *furchtbar* (' frightful ') instead of *fruchtbar* (' fruitful '). In the whole of Nature only the winter in the mountains could give her pleasure; there was nothing to remind her there of living things and propagation, but only rock, ice, and snow. She had the idea that in marriage the woman was of quite secondary importance, and an expression of hers clearly showed how much this idea was centred in her castration complex.   She said that the ring—which was to her a hated female symbol—was not fit to be a symbol of marriage, and she suggested a nail as a substitute.   Her over-emphasis of masculinity was quite clearly based on her penis envy as a little girl—an envy which appeared in a strikingly undisguised form when she was grown up.

In many women the failure to reconcile themselves to their lack of the male organ is expressed in neurotic horror at the sight of wounds.   Every wound re-awakens in their unconscious the idea of the 'wound' received in childhood. Sometimes they have a definite feeling of anxiety at the sight of wounds; sometimes this sight or the mere idea of it causes a 'painful feeling in the lower part of the body'. At the commencement of her psycho-analysis the patient whom I mentioned above as having a complicated form of vaginismus spoke of her horror of wounds before there had been any mention of the castration complex.   She said that she could look at large and irregular wounds without being particularly affected, but that she could not bear to see a cut in her skin or on another person, however small it was, if it gaped slightly and if the red colour of the flesh was visible in the depth of the cut.   It gave her an intense pain in the genital region coupled with marked anxiety, ' as though something had been cut away there '.   (Similar sensations accompanied by anxiety are found in men with a marked fear of castration.)   In many women it does not need the sight of a wound to cause feelings of the kind described; they have an aversion, associated with marked affect, to the idea of surgical operations and even to knives. Some time ago a lady who was a stranger to me and who would not give her name rang me up on the telephone and asked me if I could prevent an operation that had been arranged for the next day.   On my request for more information she told me she was to be operated on for a severe uterine hæmorrhage due to myomata.   When I told her it was not part of my work to prevent a necessary and perhaps life-saving operation she did not reply, but ex-

plained with affective volubility that she had always been
' hostile to all operations ', adding, ' whoever is once
operated on is for ever afterwards a cripple for life '.   The
wild exaggeration of this statement becomes comprehensible
if we remember that from the point of view of the unconscious
an operation of this sort has made the little girl a ' cripple '
in early childhood.

VII

A tendency with which we are well acquainted and
which we have already mentioned leads in the sphere of the
female castration complex to modifications of the woman's
aversion to that which is tabooed, and even to a conditional
admission of it and in especial to compromise formations
between impulse and repression.

In some of our patients we come across phantasies which
are concerned with the possibility of an acceptance of the
man and which formulate the conditions under which
the patient would be prepared to reconcile herself to
her femininity.   I will mention a certain proviso which I
have met with many times; it is: ' I could be content with
my femininity if I were absolutely the most beautiful of all
women '.   All men would lie at the feet of the most beautiful
woman, and the woman's narcissim would consider this
power not a bad compensation for the defect she is so
painfully aware of.   It is in fact easier for a beautiful woman
to assuage her castration complex than for an ugly one.
Nevertheless, this idea of being the most beautiful of all
women does not have the aforesaid softening effect in all
cases.   I know of a woman who said: ' I should like to be
the most beautiful of all women so that all men would adore
me.   Then I would show them the cold shoulder.'   In this
case the craving for revenge is clear enough; this remark was
made by a woman of an extremely tyrannical nature which
was based on a wholly unsublimated castration complex.

Most women, however, are not so extreme.   They are
inclined to compromise and to satisfy themselves with
relatively harmless expressions of their repressed hostility.
In this connection we are able to understand a characteristic

trait in the conduct of many women. We must keep in view the fact that sexual activity is essentially associated with the male organ, that the woman is only in the position to excite the man's libido or respond to it, and that otherwise she is compelled to adopt a waiting attitude. In a great number of women we find resistance against being a woman displaced to this necessity of waiting. In their married life these women take a logical revenge upon the man in that they *keep him waiting* on every occasion in daily life.

There is another proviso of a similar nature to the above mentioned 'If I were the most beautiful woman'. In some women we find a readiness to admit the activity of the male and their own passivity, provided that they are desired by the most manly (greatest, most important) man. We have no difficulty in recognizing here the infantile desire for the father. I have already related from one of my psycho-analyses an example of a phantastic form of this idea. I was able to follow the development of a similar phantasy through different stages in the psycho-analysis of other patients. The original desire ran: ' I should like to be a man '. When this was given up, the patient wished to be ' the only woman ' (' the only woman belonging to my father ' being originally meant). When this wish had to give way to reality, too, the idea appeared: 'As a woman I should like to be unmatchable'.

Certain compromise formations are of far greater practical importance, and though well known to psychoanalysts nevertheless merit special consideration in this connection. They concern the acknowledgement of the man, or, to be more correct, his activity and the organ serving it, under certain limiting conditions. The woman will tolerate and even desire sexual relations with the man so long as her own genital organ is avoided, or is, so to speak, considered as non-existent. She displaces her libido on to other erotogenic zones (mouth, anus) and softens her feelings of displeasure originating in the castration complex by thus turning away her sexual interest from her genital organ. The body openings which are now at the disposal of the libido are not specifically female organs. Further determinants are found in the analysis of each of this kind of cases, one only of which need be mentioned, namely, the possibility of active castration through biting by means of the mouth. Oral and anal perversions in women are thus to a considerable extent explicable as effects of the castration complex.

Among our patients we certainly have to deal more frequently with the negative counterpart of the perversions, *i.e.* with conversion symptoms which occur in relation to the specific erotogenic zones, than with the perversions themselves. Examples of this kind have already been given above. I referred among other cases to that of a young girl who had a phobia of having to do some horrible thing to her husband in the event of her marriage. The 'horrible thing' turned out to be the idea of castrating him through biting. The case showed most clearly how displacement of the libido from the genital to the mouth zone can gratify very different tendencies simultaneously. In such phantasies the mouth serves equally to represent the desired reception of the male organ and its destruction. Facts like these warn us not to be too ready to over-estimate a single determinant. Although in the preceding presentation we have estimated the castration complex as an important impelling force in the development of neurotic phenomena, we are not justified in over-valuing it in the way Adler does when he represents the 'masculine protest' as the essential *causa movens* of the neuroses. Experience that is well-founded and verified anew every day shows us that precisely those neurotics of both sexes who loudly proclaim and lay emphasis on their masculine tendencies frequently conceal —and only superficially—intense female-passive desires. Our psycho-analytic experience should constantly remind us of the over-determination of all psychical structures. It has to reject as one-sided and fragmentary every psychological method of working which does not take into full account the influence of various factors on one another. In my present study I have collected material belonging to the castration complex from a great number of psycho-

analyses. And I should like to say expressly that it is solely
for reasons of clearness that I have only occasionally alluded
to the ideas connected with female-passive instincts which
none of my patients failed to express.

VIII

Women whose ideas and feelings are influenced and
governed by the castration complex to any great extent—
no matter whether consciously or unconsciously—transplant
the effect of this complex on to their children. They
influence the psychosexual development of their daughters
either by speaking disparagingly of female sexuality to them,
or by unconsciously showing their aversion to men. The
latter method is the more permanently effective one,
because it tends to undermine the heterosexuality of the
growing girl. On the other hand, the method of depreciation can produce really traumatic effects, as when a mother
says to her daughter who is about to marry, ' What is
going to happen now is disgusting '.

It is in particular those neurotic women whose libido has
been displaced from the genital to the anal zone who
give expression to their disgust of the male body in this or a
similar manner. These women also produce serious effects
on their sons without foreseeing the result of their attitude.
A mother with this kind of aversion to the male sex injures
the narcissism of the boy. A boy in his early years is proud
of his genital organs; he likes to exhibit them to his mother,
and expects her to admire them. He soon sees that his
mother ostentatiously looks the other way, even if she does
not give expression to her disinclination in words. These
women are especially given to prohibiting masturbation on
the grounds that it is disgusting for the boy to touch his
genital organ. Whereas they are most careful to avoid
touching and even mentioning the penis, they tend to caress
the child's buttocks and are never tired of speaking of its
' bottom ', often getting the child to repeat this word. They
also take an excessive interest in the child's defæcatory
acts. The boy is thus forced into a new orientation of his

libido.   Either it is transferred from the genital to the anal zone, or the boy is impelled towards a member of his own sex —his father in the first instance—to whom he feels himself bound by a bond which is quite comprehensible to us.   At the same time he becomes a woman-hater, and later will be constantly ready to criticize very severely the weaknesses of the female sex.   This chronic influence of the mother's castration complex seems to me to be of greater importance as a cause of castration-fear in boys than occasionally uttered threats of castration.   I can produce abundant evidence for this view from my psycho-analyses of male neurotics.   The mother's anal-erotism is the earliest and most dangerous enemy of the psychosexual development of children, since she has more influence on them in the earliest years of life than the father.

To everyone of us who is a practising psycho-analyst the question occurs at times whether the trifling number of individuals to whom we can give assistance justifies the great expenditure of time, labour and patience it involves. The answer to this question is contained in what has been said above.   If we succeed in freeing such a person from the defects of his psychosexuality, *i.e.* from the difficulties of his castration complex, we obviate the neuroses of children to a great extent, and thus help the coming generation. Our psycho-analytic activity is a quiet and little appreciated work and the object of much attack, but its effect on and beyond the individual seems to us to make it an aim worth a great deal of labour.

Chapter XXIII

CONTRIBUTIONS TO THE THEORY OF THE ANAL CHARACTER [1] (1921)

THE wide field which is open to the science of psycho-analysis at the present time offers an abundance of instances of the rapid increase of psychological knowledge along the lines of purely inductive investigation. Perhaps the most remarkable and instructive of these is the development of the theory of the anal character. In 1908, about fifteen years after the appearance of his first contributions to the psychology of the neuroses, Freud published a short paper entitled 'Character and Anal Erotism'. It occupied only three pages of a journal, and was a model of condensed statement and of cautious and clear summing up. The gradually increasing number of his co-workers, among whom may be mentioned Sadger, Ferenczi, and Jones, has helped to extend the range of ascertained knowledge. The theory concerning the products of the transformation of anal erotism gained unsuspected significance when in 1913, following on Jones' important investigation on 'Hate and Anal Erotism in the Obsessional Neurosis', Freud formulated an early ' pregenital ' organization of the libido. He considered that the symptoms of the obsessional neurosis were the result of a regression of libido to this stage of development, which is characterized by a preponderance of the anal and sadistic component instincts. This threw a new light both on the symptomatology of the obsessional neurosis and on the characterological peculiarities of the person suffering

---

[1] [No. 70, A. B.]

from it—on the so-called 'obsessional character'. I might add, anticipating a future publication, that very similar anomalies of character are found in those people who tend to melancholic or manic states of mind. And the strictest possible study of the sadistic-anal character-traits is necessary before we can proceed to investigate those last mentioned diseases which are still so enigmatical to us. The present study is mainly concerned with the anal contributions to the formation of character. Jones'[1] last great work on this subject presents an abundance of valuable material, but it does not exhaust it. For the work of a single person cannot do justice to the multiplicity and complexity of the phenomena; each analyst who possesses data of his own should publish them, and so help to contribute to the body of psycho-analytical knowledge. In the same way the purpose of the following remarks is to extend the theory of the anal character-traits in certain directions. Another problem of great theoretical importance will be very frequently alluded to in this study. Up to the present we understand only very incompletely the particular psychological connections that exist between the two impulses of sadism and anal erotism which we always mention in close association with each other, almost as a matter of habit. And I shall attempt the solution of this question in a later paper.

In his first description of the anal character Freud has said that certain neurotics present three particularly pronounced character-traits, namely, a love of orderliness which often develops into pedantry, a parsimony which easily turns to miserliness, and an obstinacy which may become an angry defiance. He established the fact that the primary pleasure in emptying the bowels and in its products was particularly emphasized in these persons; and also that after successful repression their coprophilia either becomes sublimated into pleasure in painting, modelling, and similar activities, or proceeds along the path of reaction-formation to a special love of cleanliness. Finally he pointed out the unconscious equivalence of fæces and money or other

[1] 'Anal-erotic Character Traits' (1918).

valuables. Among other observations Sadger [1] has remarked that persons with a pronounced anal character are usually convinced that they can do everything better than other people. He also speaks of a contradiction in their character, namely, great perseverance side by side with the tendency to put off doing everything till the last moment.

I will pass over isolated remarks in psycho-analytic literature by other authors and turn to Jones' very thorough and comprehensive study on this subject. I might remark in advance that I do not differ from this author on any points, but that nevertheless I feel that his statements need amplification and completion in certain respects.

Jones quite rightly distinguishes two different acts in the process we usually designate as the education of the child in cleanly habits. The child has not only to be taught not to soil its body and surroundings with excreta, but it has also to be educated to perform its excretory functions at regular times. In other words, it has to give up both its coprophilia and its pleasure in the process of excretion. This double process of limitation of infantile impulses together with its consequences in the psychical sphere requires further investigation.

The child's primitive method of evacuation brings the entire surface of its buttocks and lower extremities in contact with urine and fæces. This contact seems unpleasant, even repulsive, to adults, whose repressions have removed them from the infantile reaction to these processes. They cannot appreciate the sources of pleasure on which the libido of the infant can draw, in whom the stream of warm urine on the skin and contact with the warm mass of fæces produce pleasurable feelings. The child only begins to give signs of discomfort when the excreted products grow cold against its body. It is the same pleasure which the child seeks when it handles its fæces at a somewhat later period. Ferenczi [2] has traced the further development of this infantile tendency. It must not be forgotten, moreover,

---

[1] 'Analerotik und Analcharakter' (1910).
[2] 'On the Ontogenesis of an Interest in Money' (1916).

that pleasure in the sight and smell of fæces is associated with these feelings.

The special pleasure in the *act* of excretion, which we must differentiate from pleasure in the *products* of the excretory process, comprises besides physical sensations a psychical gratification which is based on the *achievement* of that act. Now in that the child's training demands strict regularity in its excretions as well as cleanliness it exposes the child's narcissism to a first severe test. The majority of children adapt themselves sooner or later to these demands. In favourable cases the child succeeds in making a virtue out of necessity, as it were; in other words, in identifying itself with the requirements of its educators and being proud of its attainment. The primary injury to its narcissism is thus compensated, and its original feeling of self-satisfaction is replaced by gratification in its achievement, in ' being good ', in its parents' praise.

All children are not equally successful in this respect. Particular attention should be drawn here to the fact that there are certain over-compensations behind which is hidden that obstinate holding fast to the primitive right of self-determination which occasionally breaks out violently later. I have in mind those children (and of course adults also) who are remarkable for their ' goodness ', polite manners, and obedience, but who base their underlying rebellious impulses on the grounds that they have been forced into submission since infancy. These cases have their own developmental history. In one of my patients I could trace back the course of events to her earliest infancy, in regard to which, it is true, previous statements of her mother were of assistance.

The patient was the middle one of three sisters. She showed unusually clearly and completely the traits characteristic of a ' middle ' child, which Hug-Hellmuth [1] has recently described in such an illuminating way. But her refractoriness, which was associated in the clearest manner with her assertion of the infantile right of self-determination in the

---

[1] ' Vom "mittlerem " Kinde ' (1921).

sense mentioned above, went back, in the last instance, to a particular circumstance of her childhood.

When she was born her elder sister had been still under a year old. Her mother had not quite succeeded in educating the elder child to habits of cleanliness when the newcomer had imposed on her a double amount of washing, both of clothes and body. When the patient was a few months old her mother had become pregnant for the third time, and had determined to hasten the education of her second child in cleanly habits, so that she should not still be too much taken up with her when the third child was born. She had demanded obedience on its part regarding the carrying out of its needs earlier than is usual, and had reinforced the effect of her words by smacking it. These measures had produced a very welcome result for the harassed mother. The child had become a model of cleanliness abnormally early, and had grown surprisingly submissive. When she was grown up, the patient was in a constant conflict between a conscious attitude of submissiveness, resignation and willingness to sacrifice herself on the one hand, and an unconscious desire for vengeance on the other.

This brief account illustrates in an instructive manner the effect of early injuries to infantile narcissism, especially if these injuries are of a persistent and systematic nature, and force a habit prematurely upon the child before it is psychically ready for it. This psychical preparedness only appears when the child begins to transfer on to objects (its mother, etc.) the feelings which are originally bound narcissistically. Once the child has acquired this capacity it will become cleanly ' for the sake of ' this person. If cleanliness is demanded too soon, it will acquire the habit through fear. Its inner resistance will remain and its libido will continue in a tenacious narcissistic fixation, and a permanent disturbance of the capacity to love will result.

The full significance of such an experience for the psychosexual development of the child only becomes apparent if we examine in detail the course of narcissistic pleasure. Jones lays stress on the connection between the child's high self-esteem and its excretory acts. In a short paper [1] I have brought forward some examples to show that the child's idea of the omnipotence of its wishes and thoughts can proceed from a stage in which it ascribed an omnipotence of this kind to its excretions. Further experience has since convinced me that this is a regular and typical process. The patient about whose childhood I have spoken had doubtless been disturbed in the enjoyment of a narcissistic pleasure of this sort. The severe and painful feelings of insufficiency with which she was later afflicted very probably went back in the last instance to this premature destruction of her infantile 'megalomania'.

This view of the excretions as a sign of enormous power is foreign to the consciousness of normal adults. That it persists in the unconscious, however, is shown in many everyday expressions, mostly of a jocular nature; for example, the seat of the closet is often denoted as the 'throne'. It is not to be wondered at that children who grow up in a strong anal-erotic environment incorporate these kinds of comparisons which they so frequently hear, in the fixed body of their recollections and make use of them in their later neurotic phantasies. One of my patients had a compulsion to read a meaning of this kind into the German national anthem. By transposing himself in his phantasies of greatness into the Kaiser's place he pictured to himself 'the high delight' of 'bathing in the glory of the throne', *i.e.* of touching his own excreta.

Once again language gives us characteristic instances of this over-estimation of defæcation. In Spanish, the common expression for it, '*regir el vientre*' (" to rule the belly "), which is used quite seriously, clearly indicates the pride taken by the person in the functioning of his bowels.

If we recognize in the child's pride in evacuation a primitive feeling of power we can understand the peculiar feeling of helplessness we so often find in neurotically constipated patients. Their libido has been displaced from the genital to the anal zone, and they deplore the inhibition of the bowel function just as though it were a genital impotence.

[1] Cf. Chapter XVII.

In thinking of the person who is hypochondriacal about his motions one is tempted to speak of an *intestinal* impotence.

Closely connected with this pride is the idea of many neurotics, which was first described by Sadger, that they must do everything themselves because no one else can do it as well. According to my experience this conviction is often exaggerated until the patient believes that he is a unique person. He will become pretentious and arrogant and will tend to under-estimate everyone else. One patient expressed this as follows: 'Everything that is not me is dirt'. These neurotics only take pleasure in possessing a thing that no one else has, and will despise any activity which they have to share with other people.

The sensitiveness of the person with an anal character to external encroachments of every kind on the actual or supposed field of his power is well known. It is quite evident that psycho-analysis must evoke the most violent resistance in such persons, who regard it as an unheard-of interference with their way of life. 'Psycho-analysis pokes about in my affairs', one patient said, thereby indicating unconsciously his passive-homosexual and anal attitude towards his analyst.

Jones emphasizes the fact that many neurotics of this class hold fast obstinately to their own system of doing things. They refuse altogether to accommodate themselves to any arrangement imposed from without, but expect compliance from other people as soon as they have worked out a definite arrangement of their own. As an example, I might mention the introduction of strict regulations for use in the office, or possibly the writing of a book which contains binding rules or recommendations for the organization of all offices of a certain kind.

The following is a glaring example of this kind. A mother drew up a written programme in which she arranged her daughter's day in the most minute manner. The orders for the early morning were set out as follows: (1) Get up. (2) Use the chamber. (3) Wash, etc. In the morning she would knock from time to time at her daughter's door, and ask, 'How far have you got now?' The girl would then have to reply, '9' or '15', as the case might be. In this way the mother kept a strict watch over the execution of her plan.

It might be mentioned here that all such systems not only testify to an obsession for order in its inventor, but also to his love of power which is of sadistic origin. I intend later to deal with the combination of anal and sadistic impulses in detail.

Allusion may be made here to the pleasure these neurotics take in indexing and registering everything, in making up tabular summaries, and in dealing with statistics of every kind.

They furthermore show the same self-will in regard to any demand or request made to them by some other person. We are reminded of the conduct of those children who become constipated when defæcation is demanded of them, but afterwards yield to the need at a time that is agreeable to themselves. Such children rebel equally against the 'shall' (being told to empty their bowels) as against the 'must' (a child's expression for the need to defæcate); their desire to postpone evacuation is a protection against both imperatives.

The surrender of excrement is the earliest form in which the child 'gives' or 'presents' a thing; and the neurotic often shows the self-will we have described in the matter of giving. Accordingly in many cases he will refuse a demand or request made to him, but will of his own *free choice* make a person a handsome present. The important thing to him is to preserve his right of decision. We frequently find in our psycho-analyses that a husband opposes any expenditure proposed by his wife, while he afterwards hands her of his 'own free will' more than what she first asked for. These men delight in keeping their wives permanently dependent on them financially. Assigning money in portions which they themselves determine is a source of pleasure to them. We come across similar behaviour in some neurotics regarding defæcation, which they only allow to take place *in refracta dosi*. One special tendency these men and women have is to distribute food in portions according as they think best, and this habit occasionally assumes grotesque forms. For instance, there was a case of a stingy old man who fed his goat by giving it each blade of grass separately. Such people like to arouse desire and expectation in others and then to give them gratification in small and insufficient amounts.

In those instances where they have to yield to the demand of another person some of these neurotics endeavour to maintain a semblance of making a personal decision. An example of this is the tendency to pay even the smallest amounts by cheque; in this way the person avoids using current notes and coin, but creates his 'own money' in each case. The displeasure of paying out is thereby diminished by just as much as it would be increased if payment were made in coin. I should like to make it quite clear, however, that other motives are also operative here.

Neurotics who wish to introduce their own system into everything are inclined to be exaggerated in their criticism of others, and this easily degenerates into mere carping. In social life they constitute the main body of malcontents. The original anal characteristic of self-will can, however, develop in two different directions, as Jones has convincingly shown. In some cases we meet with inaccessibility and stubbornness, that is, with characteristics that are unsocial and unproductive. In others we find perseverance and thoroughness, *i.e.* characteristics of social value as long as they are not pushed to extremes. We must here once more draw attention to the existence of other instinctual sources besides anal erotism which go to reinforce these tendencies.

The opposite type has received very little consideration in psycho-analytical literature. There are certain neurotics who avoid taking any kind of initiative. In ordinary life they want a kind father or attentive mother to be constantly at hand to remove every difficulty out of their way. In psycho-analysis they resent having to give free associations. They would like to lie quite still and let the physician do all the analytical work, or to be questioned by him. The similarity of the facts disclosed by the analysis of these

cases enables me to state that these patients used in childhood to resist the act of defæcation demanded of them,
and that then they used to be spared this trouble by being
given frequent enemas or purges by their mother or father.
To them free association is a psychical evacuation, and—
just as with bodily evacuation—they dislike being asked to
perform it. They are continually expecting that the work
should be made easier or done for them altogether. I
may recall a reverse form of this resistance, which I have
likewise traced back to anal erotic sources in an earlier
paper.[1] It concerns those patients who wish to do everything themselves according to their own method in their
psycho-analysis, and for this reason refuse to carry out the
prescribed free association.

In this paper I do not intend so much to discuss
the neurotic symptom-formations arising from repressed
anal erotism, as its characterological manifestations. I shall
therefore only touch upon the various forms of neurotic
inhibition which obviously have to do with a displacement
of libido to the anal zone. The fact that avoidance of
effort is a frequent feature of the anal character needs
further discussion; and we must briefly consider what
the state of affairs is in the person with a so-called
' obsessional character '.

If the libido of the male person does not advance in
full measure to the stage of genital organization, or if it
regresses from the genital to the anal developmental phase,
there invariably results a diminution of male activity in
every sense of the word. His physiological productiveness
is bound up with the genital zone. If his libido regresses
to the sadistic-anal phase he loses his productive power,
and not only in the purely generative sense. His genital
libido should give the first impulse to the procreative act,
and therewith to the creation of a new being. If the
initiative necessary for this reproductive act is lacking, we
invariably find a lack of productivity and initiative in other
respects in his behaviour. But the effects go even beyond
this.

[1] Cf. Chapter XV.

Together with the man's genital activity there goes a positive feeling-attitude towards his love-object, and this attitude extends to his behaviour towards other objects and is expressed in his capacity for social adaptation, his devotion to certain interests and ideas, etc. In all these respects the character-formation of the sadistic-anal stage is inferior to that of the genital phase. The sadistic element, which in a normal man's emotional life is of great importance once it has undergone appropriate transformation through sublimation, appears with particular strength in the obsessional character, but becomes more or less crippled in consequence of the ambivalence in the instinctual life of such persons. It also contains destructive tendencies hostile to the object, and on account of this cannot become sublimated to a real capacity for devotion to a love-object. For the reaction-formation of too great yieldingness and gentleness which is frequently observed in such people must not be confused with a real transference-love. Those cases in which object-love and genital libido-organization have been attained to a fair extent are more favourable. If the character-trait of over-kindness mentioned above is combined with a partial object-love of this kind, a socially useful ' variety ' is produced, which in essential respects is, nevertheless, inferior to full object-love.

In individuals with more or less impaired genitality we regularly find an unconscious tendency to regard the anal function as the productive activity, and to make it appear as if the genital activity were unessential and the anal one far more important. The social behaviour of these persons is accordingly strongly bound up with money. They like to make presents of money or its equivalent, and tend to become patrons of the arts or benefactors of some kind. But their libido remains more or less detached from objects, and so the work they do remains unproductive in the essential sense. They are by no means lacking in perseverance—a frequent mark of the anal character—but their perseverance is largely used in unproductive ways. They expend it, for instance, in the pedantic observance of fixed forms, so that in unfavourable cases their preoccupation with the external form outweighs their interest in the reality of the thing. In considering the various ways in which the anal character impairs male activity we must not forget the tendency, often a very obstinate one, of postponing every action. We are well acquainted with the origin of this tendency. There is often associated with it a tendency to interrupt every activity that has been begun; so that in many cases as soon as a person begins doing anything it can already be predicted that an interruption will occur very soon.

More rarely I have found the reverse conduct. For instance, one of my patients was prevented from writing his doctor's thesis through a long-standing resistance. After several motives for his resistance had come to light we found the following one: he declared that he shrank from beginning his work because when he had once begun he could not leave off again. We are reminded of the behaviour of certain neurotics in regard to their excretions. They retain the contents of the bowel or bladder as long as they possibly can. When finally they yield to the need that has become too strong for them there is no further holding back, and they evacuate the entire contents. A fact to be particularly noted here is that there is a double pleasure, that of holding back the execreta, and that of evacuating it. The essential difference between the two forms of pleasure lies in the protracted nature of the process in the one case, and in its rapid course in the other. As regards the patient just mentioned the long-deferred beginning of the work signified a turning from pleasure in retention to pleasure in evacuation.[1]

A detail from the history of the same patient will show

[1] The tendency to retain the fæces represents a special form of adherence to fore-pleasure, and seems to me to merit special consideration. I will only mention one point concerning it in this place. Recently frequent attempts have been made to set up two opposite 'psychological types' and to bring all individuals into one or other category. We may recall in this connection Jung's 'extraverted' and 'introverted' types. The patient whom I mentioned above was undoubtedly turned in upon himself in the highest degree, but he gave up this attitude of hostility to objects more and more in the course of his analysis. This and many similar experiences go to prove that 'introversion' in Jung's sense is an infantile clinging to the pleasure in retention. We are therefore dealing with an attitude that can be acquired or given up, and not with a manifestation of a rigid psychological type.

the degree to which a preponderance of anal over genital erotism makes the neurotic inactive and unproductive. During his analysis as well he remained wholly inactive for a long period, and by means of this resistance prevented any alteration taking place in his condition and circumstances. As is often the case in obsessional patients, his sole method of dealing with his external and internal difficulties was to swear violently. These expressions of affect were accompanied by very significant behaviour. Instead of thinking about the success of his work, he used to ponder over the question of what would happen to his curses— whether they reached God or the devil, and what was the fate of sound-waves in general. His intellectual activity was thus replaced by neurotic brooding. It appeared from his associations that the brooding question about the place where noise finally got to referred also to smell, and was in the last instance of anal erotic origin (flatus).

Generally speaking, it may be said that the more male activity and productivity is hindered in neurotics, the more pronounced their interest in possession becomes, and this in a way which departs widely from the normal. In marked cases of anal character-formation almost all relationships in life are brought into the category of having (holding fast) and giving, *i.e.* of proprietorship. It is as though the motto of many of these people were: ' Whoever gives me something is my friend; whoever desires something from me is my enemy'. One patient said that he could not have any friendly feelings towards me during his treatment, and added in explanation: ' So long as I have to pay anybody anything I cannot be friendly towards him'. We find the exact reverse of this behaviour in other neurotics; their friendly feeling towards a person increases in proportion to the help he needs and asks for.

In the first and larger group envy stands out clearly as the main character-trait. The envious person, however, shows not only a desire for the possessions of others, but connects with that desire spiteful impulses against the privileged proprietor. But we will only make a passing reference to the sadistic and anal roots of envy, since both are of minor and auxiliary significance in the production of that character-trait, which originates in the earlier, oral phase of libido-development. One example will suffice to illustrate the connection of envy with anal ideas of possession, and that is the frequent envy of his analyst on the part of the patient. He envies him the position of a ' superior ', and continually compares himself with him. A patient once said that the distribution of the rôles in psycho-analysis was too unjust, for it was he who had to make all the sacrifices; he had to visit the physician, produce his associations, and to pay the money into the bargain. The same patient also had the habit of calculating the income of everyone he knew.

We have now come very close to one of the classical traits of the person with an anal character, namely, his special attitude to money, which is usually one of parsimony or avarice. Often as this characteristic has been confirmed in psycho-analytical literature, there are yet a number of features connected with it which have not received much notice, and which I shall therefore proceed to deal with.

There are cases in which the connection between intentional retention of fæces and systematic parsimony is perfectly clear. I may mention the example of a rich banker who again and again impressed on his children that they should retain the contents of the bowels as long as possible, in order to get the benefit of every bit of the expensive food they ate.

Some neurotics limit their parsimony or their avarice to certain kinds of expenditure, while in other respects they spend money with surprising liberality. There is a class of patient who avoids spending any money on ' passing ' things. A concert, a journey, a visit to an exhibition, involves expense and nothing permanent is got in return. I knew a person who avoided going to the opera for this reason; nevertheless he bought piano scores of the operas which he had not heard, because in this way he obtained something ' lasting '. Some of these neurotics avoid spending money on food, because it is not retained as a permanent possession. It is significant that there is another type of patient who readily incurs expense for food in which he has an over-great interest. These are the neurotics who are always anxiously watching their bodies, testing their weight, etc. Their interest is concerned with the question of what remains of the material introduced into their body as a lasting possession. It is evident that they identify the content of the body with money.

In other cases we find that the neurotic carries his parsimony into every part of his life; and on certain points he goes to extremes without effecting any appreciable economy. I might mention an eccentric miser who used to go about in his house with the front of his trousers unbuttoned, in order that the button-holes should not wear out too quickly. It is easy to guess that in this instance other impulses were also operative. Nevertheless it is characteristic that these could be concealed behind the anal erotic tendency to save money, and that this motive should be so much emphasized. In some patients we find a parsimony in the special instance of using toilet paper. In this a dislike of soiling a clean thing co-operates as a determining factor.

The displacement of avarice from money or the value of money to time may be observed quite frequently. Time, it may be remembered, is likened to money in a familiar saying. Many neurotics are continually worrying over waste of time. It is only the time which they spend alone or at their work that seems to them well employed. Any disturbance in their work irritates them exceedingly. They hate inactivity, pleasures, etc. These are the people who tend to exhibit the ' Sunday neuroses' described by Ferenczi,[1] i.e. who cannot endure an interruption of their work. Just as every neurotically exaggerated purpose often fails to achieve its object, so is this the case here. The patients often save time on a small scale and waste it on a great one.

Such patients frequently undertake two occupations at once in order to save time. They like, for example, to

---

[1] 'Sunday Neurosis' (1919).

plead and to insist. One might almost say that they 'cling like leeches' to other people. They particularly dislike being alone, even for a short time. Impatience is a marked characteristic with them. In some cases, those in which psycho-analytic investigation reveals a regression from the oral-sadistic to the sucking stage, their behaviour has an element of cruelty in it as well, which makes them something like vampires to other people.

We meet certain traits of character in the same people which can be traced back to a peculiar displacement within the oral sphere. Their longing to experience gratification by way of sucking has changed to a need to *give* by way of the mouth, so that we find in them, besides a permanent longing to obtain everything, a constant need to communicate themselves orally to other people. This results in an obstinate urge to talk, connected in most cases with a feeling of overflowing. Persons of this kind have the impression that their fund of thought is inexhaustible, and they ascribe a special power or some unusual value to what they say. Their principal relation to other people is effected by the way of oral discharge. The obstinate insistence described above naturally occurs chiefly by means of speech. But that function serves at the same time for the act of giving. I could, moreover, regularly establish the fact that these people could not control their other activities any more than they could their speech. Thus one frequently finds in them a neurotically exaggerated need to urinate, which often appears at the same time as an outburst of talking or directly after it.

In those features of character-formation which belong to the oral-sadistic stage, too, speaking takes the place of repressed impulses from another quarter. In certain neurotics the hostile purpose of their speech is especially striking. In this instance it serves the unconscious aim of killing the adversary. Psycho-analysis has shown that in such cases, in place of biting and devouring the object, a milder form of aggression has appeared, though the mouth is still utilized as the organ of it. In certain neurotics speaking is used to express the entire range of instinctual trends,

2 c

whether friendly or hostile, social or asocial, and irrespective of the instinctual sphere to which they originally belonged. In them the impulse to talk signifies desiring as well as attacking, killing, or annihilating, and at the same time every kind of bodily evacuation, including the act of fertilization. In their phantasies speaking is subject to the narcissistic valuation which their unconscious applies to all physical and psychical productions. Their entire behaviour shows a particularly striking contrast to reticent people with anal character-formation.

Observations of this kind most emphatically draw our attention to the varieties and differences that exist within the realm of oral character-formation, and show that the field which we are investigating is anything but limited or poor in variations. The most important differences, however, are those which depend on whether a feature of character has developed on the basis of the earlier or the later oral stage; whether, in other words, it is the expression of an unconscious tendency to suck or to bite. In the latter case we shall find in connection with such a character-trait the most marked symptoms of ambivalence—positive and negative instinctual cravings, hostile and friendly tendencies; while we may assume on the basis of our experience that the character-traits derived from the stage of sucking are not as yet subjected to ambivalence. According to my observations, this fundamental difference extends to the smallest details of a person's behaviour. At a meeting of the British Psychological Society (Medical Section) Dr. Edward Glover recently read a paper in which he gave these differences particular consideration.[1]

The very significant contrasts found in the character-formation of different individuals can be traced psycho-analytically from the fact that decisive influences on the process of formation of character have been exercised in the one case by oral impulses, and in the other case by anal ones. Equally important is the connecting of sadistic instinctual elements with the manifestation of libido flowing from the various erotogenic zones. A few examples may

[1] ' The Significance of the Mouth in Psycho-Analysis ' (1924).

roughly illustrate this point. In our psycho-analyses we are able to trace phenomena of very intense craving and effort back to the primary oral stage. It need hardly be said that we do not exclude other sources of impulse as factors in those phenomena. But the desires derived from that earliest stage are still free from the tendency to destroy the object—a tendency which is characteristic of the impulses of the next stage.

The covetous impulses which are derived from the second oral stage are in strong contrast to the unassuming character of the anally constituted person. But we must not forget that the weakness of the acquisitive tendency in the latter is balanced by his obstinate holding fast to things which he has already got.

Characteristic, too, are the differences in the inclination to share one's own possessions with others. Generosity is frequently found as an oral character-trait. In this the orally gratified person is identifying himself with the bounteous mother. Things are very different in the next, oral-sadistic stage, where envy, hostility, and jealousy make such behaviour impossible. Thus in many cases generous or envious behaviour is derived from one of the two oral stages of development; and in the same way the inclination to avarice corresponds to the succeeding anal-sadistic stage of character-formation.

There are noteworthy differences in the person's social conduct, too, according to the stage of his libido from which his character is derived. People who have been gratified in the earliest stage are bright and sociable; those who are fixated at the oral-sadistic stage are hostile and malicious; while moroseness, inaccessibility, and reticence go together with the anal character.

Furthermore, persons with an oral character are accessible to new ideas, in a favourable as well as an unfavourable sense, while the anal character involves a conservative behaviour opposed to all innovations—an attitude which certainly prevents the hasty abandonment of what has been proved good.

There is a similar contrast between the impatient importunity, haste, and restlessness of people with oral character-formation, and the perseverance and persistence of the anal character, which, on the other hand, tends to procrastination and hesitation.

The character-trait of ambition, which we meet with so frequently in our psycho-analyses, has been derived long ago by Freud [1] from urethral erotism. This explanation, however, does not seem to have penetrated to the deepest sources of that characteristic. According to my experience, and also that of Dr. Edward Glover, this is rather a character-trait of oral origin which is later reinforced from other sources, among which the urethral one should be particularly mentioned.

Besides this, it has to be noted that certain contributions to character-formation originating in the earliest oral stage coincide in important respects with others derived from the final genital stage. This is probably explicable from the fact that at these two stages the libido is least open to disturbance from an ambivalence of feeling.

In many people we find, beside the oral character-traits described, other psychological manifestations which we must derive from the same instinctual sources. These are impulses which have escaped any social modification. As examples a morbidly intense appetite for food and an inclination to various oral perversions are especially to be mentioned. Further, we meet many kinds of neurotic symptoms which are determined orally; and finally there are phenomena which have come into being through sublimation. These latter products deserve a separate investigation, which, however, would exceed the limits of this paper; hence I shall only briefly give a single example.

The displacement of the infantile pleasure in sucking to the intellectual sphere is of great practical significance. Curiosity and the pleasure in observing receive important reinforcements from this source, and this not only in childhood, but during the subject's whole life. In persons with a special inclination for observing Nature, and for many branches of scientific investigation, psycho-analysis shows a

[1] ' Character and Anal Erotism ' (1908).

close connection between those impulses and repressed oral desires.

A glance into the workshop of scientific investigation enables us to recognize how impulses pertaining to the different erotogenic zones must support and supplement one another if the most favourable results possible are to be achieved. The optimum is reached when an energetic imbibing of observations is combined with enough tenacity and ability to 'digest' the collected facts, and a sufficiently strong impulse to give them back to the world, provided this is not done with undue haste. Psycho-analytical experience enables us to recognize various kinds of divergences from this optimum. Thus there are people with great mental capacity for absorbing, who, however, are inhibited in production. Others again produce too rapidly. It is no exaggeration to say of such people that they have scarcely taken a thing in before it comes out of their mouths again. When they are analysed it often proves that these same persons tend to vomit food as soon as they have eaten it. They are people who show an extreme neurotic impatience; a satisfactory combination of forward-moving oral impulses with retarding anal ones is lacking in the structure of their character.

In conclusion, it seems to me particularly important to allude once more to the significance of such combinations. In the normal formation of character we shall always find derivatives from all the original instinctual sources happily combined with one another.

It is important, moreover, to consider the numerous possibilities of such combinations because it prevents us from over-estimating some one particular aspect, important though it may be. If we consider the problems of character-formation from the one large unifying point of view which psycho-analysis affords us, from that of infantile sexuality, then it is obvious how everything weaves itself into a whole in the characterological sphere. The realm of infantile sexuality extends over two quite different fields. It covers the entire unconscious instinctual life of the mature human being. It is likewise the scene of the very important mental impressions of the earliest years of the child, among which we have to reckon prenatal influences. Sometimes we may feel dismayed in face of the mass of phenomena which meets us in the wide field of human mentality, from the play of children and other typical products of the early activity of phantasy, through the first development of the child's interests and talents, up to the most highly valued achievements of mature human beings and the most extreme individual differentiations. But then we must remember that Freud has given us in the practice and theory of psycho-analysis an instrument with which to investigate this wide subject and to open up the road to infantile sexuality, that inexhaustible source of life.

Chapter XXV

CHARACTER-FORMATION ON THE GENITAL LEVEL OF LIBIDO-DEVELOPMENT [1]
(1925)

IN the two phases of development discussed in the preceding chapters [2] we were able to recognize *archaic types of character-formation.* They represent in the life of the individual recapitulations of primitive states which the human race has passed through at certain stages of its development. Here, as in general in biology, we find the rule holding good that the individual repeats in an abbreviated form the history of his ancestors. Accordingly, in normal circumstances the individual will traverse those early stages of character-formation in a relatively short space of time. In this chapter I shall give in very rough outline an idea of the way in which the character of men and women in its definitive form is built up on those early foundations.

According to the traditional view, character is defined as the direction habitually taken by a person's voluntary impulses. It is not part of the intention of this paper to spend much time in finding an exact definition of character. We shall, however, find it advisable not to be too much influenced by the ' habit ' of attributing great importance to the direction usually taken by these impulses of the will. For our previous discussions have already made it clear that character is a changeable thing. We shall therefore do better not to make their duration and permanence an

---

[1] [No. 106, A. B.].

[2] [These two chapters, together with the present one, were issued in book-form under the title of *Psychological Studies upon Character-Formation.*]

essential criterion of character-traits. It will be sufficient for our purposes to say that we consider the character of a person to be the sum of his instinctive reactions towards his social environment.

We have already seen that in early life the child reacts to the external world purely on the basis of its instincts. It is only by degrees that it overcomes to some extent its egoistic impulses and its narcissism and takes the step towards object-love. And, as we know, attainment of this stage of development coincides with another important event, namely, attainment of the highest level of libidinal organization—the genital level, as it is called. Believing as we do that the character-traits of men and women have their origin in definite instinctual sources, we should naturally expect that the development of a person's character would only be complete when his libido has reached its highest stage of organization and has achieved the capacity for object-love. And in fact Freud's view that a person's sexual attitude is reflected in the whole trend of his mental attitude in general finds complete confirmation from all the facts observed in this field as well.

In the first of these three essays it has been shown in detail that the individual is able to fill his place and exercise his powers fully and satisfactorily in his social environment only if his libido has attained the genital stage. But we have not as yet given special attention to that process which consists in the transition from the second stage of character-formation to the third and final one.

The first function of this third stage in the formation of character is of course to get rid of the remaining traces of the more primitive stages of development, in so far as they are unfavourable to the social behaviour of the individual. For he will not, for instance, be able to achieve a tolerant and fair-minded attitude to other people and to interests outside his own, until he has got the better of his destructive and hostile impulses springing from sadistic sources, or of his avarice and mistrust derived from anal ones. We shall therefore examine with great interest the process by means of which such a transformation takes place.

An overwhelming abundance of material connected with the processes which we have grouped under the general heading of the Oedipus complex presents itself to us, and draws our attention to this class of mental events. If we confine ourselves to the case of the male child, we find that the most powerful sources of affect in early years consist in his erotic desire for his mother and his wish to put his father out of the way. And closely allied to them are his ideas about castration. If he can successfully master the emotions centred round this subject it will have a decisive effect on the form taken by his character. I shall content myself with a very brief survey of this question, since I can refer the reader to the paper by Alexander, already published,[1] on the relations between character and the castration-complex. Generally speaking, we may say that when the child has been able to subdue his Oedipus complex with all its constituents he has made the most important step towards overcoming his original narcissism and his hostile tendencies; and at the same time he has broken the power of the pleasure-principle to dominate the conduct of his life.

At this point I will dwell in greater detail on a particular aspect of this process of change, since its significance for the formation of character has as yet received hardly any attention. This is the extensive alteration which takes place in the boy's attitude towards the body of persons of the opposite sex, *i.e.* in the first instance towards that of his mother. Originally her body was to him an object of mingled curiosity and fear; in other words, it aroused ambivalent feelings in him. But gradually he achieves a libidinal cathexis of his love-object as a whole, that is, with the inclusion of those parts of it which had formerly aroused those contrary feelings in him. If this has been achieved there arise in him expressions of his libidinal relation to his object that are inhibited in their aim— feelings of fondness, devotion, and so on—and these co-exist with his directly erotic desires for it. And indeed, during the boy's latency period, these ' aim-inhibited ' sentiments predominate over his sensual feelings. If the child's

[1] ' The Castration Complex in the Formation of Character ' (1922).

development continues to be normal, these new sentiments that have been established towards his mother next become carried over to his father. They gradually extend their field and the child adopts a friendly and well-wishing attitude, first to persons of his near environment, and then to the community at large. This process seems to me to be a very important basis for the final and definitive formation of a person's character. It occurs at the time at which he passes out of that phase of his libidinal development which Freud has called the phallic stage. It implies that he has attained a point in his object-relations where he no longer has an ambivalent attitude towards the genital organ of his heterosexual object, but recognizes it as a part of that object whom he loves as an entire person.

Whereas on the earlier levels of character-development the interests of the individual and those of the community ran counter to one another, on the genital level the interests of both coincide to a great extent.

We are thus led to the conclusion that the definitive character developed in each individual is dependent upon the history of his Oedipus complex, and particularly on the capacity he has developed for transferring his friendly feelings on to other people or on to his whole environment. If he has failed in this, if he has not succeeded in sufficiently developing his social feelings, a marked disturbance of his character will be the direct consequence. Among our patients, with every aspect of whose mental life we become acquainted in psycho-analytic treatment, there are a great number who are suffering in a greater or less degree from disturbances of this kind. The history of their early childhood never fails to show that certain circumstances occurred to prevent the development of their social feelings. We always find that the sexual impulses of such people are unaccompanied by any desire for affectionate relations. And, similarly, in their daily life they have difficulties in getting a proper contact of feeling with other people. How greatly such a favourable development of character from a social point of view depends upon the degree to which these 'affectionate' instinctual components develop is most clearly seen in a class of persons whose childhood has been in especial stamped by the circumstances of their birth.   I refer to illegitimate children.   From the very beginning these children have suffered from a want of sympathy and affection from the people about them.   If a child has no examples of love before it, it will have difficulty in entertaining any such feelings itself, and it will besides be incapable of discarding those primitive impulses which are originally directed *against* the external world.   And thus it will readily succumb to an unsocial attitude.   We see the same thing happen with the neurotic patient who, though born and educated in ordinary circumstances, feels that he is not loved, that he is the 'Cinderella' of the family.

Since we are on the topic of the definitive stage of character-formation it may be as well to obviate a possible misunderstanding.   It is not the intention of this discussion to say what exactly a 'normal' character is.   Psycho-analysis has never set up norms of this sort, but contents itself with ascertaining psychological facts.   It simply ascertains how far an individual or a group of persons has managed to travel along the line of development from the earliest stage to the latest in the structure of their character. It is precisely analytic experience which teaches us that even the most complete characterological development in a social sense merely represents a *relative* success in over-coming the more primitive types of mental structure, and that individual circumstances of an internal and external nature determine how completely the final aim will be achieved or how far that achievement will be a lasting one.

In 1913 Freud drew attention to the case of a female patient in whom at the time of the menopause there appeared, side by side with neurotic symptoms, certain phenomena of involution of character.[1]   This was the first time that such an observation had been made.   We look upon neurotic symptoms as products of a regression in the psycho-sexual sphere.   By uniting both processes under the general heading of regression, Freud was able to explain why a change in character takes place at the same time as neurotic

[1] 'The Predisposition to Obsessional Neurosis' (1913).

symptoms are formed. This observation of Freud's has often been confirmed since. But it is not only at one particular period of his life that a person's character is dependent upon the general position of his libido; that dependence exists at every age. The proverb which says ' Youth knows not virtue ' ('*Jugend kennt keine Tugend*') is expressing the truth that in early life character is still without definite form or stability. Nevertheless, we should not over-estimate the fixity of character even in later years, but ought rather to bear in mind certain psychological facts which I shall briefly touch upon now.

It was Freud who first pointed out that important changes can take place at any time in the mental make-up of the individual through the process of introjection. Women in particular tend to assimilate their character to that of the man with whom they are living. And when they change their love-object it can happen that they change their character accordingly. It is moreover worth noticing that husbands and wives who have lived long together tend to resemble one another in character.

Psycho-analysts are familiar with the fact that when a neurosis sets in it can bring with it a regressive change of character; and conversely, that an improvement in the neurosis can be accompanied by a change of character in a progressive direction. Some time ago [1] I was able to point out that in the intervals between the periodical return of symptoms persons suffering from cyclical disorders exhibit a character similar to that of obsessional neurotics, so that according to our view they progress from the oral to the anal-sadistic level.

But there are other reasons why we cannot set up a norm for character. As we know, individuals show extra-ordinarily wide variations in character, according to their social class, nationality, and race. We need only consider how widely nations or groups of people differ from one another in their sense of order, love of truth, industry, and other mental qualities. But, besides this, each group of people will vary in its behaviour at different times. A

[1] Cf. Chapter XXVI.

single nation, for instance, will change its conceptions of cleanliness, economy, justice, etc., more than once in the course of its history. Observation has shown, furthermore, that alterations in the external circumstances of a people, a social class and so on, can entail radical changes in its dominating characteristics. The effect of the Great War in this respect is still fresh in our memory. Thus we see that, as soon as suitable alterations take place in their internal or external relations, a group of people shows the same mutability of character as an individual.

In the two preceding papers I showed how the final stage of character-formation was built up on earlier phases of its development and absorbed into itself essential elements of these former phases. And we were led to attribute special importance in the formation of character to the various vicissitudes which befall the Oedipus complex. So that to set up a fixed norm for human character would be to deny not only the already acknowledged fact that character is variable but also all that we know about the way in which such variations arise.

We should be inclined to consider as normal in the social sense a person who is not prevented by any too great eccentricity in his character from adapting himself to the interests of the community. But a description like this is very elastic and allows room for a great number of variations. From the social point of view all that is required is that the character-traits of the individual should not be pushed to an excess; that he should be able, for instance, to find some sort of mean between the extremes of cruelty and over-kindness or between those of avarice and extravagance. We ought above all to avoid the mistake of setting up a norm in regard to the ratio in which the various mental qualities should be combined in any person. It need hardly be said that by this we are not intending to proclaim the ideal of the ' golden mean ' in all the relations of man to his surroundings.

It follows from what has been said that there is no absolute line of demarcation between the different kinds of character-formation. Nevertheless in practice we do find that they fall fairly naturally into distinct classes.

The best subjects for psycho-analytic investigation are those patients who exchange certain character-traits for others from time to time under the direct observation of the analyst. One young man who came to me for analysis gradually changed his attitude to such an extent under the influence of treatment that he quite got rid of certain markedly unsocial features of his character. Before that he had been unfriendly, ill-disposed, overbearing and grasping in his relation to others, and in fact had exhibited a great number of oral and anal characteristics. This attitude changed more and more as time went on. But at certain irregular intervals violent resistances appeared and were accompanied every time by a temporary relapse into that archaic phase of character-development which he had by now partly given up. On those occasions he would become disagreeable and hostile in his behaviour, and overbearing and contemptuous in his speech. From having conducted himself in a friendly and polite manner he became suspicious and irritable. While his resistance lasted all his friendly feelings towards his fellow-men—including his analyst— ceased, and he took up a completely opposite attitude towards the external world. At the same time as he reacted in this way with aversion and hatred towards human beings, he centred his desires in an unmeasured degree on inanimate objects. His whole interest was absorbed in buying things. In this way he set up as much as possible a relationship of *possession* between himself and his environment. During this time he was filled with fear that something belonging to him might get lost or stolen. His whole attitude to the external world was thus dominated by ideas of possession, acquisition, and possible loss. Directly his resistance began to diminish, his oral character-trait of covetousness and his anal one of avarice in regard to objects retreated into the background, and he began once more to entertain personal relationships towards other people and normal feelings about them which continued to develop and establish themselves.

Cases of this kind are particularly instructive, not only

because they show the connection between certain features of character and a particular level of libidinal organization, but also because they are evidence of the mutability of character; they show that the character of a person can on occasion rise to a higher level of development or sink to a lower one.

The final stage of character-formation shows traces everywhere of its association with the preceding stages. It borrows from them whatever conduces to a favourable relation between the individual and his objects. From the early oral stage it takes over enterprise and energy; from the anal stage, endurance, perseverance, and various other characteristics; from sadistic sources, the necessary power to carry on the struggle for existence. If the development of his character has been successful the individual is able to avoid falling into pathological exaggerations of those characteristics, whether in a positive or a negative direction. He is able to keep his impulses under control without being driven to a complete disavowal of his instincts, as is the obsessional neurotic. The sense of justice may serve as an illustration; in a case of favourable development this character-trait is not heightened to an excessive punctiliousness and is not liable to break out in a violent way on some trivial occasion. We have only to think of the many actions done by obsessional neurotics in the way of ‘fairness’: suppose the right hand has made a movement or touched an object, the left hand must do the same. We have already said that ordinary friendly feelings remain entirely distinct from exaggerated forms of neurotic over-kindness. And similarly it is possible to steer a middle course between the two pathological extremes of either delaying everything or always being in too great a hurry; or of either being over-obstinate or too easily influenced. As regards material goods, the compromise arrived at is that the individual respects the interests of others up to a certain point, but at the same time secures his own existence. He preserves to some extent the aggressive impulses necessary for the maintenance of his life. And a considerable portion of his sadistic instincts is employed no longer for destructive but for constructive purposes.

In the course of this general alteration of character, as presented here in rough outline, we also observe that the individual achieves a steady conquest of his narcissism. In its earlier stages his character was still in a large measure governed by his narcissistic impulses. And we cannot deny that in its definitive stage it still contains a certain proportion of such impulses. Observation has taught us that no developmental stage, each of which has an organic basis of its own, is ever entirely surmounted or completely obliterated. On the contrary, each new product of development possesses characteristics derived from its earlier history. Nevertheless, even though the primitive signs of self-love are to some extent preserved in it, we may say that the definitive stage of character-formation is *relatively* unnarcissistic.

Another change of great importance in the formation of character is that in which the individual overcomes his attitude of ambivalence (I speak again in a relative sense). Instances have already been given to show in what way a person's character avoids extremes on either side after it has attained its final stage of development. I should also like to draw attention here to the fact that as long as a severe conflict of ambivalent feelings continues to exist in a person's character, there is always a danger both for him and for his environment that he may suddenly swing from one extreme to its opposite.

Thus if a person is to develop his character more or less up to that point which we have taken to be its highest level, he must possess a sufficient quantity of affectionate and friendly feeling. A development of this sort goes hand in hand with a relatively successful conquest of his narcissistic attitude and his ambivalence.

We have seen that the customary view of character-formation did not give us any real clue to the sources of that process as a whole. Psycho-analysis, on the other hand, based on empirical observation, has demonstrated the close connection that character-formation has with the psycho-sexual development of the child, in especial with the different libidinal stages and with the successive relations of the libido to its object. And, furthermore, it has taught us that even after childhood the character of the individual is subject to processes of evolution and involution.

In psycho-analysis we view abnormal character in close and constant relation to all the other manifestations of the person's psycho-sexual life. This and the fact that character is not a fixed thing, even in adults, make it possible for us to exert a corrective influence upon pathological character-formations. Psycho-analysis is by no means simply confronted with the task of curing neurotic symptoms in the narrow sense of the word. It often has to deal with pathological deformities of character at the same time, or even in the first instance. So far our experience goes to show that the analysis of character is one of the most difficult pieces of work which the analyst can undertake, but that it has undoubtedly proved in some cases to be the most repaying. At present, however, we are not in a position to make any general judgement about the therapeutic results of character-analysis; that we must leave to future experience.

Chapter XXVI

A SHORT STUDY OF THE DEVELOPMENT OF THE LIBIDO, VIEWED IN THE LIGHT OF MENTAL DISORDERS (1924)[1]

PART I

MANIC-DEPRESSIVE STATES AND THE PRE-GENITAL LEVELS OF THE LIBIDO

INTRODUCTION

MORE than ten years have passed since I first attempted to trace the ætiology of manic-depressive disorders on psycho-analytical lines.[2] I was quite aware at the time of the shortcomings of that attempt and was at pains to make this clear in the title of my paper. But we should do well to remember how very little had been written as yet on any psycho-analytical subject. And in especial there were very few earlier works in existence on the circular insanities. Private psychotherapeutic practice offers little opportunity for the analysis of cases of this kind, so that it was not possible for any single analyst to collect and compare sufficient data on this subject.

Nevertheless, in spite of the shortcomings of that first attempt, its results have proved to be correct in certain not unimportant particulars. Freud's paper, ' Mourning and Melancholia ', confirmed my view that melancholia stood in the same relation to normal mourning for a loss as did

---

[1] [No. 105, A. B.]   [2] See Chapter VI.

morbid anxiety to ordinary fear. And we may now regard as definitely established the psychological affinity between melancholia and obsessional neuroses. Furthermore, these two illnesses show similarities in regard to the process of the disengagement of the libido from the external world. On the other hand, it had not hitherto been possible to discover anything concerning the point of divergence of melancholic and obsessional states; nor indeed had any light been shed as yet on the problem of the specific cause of the circular insanities.

After Freud had established the theory of the pre-genital levels in the organization of the libido I made an attempt to discover this specific cause. Freud had been led by the analysis of obsessional neuroses to postulate a pre-genital phase in the development of the libido which he called the sadistic-anal phase. A little later [1] he gave a detailed description of a still earlier phase, the oral or cannibalistic one. Basing my views on a large and varied collection of empiric material I was able [2] to show that certain psycho-neuroses contain clear traces of that earliest phase in the organization of the libido; and I ventured the suggestion that what we saw in melancholia was the result of a regression of the patient's libido to that same primitive oral level. But my clinical material was not very complete in this respect, and I was not able to bring forward any convincing proofs of my view.

At about the same time Freud approached the problem of melancholia from another angle, and he made the first real step towards the discovery of the mechanism of that illness. He showed that the patient, after having lost his love-object, regains it once more by a process of intro-jection (so that, for instance, the self-reproaches of a melancholiac are really directed towards his lost object).

Subsequent experience has confirmed in my mind the importance of both processes—the regression of the libido to the oral stage and the mechanism of introjection. And more than that, it has shown that there is an intimate

---

[1] In the third edition of his *Drei Abhandlungen zur Sexualtheorie*.
[2] See Chapter XII.

connection between the two. The analyses on which the present publication is based leave no doubt as to this last point. As I hope to be able to make quite clear, the introjection of the love-object is an incorporation of it, in keeping with the regression of the libido to the cannibalistic level.

Two more discoveries in this field of research must be mentioned, again in connection with Freud's name. In the first place he pointed out that in melancholia the event of underlying importance is the loss of the object which precedes the outbreak of the illness, and that this does not happen in obsessional cases. The obsessional neurotic has, it is true, a markedly ambivalent attitude towards his object and is afraid of losing it; but he does ultimately keep it. The discovery of this difference between the two pathological states is of great consequence, as I hope will become plain in the course of my study. In the second place, Freud has recently given a more definite direction to our investigation of states of manic exaltation.[1] It will become clear to the reader presently what an advance his theories represent over my first uncertain attempts in 1911.

In 1920 I was invited to read a paper on the manic-depressive psychoses at the Sixth Psycho-Analytical Congress. I was obliged to refuse, since I had no fresh data in my possession. Since that time I have had an opportunity of making an almost complete analysis of two marked cases of circular insanity, and of gaining a brief glimpse into the structure of some other cases belonging to this class. The results of those analyses confirm in a surprising way Freud's view of the structure of melancholic and manic disorders. Besides this, they bring forward a number of new points which supplement his theory in one or two important respects.

Motives of discretion impose a great deal of reserve in the publication of my psycho-analytical material. They prevent me, in especial, from giving a consecutive case-history of the two cases which I analysed thoroughly, and I can only bring forward short extracts from each. In order to preclude the possibility of a mistaken diagnosis I may say

[1] Cf. *Group Psychology and the Analysis of the Ego* (1921).

at once that both my patients had repeatedly been put in asylums or sanatoriums where they were under the observation of able psychiatrists, and that they had been examined by eminent mental specialists. The clinical picture was absolutely typical and the circular course of the illness quite characteristic in both cases, so that in point of fact there was never any doubt about the diagnosis.

In one respect my data is insufficient; and I point this fact out at once, although I do not myself attribute very great importance to it. All the manic-depressive patients I have treated, including the two recent cases I analysed completely, were male. I have only had the opportunity of making cursory psycho-analytical observations of female patients of this class, except for a quite recent case in whose analysis I am still engaged.

But I do not think it likely that an analysis of female patients would lead to any fundamentally different conclusions, especially when we consider that the patients of both sexes exhibit an extremely marked bisexuality in their symptoms, so that they doubtless have many points of similarity.

At the time when I read a part of this publication before the Seventh Psycho-Analytical Congress,[1] the interest felt in the subject was clearly shown by the fact that many of the other papers read there dealt with the same questions and arrived at conclusions strikingly similar to mine, although they approached the matter from quite a different standpoint. In especial I may mention the important contribution made by Róheim [2] in which he added a great deal to our knowledge of the psychology of cannibalism.

In the first part of this book I shall briefly examine certain problems concerning manic-depressive states—in particular the problem of the patient's relation to his love-object during his states of depression and mania and during his 'free interval'. In the second part I shall treat those problems in a broader way and shall consider the subject of the development of the libido as a whole.

[1] Held in Berlin in 1922.
[2] 'Nach dem Tode des Urvaters' (1923).

I

Melancholia and Obsessional Neurosis: Two Stages of the Sadistic-Anal Phase of the Libido

In setting out to examine the mental disorder called melancholia we shall still do well to compare it with the obsessional neuroses, since this affection, closely related to melancholia in its psychology, has to some extent been robbed of its mystery by psycho-analysis.

As early as 1911, in mentioning the similarities between the two illnesses, both as regards their clinical picture and their structure, I pointed out that obsessional symptoms were very frequently present in cases of melancholia and that obsessional neurotics were subject to states of depression. I went on to say that in both kinds of illness a high degree of ambivalence was to be found in the patient's instinctual life; and that this was most clearly seen in the want of adjustment between his emotions of love and of hate, and between his homosexual and heterosexual tendencies.

More recent researches have led me to the view that obsessional neurosis and melancholia resemble one another not only in their acute symptoms, but also have important points in common during their periods of quiescence. And therefore in my present study on melancholia I propose to take as my starting-point not the complete clinical picture, but the so-called 'free interval' which is interposed between two periods of illness.

From the point of view of the clinical observer manic-depressive states run an intermittent course, whereas obsessional states are on the whole chronic in character. Nevertheless, the latter do show a clear tendency to have considerable remissions. Indeed, in some obsessional cases the illness comes on in acute attacks which are very similar to the periodic outbreaks of the illness in melancholia. Careful observation spread over a long period of time shows us that here, as in so many other cases, the one condition shades off into the other, whereas at first we only saw an absolute cleavage between the two.

This view receives fresh confirmation as we advance deeper in our psychological inquiry. For we find that the patient who is liable to periodic fits of depression and exaltation is not really perfectly well during his ' free interval '. If we merely question such patients rather closely we learn that during long intervals of this kind they pass through depressive or hypo-manic states of mind from time to time. But what is specially interesting to the analyst is the fact that in all cycloid illnesses the patient is found to have an abnormal character-formation during his ' free interval '; and that this character-formation coincides in a quite unmistakable way with that of the obsessional neurotic. As far as my experience goes, at any rate, it does not seem possible to make a hard and fast distinction between the melancholic character and the so-called ' obsessional character '. In their ' free interval ' patients suffering from circular insanity exhibit the same characteristics as psycho-analysis has made us acquainted with in the obsessional neuroses—the same peculiarities in regard to cleanliness and order; the same tendency to take up an obstinate and defiant attitude alternating with exaggerated docility and an excess of ' goodness '; the same abnormalities of behaviour in relation to money and possessions. These character-traits furnish important evidence that these two pathological conditions have a close psychological relationship with one and the same pre-genital phase of the libido. If we assume the existence of such an extensive agreement in the characterological constitution of persons who incline to melancholia and of those who incline to an obsessional neurosis, it is quite incomprehensible to us why an illness which takes its inception from the same character-formation should be now of the one type, now of the other. It is true that we have come to the conclusion that in melancholia the patient gives up his psycho-sexual relations to his object, whereas the obsessional neurotic does in the end manage to escape that fate. But we are then faced with the problem why the object-relation is so much more labile in the one class of patients than in the other.

According to the psycho-analytic view, the fixation points that have been formed in the course of the development of the libido will determine to what level of organization the libido of the individual will advance, and to what level it will retreat in the event of a neurotic illness. And the same is true of the relation of the individual to the outer world: inhibitions in development and regressive processes are always found to be determined by earlier fixations in the sphere of the libido. Now in spite of their common relation to the anal-sadistic organization of the libido, melancholia and obsessional neurosis exhibit certain fundamental differences not only in respect of the phase to which the libido regresses at the onset of the illness, but also in respect of the attitude of the individual to his object, since the melancholiac gives it up, while the obsessional patient retains it. If, therefore, it appears that such widely divergent pathological processes can take their inception from the sadistic-anal stage, it follows that *this stage contains heterogeneous elements which we have not been able to separate out hitherto*. In other words, our knowledge of this stage of libidinal development must be insufficient. And moreover, other considerations give us good reason for believing that this is in fact the case.

Up till now we have been acquainted with three stages in the development of the libido, in each of which we were able to observe that one particular erotogenic zone was of preponderant importance. These erotogenic zones are, in order of time, the oral, the anal, and the genital. We found that the libidinal excitations belonging to anal erotism had close and manifold connections in that stage with sadistic impulses. I have already once pointed out in an earlier paper,[1] that since Freud's discovery our clinical observation has confirmed over and over again the close relationship that exists between these two instinctual spheres; and yet we have never inquired into the origin of that especial relationship. We have learnt from the psycho-

[1] See Chapter XXIII.

analysis of neurotic patients that excretory processes are employed for sadistic purposes, and have found this fact confirmed by observation of the psychology of children. We have also seen that a single character-trait—defiance, for instance—proceeds from sadistic as well as from anal sources. But these observations and others like them have not enabled us to understand the reason of that combination of sadistic and anal activities.

We can get a step nearer to the solution of the problem if we take into consideration another piece of well-ascertained psycho-analytic knowledge which I have discussed in my above-mentioned paper.[1] This is, that a complete capacity for love is only achieved when the libido has reached its genital stage. Thus we have on the one hand anal erotic processes combined with sadistic behaviour, in especial with unkind and hostile emotions which are destructive to their object; and on the other, a genital erotism combined with tendencies which are friendly to their object.

But this comparison only serves, as I have said, to bring us a step nearer to our problem, which remains unanswered so long as we do not know why, at a certain level of development, the sadistic impulses exhibit a special affinity precisely for anal erotism and not, for instance, for oral or genital erotism. Here again the empirical data of psycho-analysis may be of use to us. For they show us

1. That anal erotism contains two opposite pleasurable tendencies.

2. That similarly two opposite tendencies exist in the field of sadistic impulses.

The evacuation of the bowels calls forth a pleasurable excitation of the anal zone. To this primitive form of pleasurable experience there is presently added another, based on a reverse process—the retention of the fæces.

Psycho-analytic experience has shown beyond a doubt that in the middle stage of his libidinal development the individual regards the person who is the object of his desire as something over which he exercises ownership, and that

[1] Chapter XXIII.

he consequently treats that person in the same way as he
does his earliest piece of private property, *i.e.* the contents
of his body, his fæces.[1] Whereas on the genital level
' love ' means the transference of his positive feeling on
to the object and involves a psycho-sexual adaptation to
that object, on the level below it means that he treats
his object as though it belonged to him.   And since the
ambivalence of feelings still exists in full force on this
inferior level, he expresses his positive attitude towards
his object in the form of retaining his property, and his
negative attitude in the form of *rejecting* it.   Thus when
the obsessional neurotic is threatened with the loss of his
object, and when the melancholiac actually does lose his, it
signifies to the unconscious mind of each an expulsion of
that object in the sense of a physical expulsion of fæces.

I assume that every psycho-analyst will be able to
confirm this parallel from his own observation.   In my
above-mentioned paper [2] I have discussed it in greater
detail.   I should only like to draw attention in this place
to the fact that many neurotic persons react in an anal way
to every loss, whether it is the death of a person or the loss
of a material object.   They will react with constipation or
diarrhœa according as the loss is viewed by their unconscious
mind—whose attitude, in agreement with the ambivalence
of their emotional life, is itself naturally a variable one.
Their unconscious denies or affirms the loss by means of
the ' organ-speech ' with which we are familiar.   News of
the death of a near relative will often set up in a person a
violent pressure in his bowels as if the whole of his intestines
were being expelled, or as if something was being torn
away inside him and was going to come out through his
anus.   Without forgetting that a reaction like this is over-
determined, I should like in this place to single out this
one cause with which we are concerned.   We must regard
the reaction as an archaic form of mourning which has
been conserved in the unconscious; and we can set it side
by side with a primitive ritual, described by Róheim,[3] in

[1] Cf. Chapter XXIII.   [2] Chapter XXIII.
[3] ' Nach dem Tode des Urvaters ' (1923).

which the relatives of the deceased man defæcate on his new-made grave.

It is worth noting that certain forms of speech still preserve distinct traces of this parallel between losing something and emptying the bowels. For instance, the excrement of animals is called '*Losung*'[1] in German, and the connection between this word and 'los'[2] and the English word ' lose ' is evident.

As an illustration I should like to relate the following curious ceremonial performed by a neurotic woman. (I have already quoted this example in my above-mentioned paper.) This woman, who presented anal character-traits of an extreme kind, was as a rule unable to throw away disused objects. Nevertheless she felt impelled from time to time to get rid of one or other of them. And so she had invented a way of cheating herself, as it were. She used to go out into the wood close by, and before she left the house she would take the object that was to be thrown away—an old garment, for instance—and tuck a corner of it under her petticoat strings behind. Then she would ' lose ' the thing on her walk in the wood. She would come home by another way so as not to come across it again. Thus in order to be able to give up the possession of an object she had to let it drop from the back of her body.

Moreover, nothing is so eloquent in confirmation of our view as the utterances of children. A small Hungarian boy, whose family lived in Buda-Pesth, once threatened his nurse with these words: ' If you make me angry I'll ka-ka you across to Ofen ' (a district on the other side of the Danube). According to the child's view the way to get rid of a person one no longer liked was by means of defæcation.

This primitive idea that removing an object or losing it is equivalent to defæcation has become remote to us grown-up people; so remote, indeed, that it is only through a laborious process of psycho-analytic investigation that

---

[1] ['What has dropped off'. Cf. the English word ' droppings '.—*Trans.*]

[2] [As a suffix='without'. '*Einem loswerden*'=' to be rid of someone '.—*Trans.*]

we have been able to recover those traces of primitive thought—and even so the discovery is received by most people with an incredulous shake of the head. Nevertheless, certain psychological products, such as myths, folklore, and usages of speech, enable us to recognize that this habit of thought is the common property of the unconscious mind. Let me only mention one very general expression used by students at the German universities. If a student has been excluded by his comrades from all their official occasions on account of some misdemeanour, that is, if he has been more or less excommunicated, it is commonly said of him that '*Er gerät in Verschiss*'.[1] Here the expulsion of a person is quite openly compared to the physical expulsion of stool.

The component instinct of sadism, as it exists in the infantile libido, also shows us two opposite pleasurable tendencies at work. One of these tendencies is to *destroy* the object (or the external world); the other is to *control* it. I shall later try to show in detail that the tendency to spare the object and to preserve it has grown out of the more primitive, destructive tendency by a process of repression. For the present I shall speak of this process quite in general; but I should like to say at once that psycho-analysis has given us a perfectly sound knowledge of these stages and the succeeding ones in the development of object-love. For the moment we will confine our interest to that sadistic instinct which threatens the existence of its object. And we see that the removal or loss of an object can be regarded by the unconscious either as a sadistic process of destruction or as an anal one of expulsion.

It is worth noticing in this connection that different languages express the idea of losing something in two different ways, in agreement with the psycho-analytic view put forward. The German word '*verlieren*', the English 'to lose', and the Latin '*amittere*', correspond to the anal idea of letting something go; whereas '*ἀπολλύναι*' in Greek, '*perdere*' in late Latin, and '*perdre*' in French,

---

[1] ['He has been sent to Coventry.' '*Verschiss*' (literally 'excrement') instead of '*Verruf*' ('bad repute').—*Trans.*]

signify to ruin or destroy a thing. We may also bear in mind Freud's analytic interpretation of losing things as an unconsciously motivated tendency to put the object out of the way. His interpretation is well confirmed by those languages which directly identify losing a thing with destroying it.

Again, certain forms of speech show how closely are united in the unconscious mind anal and sadistic tendencies to abolish an object. The most widely different languages tend to express only by indirect allusion or metaphor behaviour which is based on sadistic impulses. But those metaphors are derived from activities which psychoanalytic experience has taught us to trace back to anal erotic and coprophilic instincts. A good example of this is to be found in the military reports and despatches which appeared on both sides during the late war. In them places were ' *gesäubert* ' (' cleaned ') of the enemy, trenches were ' *aufgeräumt* ' (' cleared out '); in the French accounts the word used was ' *nettoyer* ' (' to clean '), and in the English, ' cleaning up ' or ' mopping up ' was the expression.

The analysis of neurotic patients has taught us that the second, *conserving* set of tendencies that spring from anal and sadistic sources—tendencies to retain and to control the object—combine in many ways and reinforce one another. And in the same way there is a close alliance between the *destructive* tendencies coming from those two sources—tendencies to expel and to destroy the object. The way in which these latter tendencies co-operate will become especially clear in the psychology of states of melancholia. And we shall enter into this point in greater detail later on.

What I should like to do in this place is to discuss briefly the convergent action of anal and sadistic instincts in the obsessional character. We have hitherto accounted for the excessive love of cleanliness shown by such characters as being a reaction formation against coprophilic tendencies, and for their marked love of order as a repressed or sublimated anal erotic instinct. This view, though correct and supported by a great mass of empirical data, is in some

ways one-sided.   It does not take sufficiently into consideration the over-determination of psychological phenomena.

For we are able to detect in our patients' compulsive
love of order and cleanliness the co-operation of sublimated
sadistic instincts as well.   In my above-mentioned essay
I have adduced examples to show that compulsive orderliness is at the same time an expression of the patient's
desire for domination.   He exerts power over things.
He forces them into a rigid and pedantic system.   And it
not seldom happens that he makes people themselves enter
into a system of this kind.   We have only to think of
the compulsion for cleaning everything from which some
housewives suffer.   They very often behave in such a way
that nothing and no one is left in peace.   They turn the
whole house upside down and compel other persons to
submit to their pathological impulses.   In extreme cases
of an obsessional character, as it is met with in housewife's
neurosis and in neurotic exaggerations of the bureaucratic
mind, this craving for domination becomes quite unmistakable.   Or again, we need only think of the sadistic
elements that go to make up the well-known anal character-
trait of obstinacy to realize how anal and sadistic instinctual
forces act together.

In order to be able to understand more clearly what
takes place at the time of the onset of an obsessional
neurosis or of melancholia, we must once more turn our
attention to those periods of the patient's life which are
relatively free from symptoms.   The ' remission ' of the
obsessional patient and the ' interval ' of the manic-
depressive appear as periods in which his anal and sadistic
instincts have been successfully sublimated.   As soon as
something special occurs to threaten the ' loss ' of their
object in the sense already used, both classes of neurotics
react with great violence.   The patient summons up the
whole energy of his positive libidinal fixations to combat
the danger that the current of feeling hostile to his object
will grow too strong.   If the conserving tendencies—those
of retaining and controlling his object—are the more
powerful, this conflict around the love-object will call forth

phenomena of psychological compulsion. But if the opposing sadistic-anal tendencies are victorious—those which aim at destroying and expelling the object—then the patient will fall into a state of melancholic depression.

We shall not be surprised to find that obsessional symptoms make their appearance in a melancholia and that states of depression occur in an obsessional neurosis. In cases of this sort the destructive or the conserving tendency, as the case may be, has not been able to carry the day completely. As a rule, however, either the one or the other—the tendency to manic-depressive symptoms or the tendency to show signs of obsessional behaviour— occupies the foreground of the clinical picture. But we are not yet in a position to get a deeper insight into the causes of this interplay of the two sets of symptoms.

Psycho-analytic experience and the direct observation of children have established the fact that that set of instincts which aims at the destruction and expulsion of the object is ontogenetically the elder of the two. In the normal development of his psycho-sexual life the individual ends by being capable of loving his object. But the road which he traverses, beginning from the auto-erotism of his infancy and ending with a complete object-love, still needs to be studied more exactly. But this much may be said to be certain: the child's libido is without an object (auto-erotic) to begin with. Later, it takes its ego as its first object; and not till after that does it turn towards external objects. But even then it retains the quality of ambivalence for some time; and it is only at a relatively late period of his childhood that the individual is capable of having a completely friendly attitude towards his object.

When we compare the course taken by the libido in obsessional neurosis and in melancholia, we can see at once that in the obsessional neurotic, in spite of the insecurity of his relations to his object, it has never deviated so far in a regressive direction from the normal goal of its development as it has in the case of the melancholiac. For at the onset of his illness the depressive patient has completely broken off all object-relations.

Psycho-analytic experience has already obliged us to assert the existence of a pre-genital, anal-sadistic stage of libidinal development; and we now find ourselves led to assume that that stage includes two different levels within itself. On the later level the conserving tendencies of retaining and controlling the object predominate, whereas on the earlier level those hostile to their object—those of destroying and losing it—come to the fore. The obsessional neurotic regresses to the later of these two levels, and so he is able to maintain contact with his object. During his quiet periods of remission he is able to a great extent to sublimate his sadistic and anal impulses so that his relation to the external world may even appear normal to the ordinary eye. The same thing may happen in melancholia. Even clinical psychiatry admits that a melancholic may get ' well ', *i.e.* recover his mental health. For during the period when his symptoms are absent the manic-depressive patient can transform his instincts in the same way as the obsessional neurotic. But as soon as his ego enters into an acute conflict with his love-object he gives up his relation to that object. And now it becomes evident that the whole of his sublimations and reaction-formations which are so similar to those of the ' obsessional character ' are derived from the lower level of the anal-sadistic stage of his libidinal development.

This differentiation of the anal-sadistic stage into a primitive and a later phase seems to be of radical importance. For at the dividing line between those two phases there takes place a decisive change in the attitude of the individual to the external world. Indeed, we may say that this dividing line is where ' object-love ' in the narrower sense begins, for it is at this point that the tendency to preserve the object begins to predominate.

Nor is such a differentiation of merely theoretical interest. It not only serves to give us a clear picture of a particular period of the child's psycho-sexual development; it also assists us in getting a deeper insight into the regressive movement of the libido in the psycho-neuroses. We shall see later that the process of regression in melancholia does not stop at the earlier level of the anal-sadistic stage, but goes steadily back towards still more primitive organizations of the libido. It thus appears as though when once the dividing line between the two anal-sadistic phases has been crossed in a regressive direction the effects are especially unfavourable. Once the libido has relinquished its object-relations it seems to glide rapidly downwards from one level to the next.

In regarding this dividing line as extremely important we find ourselves in agreement with the ordinary medical view. For the division that we psycho-analysts have made on the strength of empirical data coincides in fact with the classification into neurosis and psychosis made by clinical medicine. But analysts, of course, would not attempt to make a rigid separation between neurotic and psychotic affections. They are, on the contrary, aware that the libido of any individual may regress beyond this dividing line between the two anal-sadistic phases, given a suitable exciting cause of illness, and given certain points of fixation in his libidinal development which facilitate a regression of this nature.

II

OBJECT-LOSS AND INTROJECTION IN NORMAL MOURNING AND IN ABNORMAL STATES OF MIND

Having taken as the starting-point of our investigations the 'free interval' in periodical depressive and manic states, we may now proceed to inquire into the event which ushers in the actual melancholic illness—that event which Freud has called the 'loss of object'—and into the process, so closely allied to it, of the introjection of the lost love-object.

In his paper, 'Mourning and Melancholia', Freud described in general outlines the psychosexual processes that take place in the melancholic. He was able to obtain an intuitive idea of them from the occasional treatment of depressive patients; but not very much clinical material has

been published up till now in the literature of psycho-
analysis in support of this theory. The material which I
shall bring forward in this connection is, however, intended
not merely to illustrate that theory but to prepare the way
for a systematic inquiry into the pathological processes of
melancholia and into the phenomena of mourning. As we
shall see, the psychology of melancholia and of mourning
are not as yet sufficiently understood.[1]

Now and then we come across cases of marked melancholic depression where the processes of object-loss and
introjection can be recognized without making any psycho-
analysis. But we must not forget that this would not have
been possible if Freud had not drawn our attention to the
general features of the psychological situation.

Dr. Elekes of Klausenburg has recently communicated
to me the following peculiarly instructive case from his
psychiatric practice in an asylum. A female patient was
brought to the asylum on account of a melancholic depression.
She repeatedly accused herself of being a thief. In reality
she had never stolen anything. But her father, with whom
she lived, and to whom she clung with all an unmarried
daughter's love, had been arrested a short while before for a
theft. This event, which not only removed her father from
her in the literal meaning of the word but also called forth
a profound psychological reaction in the sense of estranging
her from him, was the beginning of her attack of melancholia.
The loss of the loved person was immediately succeeded by
an act of introjection; and now it was the patient herself
who had committed the theft. This instance once more
bears out Freud's view that the self-reproaches of melancholia are in reality reproaches directed against the loved
person.

It is easy enough to see in certain cases that object-loss
and introjection have taken place. But we must remember
that our knowledge of these facts is purely superficial, for
we can give no explanation of them whatever. It is only

[1] Medical discretion forbids me to give in full the analytic material of cases
at my disposal. I must therefore confine myself to the reproduction of instructive
extracts from various cases. This method has the advantage of making the material
less difficult to survey.

by means of a regular psycho-analysis that we are able to perceive that there is a relationship between object-loss and tendencies, based on the earlier phase of the anal-sadistic stage, to lose and destroy things; and that the process of introjection has the character of a physical incorporation by way of the mouth. Furthermore, a superficial view of this sort misses the whole of the ambivalence conflict that is inherent in melancholia. The material which I shall bring forward in these pages will, I hope, help to some extent to fill in this gap in our knowledge. I should like to point out at once, however, that our knowledge of what takes place in normal mourning is equally superficial; for psycho-analysis has thrown no light on that mental state in healthy people and in cases of transference-neurosis. True, Freud has made the very significant observation that the serious conflict of ambivalent feelings from which the melancholiac suffers is absent in the normal person. But how exactly the process of mourning is effected in the normal mind we do not at present know. Quite recently, however, I have had a case of this sort which has at last enabled me to gain some knowledge of this till now obscure subject, and which shows that in the normal process of mourning, too, the person reacts to a real object-loss by effecting a temporary introjection of the loved person. The case was as follows:[1]

The wife of one of my analyzands became very seriously ill while he was still under treatment. She was expecting her first child. At last it became necessary to put an end to her pregnancy by a Cæsarian section. My analyzand was hurriedly called to her bedside and arrived after the operation had been performed. But neither his wife nor the prematurely born child could be saved. After some time the husband came back to me and continued his treatment. His analysis, and in especial a dream he had shortly after its resumption, made it quite evident that he had reacted to his painful loss with an act of introjection of an oral-cannibalistic character.

One of the most striking mental phenomena exhibited

---

[1] The person concerned has authorized me to make use of this observation in view of its scientific value.

by him at this time was a dislike of eating, which lasted for weeks. This feature was in marked contrast to his usual habits, and was reminiscent of the refusal to take nourishment met with in melancholiacs. One day his disinclination for food disappeared, and he ate a good meal in the evening. That night he had a dream in which he was present at the *post-mortem* on his late wife. The dream was divided into two contrasting scenes. In the one, the separate parts of the body grew together again, the dead woman began to show signs of life, and he embraced her with feelings of the liveliest joy. In the other scene the dissecting-room altered its appearance, and the dreamer was reminded of slaughtered animals in a butcher's shop.

The scene of the dissection, twice presented in the dream, was associated with his wife's operation (*sectio Caesaris*). In the one part it turned into the re-animation of the dead body; in the other it was connected with cannibalistic ideas. The dreamer's association to the dream in analysis brought out the remarkable fact that the sight of the dissected body reminded him of his meal of the evening before, and especially of a meat dish he had eaten.

We see here, therefore, that a single event has had two different sequels in the dream, set side by side with one another, as is so often the case when a parallel has to be expressed. Consuming the flesh of the dead wife is made equivalent to restoring her to life. Now Freud has shown that by introjecting the lost object the melancholiac does indeed recall it to life; he sets it up in his ego. In the present case the widowed man had abandoned himself to his grief for a certain period of time as though there were no possible escape from it. His disinclination for food was in part a playing with his own death; it seemed to imply that now that the object of his love was dead life had no more attraction for him. He then began to work off the traumatic effect of his loss by means of an unconscious process of introjection of the loved object. While this was going on he was once more able to take nourishment, and at the same time his dream announced the fact that the work of mourning had succeeded. The process of mourning thus brings with it the consolation: ' My loved object is not gone, for now I carry it within myself and can never lose it '.

This psychological process is, we see, identical with what occurs in melancholia. I shall try to make it clear later on that melancholia is an archaic form of mourning. But the instance given above leads us to the conclusion that the work of mourning in the healthy individual also assumes an archaic form in the lower strata of his mind.

At the time of writing I find that the fact that introjection takes place in normal mourning has already come near discovery from another quarter. Groddeck [1] cites the case of a patient whose hair went grey at the time of his father's death, and he attributes it to an unconscious tendency on the part of the patient to become like his father, and thus as it were to absorb him in himself and to take his place with his mother.

And here I find myself obliged to contribute an experience out of my own life. When Freud published his ' Mourning and Melancholia ', so often quoted in these pages, I noticed that I felt a quite unaccustomed difficulty in following his train of thought. I was aware of an inclination to reject the idea of an introjection of the loved object. I combated this feeling in myself, thinking that the fact that the genius of Freud had made a discovery in a field of interest so much my own had called forth in me an affective ' no '. It was not till later that I realized that this obvious motive was only of secondary importance compared with another. The facts were these:

Towards the end of the previous year my father had died. During the period of mourning which I went through certain things occurred which I was not at the time able to recognize as the consequence of a process of introjection. The most striking event was that my hair rapidly turned very grey and went black again in a few months' time. At the time I attributed this to the emotional crisis I had been through. But I am now obliged to accept Groddeck's view, quoted above, concerning the deeper connection

[1] In his *Buch vom Es* (1923), p. 24.

between my hair turning grey and my state of mourning. For I had seen my father for the last time a few months before his death, when I was home from the war on a short leave. I had found him very much aged and not at all strong, and I had especially noticed that his hair and his beard were almost white and were longer than usual on account of his having been confined to his bed. My recollection of my last visit to him was closely associated with this impression. Certain other features in the situation, which I am unfortunately unable to describe here, lead me to attribute my temporary symptom of turning grey to a process of introjection. It thus appears that my principal motive in being averse to Freud's theory of the pathological process of melancholia at first was my own tendency to employ the same mechanism during mourning.

Nevertheless, although introjection occurs in mourning in the healthy person and in the neurotic no less than in the melancholiac, we must not overlook the important differences between the process in the one and in the other. In the normal person it is set in motion by real loss (death); and its main purpose is to preserve the person's relations to the dead object, or—what comes to the same thing—to compensate for his loss. Furthermore, his conscious knowledge of his loss will never leave the normal person, as it does the melancholiac. The process of introjection in the melancholiac, moreover, is based on a radical disturbance of his libidinal relations to his object. It rests on a severe conflict of ambivalent feelings, from which he can only escape by turning against himself the hostility he originally felt towards his object.

Recent observations, those of Freud in the first instance, have shown that introjection is a far commoner psychological process than has hitherto been supposed. I should like to refer in particular to a remark of Freud's [1] concerning the psycho-analysis of homosexuality.

He expresses the view (though he does not support it with any clinical material) that we should be able to trace certain cases of homosexuality to the fact that the subject

[1] Cf. his *Group Psychology*, p. 66.

has introjected the parent of the opposite sex. Thus a young man will feel an inclination towards male persons because he has assimilated his mother by means of a psychological process of incorporation and consequently reacts to male objects in the way that she would do. Up till now we have been chiefly acquainted with another ætiology of homosexuality. The analysis of such cases has shown that as a rule the person has had a disappointment in his love for his mother and has left her and gone over to his father, towards whom he henceforward adopts the attitude usually taken by the daughter, identifying himself like her with his mother. A short time ago I had a case in which I was able to establish the presence of both these possible lines of mental development. The patient had a bisexual libidinal attitude, but was in a homosexual phase at the time he came to me for analysis. Twice before— once in early childhood and once during puberty—he had passed through a homosexual phase. It was only the second of these that set in with what must be described as a complete process of introjection. On that occasion the patient's ego was really submerged by the introjected object. I shall give a short abstract of his analysis, for it seems to me that the material is not only important for an understanding of the process of introjection, but also throws light on certain phenomena of mania and melancholia.

The patient was the younger of two children and had been a spoilt child in every sense of the word in his infancy. His mother had continued to suckle him well on into his second year, and even in his third year she still occasionally gave way to his desire, vehemently urged, to be fed at the breast. She did not wean him till he was three years old. At the same time as he was being weaned—a process which was achieved with great difficulty—a succession of events took place which robbed the spoilt child all at once of the paradise he had lived in. Up till then he had been the darling of his parents, of his sister, who was three years his senior, and of his nurse. Then his sister died. His mother withdrew into an abnormally severe and long period of mourning and thus became still more estranged from him than the weaning had already made her. The nurse left them. His parents could not bear to go on living in the same house, where they were constantly being reminded of their dead child, and they moved into an hotel and then into a new house. This series of events deprived the patient of all the things he had hitherto enjoyed in the way of maternal solicitude. First his mother had withdrawn the breast from him. Then she had shut herself off from him psychologically in mourning for her other child. His elder sister and his nurse were gone. Finally the house, that important symbol of the mother, was given up. It is not surprising that the small boy should have turned towards his father for love at this point. Besides this, he fixed his inclinations on a friendly neighbour, a woman who lived near their new house, and he made a great show of his preference for her over his mother. The splitting up of his libido—one part going to his father, the other to a woman who was a mother-surrogate—had already become evident. In the years following this period he became attached by a strong erotic interest to boys older than himself who resembled his father in their physical characteristics.

In his later childhood, as his father began to give way to drink more and more, the boy withdrew his libido from him and once more directed it towards his mother. He maintained this position for several years. Then his father died, and he lived alone with his mother, to whom he was devoted. But after a short period of widowhood she married again and went travelling with her husband for quite a long time. In doing this she had once more repulsed her son's love. And at the same time the boy's feelings of hatred were aroused against his step-father.

A new wave of homosexual feeling came over the half-grown boy. But this time he was attracted by a different type of young man, one which closely resembled that of his mother in certain physical qualities. The kind of youth he had loved on the first occasion, and the kind he loved now, exactly represented the contrast between his father and his mother in respect of their determining physical characteristics. It must be mentioned that the patient was himself entirely of his mother's type. His attitude towards this second type of young man for whom he now had a preference was, in his own words, tender, loving, and full of solicitude, like a mother.

Several years later the patient's mother died. He was with her during her last illness and she died in his arms. The very great effect which this experience had on him was caused by the fact that in a deeper stratum of his mind it represented the complete reversal of that unforgotten situation in which he, as an infant, had lain at his mother's breast and in her arms.

No sooner was his mother dead than he hurried back to the neighbouring town where he lived. His state of feeling, however, was by no means that of a sorrowing son; he felt, on the contrary, elated and blissful. He described to me how he was filled with the feeling that now he carried his mother safely in himself, his own for ever. The only thing that caused him uneasiness was the thought of her burial. It was as if he was disturbed by the knowledge that her body was still visible and lying in the house she had died in. It was not till the funeral was over that he could give himself up to the feeling that he possessed his mother for evermore.

If it were possible for me to publish more details from the analysis of this patient, I could make this process of incorporating the mother still more evident. But enough has been said to make its occurrence quite clear.

In this instance the process of introjecting the loved object began when the patient lost his mother through her second marriage. He was unable to move his libido away on to his father, as he had done in his fourth year; and his step-father was not qualified to attach his libido to himself. The last object of his infantile love that was left—his mother—was also the first. He strove against this heaviest loss that could befall him by employing the mechanism of introjection.

It is astonishing to find that this process of introjection should have resulted in such a feeling of happiness, in direct contradiction to its effect on the melancholiac upon whose mind it weighs so heavily. But our surprise is lessened when we recollect Freud's explanation of the mechanism of melancholia. We have only to reverse his statement that ' the shadow of the lost love-object falls upon the ego ' and say that in this case it was not the shadow but the bright radiance of his loved mother which was shed upon her son. In the normal person, too, feelings of affection easily oust the hostile ones in regard to an object he has (in reality) lost. But it is otherwise in the case of the melancholiac. For here we find so strong a conflict based on libidinal ambivalence that every feeling of love is at once threatened by its opposite emotion. A ' frustration ', a disappointment from the side of the loved object, may at any time let loose a mighty wave of hatred which will sweep away his all too weakly-rooted feelings of love. Such a removal of the positive libidinal cathexes will have a most profound effect: it will lead to the giving up of the object. In the above-cited case, which was not one of melancholia, however, the loss *in reality* of the object was the primary event, and the alteration in the libido only a necessary consequence of it.

III

THE PROCESS OF INTROJECTION IN MELANCHOLIA: TWO STAGES OF THE ORAL PHASE OF THE LIBIDO

The following particularly instructive example may serve as a starting-point for further inquiry into the process of introjection.

The patient in question had already had several typical attacks of melancholia when he first came to me, and I began his analysis just as he was recovering from an attack of this kind. It had been a severe one, and had set in under rather curious circumstances. The patient had been fond of a young girl for some time back and had become engaged to her. Certain events, which I will not go into here, had caused his inclinations to give place to a violent resistance. It had ended in his turning away completely from his love-object—whose identification with his mother became quite evident in his analysis—and succumbing to a depressive condition accompanied by marked delusions. During his convalescence a *rapprochement* took place between him and his fiancée, who had remained constant to him in spite of his having left her. But after some time he had a brief relapse, the onset and termination of which I was able to observe in detail in his analysis.

His resistance to his fiancée re-appeared quite clearly during his relapse, and one of the forms it took was the following transitory symptom: During the time when his state of depression was worse than usual, he had a compulsion to contract his *sphincter ani*. This symptom proved to be over-determined. What is of most interest here is its significance as a convulsive holding fast to the contents of the bowels. As we know, such a retention symbolizes possession, and is its prototype in the unconscious. Thus the patient's transitory symptom stood for a retention, in the physical sense, of the object which he was once more in danger of losing. It had another determinant which I shall briefly notice. This was his passive homosexual attitude towards his father. Whenever he turned away from his mother or from a mother-substitute he was in danger of adopting this attitude; and his symptom was a defence not only against an object-loss but against a move towards homosexuality.

We have followed Freud in assuming that after he has lost his object the melancholiac attempts some kind of restitution of it. In paranoia this restitution is achieved by the specific mechanism of projection. In melancholia the mechanism of introjection is adopted, and the results are different. In the case of my patient the transitory symptom mentioned above, which was formed at the beginning of a brief remission of his illness, was not the end of the matter. A few days later he told me, once more of his own accord, that he had a fresh symptom which had, as it were, stepped into the shoes of the first one. As he was walking along the street he had had a compulsive phantasy of eating the excrements that were lying about. This phantasy turned out to be the expression of a desire to take back into his body the love-object which he had expelled from it in the form of excrement. We have here, therefore, a literal confirmation of our theory that the unconscious regards the loss of an object as an anal process, and its introjection as an oral one.

The tendency to coprophagia seems to me to contain a symbolism which is typical for melancholia. My own observations on a number of cases have always shown that the patient makes his love-object the target of certain impulses which correspond to the lower level of his anal-sadistic libidinal development. These are the impulses of expelling (in an anal sense) and of destroying (murdering). The product of such a murder—the dead body—becomes identified with the product of expulsion—with excrement. We can now understand that the patient's desire to eat excrement is a cannibalistic impulse to devour the love-object which he has killed. In one of my patients the idea of eating excrement was connected with the idea of being punished for a great sin. Psychologically speaking, he was right. For it was in this way that he had to make up for a certain crime whose identity with the deed of Oedipus we shall presently learn to understand.[1] I should like in this place to mention Róheim's interesting remarks [2] on the subject of necrophagia. What he has said makes it very probable that in their archaic form mourning rites consisted in the eating of the dead person.

The example given above is unusual in the easy and simple way in which it discloses the meaning of melancholic symptoms as an expulsion and a re-incorporation of the love-object. To show to what a degree these impulses can be rendered unrecognizable, I will give a second instance, taken from the psycho-analysis of another patient.

This patient told me one day that he had noticed a

[1] Dr. J. Hárnik has pointed out that in Egypt a prayer is often put on gravestones in which the dead man asks that he may be spared the punishment of having to eat excrement. Cf. Erman, *Religion der Ägypter*.

[2] Communicated to the Psycho-Analytical Congress in 1922.

curious tendency that he had during his states of depression. At the beginning of those states he used to go about with his head lowered, so that his eyes were fixed on the ground rather than on the people about him. He would then begin to look with compulsive interest to see whether any mother-of-pearl buttons were lying in the street. If he found one he would pick it up and put it in his pocket. He rationalized this habit by saying that at the beginning of his depression he had such a feeling of inferiority that he had to feel glad if he even so much as found a button in the street; for he did not know whether he would ever again be capable of earning enough money to buy the least thing for himself. In the wretched condition he was in, he said, even those objects which other people left about must have a considerable value for him.

This explanation was contradicted by the fact that he passed by other objects, especially buttons made of other material, with a certain feeling of contempt. His free associations gradually led us to the deeper motives of his strange inclination. They showed that he connected the mother-of-pearl of which the buttons were made with the idea of brightness and cleanness, and then of special worth. We had thus arrived at his repressed coprophilic interests. I may remind my readers of Ferenczi's excellent paper on this subject.[1] In it he shows how the child first takes pleasure in substance that is soft and yielding, then in hard and granular material, and finally in small, solid objects with a clean and shining surface. In the unconscious these objects all remain equivalent to excrement.

The mother-of-pearl buttons stood, then, for excrement. Having to pick them up from the road reminds us of the obsessional impulse in the case described before, in which there was a direct compulsion to pick up excrement from the street and eat it. A further point of similarity between the two may be noted, namely, that people lose buttons off clothes just as they let fæces drop.[2] In both instances,

---

[1] 'On the Ontogenesis of an Interest in Money' (1914).
[2] Regarding this assimilation of ideas, cf. the case described in Section I. of this chapter.

therefore, the action is concerned with taking up and keeping a lost object.

In one of his next analytic hours the patient resumed this theme and said that what he had told me was not the only strange impulse he had had in his states of depression. During his first attack of this kind he had gone to Professor Y.'s nursing home at X. One day two relatives of his had come to take him out for a walk. They had shown him the public gardens and buildings and other things, but he had been utterly uninterested in them. But on his way back he had stopped in front of a shop-window in which he saw some pieces of Johannis bread.[1] He felt a strong desire to buy some of it, and had done so.

The patient at once had an association to this story, which was as follows: In the little town in which he lived as a child there was a small shop opposite his house. The shop was owned by a widow, whose son was a play-mate of his. He recollected that this woman used to give him Johannis bread. At that time he had already had the fateful experience which was the origin of his later illness — a profound disappointment in his love-relations from the side of his mother. In his childhood memories this woman across the road was set up as a model and contrasted with his 'wicked' mother. His automatic impulse to buy Johannis bread in a shop and to eat it had as its immediate significance his desire for maternal love and care. That he should have selected precisely Johannis bread as a symbol for this was because its long shape and brown colour reminded him of fæces. Thus we once more meet with the impulse to eat excrement as an expression of the desire for a lost love-object.

The patient had another association that went back to his childhood days. A road was being constructed in his native town and the workmen had dug up some shells. One side of them was covered with earth and looked dirty, but the other side glistened like mother-of-pearl. Here again the patient's associations took him back to his native place, which

[1] [A fancy bread.—*Trans.*]

he undoubtedly identified with his mother. These shells were the precursors of the mother-of-pearl buttons about which he had his obsession. The idea of mother-of-pearl shells, moreover, proved in analysis to be a means of representing his ambivalent attitude towards his mother. The word 'mother-of-pearl' expressed his high esteem for his mother as a 'pearl'. But the smooth, shining surface was deceptive—the other side was not so beautiful. In likening this other side, which was covered with dirt (excrement) to his 'wicked' mother, from whom he had had to withdraw his libido, he was abusing her and holding her up to scorn.[1]

The instances given above may suffice for the present. They help us to understand psycho-analytically the course run by melancholia in its two phases—the loss and the re-incorporation of the love-object. Each of these phases, however, calls for further examination.

We have already said that the tendency to give up the love-object has its source in the fixation of the libido on the earlier phase of the anal-sadistic level. But if we find that the melancholiac is inclined to give up that position in favour of a yet more primitive one, namely, the oral level, then we must suppose that there are also certain fixation points in his libidinal development which date back to the time when his instinctual life was still mainly centred in the oral zone. And psycho-analytic observations bear out this supposition fully. A few examples may serve as an illustration.

In dealing with melancholic cases I have repeatedly come across strong perverse cravings which consisted in using the mouth in place of the genitals. The patients satisfied these cravings in part by practising *cunnilinctus*.

[1] Before leaving this subject I should like to add that the shell is a universal female symbol.

We learn from Róheim that in many places shells are employed as money. This use of them is once more connected with them as a symbol of the female genitals. It is worth noting that they are never used in this way in the place in which they are found. Only shells coming from a distance can be used as money. This fact seems to be the expression of a widely extended fear of incest, and parallel to the law of exogamy. A woman belonging to the same tribe or a shell found on the shore near by both represent the forbidden genitals of the mother.

Moreover, shells are also likened to excrement, since they are cast up by the sea as are sea-amber and other substances. (These notes are taken in part from a discussion that took place at a meeting of the Berlin Psycho-Analytical Society.)

But they chiefly used to indulge in very vivid phantasies based on cannibalistic impulses. They used to phantasy about biting into every possible part of the body of their love-object—breast, penis, arm, buttocks, and so on. In their free associations they would very frequently have the idea of devouring the loved person or of biting pieces off his body; or they would occupy themselves with necrophagic images. They sometimes produced these various phantasies in an uninhibited and infantile way, sometimes concealed them behind feelings of disgust and terror. They also often exhibited a violent resistance against using their teeth. One of them used to speak of a ' chewing laziness ' as one of the phenomena of his melancholic depression. It even appears that the consequent disuse of the teeth can actually cause them to become diseased. I showed some years ago (in 1917), in cases of melancholia where the patient absolutely declines to take nourishment, that his refusal represents a self-punishment for his cannibalistic impulses. At a recent meeting of the British Psycho-Analytical Society, Dr. James Glover spoke about a case of periodic melancholia which exhibited cannibalistic impulses of this kind; and he gave in especial an analytic account of the way in which those impulses became transformed into suicidal tendencies.[1]

In their pathological symptoms, their phantasies and their dreams, melancholic patients supply us with a great number and variety of oral-sadistic tendencies both conscious and repressed. These tendencies are one of the main sources of the mental suffering of depressive patients, especially in the case where they are turned against the subject's ego in the shape of a tendency to self-punishment. It is to be noticed that this situation is in contrast to some neurotic conditions of mind in which particular symptoms can be seen to be substitutive forms of gratification of the oral zone. I have described cases of this type in my paper

[1] One of my patients had made a deep cut in his throat and nearly succeeded in killing himself. His attempted suicide was really an attack on his introjected love-object, combined with an impulse to punish himself. In his analysis he produced phantasies connected with the sacrifice of Isaac, the theme of which is, of course, the father at the altar about to slay his own son with his knife.

on the earliest pre-genital level of the libido.[1]   And there are besides certain perversions in which oral erotism provides a considerable amount of pleasure.   Even taking into account the masochistic pleasure-value of its symptoms, we must nevertheless lay stress upon the fact that melancholia brings with it a very high degree of displeasure compared to other mental illnesses.   If we observe attentively the depressive patient's chain of associations we shall discover that the excessive amount of displeasure he feels is allied to that stage of libidinal development to which he has regressed after he has lost his object.   For we shall notice that he has a peculiar longing to use his mouth in a manner quite at variance with the biting and eating phantasies mentioned above.   I will give an instance.

At a time when he was recovering from his depression a patient told me about his day-dreams.   In these he was at times impelled to imagine that he had a female body. He would employ all sorts of devices to create in himself the illusion that he had a woman's breasts, and would take special pleasure in the phantasy that he was suckling an infant.   Although he played the part of the mother in this phantasy, he would sometimes exchange his rôle for that of the child at her breast.   His fixation on the mother's breast found expression in two ways—in a great number of symptoms connected with the oral zone, and in a very marked desire to lean his head against something soft like a woman's breast.   Thus, for instance, he used to behave in a very curious way with the cushion on the sofa during analysis.   Instead of leaving it where it was and laying his head on it, he used to take it up and put it over his face. His associations showed that the cushion represented the breast being brought close to his head from above.   The scene with the cushion repeated a pleasurable situation in his infancy.   He had, moreover, seen his younger brother in this position later on and had connected feelings of intense jealousy with that spectacle.

Another melancholic patient I had said that during his deepest fits of depression he had the feeling that a woman

[1] Cf. Chapter XII.

2 F

might free him from his suffering if she expended on him a special maternal love and solicitude. The same type of conative idea was present here. I have repeatedly been able to analyse the meaning of an idea like this, and I can remember a case in point which I described in an earlier paper. A young man suffering from depression—though not a melancholic one—used to feel himself almost miraculously soothed by drinking a glass of milk which his mother handed to him. The milk gave him a sensation of something warm, soft, and sweet, and reminded him of something he had known long ago. In this instance the patient's longing for the breast was unmistakable.

All my psycho-analytic observations up till now lead me to the conclusion that the melancholiac is trying to escape from his oral-sadistic impulses. Beneath these impulses, whose manifestations colour the clinical picture, there lurks the desire for a pleasurable, sucking activity.

We are thus obliged to assume that there is a differentiation within the oral phase of the libido, just as there is within the anal-sadistic phase. On the primary level of that phase the libido of the infant is attached to the act of sucking. This act is one of incorporation, but one which does not put an end to the existence of the object. The child is not yet able to distinguish between its own self and the external object. Ego and object are concepts which are incompatible with that level of development. There is as yet no differentiation made between the sucking child and the suckling breast. Moreover, the child has as yet neither feelings of hatred nor of love. Its mental state is consequently free from all manifestations of ambivalence in this stage.

The secondary level of this phase differs from the first in that the child exchanges its sucking activity for a biting one. In this place I should like to mention a private communication made to me by van Ophuijsen, which supplies an important addition to our knowledge of the mechanism of melancholia.[1] Psycho-analytic observation has led him

---

[1] In the same way, in his paper, ' On the Origin of the Feeling of Persecution ' (1920), van Ophuijsen has thrown light on the relations of paranoia to the anal-sadistic phase.

to believe that certain neurotic phenomena are due to a regression to the age when the teeth were being formed, and furthermore that biting represents the original form taken by the sadistic impulses.   Undoubtedly the teeth are the first instruments with which the child can do damage to the outer world.   For they are already effective at a time when the hands can at most only assist their activity by seizing and keeping hold of the object.   Federn [1] has derived sadism from genital sensations, and no doubt the observations on which he bases his view are correct.   Nevertheless phenomena connected with the genital zone cannot be as primary as those connected with the oral zone.   The fact is, that what we call the sadistic impulses spring from a number of different sources, among which we may mention in especial the excremental ones.   We must also bear in mind the close association of sadism with the muscular system.   But there is no doubt that in small children far and away the most powerful muscles of the body are the jaw muscles.   And, besides, the teeth are the only organs they possess that are sufficiently hard to be able to injure objects around them.

In the biting stage of the oral phase the individual incorporates the object in himself and in so doing destroys it. One has only to look at children to see how intense the impulse to bite is—an impulse in which the eating instinct and the libido still co-operate.   This is the stage in which cannibalistic impulses predominate.   As soon as the child is attracted by an object, it is liable, indeed bound, to attempt its destruction.   It is in this stage that the ambivalent attitude of the ego to its object begins to grow up.   We may say, therefore, that in the child's libidinal development the second stage of the oral-sadistic phase marks the beginning of its ambivalence conflict; whereas the first (sucking) stage should still be regarded as pre-ambivalent.

The libidinal level, therefore, to which the melancholiac regresses after the loss of his object contains in itself a conflict of ambivalent feelings in its most primitive and therefore most unmodified form.   On that level the indi-

[1] ' Beiträge zur Analyse des Sadismus und Masochismus ' (1913).

vidual threatens to destroy his libidinal object by devouring it. It is only gradually that the ambivalence conflict assumes a milder aspect and that the libido consequently adopts a less violent attitude towards its object. Nevertheless this ambivalent attitude remains inherent in the tendencies of the libido during the subsequent phases of its development. We have already discussed its importance in the anal-sadistic phase. But even in the structure of neuroses based on the genital phase we meet this ambivalence everywhere in the patient's emotional life. It is only the normal person—the person who is relatively far removed from the infantile forms of sexuality—who is in the main without ambivalence. His libido has, as it were, reached a post-ambivalent stage and has thus achieved a full capacity for adapting itself to the external world.

It now becomes evident that we ought also to distinguish two stages within the genital phase of the libido, just as we did within its two pre-genital phases. And this leads us to a result which seems to coincide perfectly with Freud's recently published view [1] that there exists an early stage of the genital phase—what he calls a ‘ phallic ’ stage. Thus it would seem that the libido passes through six stages of development in all. But I should like to state explicitly that I do not consider the above classification either as final or exhaustive. It only presents a general picture of the continuous evolution of the libido in so far as our present-day psycho-analytic knowledge has been able to throw light on that slow and laborious process. Nevertheless in my opinion the transition from the earlier stage to the later one within each of the three main developmental phases of the libido is by no means a process of minor importance. We have long since become acquainted with the significance that the change from one preponderating erotogenic zone to another has for the normal psychosexual development of the individual and for the formation of his character. We now see that within each of those three main periods a process takes place which is of great importance for the gradual attainment by the individual of complete object-

[1] ‘ The Infantile Genital Organization of the Libido ’ (1923).

love. Within the first—the oral—period, the child exchanges its pre-ambivalent libidinal attitude, which is free
from conflict, for one which is ambivalent and preponderantly
hostile towards its object. Within the second—the anal-
sadistic—period, the transition from the earlier to the later
stage means that the individual has begun to spare his
object from destruction. Finally, within the third—the
genital—period, he overcomes his ambivalent attitude and
his libido attains to its full capacity both from a sexual and
a social point of view.

The above account does not by any means cover the
whole of the changes that take place in the relations between
the individual and the external world. Those changes will
have to form the subject of a thorough investigation in a
later part of my study.

IV

Notes on the Psychogenesis of Melancholia

We are now in a position to understand why it is that
the ambivalence of his instinctual life involves the melancholiac in quite especially grave conflicts which strike at the
roots of his relation to his love-objects. The act of turning
away from that original object round whom his whole
emotional life revolved does not end there. It extends
to other people; first to those in his immediate vicinity,
then to a wider circle, and finally to every human being.
And the withdrawal of his libido goes even further. It
affects everything which had formerly interested him. His
profession, his hobbies, his pursuits, scientific and otherwise, the whole field of nature—everything has lost its
attraction for him. We find an equally extensive detachment of the libido from the external world in another illness,
namely, dementia præcox or schizophrenia; but in this
case the individual accepts his complete loss of interest
with a dull indifference, whereas the melancholiac complains
of that loss, and indeed tends to connect his feelings of
inferiority with it.

When we penetrate more deeply into the mental life of the melancholiac, however, we find that that very person who, in his state of depression, lamented the loss of all his interests, was all along predisposed to such a loss by the unusually high degree of ambivalence of his emotional life. Long before the first onset of his illness he had been carrying on his profession, his mental interests, and so on, in a forced and spasmodic manner, and this involved a danger that he might suddenly give them up. But these are not the only effects of ambivalence in melancholia. When the libidinal cathexis has been withdrawn from the object, it is directed, as we know, to the ego, while at the same time the object is introjected into the ego. The ego must now bear all the consequences of this process; henceforward it is mercilessly exposed to the ambivalence of the libidinal impulses. It is only a superficial observation that leads us to believe that the melancholiac is exclusively filled with a tormenting self-contempt and a craving to belittle himself. An attentive examination will show that we may equally truly say the opposite of him. As we shall see presently, the interchangeability of depressive and manic states in the melancholic patient hinges on this ambivalent attitude of his libido towards his ego. At present, however, our task is to establish the existence of such an ambivalence towards the ego and to show how it manifests itself during the depressive phase. It is only in this way that we can hope to gain an understanding of the symptoms of melancholia.

As far as I know, orthodox clinical psychiatry has failed to notice this important characteristic of melancholia. Freud, however, recognized it.[1] Speaking of these patients he says: ' Moreover, they are far from evincing towards those around them the attitude of humility and submission that alone would befit such worthless persons; on the contrary, they give a great deal of trouble, perpetually taking offence and behaving as if they had been treated with great injustice '. But, as we shall see, the facts warrant us in going even further than this.

[1] ' Mourning and Melancholia ' (1917).

Naturally the characteristics under discussion are much more noticeable in some cases than in others. But speaking generally we may say that the melancholiac has a feeling of superiority which is observable even during his free interval. He has this feeling towards his family, his friends, his fellow-workers, and the world at large. And the analyst who treats him gets a good share of it. One of my patients used always to walk into my room with an air of lofty condescension in his look and carriage. Patients like these are especially fond of displaying a superior scepticism about the discoveries of psycho-analysis. In another patient this attitude used to alternate with an exaggerated attitude of humility. In this second state of mind he would, for instance, have the phantasy of falling down in front of me, embracing my knees, and imploring me to help him.

We all know how inaccessible melancholic patients are to any criticism on the part of the analyst of their ways of thought; and of course their delusional ideas are especially resistant to any such interference. A patient once said to me that whenever his physician had tried to make him see how unfounded his self-reproaches were, he ' had not even heard him '. What makes of a phantasy a delusional idea, and what prevents that delusion from being open to correction, is the purely narcissistic character of the train of thought. Besides this, there is another factor which determines the behaviour of the melancholiac, and that is his contempt for other people who apply the standards of reality to his ideas.

One of the most marked defects of clinical psychiatry is its predilection for characterizing the pathological ideas of melancholiacs as ' delusions of inferiority ', when in fact those ideas include a great deal of self-appreciation on the part of the sufferer, especially in regard to the importance and effect of his own thoughts, feelings, and behaviour. A good example of this is the idea not uncommonly met with in melancholiacs that they are the greatest sinners of all, that they are guilty of every sin committed since the beginning of the world. Every delusion of this kind contains, besides the introjected reproach aimed at the love-object, a tendency on the part of the melancholiac to represent his feelings of hatred as enormously powerful and himself as a monster of wickedness.

Thus melancholia presents a picture in which there stand in immediate juxtaposition yet absolutely opposed to one another self-love and self-hatred, an overestimation of the ego and an underestimation of it—the manifestations, that is, of *a positive and a negative narcissism*. We have already learned to understand in a quite general way this striking relation of the libido to the ego. But we must now go a step further and look for the factors in the life of the melancholiac that have caused so grave a deviation from the psychological norm. We must endeavour to ascertain how that psychological process which Freud was able to discover is actually carried out in the patient's unconscious and what were the events which directed his libido into those channels. In other words, we must deal with the problem of the choice of neurosis, and we have to ask ourselves why it is that these persons have not become hysterics or obsessional neurotics but manic-depressive patients. To expect to find a complete solution of the problem would be to under-estimate its difficulty. But we may perhaps hope to approach that distant goal a little nearer.

There can be no doubt that an attack of melancholic depression is ushered in by a disappointment in love. In analysing patients who have been through several periods of depression we find that each fresh attack was immediately preceded by an experience of this sort. I need hardly say that I do not use the expression ' disappointment in love ' in the ordinary sense of an unhappy love affair only. The events which culminate in the person's loss of object are often a great deal more obscure. Only a thorough analysis can discover the causal connections between the event and the illness. Such an analysis invariably shows that that event had a pathogenic effect because the patient was able to regard it in his unconscious as a repetition of an original infantile traumatic experience and to treat it as such. In no other form of neurosis, it seems to me, does the compulsive tendency to repeat an experience operate so strongly as in manic-depressive illnesses. How powerful this repetition-compulsion in melancholiacs becomes is evident when we consider to what frequent recurrences of their manic-depressive states they are exposed.

It is no part of my intention in this essay, based as it is on a very limited number of psycho-analyses, to make a general and final pronouncement about the psychogenesis of the circular insanities. Nevertheless I believe that the material at our disposal does warrant us in making certain statements of whose provisional and incomplete character I am fully aware. I think it is permissible to point out a number of ætiological factors in this disease. But I should like to make it quite clear that it is only when those factors are all present together that a melancholic depression with its specific symptoms will result. Each one taken by itself could enter into the ætiology of some other psycho-neurosis.

The factors are these:

1. A constitutional factor.—In accordance with my experience in clinical psychiatry, and more especially in psycho-analysis, I should say that there is no direct inheritance of a tendency to develop manic-depressive states as such. This only happens in a small proportion of melancholic cases. Among those of my patients who suffered from manic-depressive states according to the strict clinical diagnosis I did not have a single one in whose family there was another member who was subject to any grave disorder of the same kind. On the other hand, neuroses of other kinds abounded. I am therefore much more inclined to think that what really is constitutional and inherited is an over-accentuation of oral erotism, in the same way that in certain families anal erotism seems to be a preponderant factor from the very beginning. An inherited pre-disposition of this kind would help to bring the next factor into operation, namely:

2. A special fixation of the libido on the oral level.—People with a constitutional intensification of this sort of their oral erotism are very exacting in their demands to have their special erotogenic zone gratified, and react with great displeasure to every frustration in this connection. The excessive pleasure they derive from sucking persists

in many forms throughout life. They get abnormal pleasure from eating, and especially from the use of the jaws. One of my patients described to me quite spontaneously what a great pleasure he got from opening his mouth wide. Others speak of the contraction of the muscles of the jaw as being especially pleasurable. People like these are insatiable in their demands for exchanges of affection of an oral nature. As a child one of my patients had been so vehement in this method of demonstrating his love that at last his mother had been able to bear it no longer and had checked him on the rather ill-chosen pretext that she did not like that kind of thing. Shortly after, the child's observant eye had caught her exchanging the same tokens of love with his father. This observation, together with others, had had the effect of arousing and fostering in him an abnormally large amount of hostile feeling. Another patient said that whenever he thought of his childhood he had a stale kind of taste in his mouth that reminded him of a gruel soup which he used to be given and which he disliked very much. His analysis showed that this sensation was an expression of his jealousy of his younger brother, whom he used to see being suckled by his mother at a time when he had to drink soup and slops. In the depths of his heart he envied his brother that intimate relation with his mother which he himself no longer enjoyed. In his depressive states he would be overcome by longing for his mother's breast, a longing that was indescribably powerful and different from anything else. If the libido still remains fixated on this point when the individual is grown up, then one of the most important conditions for the appearance of a melancholic depression is fulfilled.

3. A severe injury to infantile narcissism brought about by successive disappointments in love.—We are accustomed to hear of events in the childhood of the neurotic which caused him to be disappointed in his desire for love, although of course experiences of this sort are not in themselves sufficient to provide the basis for a melancholia. As regards this factor several of my melancholic cases disclosed a remarkable similarity in the scheme of significant events.

The child had felt that he was his mother's favourite and had been secure of her love. He had then suffered a disappointment at her hands and had with difficulty recovered from its shattering effect. Later on, he had had fresh experiences of the same sort which had made him feel that his loss was an irreparable one, especially as there had been no suitable female person on to whom he could carry over his libido. Furthermore, his attempt to direct it towards his father had failed, either straight away or after some time. Thus as a child he had got the impression of being completely deserted. And it was this feeling that had given rise to his first attacks of depression. A dream-analysis which I shall give later on will leave no doubt possible as to this. The constantly repeated attempts of the melancholiac to gain love from a person of the opposite sex are intimately bound up with this early disappointment from both sides.

4. The occurrence of the first important disappointment in love before the Oedipus-wishes have been overcome.—It has invariably been my experience that the boy is most deeply and permanently affected by the great disappointment in love which he receives from his mother if it comes at a time when his libido has not adequately overcome the narcissistic stage. In this stage his incestuous desires have awakened and his revolt against his father is in full activity. But the repressive forces have as yet gained no control over his Oedipus impulses. If the child is suddenly subjected to a mental trauma such as we have described just as he is making his first important step towards object-love, the consequences are especially serious. And since at that date his oral-sadistic instincts are still in force, a permanent association will be established between his Oedipus complex and the cannibalistic stage of his libido. This will facilitate a subsequent introjection of both his love-objects—that is, his mother in the first place and in the second place his father.

5. The repetition of the primary disappointment in later life.—This is the exciting cause of the onset of a melancholic depression.

We have been led to assume that the psychogenesis of melancholia is closely bound up with disappointments in the patient's early life or after; and we ought consequently to expect to find in him extremely strong hostile feelings towards all those persons who have so fatally thwarted his narcissistic desire for love.   But since all his subsequent disappointments derive their importance from being repetitions of his original one, the whole sum of his anger is ultimately directed against one single person—against the person, that is, whom he had been most fond of as a child and who had then ceased to occupy this position in his life. Freud has already shown that the self-reproaches of the melancholiac are in reality aimed at the love-object he has relinquished.   And we shall therefore be prepared to discover that his self-criticisms, and more especially his delusions, are complaints directed against that former object.

In this connection we may consider a characteristic of melancholia which would seem to put it in a place apart from the other neuroses.   My analyses showed that the ambivalent attitude of the male patients, with its hostile, cannibalistic impulses, was mainly directed against the mother, whereas we know that in other neurotic conditions the father is pre-eminently the object of the patient's hostile tendencies. The disappointment which the melancholiac has suffered as a child at the hands of his mother while he was still in a markedly ambivalent state of feeling has affected him in such a permanent way and made him so hostile to her that even his hatred and jealousy of his father has become of minor importance.   In every male melancholiac I have hitherto analysed I have been able to satisfy myself that the patient's castration complex was quite predominantly connected with his mother, whereas in other kinds of patients it is usually much more in evidence in relation to the father.   Nevertheless I was able to discover that its connection with the mother was a secondary one and the result of a tendency to invert the Oedipus situation.   When thoroughly analysed the hostility of the melancholiac towards his mother is seen to have roots in the Oedipus complex.   In fact, his ambivalence really applies to both parents alike.   And his father is also the object of a process of introjection.   Many melancholic symptoms, as, for instance, certain self-reproaches, show their original relation to both parents quite clearly. What I have just said does not invalidate my previous statement that in melancholia the whole psychological process centres *in the main* round the mother; it only seeks to emphasize the fact that the process has more than one determinant.

A careful analysis of the self-criticisms and self-reproaches—especially those of a delusional nature—uttered by melancholic patients will show that the process of introjection takes two forms:

1. The patient has introjected his original love-object upon which he had built his ego ideal; so that that object has taken over the rôle of conscience for him, although, it is true, a pathologically formed one. Our material goes to show that the pathological self-criticism of the melancholiac emanates from this introjected object.[1] One of my patients used to be continually taking himself to task and repeating the same reproaches against himself; and in doing this he copied exactly the tone of voice and actual expressions that he had often heard his mother use when she had scolded him as a little boy.

2. The content of those self-reproaches is ultimately a merciless criticism of the introjected object. A patient of mine used to pass judgement on himself in the following words: 'My whole existence is based on deceit'. This reproach turned out to be determined by certain elements in the relationship of his mother and father.

I will give an example to illustrate the way in which these two forms of introjection work in with one another. The patient I have just spoken about used to say that he was utterly incapable and could never lead a useful life. Analysis showed that this complaint was an exaggerated criticism of his father's quiet and inactive character, in contrast to whom his mother was for him the ideal of practical efficiency. He felt that he himself took after his father.

---

[1] Freud's *The Ego and the Id* appeared shortly after I had written this part of my book. In it he gives such a lucid account of the process that I need only refer the reader to its pages. To give a résumé of it would only be to render it less clear.

His criticism of himself therefore stood for an unfavourable judgement passed by his introjected mother on his introjected father. We have here a very instructive instance of a twofold process of introjection.

If we take this view we are able to understand another symptom this patient had—a delusional self-reproach. During his last period of depression he had been put in an asylum. One day he declared that he had introduced lice into the place. He grew more and more agitated and bewailed the enormity of his act, saying that he had infected the whole house with lice. He tried to demonstrate the presence of the lice to the house-physician. He saw them in every particle of dust and in every shred of material. The analysis of this delusion brought to light the special symbolic importance of lice to him. In dream-symbolism and all other forms of phantasy small animals represent children. A house which is full of lice thus means a house (his father's and mother's house) which is full of children. As a child the patient had been deprived of his mother's love because a great many younger brothers and sisters had been born. One of the determinants of his introjected complaint had been the thought, 'My wicked mother, who once pretended to love me so much, has filled the whole house with children'. Furthermore, if we consider that the house is a symbol of the mother, we can see that he is also blaming his father for having procreated the children. Thus in this example also the patient's accusations against both his parents have been condensed into a single accusation directed against himself.

I should like to remark in this place that the complaints of the melancholiac against his love-object are not all of them uttered in this introjected form. Apart from that form, which is specific for his illness, he has other means of expression at his disposal; and he makes use of these in his free intervals as well. I will give an instance.

Just before the onset of his first severe depression one of my patients was seized with an obsessive interest in prostitutes. He used to spend many hours of the night watching the women in the streets, but he never entered into closer relations with them. Analysis showed that he was repeating in a compulsive way certain observations he had made as a child. Prostitutes represented his mother in a derogatory sense—his mother who had let his father understand her sexual desires by means of certain looks and gestures. In comparing her to a prostitute he was revenging himself for having been disappointed by her. His reproach was meant to say, 'You are only a sensual woman, not a loving mother'. On the other hand, his nocturnal perambulation of the streets represented an identification with the prostitutes (his mother). Here we have once more the mechanism of introjection.

Another patient depicted his mother as unloving and cruel in his phantasies. In this case the patient's association of his castration complex with the female—that is, with his mother—was especially noticeable. For instance, in his phantasies he likened the vagina to the jaws of a crocodile. This was an unambiguous symbol of castration by biting.

If we want to realize the full strength of the melancholiac's hostility towards his mother, and to understand the particular character of his castration complex, we must keep in mind Stärcke's theory that the withdrawal of the mother's breast is a 'primal castration'.[1] As the analysis of many of his symptoms shows, the melancholiac wants to revenge himself on his mother for this by castrating her in his turn, either taking away her breasts or her imaginary penis. In his imagination he always chooses biting as the means of doing it, as I have already shown in some of the phantasies produced by such patients. I should like once more to lay stress on the ambivalent character of those phantasies. They involve on the one hand a total or partial incorporation of the mother, that is, an act of positive desire; and on the other, her castration or death, that is, a negative desire tending to her destruction.

Up till now we have been examining the process of introjection and some of its effects, and we may shortly sum up our conclusions as follows: When melancholic persons suffer an unbearable disappointment from their

[1] 'The Castration Complex' (1921).

love-object they tend to expel that object as though it were fæces and to destroy it. They thereupon accomplish the act of introjecting and devouring it—an act which is a specifically melancholic form of narcissistic identification. Their sadistic thirst for vengeance now finds its satisfaction in tormenting the ego—an activity which is in part pleasurable. We have reason to suppose that that period of self-torment lasts until lapse of time and the gradual appeasement of sadistic desires have removed the love-object from the danger of being destroyed. When this has happened the object can, as it were, come out of its hiding-place in the ego. The melancholiac can restore it to its place in the outer world.

It seems to me to be of no little psychological interest to be able to establish the fact that in his unconscious the melancholiac regards this liberation from his object as once more an act of evacuation. During the time when his depression was clearly beginning to diminish, one of my cases had a dream in which he expelled with the greatest sensation of relief a stopper that was sticking in his anus.[1] This act of expulsion concludes the process of that archaic form of mourning which we must consider melancholia to be. We may truly say that during the course of an attack of melancholia the love-object goes through a process of psychological metabolism within the patient.

V

THE INFANTILE PROTOTYPE OF MELANCHOLIC DEPRESSION

An examination of the material before us has led us to the view that in the last resort melancholic depression is derived from disagreeable experiences in the childhood of the patient. It is therefore natural that we should be particularly interested in the original emotional reactions of the child to such traumatic experiences. We may justifiably assume that those experiences caused feelings of an unhappy character,

---

[1] The over-determination of this symbol—its passive homosexual significance—need not occupy us here.

but we have not up till now got any direct idea, any living picture, of the child's actual state of mind at the time. Owing to special circumstances, as will be seen, I was able in one case to get some very instructive information on this subject.   After going through a depressive attack my patient had had a free interval which had lasted some time. He had become attached to a young girl, when certain events awoke in him the causeless fear that he was once more in danger of losing what he loved.   At this time he dreamt several times about losing a tooth—a very obvious symbolic occurrence which typified both his fear of castration and of an object-loss (evacuation).   One night this dream was succeeded by another, which I give here:

' I was in some place with Herr Z.'s wife.   In the course of the dream I somehow got mixed up in some theft of books.   The dream was a long one.   I remember the painful feeling in it better than its content.'

Herr Z. was an acquaintance of the dreamer and a periodic drinker.   He caused his wife a great deal of unhappiness, and on the day before his dream my patient had got to hear of another instance of this.   His dream was connected with his waking life at this point.   Stealing books symbolized stealing his mother, whom he thus took away from his father who tormented her.   But it also represented castrating his father.   We have here a straightforward Oedipus dream, only interesting to us because the theme of theft is the active complement to that of the loss of a tooth in the first dream of the same night.   The importance of the dream in the patient's analysis lay not so much in the things that happened in it as in the aforesaid feeling which accompanied it.   For my patient told me that when he had woken up it had struck him that that feeling was familiar to him.   He knew it in connection with a particular dream which he had repeatedly dreamt when he was about five years old.   He said that up till now he had never thought of that dream in the whole course of his long analysis.   But now he remembered it quite plainly, and what he especially noticed about it was this dreadful, tormenting feeling which his recent dream had also had.   He told me it as follows:

2 G

'I was standing in front of my parents' house, where I was born. A line of carts came up the street. The street was otherwise quite still and deserted. Each waggon had two horses in front of it. A driver walked beside the horses and beat them with his whip. The cart had tall sides so that I could not see what was inside. There was something mysterious about it. Underneath it there hung a man, tied up and dragged along by a rope. There was a rope round his neck, and he could only manage to draw a little breath with great difficulty and at long intervals. The sight of this man who could neither go on living nor die affected me very much. Then I saw to my horror that two more carts followed the first one and each presented the same terrible spectacle.'

The analysis of this dream proceeded in the face of unusually strong resistances and took up the whole of our time for several weeks. During this part of the analytic work the patient was dominated by what he described as the 'tormenting' feeling-tone of the dream, which he once very significantly called a 'scene in Hell'.

The dream-analysis first led us to recognize the driver as his father, whom he had always spoken of as a hard and repellent man. On this superficial level the beating of the horses referred to the frequent corporal punishment his father had administered to him. According to him, the patient wanted to protest in the dream against the horses being beaten, and against the horrible way in which the bound man was being treated, but he felt too much intimidated. His feelings of pity betrayed the fact that he identified himself with the unfortunate man. It was evident that the dreamer was represented in at least three different figures: as the onlooker, as the horse, and as the bound man.

At this point the work of interpretation ceased for the time being, since a fresh dream engaged our attention in the following hour. This new dream was concerned with the young girl we have already mentioned, and whom we will call E. It was this:

'I saw a part of E.'s naked body, only the middle part. Her breasts and her genitals were covered. This part of the body formed a flat surface and had no navel. Where the navel ought to have been something suddenly grew out like a male organ. I touched it and asked E. whether it was sensitive. It now began to swell a little, and I got frightened and woke up.'

In this dream, the analysis of which proceeded with some interruptions, the female body was endowed with male attributes, and the dreamer was frightened at seeing the female penis swelling up. Another determinant was the dreamer's interest in the breasts (the body with its swelling protuberance). The whole female body was represented as a breast. The meaning of the dream becomes still more evident when we know that E. was for the patient the ideal of motherhood. So that we have once more the intense longing of the melancholiac for the happy state when he was still at his mother's breast. I pass over certain other determinants of the dream in this place.

Going back to his childhood dream, the patient compared the impression the scene made on him with the petrifying sight of the Gorgon's head.[1] He had the same feeling of terror in his old dream as in the recent one we have just interpreted in outline.

The patient's associations led us through a succession of impressions of childhood—among them the sight of a hanged man—to certain infantile observations of his parents' married life that had already come into his analysis. It became evident that the driver who was using the whip stood for his father having coitus with his mother ('beating' in its typical symbolic sense). Then, however, it turned out that the hanging man was a man who was in the position of succubus and being crushed during copulation (his difficulty in breathing). It was clear that this was an inversion of the man's position as actually observed by the child.

During the following days of analysis the patient was often in a depressed state of mind, rather as he had been in his early dream. Without having referred to that dream, he one day said that he felt like a 'five-year-old boy who

[1] Cf. Freud's analysis of this myth in ' The Infantile Genital Organization of the Libido ' (1923).

had somehow lost his way '—and as if he was in need of protection but could not find any. Immediately afterwards he called his depression 'infernal', just as he had said that his early dream was a 'scene in Hell'. The words he used, however, did not merely serve to express the excess of his sufferings; it also had reference to a particular circumstance associated with the onset of his last severe attack of depression. It had begun immediately after he had been reading a book, the *Enfer* ('Hell') of Barbusse, about which all that need be said here is that it contains a description of certain intimate scenes whose action is observed from an adjoining room. This gave a clue to the situation which had excited such stormy feelings in him in his early childhood. A trifling incident that took place at that time showed how greatly subject he had been to the recurrence of that impression of childhood terror. On one occasion he had heard his parents say something softly to one another, and he had become frightened and had 'automatically' made an effort to force out of his mind a rising recollection of 'something terrible'. He noticed that he had a similar strong feeling of repugnance whenever he thought of the bound man in the dream. During the next few days his analysis brought to light a number of such repressed observations; and his affect became less violent, in especial his horror at the sight of the bound man. At the same time he began to get a clear general view of that decisive period of his childhood. He said: 'Even as a child I was always mourning for something. I was always grave and reserved. In the photographs of myself as a small child I already look thoughtful and sad.'

I shall omit many details of the dream-analysis and only add the following remarks: Going back to the 'hanging man', the patient said one day, 'his head was tied somewhere near the navel', meaning near the middle of the cart. A number of associations now made it evident that in his unconscious he had an infantile sexual theory that the imaginary penis of the female was concealed in her navel. And now we were able to return to the analysis of his dream about a female body without a navel out of which a penis grew. The principal motive of the early dream was the following wish: ' My mother is to pay my father back for what he has done to her (in copulating with her) and to me (in beating me). She is to throw herself on top of him, as he did on her, and she is to use her concealed penis to strangle him as he lies underneath her.'

During the next few days the patient happened to see a relative of his who for certain reasons had the significance of a father for him. He suddenly found himself having the phantasy that he might push this man into some dark doorway and strangle him with his hands. This act clearly represented the Oedipus act and was at the same time an allusion to the theme of suffocation in the dream. It may be worth adding that in his most recent depressive attack the patient had made serious preparations for hanging himself with a rope.

The above extract from the analysis of a dream has thus enabled us to reconstruct a vivid picture of the patient's state of feeling at the early age of five. I should be inclined to speak of a ' primal parathymia ' ensuing from the boy's Oedipus complex. We see with impressive clearness how much the child longed to gain his mother as an ally in his struggle against his father, and his disappointment at having his own advances repulsed combined with the violent emotions aroused in him by what he had observed going on in his parents' bedroom. He nursed terrible plans of revenge in his breast, and yet the ambivalence of his feelings prevented his ever putting them into practice. Unable either to achieve a complete love or an unyielding hatred, he succumbed to a feeling of hopelessness. In the years that followed he made repeated attempts to attain a successful object-love; and every failure to do so brought with it a state of mind that was an exact replica of his primal parathymia. It is this state of mind that we call melancholia.

An instance may show how ready the melancholiac is even during his free intervals to be disappointed, betrayed, or abandoned by his love-object. A patient who had married a considerable time after a depressive attack was constantly looking forward, without the slightest cause, to his wife's infidelity as to a self-evident occurrence. Once, as he was talking about a man, somewhat younger than himself, who was living in the same building, his first association was ' My wife will have an affair with him and betray me '. His analysis showed that his mother had been ' unfaithful ' to him and had transferred her ' favours ' to his younger brother—*i.e.* she had nursed him at the breast. This brother occupied for him the position of father in his Oedipus complex. In each symptom of his various depressive periods he faithfully repeated all those feelings of hatred, rage, and resignation, of being abandoned and without hope, which had gone to colour the primal parathymia of his early childhood.

VI

Mania

In our discussion so far I have dealt with the melancholic phase of the circular insanities and have neglected the manic phase. This is partly due to the nature of the material that has presented itself to me for observation; and partly to the fact that psycho-analysis has enabled us to understand the psychological processes of melancholia irrespective of any closer knowledge of those involved in mania, whilst this latter phase would remain a mystery to us did we not already possess the key to it in virtue of our analytic knowledge of depression. It is for these reasons, no doubt, that Freud, in investigating this illness, has penetrated so much more deeply into the nature of the depressive states than into that of the manic ones. I should like to say at once that I am able to add to the knowledge gained by Freud on this subject only in a very slight degree and in but few respects.

In clinical psychiatry the manic state has always been likened to a state of intoxication in which all existing inhibitions are swept away. Freud, in one of his most recent publications,[1] has put forward a view of it which at at any rate renders its relation to melancholic depression more comprehensible. We know that one of the principal respects in which the two conditions differ from one another is in the relation of the individual to his super-ego. According to Freud's view, the child forms its super-ego by introjecting the objects of its libido into its ego, of which they henceforward form an organic part. The super-ego takes on those functions of criticizing the behaviour of the ego which form the individual into a social being. Of those functions, the one we call *conscience* interests us most at present. The super-ego instructs the ego by means of that function as to what it may or may not do, in the same way as the persons in authority over it used formerly to do.

In melancholia we see the super-ego exercising this function of criticism with an excessive severity. In mania, on the other hand, we see it use no such harsh criticism of the ego. On the contrary, the individual has a sense of self-importance and power instead of those feelings and delusions of inferiority that characterized his depressive state. One of my patients believed during his states of depression that he was utterly devoid of every intellectual capacity and could not perform even the simplest practical action; but when a phase of reactive hypo-mania set in he became all of a sudden a great inventor in his own opinion. We see that the manic patient has thrown off the yoke of his super-ego, which now no longer takes up a critical attitude towards the ego, but has become merged in it. The difference between ego and super-ego has now disappeared. For this reason Freud takes the view that in the manic condition the patient is celebrating a triumph over the object he once loved and then gave up and introjected. The ' shadow of the object ' which had fallen on his ego has passed away. He is able to breathe freely once more, and he gives himself up to his sense of regained freedom with a kind of frenzy. We are reminded of our earlier observation that the circular type of patient has a very highly ambivalent attitude towards his ego. And we may

[1] *Group Psychology* (1921).

add to Freud's statement and say that the withdrawal of his super-ego allows his narcissism to enter upon a positive, pleasurable phase.

Now that his ego is no longer being consumed by the introjected object, the individual turns his libido to the outer world with an excess of eagerness. This change of attitude gives rise to many symptoms, all of them based on an increase in the person's oral desires. A patient of mine once called it a 'gobbling mania'. This appetite is not confined to the taking of nourishment alone. The patient 'devours' everything that comes his way. We are all familiar with the strength of the erotic cravings of the manic patient. But he shows the same greed in seizing on new impressions from which, in his melancholic state, he had cut himself off. Whereas in his depressive phase he had felt that he was dispossessed and cast out from the world of external objects, in his manic phase he as it were proclaims his power of assimilating all his objects into himself. But it is characteristic that this pleasurable act of taking in new impressions is correlated to an equally pleasurable act of ejecting them almost as soon as they have been received. Anyone who has listened to the associations of a manic patient will recognize that his flight of ideas, expressed in a stream of words, represents a swift and agitated process of receiving and expelling fresh impressions. In melancholia we saw that there was some particular introjected object which was treated as a piece of food that had been incorporated and which was eventually got rid of. In mania, *all* objects are regarded as material to be passed through the patient's 'psychosexual metabolism' at a rapid rate. And it is not difficult to see from the associations of the manic patient that he identifies his uttered thoughts with excrement.

Freud has pointed out and discussed the psychological relationship of melancholia and normal mourning; but he does not find anything in the normal mind which is analogous to the reversal from melancholia to mania. I believe we are now in a position to point to such an analogy. It is an occurrence which is observable in normal mourning, and has, I suspect, a general application, although I cannot at present be sure of this. We find, namely, that when the mourning person has gradually detached his libido from his dead object by means of the 'work of mourning' he is aware of an increase in his sexual desires. He manifests this in sublimated forms as well, such as showing greater enterprise, enlarging his circle of intellectual interests, and so on. Such an increase of libidinal desire after a loss of object will set in at an interval of time which varies with the course that the 'work of mourning' runs in each case.

At the Psycho-Analytical Congress of 1922, at which I put forward this view, Róheim also read his paper [1] on primitive mourning ceremonies, in which he showed conclusively that in primitive man the period of mourning is followed by an outbreak of the libido, which is brought to an end by yet another symbolic killing and eating of the dead person, this time performed with evident and undisguised pleasure—is ended, in other words, by a repetition of the Oedipus act. Now the manic phase which follows upon pathological mourning (melancholia) contains the same impulse once more to incorporate and expel the love-object, in the same way as Róheim has shown to be the case in primitive mourning rites. So that the increase in libidinal activities which set in at the end of normal mourning, as described above, shows like a faint replica of archaic mourning customs.

I had a patient in whom certain events brought on a parathymic condition when he was already well forward in his analysis. It passed off much more lightly than his earlier attacks of depression had done, and resembled in some of its main features an obsessional condition.[2] This state was followed by a very slight deviation in the direction of mania. It passed over after a few days, and then the patient told me that during that short period he had felt the desire to indulge in some form of excess. He said: 'I had the feeling that I must eat a great deal of meat—that I must

---

[1] 'Nach dem Tode des Urvaters' (1923).

[2] The next section contains one or two further remarks concerning this kind of modification of the symptoms.

go on eating till I was absolutely glutted '. He had thought of it as a yielding to a kind of intoxication or orgy.

In this instance it was quite evident that the patient's manic state was ultimately nothing else than an orgy of a cannibalistic character. His words, quoted above, are convincing evidence of the correctness of Freud's view that in mania the ego is celebrating the festival of its liberation. That celebration takes the form in phantasy of a wild excess in eating flesh, as to whose cannibalistic significance enough has already been said, I trust, to leave no room for doubt.

Like melancholia, the reactive manic parathymia takes a certain length of time in which to work itself off. Gradually the narcissistic requirements of the ego diminish and larger quantities of libido are set free and can be transferred to external objects. Thus, after both phases of the illness have passed off, the libido is able to attain a relatively real relation to its objects. That this relation remains incomplete has already been fully shown in the chapter dealing with the fixation of the libido in the anal-sadistic phase.

In this phase we must consider a point which has already been discussed in connection with melancholia. Freud has drawn a very instructive parallel between mania and the celebration of a festival by the ego; and he has associated that festival with the totem-feast of primitive people, that is, with man's ' primal crime ', which consisted in killing and eating the primal father. What I must here point out is that the criminal phantasies of the manic patient are for the most part directed against his mother. A striking illustration of this was given by one of my patients who had a delusion during his manic excitement that he was the emperor Nero. He afterwards accounted for this by the fact that Nero had killed his own mother, and had also had the idea of burning the city of Rome (as a mother-symbol). Let me once more add that those emotions directed towards the mother are of a secondary kind; they were in the first instance aimed at the father, as became quite evident in the course of the analysis referred to above.

We are now, therefore, able to some extent to understand the reactive state of exaltation following upon melancholia as a pleasurable emancipation on the part of the individual from the painful relation in which he has hitherto been to his introjected object of love. But we know that an attack of mania can come on without having been preceded by a melancholia. However, if we remember what has been said in the previous chapter, we shall not be quite at a loss to account for this fact. In that chapter we showed that certain definite psychological traumas in the early childhood of the patient caused a state of mind in him which we called the ' primal parathymia '. In ' pure ' mania, which is frequently of periodic occurrence, the patient seems to me to be shaking off that primal parathymia without having had any attack of melancholia in the clinical sense. But lack of suitable data forbids me to make any definite statements in this connection.

This paper took as its starting-point a comparison of melancholia with obsessional neuroses. Returning to this comparison, we are now able to explain the difference in the course run by the two illnesses and to say that manic-depressive states, which set in in an acute form and are intermittent and liable to relapses, represent an expulsion of the love-object repeated at certain intervals of time; whereas obsessional states, which have a more chronic character and allow of remissions, correspond to a dominant tendency to keep possession of the object.

If we follow the lines of thought of Freud and Róheim, we may say that each of the two illnesses presents a different attitude of the individual towards that primal crime which he has not enacted in reality. In melancholia and mania he carries out that crime from time to time on a psychological plane, just as primitive people perform it in a ceremonial way at their totem-feasts. In the obsessional neurosis he carries on a constant struggle against its commission. His morbid anxiety bears witness on the one hand to his impulse to do that deed, and on the other, to the yet more powerful inhibition of his criminal impulses.

What has been said has not, I know, presented a complete answer to the problems of mania and melancholia. The empirical material of psycho-analysis is not as yet sufficient to enable us to find any such answer. But I should like to remind the reader that this paper does not profess to deal in the first instance with the psychological aspect of those two mental disorders. Its principal aim is to show that certain things which we discover in manic-depressive patients find their place in the sexual theory of psycho-analysis. But I should not like to close this section without once more acknowledging that the problem of the choice of neurosis in the circular insanities still awaits its final solution.

VII

THE PSYCHO-ANALYTIC THERAPY OF MANIC-DEPRESSIVE STATES

After what has been said in the foregoing section it is not difficult to understand what the aim of a treatment of melancholia should ideally be. It should be to do away with the regressive libidinal impulses of the individual and to effect a progression of his libido until it reaches the stage of genital organization and complete object-love. The question is, Can that aim be in any way brought nearer by psycho-analysis? In this section I should like to try to answer that question, basing my views exclusively on the facts so far collected. For it would be as inadvisable to incline to a premature optimism as regards psycho-analysis as to adopt the traditional attitude of nihilism maintained by clinical psychiatry. As far back as 1911 I pointed out that in certain stages of his illness, and especially during his free interval, the melancholiac is capable of establishing a sufficient amount of the transference necessary for therapeutic results to justify us in attempting to treat him. And on Freud's advice I have recently started psycho-analysing melancholiacs at a time when they were just coming out of a depressive state and entering upon a free interval. I need hardly add that I would not in these circumstances attribute any continued improvement on the patient's part to the treatment he has begun to receive. An improvement of this sort will take place of itself in every case, but it never enables the patient to attain to that complete object-love which is the touchstone of real mental health.   Moreover, this is not, in my opinion, what a psycho-analytic treatment is aiming at fundamentally.   What its aim really is I have already briefly outlined above.   It ought, in the first place, to do more for the patient than merely remove his symptoms, and it ought furthermore to safeguard him from a return of his illness.   If this first requisite is satisfied we shall see many changes take place in his whole mental life such as did not use to occur spontaneously during his free interval.   Here, therefore, we shall have an objective criterion of the success of the treatment.   But so far as the second requisite is concerned a long period of time and continuous and careful observation will be necessary before we can say whether or no the danger of a fresh onset of the illness has been successfully averted.

The psycho-analyses of melancholic cases which I have recently been carrying on are none of them completely finished, so that there is no question of making any prophecy about the lasting nature of analytic treatment.   All I can do is to place on record those changes which it undeniably did bring about.   They are these:

1. The patient's capacity for transference is sometimes quite visibly increased immediately after some piece of analytic work has been accomplished.   In the case of the patient whose childhood dream we have discussed [1] his whole attitude to the analyst changed under the influence of this part of the analysis.   And, as we know, important changes cannot be effected in the patient until he succeeds in establishing a transference on to his analyst.

2. The patient's narcissistic and negative attitude towards certain persons or towards his whole environment and his high degree of irritability in regard to them are diminished in a way which never happened before during his free interval.

3. In one instance the patient's attitude towards the female sex was greatly modified.   His obsessive interest in

[1] Cf. Section V.

prostitutes disappeared, and he gradually became able to direct his libido on to one particular person in a quite normal way.   This was the patient's first successful attempt to do this after a great number of failures.

4. The same patient used to harp upon his own inferiority in a self-tormenting manner even during his interval.   But after we had succeeded in analysing the process of introjection in him a good way, he suddenly told me that he felt very much relieved.   As he said, he no longer regarded himself as a ' monstrosity '.   And this new outlook, which began nine months ago, has been maintained up till the present time.

5. The most important criterion seems to me to be the formation of transitory symptoms.   As has already been said, patients often exhibit mild parathymias in their free interval, which, slight as they are, bear all the essential marks of true melancholia or mania.   It happened that two of my patients, both of whom I had been treating for over a year and a half, were exposed to a series of severe emotional shocks due to external events.   Before their analysis and in the beginning part of it they had invariably reacted to disturbances of this sort with marked melancholic symptoms.   But later on I observed that the new symptoms which the patients produced on such occasions bore a different stamp.   And the regularity with which this happened precluded the possibility of chance.   On such occasions something in the patient seemed to urge him towards a renewed attack of depression.   If, for instance, he was obliged to make an important decision concerning his practical life, he would show an inclination to take refuge once again in his illness.   But he did not actually make the first and essential step towards melancholia; he did not give up his object.   He did form a fresh symptom, it is true, but it was an obsessional one or a phobia or a hysterical conversion.   I could not avoid having the impression that the patient no longer produced a genuine melancholic depression.   That a psychoneurosis should have ascended from a melancholic to a hysterical level seems to me a significant and noteworthy achievement.

And the fact that the patient's object-love has shown itself more resistant than before to external influences is undoubtedly of the greatest practical consequence.[1]

I pass over many of the minor improvements that were observable in my patients because they seem to me to have no very great theoretical importance. Nevertheless I should like to point out once more that I had to deal with especially severe cases that had had repeated relapses. I got the decided impression that younger patients who have not had a great many attacks of illness, and have not, in consequence, withdrawn so much from the real world, would very probably respond more rapidly and effectively to treatment. Later on I shall have a few more things to say about the cases I have had for treatment.

Since I myself do not possess sufficient experience to make any judgement about the lasting effects of analytic therapy in melancholic cases, I am all the more happy to be able to quote an opinion from an authoritative quarter. In a private communication Professor Freud has told me that he has had two cases of this kind in which the cure has been permanent. One of these has had no relapse now for over ten years.

I feel I cannot leave this question of therapeutic results without bringing up for consideration the subjective value which psycho-analytic treatment has for depressive patients in especial. The mental relief which it brings them is often quite astonishing, and the patients themselves lay much stress on it. Nor should we forget that it is precisely this class of person who is as a rule the most inaccessible to any outside influence. It therefore seems to me that, while maintaining a due reserve in the evaluation of its therapeutic results in this field, we cannot deny that psycho-analysis does exercise an effect on patients suffering from the circular insanities. Nor do I believe that we are in danger of overestimating the extent of our results. For the method of psycho-analysis itself, which discloses to us

[1] In the second part of this paper, which deals with the development of object-love, I discuss this question in greater detail, and adduce examples from actual cases.

in all their strength the resistances of the patients, and which in each individual case obliges us to conduct a wearisome and difficult technical procedure of many months' duration, offers the best guarantee against entertaining too great hopes in regard to the success of our therapeutic endeavours.

PART II

ORIGINS AND GROWTH OF OBJECT-LOVE

In the first part of this study I have attempted to throw light on the psychology of certain pathological states of mind and to add something to our knowledge of the sexual life of the individual. But in doing this I have confined myself to the theory of the pregenital levels of the libido. That part of sexual theory deals with the transformations which the individual undergoes in regard to his sexual aim during the course of his psychosexual development. Since Freud's classical work on this subject [1] we are accustomed to distinguish the sexual *aims* of the individual from those processes which concern his relations to his sexual *object*. What we have so far said about the ontogenesis of object-love does not sufficiently cover the field of facts. This is especially so in those pathological states which, in accordance with Freud, we group together under the name of the 'narcissistic neuroses'. In analysing them we meet with a number of psychosexual phenomena which our theory must take account of. And I propose in the following section to attempt to do this.

In thus tracing separately the development of the relation of the individual to his love-object we shall not overlook the close and manifold psychological connections which exist between it and the subject of our earlier investigations. Those connections will, on the contrary, become much more evident in this way than before. And

---

[1] *Drei Abhandlungen zur Sexualtheorie* (1905).

just as in the previous section we were led to discuss at some length certain important aspects of object-relations, such, for instance, as ambivalence in man's instinctual life, so now there can be no question of treating particular subjects as isolated problems. And indeed we shall most easily be able to see in what respects the history of the development of object-love requires amplification if we begin by giving a short summary of the theory of the stages of libidinal organization.

We have recognized the presence of two different pleasurable tendencies in the anal-sadistic phase: a more primitive one of expelling the object (evacuation) and destroying it, and a later one of retaining and controlling it. Thus we have been led on empirical grounds to believe that there is a differentiation within the anal-sadistic phase which before had been supposed to be homogeneous. We have come to the conclusion that the melancholic patient regresses to the lower level of that phase but does not make a halt there. His libido tends towards a still earlier phase—the cannibalistic phase—in which his instinctual aim is to incorporate the object in himself. In his unconscious he identifies the love-object he has lost and abandoned with the most important product of bodily evacuation—with his fæces—and re-incorporates it in his ego by means of the process we have called introjection. But he cannot, even by regressing so far, escape from the conflict of his ambivalent feelings. That conflict, on the contrary, increases in strength, until there begins to arise in him a tendency to regress to a still more primitive stage of libidinal development whose sexual aim is that of sucking. This stage we have considered as *pre-ambivalent*. Thus we have been led to distinguish two levels in the oral phase as well as in the anal one. Finally we have been able to observe a similar differentiation within the later, genital phase. And it is only the most recent of those two levels that we have been able to regard as free from ambivalence, or *post-ambivalent*.

By assuming that each of the three main phases of the libido is differentiated into two stages we have been able, so far at least, to account satisfactorily for the observed facts concerning the changes undergone by the individual in regard to his sexual aim.   And we have also been able to find a more definite genetic connection between certain kinds of illness and certain levels of the libido than has hitherto been possible.   But we will not try to conceal the very considerable gaps that still exist in our knowledge in this respect.   For instance, we have up till now not succeeded in finding a connection of this sort for paranoic conditions. This is a point to which we shall return later.

Up till now much less has been known about the development of object-love.   Just as we have hitherto been accustomed to distinguish three phases in the development of the libido, so we have recognized three phases in the relationship of the individual to his object.   And here once more it is to Freud that we owe the first discoveries of importance.   He grouped the development of that relationship into an auto-erotic phase belonging to earliest infancy in which the individual has no object, a narcissistic phase in which the individual is his own love-object, and a phase in which there is object-love in the true sense of the word.   In the following discussion I shall try to show how far we are able to add new knowledge to this part of our sexual theory.

The new contributions which I hope to be able to make are derived from a particular field of psycho-analytic empiricism, namely, from the study of the ' narcissistic neuroses ' and of certain neuroses belonging to those levels of object-love which are closely related to the narcissistic neuroses in a certain respect.

The manic-depressive cases whose analysis formed the groundwork of the first part of this study are of considerable assistance in helping us to solve our present problem also. At the time that I was analysing those cases it happened that I was also having two female patients under long treatment of whose neurotic condition I should like to give a brief account in these pages.   The clinical picture they presented was quite different from melancholia, but it will soon become evident why I have placed them side by side with the latter.

The first of these patients, whom I shall call X, presented a very complicated clinical picture, and I shall only reproduce the most outstanding features of it. Foremost of these was a marked *pseudologia phantastica* dating back to her sixth year. Besides this, she had severe impulses of kleptomania going back to the same time. And lastly, she suffered from attacks of despair which could be occasioned by the slightest thing and which found utterance in uncontrollable fits of weeping of many hours' duration. This compulsive weeping had two main determinants. It was, in the first place, derived from her castration complex, and represented the loss of her masculinity with all that this involved, such as envy of her more favoured younger brother, and so on. During menstruation, which used to excite her castration complex in a typical way, she scarcely ever stopped crying.[1] The second determinant of her crying fits was connected with her relation to her father whose loss she was mourning, not in a real sense because he was dead, but in a psychological one. It was in connection with this psychological loss of him that the earliest symptoms of her neurosis had appeared. As a child she had early developed an especially strong transference-love towards her father, but, as her analysis showed, it had suffered a sudden check in the first half of her sixth year. At that time she had been convalescing from an illness and had shared her parents' bedroom. There she had had an opportunity of seeing her mother and father having sexual intercourse, and of observing her father's body. This increased her scoptophilic tendencies greatly, until they were overtaken by an intense repression. I should like to mention one especial consequence which those experiences had in her case in addition to those familiar to all analysts. This was that she complained of having lost all emotional contact with her father, and indeed of being unable to form any kind of mental image of him. She was conscious neither of affectionate feelings nor of sensual ones towards him. But we were able to infer from a quantity of neurotic material that she

---

[1] It may be mentioned in passing that this copious flow of tears represented her unconscious wish to urinate like a man.

had a quite specialized compulsive interest in one particular part of his body, namely, his penis.   He had ceased to exist for her as a whole person; only one part of him had remained, and this formed the object of her compulsive looking.[1]   Besides this, she unconsciously identified herself now with him, now with his genitals, which had become for her his representative.   Her kleptomanic impulses were in a great measure derived from her active castration tendency directed against her father.   The unconscious aim of her thefts was to rob him of his envied possession so as to have it herself or to identify herself with it.   That those thefts were connected with the person of her father was made evident in many ways.   For instance, she had on one occasion taken an enema tube out of his room and had used it —as a substitute for his male member—for anal-erotic purposes.   She used to 'castrate' him in other ways, by taking money [*Vermögen*] [2] out of his purse, and by stealing his pens, pencils, and other male symbols, as is so common in cases of kleptomania.

The patient's castration complex also proved to be an important motive of her *pseudologia*.   Just as her klepto-manic impulses expressed the idea, ' I seize by force or fraud what has been withheld from me or taken away from me ', we might formulate one of the main determinants of her lying in this way: ' I do possess that desired part of the body, and so I am equal to my father '.   It is particularly interesting to learn from the patient that telling these imaginary facts gave her strong sexual excitement and a sensation as if something was growing and swelling out of her abdomen.   This sensation was connected with a feeling of physical strength and activity; and in the same way the act of lying made her feel mentally powerful and superior to others.

Her relation to her father, as I have roughly sketched it, was in keeping with her attitude to the rest of her environment.   She had no real mental contact whatever with

---

[1] This took the form of looking for the outline of his genitals underneath his clothes.

[2] [='means', is also used in the sense of 'capacity', and thus comes to stand for ' sexual potency ' in German.—*Trans*.]

anyone.   Telling lies had for many years represented for her her sole mental relation with the external world.

As we have said, she had arrived at this position, so far removed from a regular and complete object-love, through a regression from such an object-love.   She did nevertheless maintain some kind of relation to her objects, and she clung to them with the utmost tenacity.   Further analysis of her kleptomania, together with analysis of one or two other cases, threw light on the nature of her peculiar and incomplete form of object-love.   Her dreams and day-dreams contained ever-recurring images of castration by means of biting.   The aim of her phantasies was not to incorporate her love-object as a whole but to bite off and swallow a part of it and then to identify herself with the part.   Such a partial incorporation of the object seems to occur in other cases of kleptomania as well.   I will give another example.

A female patient whom I shall call Y was suffering from a grave neurosis whose most marked symptom was severe hysterical vomiting.   In addition she exhibited very strong kleptomanic tendencies which in her case too were found to be determined by her castration complex. Her habit of stealing had grown up around an incorrigible inclination she had had in childhood to pull everything out with her hands, especially flowers and hair.   But this impulse was itself a modification of a desire to bite off everything that ' stuck out '.   Even when she was grown up she had phantasies of this kind.   As soon as she got to know a man she had a compulsive idea of biting off his penis.   Her neurotic vomiting was closely related to these oral-sadistic impulses.   In her case, too, her father had lost all value for her as a person.   Her libidinal interest was focussed on his penis alone.   And when he had died she too had been unable to feel any sorrow.   But she had had a vivid phantasy of stealing his penis by biting it off, and of keeping it.   In her day-dreams she used to have a great many phantasies of copulating with a penis ' without any man belonging to it '.

Another similarity between these two patients was that in each case the mother also was represented by only one part

of her body, namely, her breasts. They had obviously
been identified in the child's mind with the supposed penis
of the female. She was alternatively represented by her
buttocks, which in their turn stood for her breasts. The
relation of this image to oral erotism (pleasure in biting)
was more than evident, and could be supported by many
examples, one of which I shall give. X once dreamed as
follows: 'I was eating away at a piece of meat, tearing it
with my teeth. At last I swallowed it. Suddenly I noticed
that the piece of meat was the back part of a fur coat
belonging to Frau N.'.

It is not difficult to understand the 'back part' as a
displacement from before backwards. In the same way
we can understand the frequent symbolic use made of fur
as an allusion to the female genital. Frau N.'s surname
was in fact the name of an animal, and of an animal which
frequently symbolized her mother in this patient's dreams.

'Displacement backwards' was a process that constantly occurred in the mental images of both patients.
Both had a feeling of disgust at their mother, and in their
phantasies and certain symptoms both likened her to the
essence of all that is most disgusting, namely, excrement.
Thus the mother was represented in imagination by a piece
of the body that had left it, *i.e.* a penis, and fæces.

In both cases the libido had undergone a considerable
degree of narcissistic regression, though by no means a
complete one. What had happened was that—until
analysis set this right—its capacity for object love had been
imperfectly developed in a certain respect or had regressed
to a stage of imperfect development. The stage in question
must have lain somewhere between narcissism and object-
love. Another fact which was to be noticed about both
cases, and which I later on observed in other persons,
pointed in the same direction. This was that the libido
was in an unmistakable state of ambivalence towards its
object and showed a strong tendency to inflict injuries on
it. Nevertheless, that destructive tendency had already
been subjected to limitations. At this stage the sexual
aim of the individual must have been to deprive his object

of a part of its body, *i.e.* to attack its integrity without destroying its existence. We are put in mind of a child which catches a fly and, having pulled off a leg, lets it go again. We must once more emphasize the fact that the pleasure in biting is very markedly associated with this form of object-relation which had hitherto escaped our notice.

I have been able to ascertain the presence of similar psychological processes in the two manic-depressive patients about whom I have spoken in greater detail in the first part of this study. But the really valuable evidence for this only appeared when their gravest symptoms were beginning to pass off. So long as these were present the cannibalistic, destructive tendencies of the libido manifested themselves in many ways. During the period of recovery one of the patients used very often to have a phantasy of biting off the nose, or the lobe of the ear or the breast, of a young girl whom he was very fond of. At other times he used to play with the idea of biting off his father's finger. And once, when he believed that I was not going to continue his analysis, he all of a sudden had the same thought about me. This idea of biting off a finger was found to have a great number of determinants besides its obvious significance of castration. What chiefly interests us here is the ambivalence expressed in the phantasy. For although in it the patient's physician—as the substitute of his father—was to be maimed by having a piece of his body bitten off, we must not see the hostile side of the phantasy only and overlook its friendly tendency which was expressed in the patient's desire to spare the existence of the object except for one part, and again in his desire to keep that part as his own property for ever. We may thus speak of an impulse of *partial incorporation* of the object. The patient just referred to once said that he would like to 'eat up' the young girl in question (whom he identified with his mother) 'mouthful by mouthful'. And the following incident will show how greatly occupied his mind was in this stage of his analysis with the idea of biting off things. On one occasion he was speaking about a man under whom he was working who represented both his father and his mother in his unconscious and towards whom he had an extremely ambivalent attitude. As often happened with him his free associations flowed over into phantasies of a markedly concrete kind, which would at times be interrupted by an affective ' blocking '. A ' blocking' of this nature occurred as he was speaking about his superior. In accounting for that stoppage in his associations he said, ' Now [*i.e.* in the phantasied situation] I must first tear out his beard with my teeth; I can't get any further till I've done that '. The patient was thus himself saying that there was no possible way of avoiding the intrusion of those phantasies which belonged unmistakably to the class of partial cannibalism.

Complete and unrestricted cannibalism is only possible on the basis of unrestricted narcissism. On such a level all that the individual considers is his own desire for pleasure. He pays no attention whatever to the interests of his object, and destroys that object without the least hesitation.[1] On the level of partial cannibalism we can still detect the signs of its descent from total cannibalism, yet nevertheless the distinction between the two is sharply marked. On that later level the individual shows the first signs of having some care for his object. We may also regard such a care, incomplete as it is, as the first beginnings of object-love in a stricter sense, since it implies that the individual has begun to conquer his narcissism. But we must add that on this level of development the individual is far from recognizing the existence of another individual as such and from ' loving ' him in his entirety, whether in a physical or a mental way. His desire is still directed towards removing a part of the body of his object and incorporating it. This, on the other hand, implies that he has resigned the purely narcissistic aim of practising complete cannibalism.

Now that we have become alive to certain occurrences relating to infantile development, there will not be wanting confirmatory evidence obtained from the direct observation

[1] The cannibalism of primitive people after which we have named this phase of the infantile libido cannot be said to be unrestricted in this way. It is not at all the case that any one person can kill and eat any other. The selection of the victim has a strict affective determination.

of the child. Our inquiries have, moreover, led us a certain distance forward into unknown country, and we are glad to come upon some traces of earlier exploration. Several years ago two psycho-analysts, whose reliability as observers is not open to question, have each independently added to our knowledge of the psychology of paranoic delusions of persecution. Both van Ophuijsen [1] and Stärcke [2] discovered during the course of their psycho-analytic practice that in paranoia the 'persecutor' can be traced back to the patient's unconscious image of the fæces in his intestines which he identifies with the penis of the 'persecutor', *i.e.* the person of his own sex whom he originally loved. Thus in paranoia the patient represents his persecutor by a part of his body, and believes that he is carrying it within himself. He would like to get rid of that foreign body but cannot.

I must admit that I did not at the time recognize the full importance of van Ophuijsen's and Stärcke's discovery. It was an isolated one, and did not fit easily into the general body of known facts, although the relations between paranoia and anal-erotism had already been recognized by Ferenczi. Now, however, it finds its place in a wider scheme and is thus seen to possess a very great significance.

When the paranoiac has lost his libidinal relations to his object and to all objects in general, he tries as far as he can to compensate for the loss which to him amounts to a destruction of the world. As we know since Freud's analysis of the case of Schreber, he proceeds to reconstruct his lost object. We may now add that in this process of reconstruction the paranoiac incorporates a part of his object. In doing this he undergoes much the same fate as the melancholiac who has introjected the whole of his object by a process of incorporation. Nor can he, either, escape his ambivalence in this way. Like the melancholiac, therefore, he tries to get rid of that part of his object which he has taken into himself. And on the psychosexual developmental level on which he is this can only be an anal process for him. To a paranoiac, therefore, the love-object is

---

[1] ' On the Origin of the Feeling of Persecution ' (1920).
[2] ' The Reversal of the Libido-Sign in Delusions of Persecution ' (1919).

equivalent to fæces which he cannot get rid of. The introjected part of his love-object will not leave him, just as in the case of the melancholiac the object, which has been introjected *in toto*, continues to exercise its despotic power from within.

We have thus come to the conclusion that the melancholiac incorporates his abandoned love-object as a whole, whereas the paranoiac only introjects a part of his. In the latter case there is another alternative to be considered, namely, that this partial introjection need not be effected in an oral way but can be thought of as an anal process. Pending a more complete understanding of the situation we may put forward the view—though with all due hesitation—that in respect of its sexual aim the libido of the paranoiac regresses to the earlier of the two sadistic-anal stages, while in respect of its attitude towards its object it goes back to the stage of partial introjection. Whether that introjection takes place in an oral or an anal way must be left an open question. We meet with a similar state of affairs in melancholiacs during their period of convalescence. Nor can we as yet say why it is that in the latter case regular paranoic delusions are not formed. This difference may be due to the different effects of introjection according as it is total or partial in its extent, and oral or anal in its means. We shall have no certainty on this subject until we know more about the part played by the ego in those two forms of illness.

Another point to be noted in regard to the part of the body that has been introjected is that the penis is regularly assimilated to the female breast, and that other parts of the body, such as the finger, the foot, hair, fæces, and buttocks, can be made to stand for those two organs in a secondary way, as has already been shown.[1] If we suppose that there is such a stage of 'partial love' as we have depicted in the development of object-love, further facts are opened to us and we begin to understand a certain peculiarity of sexual

---

[1] A remarkable parallel to this ' partial love ' is seen in the ' partial identification' of the individual with his love-object, as Freud has briefly outlined it in his *Group Psychology* (p. 64).

perversions to which Sachs has recently drawn our attention once again:[1] I refer to the pervert's concentration of
interest on certain bodily parts of his object, the choice of
which often seems very curious to us. This peculiarity is
most strikingly exhibited in the fetishist. To him the whole
person is often only an accidental appendage to one particular
part of his body which alone exercises an irresistible attraction over him. Many years ago, as I was attempting for
the first time to investigate a case of foot and corset fetishism[2]
by means of psycho-analysis, Freud suggested to me that I
should introduce the idea of a partial repression so as to
account for the phenomena in question. In the light of our
present knowledge this psychological process, by means of
which the greater part of the object is reduced to insignifi-
cance and excessive value is attached to the remaining part,
is seen to be the consequence of a regression of the libido
to this supposed stage of 'partial love'; and it ceases to be
an isolated event found in a certain kind of illness, and falls
into place among a large number of allied psychological
phenomena. It is not the intention of this study to go more
deeply into the symptoms of fetishism. But it may be
useful to point out that those parts of the body on which
the fetishist tends to concentrate his inclinations are the
same as those we meet with as the objects of 'partial
love'.

Our clinical observations have long since made us
acquainted with a stage in the development of object-love
in which the individual already spares his object in a great
measure; and we meet with it again in the neuroses as a
regressive phenomenon belonging to the sexual life of
obsessional patients. In this stage the individual is not yet
able to love anyone in the full sense of the word. His
libido is still attached to a part of its object. But he has
given up his tendency to incorporate that part. Instead,
he desires to rule and possess it. Distant as the libido still
is at this stage from the ultimate goal of its development,

[1] 'Zur Genese der Perversionen' (1923).
[2] Cf. my earlier essay, 'Notes on the Analysis of a Case of Foot and Corset
Fetishism', on p. 125 of this book.

it has yet made an important step forward in so far as such a proprietorship is, as it were, *exteriorized*. Property no longer means that which the individual has incorporated by devouring. It is situated outside his body now. In this way its existence is recognized and safeguarded. This implies that the individual has accomplished an important piece of adaptation to the external world. Such a change has the greatest practical significance in a social sense. It makes possible for the first time joint ownership of an object; whereas the method of devouring the object could only secure it for one person alone.

This position of the libido in respect of its object has left traces in the forms of speech of various languages, as in the German word *besitzen*,[1] for instance, and in the Latin *possidere*. A person is thought of as *sitting on* his property, and thus as still keeping in close contact with it. This attitude can easily be observed in children. We often notice how a child will take an object that is specially dear to him to bed with him at night and will lie on top of it. In animals, too, and especially in dogs, the same thing can be seen. They will endeavour to place an object in security by covering it with their bodies. I have noticed this in my own dog. As soon as a stranger came to stay in the house he would fetch his muzzle—an object, that is, that belonged exclusively to him—and would lie down upon it.[2]

Further psycho-analytic study of the obsessional neuroses will, no doubt, furnish us with more information concerning this stage of object-love. The especially intense nature of active and passive castration-images in obsessional patients and their peculiar attitude to questions of possession make it seem very probable that there is a connection between that illness and the stage of partial love.

Psycho-analysis has taught us that the unconscious of the adult person contains many traces of the earlier stages of his psychosexual life. In the healthy person we come across such traces chiefly in his dreams. In the same

---

[1] [' To possess.' *Sitzen*=to sit.—*Trans*.]

[2] We may compare with this the phantasies of little Hans (Freud, 'Analysis of a Phobia in a Five-year-old Boy ', 1909), in which he takes the giraffe, who represents his mother, away from his father and then sits down upon it.

way the stage of partial love leaves traces behind in the unconscious.

An example of this is seen in the familiar dreams about a tooth dropping out. Every analyst is aware of the manifold symbolic meaning of such a dream. The tooth that drops out symbolizes on the one hand castration, and on the other some person whom the dreamer knows and whose death he desires in the dream. Thus a near friend or relative is made equivalent to a part of the body which has to be expelled. We see at once the resemblance with the psychology of delusions of persecution. We should particularly note the ambivalence of the subject's feelings which is manifested in his identification of a person with a part of his own body. To compare another person with a part of one's own body which is the object of a specially high narcissistic estimation is without doubt a proof of exceptional love. In German we often call a loved person ' my heart ' (mein Herz); and we say of a mother that she loves her child as the ' apple of her eye '. When a man likens someone to his tooth, as so often occurs in dreams, it is as much as to say that although he is loth to lose a part of himself he nevertheless can do without it since he possesses plenty more. Indeed, the dreamer often observes that the loss of his tooth or its extraction is quite painless; from which it may be inferred that the loss of that person would not be so very painful to him after all. Furthermore, we must not forget that underlying symbolic castration there is an unconscious wish for the loss of that part of the body upon which the narcissism of man is as a rule centred. The hostile significance of the comparison, however, is most clearly seen where the part employed as the equivalent of the person is excrement.

Thus it is clear that the stage of partial love has left traces behind it even in the mind of the healthy person. He represents the love-object that is cathected with his ambivalent feelings by a single part of its body, which he has introjected into his own.

As my two female patients, X and Y, whose case I have described, gradually approached a normal condition of object-love under the influence of psycho-analysis, they passed through a stage of development that seemed to be the next modification of the stage we have been discussing. As will be remembered, the patient X had been dominated by an idea which had constantly recurred in varying forms in her dreams and phantasies, and which was concerned with the acquisition of her father's penis; and we recollect that she had identified the whole of herself with that part of his body. At a certain point in her recovery, when she had pretty well overcome her kleptomanic impulses and her *pseudologia*, her phantasies took another form. As a particularly clear example of this later form, I may mention a dream she had in which she saw her father's body and noticed the absence of the pubic hair (a part of his body which had always stood for his genitals in a number of earlier dreams). Now, therefore, she was dreaming of her father as an entire person *except* for one part of his body. We are struck by the contrast between this and certain expressions of her neurosis that have been mentioned earlier. Before, when she had had a compulsion to stare at her father's genitals, her love-interest had been turned away from all the rest of him. Now she was repressing what had then exercised a compulsive power in her consciousness.

I have come across dreams like the one above in other people. One patient, a woman, who had a strongly ambivalent attitude towards me, expressed her transference in a dream in which she represented me without any genitals The hostile tendency—the desire to castrate her object— is obvious. But the dream had another determinant, which was to be found in her likening me to her father whom she was allowed to love but not to desire in a genital sense. She could only love her analyst, as her father's substitute, so long as the genital aspect was excluded. And the dream-censorship took means accordingly to prevent her from over-stepping the incest-barrier.

Such a positive erotic attitude towards the object, but with the exclusion of the genitals, seems to be a typically hysterical expression of the incest-prohibition. As early as in the first edition of his *Drei Abhandlungen zur Sexual-*

theorie, Freud pointed out that hysterics reject the normal, genital sexual aim, and put in its place other, ' perverse ' aims. We shall remain in agreement with his view in proposing to set up a stage of object-love with the exclusion of the genitals.[1] The rejection of the genital zone applies to the subject's own body as well as to that of his object. This situation is to a great extent responsible for two very general and, from a practical point of view, important symptoms—impotence in men and frigidity in women. In it the individual cannot love his object completely because of the presence of its genitals.

We know from the psycho-analysis of neurotics that such an inhibition of the libido in both sexes proceeds from the castration complex. In the man, anxiety about his own male organ and horror at the absence of any such organ in the female bring about the same result as is effected in the woman by her still unmastered pain at having been deprived of her genitals and by her castration-desires directed against the male. We must not forget, too, that the genitals are more intensely cathected by narcissistic love than any other part of the subject's own body. Thus everything else in the object can be loved sooner than the genitals. On the level of the ' phallic ' organization of the libido, as Freud calls it, the last great step in its development has obviously not yet been made. It is not made until the highest level of the libido—that which alone should be called the genital level—is attained. Thus we see that the attainment of the highest level of the organization of the libido goes hand in hand with the final step in the evolution of object-love.

The table appended below is intended to facilitate a survey of the various stages of sexual organization and of object-love which the individual traverses. I should like to make it quite clear that it is of a purely provisional nature and that it by no means implies that those stages are only six in number. We can compare it to a time-table of

[1] Such a stage of object-love with genital exclusion seems to coincide in time with Freud's ' phallic stage ' in the psychosexual development of the individual, and moreover to have close internal relations with it. We may look upon hysterical symptoms as the obverse of those libidinal impulses which belong to object-love with genital exclusion and to the phallic organization.

express trains in which only the larger stations at which they stop are given. The halting-places that lie between cannot be marked in a summary of this kind. I should also like to say that the stages placed on the same horizontal level in each column do not necessarily coincide in time.

Stages of Libidinal Organization.	Stages of Object-love.	
VI. Final Genital Stage	Object-love	(Post-ambivalent)
V. Earlier Genital Stage (phallic)	Object-love with exclusion of genitals	
IV. Later Anal-sadistic Stage	Partial love	
III. Earlier Anal-sadistic Stage	Partial love with incorporation	(Ambivalent)
II. Later Oral Stage (cannibalistic)	Narcissism (total incorporation of object)	
I. Earlier Oral Stage (sucking)	Auto-erotism (without object)	(Pre-ambivalent)

The table gives a brief survey of the psychosexual development of man in two respects. It considers the movement of his libido in respect of his sexual aim and of his sexual object. Among other important phenomena belonging to this process of development there is one in especial that I have omitted to deal with, and that is the formation of the inhibitions of the instincts. I should therefore like to add a few short remarks on this subject.

We regard the earliest, auto-erotic stage of the individual as being still exempt from instinctual inhibitions, in accordance with the absence of any real object relations. In the stage of narcissism with a cannibalistic sexual aim the first evidence of an instinctual inhibition appears in the shape of morbid anxiety. The process of overcoming the cannibalistic impulses is intimately associated with a sense of guilt which comes into the foreground as a typical inhibitory phenomenon belonging to the third stage. The third stage, whose sexual aim is the incorporating of a part of the object, is left behind when feelings of pity and disgust arise in the individual and cut off this form of libidinal activity. In the next stage—that of object-love with the exclusion of the genitals—inhibition takes the form of feelings of shame. Finally, in the stage of real object-love we find social feelings of a superior kind regulating the instinctual life of the

individual. This brief and generalized outline will serve
to show that a further inquiry is needed into the origin of
the inhibitions of the libido, but that psycho-analysis can
doubtless give us the key to the solution of this problem
as well.

I should only like to say a few more words about one
event in that complicated process. In the stage of 'partial
love with incorporation ', as we have seen, the love-object
is represented by one part of itself. The small child has
an ambivalent attitude towards that part (penis, breast,
excrement, etc.); that is, he desires it and rejects it at the
same time. It is not until he has completely given up his
tendency to incorporate objects—a change which, according
to our scheme, does not happen until the fourth stage—that
he adopts a contemptuous attitude towards those parts, and
especially towards excrement. In this stage excrement
becomes for him the representative of everything that he
does not want to keep; so that he identifies the person
whom he rejects with disgust with fæces (as in the case of
X and Y). And the mere idea of putting excrement into
the mouth is now the very essence of all that is disgusting.
In certain illnesses we can observe a serious process of
regression taking place in which the individual once more
has as his sexual aim the eating of fæces. For in our
unconscious we retain our original narcissistic estimation
of the value of excrement.

I have already attempted in an earlier paper [1] to give
some coherent account of the relation between the various
forms of psychoneurosis and the different levels of libidinal
development, as far as the state of our knowledge then
permitted. My attempt was a very imperfect one and far
from being a final explanation of the facts. Even at the
present day we know almost as little as we did then; and
we can only hope to have made an addition to our knowledge in two points, and that with every reserve.

In the first place we may assume that in melancholia
the subject's capacity for object-love is especially poorly
developed, so that if he falls ill his tendency to incorporate

[1] See Chapter XVIII.

2 I

his object in a cannibalistic way gets the better of him—an occurrence which would coincide with a regression of his libido to the second stage as tabulated above. In the second place, it would seem that in paranoic states the libido has stopped in its regressive movement at the stage of partial incorporation (the third stage). This also seems to be true of kleptomanic conditions. And perhaps the main difference between the wish contained in each of those illnesses is that the kleptomaniac has taken as his sexual aim an *oral* incorporation of his object, while the paranoiac has made his its *anal* incorporation.

Only steady and persistent psycho-analytical work, especially in regard to the narcissistic psychoneuroses, can gradually give us a more complete view of man's psycho-sexual development. Meanwhile, until we have collected a greater number of thorough analyses to confirm and amplify the theoretic assumptions made in this paper, it may not be superfluous to consider the *prima facie* arguments in favour of those assumptions.

To begin with, we must remember that the results of our examination have been obtained by strictly empirical methods. I do not think that I have anywhere allowed myself to abandon the ground of empirical fact for that of speculative reasoning. At any rate I can say that I have never attempted to produce a complete and a well-rounded-off theory, but that on the contrary I have myself drawn attention to faults and shortcomings in my own suggestions.

In the next place, I should like to point out the simplicity of that process of development whose existence we have assumed. It follows along the same lines as the processes involved in organic growth: what was at first a *part* grows into a *whole*, and what was at first a *whole* shrinks to a *part* and finally loses all value or continues its existence as a mere rudiment.

But we can carry this parallel with biological processes further still. We have long since learned to apply the biogenetic principle of organic life to the mental (psycho-sexual) development of man. Psycho-analysis is constantly finding confirmation of the fact that the individual re-capitulates the history of his species in its psychological aspects as well. A great quantity of empirical data, however, warrants us in laying down yet another law concerning man's psychosexual development. This is that it lags a long way behind his somatic development, like a late version or repetition of that process. The biological model upon which the developmental processes discussed in this paper are based takes place in the earliest embryonic period of the individual, whereas the psychosexual processes extend over a number of years of his extra-uterine life, namely, from his first year to the period of puberty.

If we turn to the field of embryology we can without difficulty recognize that there is an extensive similarity between the gradual development of man's psychosexual life, as we have examined it in this paper, and the organic development of his early embryonic life. In the first period of his extra-uterine life his libido is, according to our view, predominantly attached to the mouth as an erotogenic zone. The first vital relation of the infant to external objects consists in sucking up into its mouth a substance that is suitable for it and accessible to it. In its embryonic life, the first organ that is formed in connection with the earliest simple process of cell-division is the so-called blastopore, an organ which is permanently retained and keeps its function in low forms of the animal world such as the Cœlenterata.

It is a long time before the sexual organs (in the narrower sense of the word) of the child take over the leading part in its sexual life. Before this state is reached the intestinal canal, and especially the apertures at either end, becomes possessed of an important erotogenic significance, and sends out strong stimuli to the nervous system. This state also has its prototype in the embryo. For a time there exists an open connection between the intestinal canal (rectum) and the caudal part of the neural canal (*canalis neurentericus*). The path along which stimuli may be transmitted from the intestinal canal to the nervous system might thus be said to be marked out organically.

But what is most clearly visible is the biological prototype of the child's oral-sadistic (cannibalistic) and anal-sadistic phases. Freud [1] has already alluded to this fact; and I will quote the passage here: ' The sadistic-anal organization can easily be regarded as a continuation and development of the oral one. The violent muscular activity, directed upon the object, by which it is characterized, is to be explained as an action preparatory to eating. The eating then ceases to be a sexual aim and the preparatory action becomes a sufficient aim in itself. The essential novelty, as compared with the previous stage, is that the receptive passive function becomes disengaged from the oral zone and attached to the anal zone.' He goes on to speak of parallel processes in the field of biology but does not specify which they are. In this connection I should like to lay particular stress on a striking parallel between the organic and the psychosexual development of the individual.

At first the blastopore is situated at the anterior end (cephalic end) of the primitive streak. In the embryos of certain animals we can observe that the original mouth-opening closes up at the anterior end and becomes enlarged at the posterior end. In this way it gradually approaches the tail, which is in process of formation, and finally comes to rest there as the anus. This direct derivation of the anus from the blastopore appears as the biological prototype of that psychosexual process which Freud has described and which occurs somewhere about the second year of the life of the individual.

At about the same time as the anus is being formed in the embryo we can observe the muscular system of the body developing. In this process the jaw muscles are far in advance of the limb muscles. The development of the anus and of the jaws is closely connected. We may also remark that in extra-uterine life the jaw muscles are able to perform powerful and effective movements much earlier

[1] Cf. ' From the History of an Infantile Neurosis ' (1918).

than other muscles, such as the muscles of the trunk or of the limbs.

We recognized as the fourth stage of the psychosexual development of the individual that in which he has as his sexual aim the retention and control of his object. Its correlate in biological ontogenesis is to be found in the formation of the intestinal mechanisms for retaining what has been taken into the body. These consist in constrictions and enlargements, annular contractures, branching passages, divagations ending blindly, manifold convolutions, and finally the voluntary and involuntary sphincter muscles of the anus itself. At the time that this complicated arrangement for the retention of objects is being formed there is as yet no sign of the appearance of the uro-genital apparatus.

We have seen that the genital organization of the libido falls into two stages which correspond to two stages in the development of object-love. Here once more the organic development of the individual supplies the model. The genital organs are at first ' indifferent ', and it is only later on that they become differentiated into ' male ' and ' female '. This applies to the generative glands as well as to the organs of copulation. In the same way we have detected a gradual process of differentiation in the psychosexual life of the individual.

Until a wider and more profound psycho-analytic knowledge shall have enabled us to come to valid conclusions concerning psychosexual development, I trust that the above instances of parallelism with biological processes may lend a certain support to my endeavour to give an account of the evolution of object-love in the human individual.

BIBLIOGRAPHY OF SCIENTIFIC
PUBLICATIONS [1]

C. = Centralblatt für Nervenheilkunde und Psychiatrie.
Z. = Zentralblatt für Psychoanalyse.
I.Z. = Internationale Zeitschrift für (ärztliche) Psychoanalyse.
J. = Jahrbuch der Psychoanalyse (Jahrbuch für psychoanalytische und psychopathologische Forschungen).
I.J. = International Journal of Psycho-Analysis.
B. = Berlin Psycho-Analytical Society.

1900

1. Normentafel zur Entwicklungsgeschichte des Huhnes (with Prof. Keibel). *Normentafeln zur Entwicklungsgeschichte der Wirbeltiere*, Heft 2. Jena.

1901

2. Beiträge zur Entwicklungsgeschichte des Wellensittichs. (Inaugural Dissertation.) *Anatomische Blätter* (Anatomical Institute, Freiburg), Heft LVI/LVII. (Wiesbaden, I. F. Bergmann.)

1902

3. Beiträge zur Kenntnis des Delirium tremens der Morphinisten. *C.*, Jahrg. xxv., June, S. 369-80.

1904

4. Über Versuche mit 'Veronal' bei Erregungszuständen der Paralytiker. *C.*, Jahrg. xxvii., March, S. 176-80.

5. Cytodiagnostische Untersuchungen bei Dementia paralytica (with Dr. Ziegenhagen). Psychiatrischer Verein, Berlin, March 19. Author's Abstract in *C.*, Jahrg. xxvii., May, S. 323-24.

6. Über einige seltene Zustandsbilder bei progressiver Paralyse : Apraxie, transkortikale sensorische Aphasie, subkortikale sensorische Aphasie, sensorisch-motorische Asymbolie. *Allgemeine Zeitschrift für Psychiatrie*, Band lvi. Heft 4, June, S. 502-23.

7. Vorstellung eines Kranken mit Hemianopsie und Rotgrünblindheit im erhaltenen Gesichtsfeld. Psychiatrischer Verein, Berlin, June 18. Author's Abstract in *C.*, Jahrg. xxvii., September, S. 578-79.

---

[1] The most important works are marked with an asterisk.—E. J.

1907

8. Beiträge zur Kenntnis der motorischen Apraxie auf Grund eines Falles von einseitiger Apraxie. *C.*, N.F. Bd. xviii., March, S. 161-76.

9. Über die Bedeutung sexueller Jugendträumen für die Symptomatologie der Dementia Præcox. Annual Meeting of the Deutscher Verein für Psychiatrie in Frankfort, April 27. *C.*, N.F. Bd. xviii., June, S. 409-15.

*10. Das Erleiden sexueller Träumen als Form infantiler Sexualbetätigung. *C.*, N.F. Bd. xviii., November, S. 854-65.

1908

*11. Die psychosexuellen Differenzen der Hysterie und der Dementia præcox. First International Psycho-Analytical Congress, Salzburg, April 26. *C.*, N.F. Bd. xix., July, S. 521-33.

*12. Die psychologischen Beziehungen zwischen Sexualität und Alkoholismus. *Zeitschrift für Sexualwissenschaft*, No. 8, August, S. 449-58. (*I.J.* vol. vii. pp. 2-10.)

13. Die Stellung der Verwandtenehen in der Psychologie der Neurosen. Gesellschaft für Psychiatrie und Nervenkrankheiten, Berlin, November 9. (Author's abstract and discussion, *Neurologisches Centralblatt*, Jahrg. xxvii., S. 1150-52.) *J.*, Bd. i., 1909, S. 110-18.

1909

*14. Traum und Mythus : Eine Studie zur Völkerpsychologie. *Schriften zur angewandten Seelenkunde*, Heft 4, pp. 73. (Wien, Deuticke.) English translation, 1913 (New York, Nervous and Mental Disease Monograph Series, No. 15). Dutch Translation, 1914 (Leiden, S. C. van Doesburgh).

15. Freuds Schriften aus den Jahren 1893–1909. (Collective Review.) *J.*, Bd. i. S. 546-74.

16. Bericht über die österreichische und deutsche psychoanalytische Literatur bis zum Jahre 1909. (Collective Review.) *J.*, Bd. i. S. 575-94.

1910

*17. Über hysterische Traumzustände. *J.*, Bd. ii. S. 1 ja.

18. Bemerkungen zur Analyse eines Falles von Fuss- und Korsettfetischismus. Second International Psycho-Analytical Congress, Nuremberg, March 30. (Abstract, Z., Jahrg. i. Heft 2, November, S. 129) *J.*, Bd. iii., 1912, S. 557-67.

19. Historisches Referat über die Psychoanalyse. *B.*, April 29.

20. Psychoanalyse eines Falles von Hysterie mit ungewöhnlichem Hervortreten der Inzestfixierung. *B.*, June 7.

21. Über sadistische Phantasien im Kindesalter (kasuistische Beiträge). *B.*, August 31.

22. Inzest und Inzestphantasien in neurotischen Familien. Kasuistische Mitteilungen über wirkliche Sexualbeziehungen innerhalb neurotischer Familien und über Krankheitssymptome auf der Basis der Inzestphantasien. *B.*, November 12.

23. Mitteilung zweier Ödipus-Träume. *B.*, December 8.

1911

24. Psychoanalyse einer Zwangsneurose. *B.*, February 9.

25. Einige Bemerkungen über den Mutterkultus und seine Symbolik in der Individual- und Völkerpsychologie. *Z.*, Jahrg. i. Heft 12, September, S. 549-50.

*26. Die psychosexuelle Grundlage der Depressions- und Exaltationszustände. Third International Psycho-Analytical Congress, Weimar, September 21. (Abstract, *Z.*, Jahrg. ii. Heft 2, November 1911, S. 101-2.) Published *in extenso* under the title : Ansätze zur psychoanalytischen Erforschung und Behandlung des manisch-depressiven Irreseins und verwandter Zustände. *Z.*, Jahrg. ii. Heft 6, March 1912, S. 302-15.

27. Über die Beziehungen zwischen Perversion und Neurose. (Abstract of the first of Freud's 'Drei Abhandlungen zur Sexualtheorie'.) *B.*, October 30.

28. Über die determinierende Kraft des Namens. *Z.*, Jahrg. ii. Heft 3, December 1911, S. 133-34.

29. Eine Traumanalyse bei Ovid. *Z.*, Jahrg. ii. Heft 3, December 1911, S. 159-60.

*30. Giovanni Segantini : Ein psychoanalytischer Versuch. *Schriften zur angewandten Seelenkunde*, Heft 11, pp. 65. New enlarged edition, 1925. (Wien, Deuticke.) Russian Translation, 1913 (Odessa). Italian Translation, 1926.

1912

31. Aus der Analyse eines Falles von Grübelzwang. *B.*, March 14.

32. Über ein kompliziertes Zeremoniell neurotischer Frauen. *Z.*, Jahrg. ii. Heft 8, May, S. 421-25.

33. Eine besondere Form sadistischer Träume (Massenmord-Träume). *B.*, May 18.

*34. Amenhotep IV. (Echnaton). Psychoanalytische Beiträge zum Verständnis seiner Persönlichkeit und des monotheistischen Aton-Kultes. *B.*, July. *Imago*, Band i. Heft 4, S. 334-60.

35. Über neurotische Lichtscheu. *B.*, October.

1913

36. Psychosexuelle Wurzeln des neurotischen Kopfschmerzes. *B.*, February and March.

37. Sollen wir die Patienten ihre Träume aufschreiben lassen ? *I.Z.*, Jahrg. i. Heft 2, March, S. 194-96.

38. Eine Deckerinnerung, betreffend ein Kindheitserlebnis von scheinbar ätiologischer Bedeutung. *I.Z.*, Jahrg. i. Heft 3, May, S. 247-51.

39. Zur Psychogenese der Strassenangst im Kindesalter. *I.Z.*, Jahrg. i. Heft 3, May, S. 256-57.

40. Einige Bemerkungen über die Rolle der Grosseltern in der Psychologie der Neurosen. *I.Z.*, Jahrg. i. Heft 3, May, S. 224-27.

41. Beobachtungen über die Beziehungen zwischen Nahrungstrieb und Sexualtrieb. *B.*, June.

42. Psychische Nachwirkungen der Beobachtung des elterlichen Geschlechtsverkehrs bei einem neunjährigen Kinde. *I.Z.*, Jahrg. i. Heft 4, July, S. 364-66.

*43. Über Einschränkungen und Umwandlungen der Schaulust bei den Psychoneurotikern nebst Bemerkungen über analoge Erscheinungen in der Völkerpsychologie. Fourth International Psycho-Analytical Congress, Munich, September 7. (Includes No. 35.) *J.*, Band vi., 1914, S. 25-88.

44. Über eine konstitutionelle Grundlage der lokomotorischen Angst. *B.*, October. *I.Z.*, Jahrg. ii. Heft 2, March 1914, S. 143-50.

45. Über neurotische Exogamie: Ein Beitrag zu den Übereinstimmungen im Seelenleben der Neurotiker und der Wilden. *B.*, November 8. *Imago*, Band iii. Heft 6, S. 499-501.

46. Ohrmuschel und Gehörgang als erogene Zone. *B.*, December. *I.Z.*, Jahrg. ii. Heft 1, March 1914, S. 27-29.

1914

47. Kritik zu C. G. Jung, Versuch einer Darstellung der psychoanalytischen Theorie. *B.*, January. *I.Z.*, Jahrg. ii. Heft 1, January, S. 72-82.

48. Zur Bedeutung der Analerotik. *B.*, February.

49. Zum Verständnis ' suggestiver ' Arzneiwirkungen bei neurotischen Zuständen. *I.Z.*, Jahrg. ii. Heft 4, July, S. 377-78.

50. Eigentümliche Formen der Gattenwahl, besondere Inzucht und Exogamie. Ärztliche Gesellschaft für Sexualwissenschaft, Berlin, July 3.

51. Spezielle Pathologie und Therapie der nervösen Zustände und der Geistesstörungen. (Collective Review.) *J.*, Band vi., 1914, S. 343-63.

1916

*52. Untersuchungen über die früheste prägenitale Entwicklungsstufe der Libido. *I.Z.*, Jahrg. iv. Heft 2, S. 71-97.

1917

53. Einige Belege zur Gefühlseinstellung weiblicher Kinder gegenüber den Eltern. *I.Z.*, Jahrg. iv. Heft 3, S. 154-55.

*54. Über Ejaculatio præcox. *I.Z.*, Jahrg. iv. Heft 4, S. 171-86.

55. Das Geldausgeben im Angstzustand. *I.Z.*, Jahrg. iv. Heft 5, S. 252-53.

1918

56. Dreikäsehoch. Zur Psychoanalyse des Wortwitzes. *Imago*, Band v. Heft 4, S. 294-95.

57. Zur Psychoanalyse der Kriegsneurosen: Contribution to the Discussion on War Neuroses at the Fifth International Psycho-Analytical Congress, Budapest, September 28. Published with Contributions by Prof. Dr. Sigm. Freud, Dr. S. Ferenczi, Dr. Ernst Simmel, and Dr. Ernest Jones, as No. 1 of the *Internationale Psychoanalytische Bibliothek*, S. 31-41. (Internationaler Psychoanalytischer Verlag, 1910. English translation, International Psycho-Analytical Press, 1921.)

*58. Über eine besondere Form des neurotischen Widerstandes gegen die psychoanalytische Methodik. *B.*, February 6. *I.Z.*, Jahrg. v. Heft 3, October, S. 173-80.

59. Tiertotemismus. *B.*, March 16.

60. Über den weiblichen Kastrationskomplex. *B.*, April 17.

61. Bemerkungen zu Ferenczi's Mitteilung über ' Sonntagsneurosen '. *I.Z.*, Jahrg. v. Heft 3, October, S. 203-4.

62. Zur Prognose psychoanalytischer Behandlungen in vorgeschrittenem Lebensalter. *B.*, November 6. *I.Z.*, Jahrg. vi. Heft 2, June 1920, S. 113-17.

63. Zur narzistischen Bewertung der Exkretionsvorgänge in Traum und Neurose. *B.*, December 18. *I.Z.*, Jahrg. vi. Heft 1, March 1920, S. 64-67.

1920

64. Der Versöhnungstag. Comments on Reik's ' Probleme der Religionspsychologie '. *Imago*, Band vi. Heft 1, S. 80-90.

65. Paper read before the University Clinic, Halle, July 10.

66. Über die Sexualität des Kindes. Ärztliche Gesellschaft für Sexualwissenschaft, Berlin, May 21. *Archiv für Frauenkunde* (Sexualwissenschaftliches Beiheft), Band vi., 1920, Heft 3/4, S. 278 *et seq.*

*67. Äusserungsformen des weiblichen Kastrationskomplexes. Sixth International Psycho-Analytical Congress, The Hague, September 8. (Abstract, *I.Z.*, Jahrg. vi. S. 391-92.) Published *in extenso*, *I.Z.*, Jahrg. vii. Heft 4, December 1921, S. 422-52. (*I.J.*, vol. iii. pp. 1-29.)

68. Technisches zur Traumdeutung. *B.*, September 24.

69. Die Psychoanalyse als Erkenntnisquelle für die Geisteswissenschaften. *Die neue Rundschau*, Jahrg. xxxi. of the *Freien Bühne*, October, Heft 10, S. 1154-74.

1921

70. Ergänzung zur Lehre vom Analcharakter. *B.*, January 20. *I.Z.*, Jahrg. ix. Heft 1, March 1923, S. 27-47. (*I.J.*, vol. iv. pp. 400-18.)

71. Zwei Fehlhandlungen einer Hebephrenen. *I.Z.*, Jahrg. vii. Heft 2, June, S. 208.

72. Beitrag zur ' Tic-Diskussion '. *B.*, June 2. *I.Z.*, Jahrg. vii. Heft 3, October, S. 393-95.

73. Spezielle Pathologie und Therapie der Neurosen und Psychosen. (Collective Review with Dr. J. Hárnik.) ' Bericht über die Fortschritte der Psychoanalyse in den Jahren 1914–1919 ', S. 141-63. (Internationaler Psychoanalytischer Verlag, 1921.) (*I.J.*, vol. i. pp. 280-85.)

74. Literatur in spanischer Sprache. ' Bericht über die Fortschritte der Psychoanalyse in den Jahren 1914–1919 ', S. 366-67. (Internationaler Psychoanalytischer Verlag, 1921.) (*I.J.*, vol. i. pp. 457-58.)

75. Klinische Beiträge zur Psychoanalyse aus den Jahren 1907–1920. Includes the above-mentioned numbers 9, 10, 11, 12, 14, 17, 18, 26, 28, 32, 37, 38, 39, 40, 42, 43, 44, 45, 46, 47, 52, 53, 54, 55, 58, 61, 62, 63. *Internationale Psychoanalytische Bibliothek*, No. 10. (Internationaler Psychoanalytischer Verlag, 1921.)

1922

*76. Vaterrettung und Vatermord in den neurotischen Phantasiengebilden. *I.Z.*, Jahrg. viii. Heft 1, March, S. 71-77. (*I.J.*, vol. iii. pp. 467-74.)

77. Paper read before a Psycho-Analytical Circle in Leipzig, May 27.

78. Über Fehlleistung mit überkompensierender Tendenz. *I.Z.*, Jahrg. viii. Heft 3, October, S. 345-48. (*I.J.*, vol. v. pp. 197-200.)

79. Fehlleistung eines Achtzigjährigen. *I.Z.*, Jahrg. viii. Heft 3, October, S. 350. (*I.J.*, vol. iv. p. 479.)

80. Die Spinne als Traumsymbol. *I.Z.*, Jahrg. viii. Heft 4, December, S. 470-75. (*I.J.*, vol. iv. pp. 313-17.)

81. Neue Untersuchungen zur Psychologie der manisch-depressiven Zustände. Seventh International Psycho-Analytical Congress, Berlin, September 27. (Abstract: *I.Z.*, Jahrg. viii. S. 492-93.)

1923

82. Zwei Beiträge zur Symbolforschung: Zur symbolischen Bedeutung der Dreizahl; Der 'Dreiweg' in der Ödipus-sage. *Imago*, Band ix. Heft 1, S. 122-26.

83. Eine infantile Theorie von der Entstehung des weiblichen Geschlechtes. *I.Z.*, Jahrg. ix. Heft 1, March, S. 75-76.

84. Die Wiederkehr primitiver religiöser Vorstellungen im Phantasienleben des Kindes. Oriental Department of the University, Hamburg, March 3.

85. Kastrationsphantasien bei zwei kleinen Knaben. *B.*, March 13.

86. Der Kastrationskomplex in der Analyse eines Bisexuellen. *B.*, March 13.

87. Anfänge und Entwicklung der Objektliebe. *B.*, March 27.

88. Zum Introjektionsvorgang bei Homosexualität. *B.*, May 8.

89. (With Dr. Helene Deutsch) Über Phantasien der Kastration durch Beissen. *B.*, June 5.

90. Aus der Analyse eines Asthmatikers. *B.*, June 30.

91. Ein Beitrag zur Psychologie der Melancholie. *B.*, June 30.

92. Ein Beitrag zur Prufungssituation im Traume. *B.*, June 30.

93. Psycho-Analytic Views on some Characteristics of Early Infantile Thinking. Seventh International Congress of Psychology, Oxford, July 31. *Proceedings and Papers of the Congress*, pp. 263-67 (German) (Cambridge University Press, 1924). *British Journal of Medical Psychology*, vol. iii. Part 4, 1923, pp. 283-87 (English).

94. Zwei neue kindliche Sexualtheorien. *B.*, November 6.

95. Die Geschichte eines Hochstaplers im Lichte psychoanalytischer Erkenntnis. *B.*, November 13. *Imago*, Band xi. Heft 4, 1925, S. 355-370.

96. Zur Symbolik des Hauses, besonder des Neubaus. *B.*, December 4. (Abstract: *I.Z.*, Jahrg. x. Heft 1, March 1924, S. 107.)

1924

97. Über unbewusste Strömungen im Verhältnis der Eltern zum Kinde. Paper read in Hamburg, January 5.

98. Umwandlungsvorgänge am Ödipuskomplex im Laufe einer Psychoanalyse. *B.*, March 29.

99. Beiträge der Oralerotik zur Charakterbildung. Eighth International Psycho-Analytical Congress, Salzburg, April 21. (Abstract: *I.Z.*, Jahrg. x. S. 214.) (*I.J.*, vol. vi. pp. 247-58.)

100. Über die Psychologie der modernen Kunstrichtungen. Paper read before an Art Circle in Berlin.

101 Zur Charakterbildung auf der 'genitalen' Entwicklungsstufe. *B.*, September 23.

102. Analyse einer Zwangsneurose. First German Psycho-Analytical Congress, Würzburg, October 12.

103. Über eine weitere Determinante der Vorstellung des zu kleinen Penis. *B.*, October 21.

104. Phantasien der Patienten über den Abschluss der Analyse. *B.*, November 11.

*105. Versuch einer Entwicklungsgeschichte der Libido auf Grund der Psychoanalyse seelischer Störungen. [1. *Teil:* Die manisch-depressiven Zustände und die prägenitalen Organisationsstufe der Libido. Einleitung. 1. Melancholie und Zwangsneurose. Zwei Stufen der sadistisch-analen Entwicklungsphase der Libido. 2. Objektverlust und Introjektion in der normalen Trauer und in abnormen psychischen Zuständen. 3. Der Introjektionsvorgang in der Melancholie. Zwei Stufen der oralen Entwicklungsphase der Libido. 4. Beiträge zur Psychogenese der Melancholie. 5. Das infantile Vorbild der melancholischen Depression. 6. Die Manie. 7. Die psychoanalytische Therapie der manisch-melancholischen Zustände (includes Nos. 81 and 91). 11. *Teil.* Anfänge und Entwicklung der Objektliebe (corresponds to No. 87).] *Neue Arbeiten zur ärztlichen Psychoanalyse*, Heft 11, pp. 96. (Internationaler Psychoanalytischer Verlag.)

1925

*106. Psychoanalytische Studien zur Charakterbildung. [Contains the above-mentioned Nos. 70 and 99. Further: Zur Charakterbildung auf der 'genitalen' Entwicklungsstufe. (*I.J.*, vol. vii. pp. 214-22).] *Internationale Psychoanalytische Bibliothek*, No. xvi. pp. 64. (Internationaler Psychoanalytischer Verlag.)

107. Zur Verdrängung des Ödipuskomplexes. *B.*, January 20.

108. Paper read before a Psycho-Analytical Circle in Leipzig, February 21.

109. Die Bedeutung von Wortbrücken für die neurotische Symptombildung. *B.*, February 26.

110. Eine unbeachtete kindliche Sexualtheorie. *I.Z.*, Jahrg. xi. Heft 1, March, S. 85-87. (*I.J.*, vol. vi. pp. 444-46.)

111. Psychoanalyse und Gynäkologie. Gesellschaft für Gynäkologie und Geburtshilfe, Berlin, March 13. (Abstract: *I.Z.*, Jahrg. xi. S. 126.) *Zeitschrift für Geburtshilfe und Gynäkologie*, Bd. lxxxix. S. 451-58.

112. Koinzidierende Phantasien bei Mutter und Sohn. *I.Z.*, Jahrg. xi. Heft 2, June, S. 222. (*I.J.*, vol. vii. p. 79.)

113. Die Psychoanalyse schizophrener Zustände.   Leidsche Vereeniging voor Psychopathologie en Psychoanalyse, Leyden, May 27 and 29.

114. Das hysterische Symptom.   Nederlandsche Maatschappy ter Bevordering der Geneeskunst, Hague, May 28.

115. Psychoanalytische Bemerkungen zu Coué's Verfahren der Selbstmeisterung.   *I.Z.*, Jahrg. xii. Heft 2, 1926, S. 131-54.   (*I.J.*, vol. vii. pp. 190-213.)

LIST OF BOOKS AND PAPERS REFERRED TO

ALEXANDER, F., 'The Castration Complex in the Formation of Character', *International Journal of Psycho-Analysis*, vol. iv. (First published in German, *Internationale Zeitschrift für Psychoanalyse*, Bd. viii., 1922.)

BLEULER, E., *Dementia Praecox, oder Gruppe der Schizophrenien*, Vienna, 1911.

BREUER, Jos., and FREUD, SIGM., *Studien über Hysterie*, Vienna, 1895; fourth edition, 1922.

BRILL, A. A., 'Ein Fall von periodischer Depression psychogenen Ursprungs', *Centralblatt für Nervenheilkunde und Psychiatrie*, Bd. i., 1911.

EDER, M. D., 'Augenträume', *Internationale Zeitschrift für Psychoanalyse*, Bd. i., 1913.

EISLER, M. J., 'Pleasure in Sleep and Disturbed Capacity for Sleep', *The International Journal of Psycho-Analysis*, vol. iii., 1922. (First published in German, *Internationale Zeitschrift für Psychoanalyse*, Bd. vii., 1921.)

FEDERN, PAUL, 'Beiträge zur Analyse des Sadismus und Masochismus', *Internationale Zeitschrift für Psychoanalyse*, Bd. i., 1913.

FERENCZI, SANDOR, 'On the Ontogenesis of an Interest in Money', *Contributions to Psycho-Analysis*, Boston, 1916. (First published in German, *Internationale Zeitschrift für Psychoanalyse*, Bd. ii., 1914.)
'Psycho-Analytical Observations on Tic', *Further Contributions to the Theory and Technique of Psycho-Analysis*, London, 1926. (First published in German, *Internationale Zeitschrift für Psychoanalyse*, Bd. vii., 1921.)
'Sunday Neuroses', *Further Contributions to the Theory and Technique of Psycho-Analysis*, London, 1926. (First published in German, *Internationale Zeitschrift für Psychoanalyse*, Bd. v., 1919.)
'Symbolic Representation of the Pleasure and Reality Principles in the Oedipus Myth', *Contributions to Psycho-Analysis*, Boston, 1916. (First published in German, *Imago*, Bd. i., 1912.)

FOREL und JULIUSBURGER, 'Über Blastophthorie', *Zeitschrift für Sexualwissenschaft*, Bd. i., 1908.

FREUD, SIGM., 'Analysis of a Phobia in a Five-year-old Boy', *Collected Papers*, vol. iii. (First published in German, *Jahrbuch für psychoanalytische und psychopathologische Forschungen*, Bd. i., 1909.)
'Animismus, Magie, und Allmacht der Gedanken', *Imago*, Bd. ii.,

1913. (Reprinted as part of *Totem und Tabu*, Vienna, 1913 ; third edition, 1922.)

' Character and Anal Erotism ', *Collected Papers*, vol. ii. (First published in German, *Psychiatrisch-neurologische Wochenschrift*, Bd. ix., 1908.)

Collected Papers, 4 vols., London, 1924-25.

' Contributions to the Psychology of Love ', *Collected Papers*, vol. iv. (First published in German, *Jahrbuch für psychoanalytische und psychopathologische Forschungen*, Bd. ii., 1910 ; Bd. iv., 1912 ; *Sammlung kleiner Schriften*, Vierte Folge, 1918.)

Der Witz und seine Beziehungen zum Unbewussten, Vienna, 1905 ; fourth edition, 1925.

Die Traumdeutung, Vienna, 1900 ; seventh edition, 1922.

Drei Abhandlungen zur Sexualtheorie, Vienna, 1905 ; sixth edition, 1925.

' Fragment of an Analysis of a Case of Hysteria ', *Collected Papers*, vol. iii. (First published in German, *Monatsschrift für Psychiatrie und Neurologie*, Bd. xxviii. Heft 4, 1905.)

' From the History of an Infantile Neurosis ', *Collected Papers*, vol. iii. (First published in German, *Sammlung kleiner Schriften*, Vierte Folge, 1918.)

' General Remarks on Hysterical Attacks ', *Collected Papers*, vol. ii. (First published in German, *Zeitschrift für Psychotherapie und medizinische Psychologie*, 1909.)

Group Psychology and the Analysis of the Ego, London, 1922. (First published in German, 1921.)

' Hysterical Phantasies and their Relation to Bisexuality ', *Collected Papers*, vol. ii. (First published in German, *Zeitschrift für Sexualwissenschaft*, Bd. i., 1908.)

' Mourning and Melancholia ', *Collected Papers*, vol. iv. (First published in German, *Internationale Zeitschrift für Psychoanalyse*, Bd. iv., 1917.)

' My Views on the Part Played by Sexuality in the Aetiology of the Neuroses ', *Collected Papers*, vol. i. (First published in German, Löwenfeld's *Sexualleben und Nervenleiden*, 1905.)

' Notes upon a Case of Obsessional Neurosis ', *Collected Papers*, vol. iii. (First published in German, *Jahrbuch für psychoanalytische und psychopathologische Forschungen*, Bd. i., 1909.)

' Obsessive Acts and Religious Practices ', *Collected Papers*, vol. ii. (First published in German, *Zeitschrift für Religionspsychologie*, Bd. i., 1907.)

' On Narcissism : An Introduction ', *Collected Papers*, vol. iv. (First published in German, *Jahrbuch für psychoanalytische und psychopathologische Forschungen*, Bd. vi., 1914.)

' Psycho-Analytic Notes upon an Autobiographical Account of a Case of Paranoia (Dementia Paranoides) ', *Collected Papers*, vol. iii. (First published in German, *Jahrbuch fur psychoanalytische und psychopathologische Forschungen*, Bd. iii., 1911.)

' Psychogenic Visual Disturbance according to Psycho-Analytical Conceptions ', *Collected Papers*, vol. ii. (First published in German, *Ärztliche Standeszeitung*, Vienna, 1910.)

' Sexuality in the Aetiology of the Neuroses ', *Collected Papers*, vol. i. (First published in German, *Wiener klinische Rundschau*, 1898, Nos. 2, 4, 5, and 7.)

' The Antithetical Sense of Primal Words ', *Collected Papers*, vol. iv. (First published in German, *Jahrbuch für psychoanalytische und psychopathologische Forschungen*, Bd. ii., 1910.)

The Ego and the Id, London, 1927. (First published in German, 1923.)

' The Infantile Genital Organization of the Libido ', *Collected Papers*, vol. ii. (First published in German, *Zeitschrift für Psychoanalyse*, Bd. ix., 1923.)

' The Predisposition to Obsessional Neurosis ', *Collected Papers*, vol. ii. (First published in German, *Internationale Zeitschrift für Psychoanalyse*, Bd. i., 1913.)

' The Taboo of Virginity ', *Collected Papers*, vol. iv. (First published in German, *Sammlung kleiner Schriften*, Vierte Folge, 1918.)

' The Uncanny ', *Collected Papers*, vol. iv. (First published in German, *Imago*, Bd. v., 1919.)

Totem und Tabu, Vienna, 1913 ; third edition, 1922.

' Über einige Übereinstimmungen im Seelenleben der Wilden und der Neurotiker ', *Imago*, Bd. i. and ii., 1912 and 1913. (Reprinted as *Totem und Tabu*, Vienna, 1913 ; third edition, 1922.)

Zur Psychopathologie des Alltagslebens, Berlin, 1904 ; tenth edition, Vienna, 1924. (First published in *Monatsschrift für Psychiatrie und Neurologie*, Bd. x., 1901.)

GLOVER, EDWARD, ' The Significance of the Mouth in Psycho-Analysis ', *British Journal of Medical Psychology*, vol. iv., 1924.

GRODDECK, GEORG, *Das Buch vom Es*, Vienna, 1923.

HUG-HELLMUTH, ' Vom " mittleren " Kinde ', *Imago*, Bd. vii., 1921.

JEKELS, LUDWIG, ' Einige Bemerkungen zur Trieblehre ', *Internationale Zeitschrift für Psychoanalyse*, Bd. i., 1913.

JONES, ERNEST, ' Anal-Erotic Character Traits ', *Papers on Psycho-Analysis*, third edition, London, 1923. (First published in *Journal of Abnormal Psychology*, vol. xiii., 1918.)

' Einige Fälle von Zwangsneurose ', *Jahrbuch für psychoanalytische und psychopathologische Forschungen*, Bd. v., 1913.

' Hate and Anal Erotism in the Obsessional Neurosis ', *Papers on Psycho-Analysis*, third edition, London, 1923. (First published in German, *Internationale Zeitschrift für Psychoanalyse*, Bd. i., 1913.)

Papers on Psycho-Analysis, London, 1912 ; third edition, 1923.

' Psycho-Analytic Notes on a Case of Hypomania ', *Bulletin of the Ontario Hospitals for the Insane*, 1910.

JUNG, C. G., *Über die Psychologie der Dementia Præcox*, Halle, 1907.

LIEPMANN, *Über Ideenflucht*, Halle, 1904.

LOEWENFELD, ' Über traumartige und verwandte Zustände ', *Centralblatt für Nervenheilkunde und Psychiatrie*, 1909.

MAEDER, A., ' Psychoanalyse bei einer melancholischen Depression ', *Centralblatt für Nervenheilkunde und Psychiatrie*, 1910.

VAN OPHUIJSEN, J. H. W., ' Beiträge zum Männlichkeitskomplex der Frau ', *Internationale Zeitschrift für Psychoanalyse*, Bd. iv., 1917.
' On the Origin of the Feeling of Persecution ', *The International Journal of Psycho-Analysis*, vol. i., 1920. (First published in German, *Zeitschrift für Psychoanalyse*, Bd. vi., 1920.)

RANK, OTTO, *Das Inzestmotiv in Dichtung und Sage*, Vienna, 1912.
Der Künstler : Ansätze zu einer Sexualpsychologie, Vienna, 1907.
Der Mythus von der Geburt des Helden, Vienna, 1909.
' Die Nacktheit in Sage und Dichtung ', *Imago*, Bd. ii., 1913.

REITLER, R., ' Zur Augensymbolik ', *Internationale Zeitschrift für Psychoanalyse*, Bd. i., 1913.

RIKLIN, F., *Wunscherfüllung und Symbolik im Märchen*, Vienna, 1908.

RÓHEIM, G., ' Nach dem Tode des Urvaters ', *Imago*, Bd. ix., 1923.

ROHLEDER, ' Über Masturbatio interrupta ', *Zeitschrift für Sexualwissenschaft*, 1908.

SACHS, H., ' Zur Genese der Perversionen ', *Internationale Zeitschrift für Psychoanalyse*, Bd. ix., 1923.

SADGER, I., ' Analerotik und Analcharakter ', *Die Heilkunde*, 1910.
' Die Bedeutung der psychoanalytischen Methode nach Freud ', *Centralblatt für Nervenheilkunde und Psychiatrie*, 1907.
' Haut-, Schleimhaut-, und Muskelerotik ', *Jahrbuch für psychoanalytische und psychopathologische Forschungen*, Bd. iii., 1912.
' Über sexualsymbolische Verwertung des Kopfschmerzes ', *Zentralblatt für Psychoanalyse*, Bd. ii., 1912.
' Über Urethralerotik ', *Jahrbuch für psychoanalytische und psychopathologische Forschungen*, Bd. ii., 1910.

SCHREBER, *Denkwürdigkeiten eines Nervenkranken*, Leipzig, 1903.

STAERCKE, AUG., ' The Castration Complex ', *The International Journal of Psycho-Analysis*, vol. ii., 1921. (First published in German, *Internationale Zeitschrift für Psychoanalyse*, Bd. vii., 1921.)
' The Reversal of the Libido-Sign in Delusions of Persecution ', *The International Journal of Psycho-Analysis*, vol. i., 1920. (First published in German, *Zeitschrift für Psychoanalyse*, Bd. v., 1919.)

STEKEL, W., *Die Sprache des Traumes*, Wiesbaden, 1911.
Nervöse Angstzustände und ihre Behandlung, Vienna, 1908.

STORFER, A. J., 'Jungfrau und Dirne', *Zentralblatt fur Psychoanalyse*, Bd. ii., 1912.
   Marias jungfräuliche Mutterschaft, Berlin, 1914.

VON WINTERSTEIN, H., 'Psychoanalytische Anmerkungen zur Geschichte der Philosophie', *Imago*, Bd. ii., 1913.

INDEX

THE END